About the authors

Alana Lentin is a senior lecturer in the Department of Sociology, University of Sussex, UK.

Gavan Titley is a lecturer in the School of English, Media and Theatre Studies, National University of Ireland, Maynooth, Ireland.

D1488827

THE CRISES OF MULTICULTURALISM

racism in a neoliberal age

Alana Lentin and Gavan Titley

Zed Books

LONDON · NEW YORK

The Crises of Multiculturalism: Racism in a neoliberal age was first published in 2011 by Zed Books Ltd, 7 Cynthia Street, London N1 9JF, UK, and Room 400, 175 Fifth Avenue, New York, NY 10010, USA

www.zedbooks.co.uk

Set in Monotype Sabon and Gill Sans Heavy by Ewan Smith, London
Index: ed.emery@thefreeuniversity.net
Cover designed by Stuart Tolley
Printed and bound in Great Britain by Mimeo Ltd, Huntingdon, Cambridgeshire, PE29 6XX

MIX
Paper from
responsible sources
FSC
www.fsc.org   FSC® C019549

Distributed in the USA exclusively by Palgrave Macmillan, a division of St Martin's Press, LLC, 175 Fifth Avenue, New York, NY 10010, USA

A catalogue record for this book is available from the British Library
Library of Congress Cataloging in Publication Data available

ISBN 978 1 84813 580 2 hb
ISBN 978 1 84813 581 9 pb

Contents

Preface by Gary Younge

On 15 February 2006 in Strasbourg the head of the European Commission, José Manuel Barroso, delivered a stout defence of freedom of speech, democratic values and modernity on the continent. With the embers from heated exchanges over a Danish newspaper's decision to publish cartoons of Muhammad still glowing, Barroso laid out the consequences of privileging sensitivity towards 'others' over core values that define 'us'. If Europe failed to defend its principles in the face of such an onslaught, he argued, 'we are accepting fear in our society [...] I understand that offended many people in the Muslim world but is it better to have a system in which some excesses are allowed or to be in some countries where they don't even have the right to say this [...] I defend the democratic system.'

On the very same day in the House of Commons the British government employed fear of terrorism to limit existing freedoms, expanding state power to make 'glorification' of terrorism a criminal offence. Laying out the consequences of privileging freedom over security, the then prime minister, Tony Blair, later explained that the law 'will allow us to deal with "those" people and say: Look, we have free speech in this country, but don't abuse it'. For certain groups the price for belonging and conditions for banishment have shifted dramatically in Western nations, particularly but by no means exclusively in Europe, in recent years. Citizenship is no longer enough. The clothes you wear, the language you speak, the way you worship, have all become grounds for dismissal or inclusion. These terms are not only not applied equally to all, they are not even intended to be. In a series of edicts, popular, political and judicial, their intention is not to erase all differences but act as a filter for certain people who are considered dangerously different.

To achieve this certain groups and behaviours must first be pathologized so that they might then be more easily particularized. The pathologization has been made easier over the past decade by the escalation of terrorist acts or attempts in the USA and Europe in the name of radical Islam. 'Terror is first of all the terror of the next attack,' explains Arjun Appadurai in *Fear of Small Numbers*. 'Terror

[...] opens the possibility that anyone may be a soldier in disguise, a sleeper among us, waiting to strike at the heart of our social slumber.'

But in truth terrorism, and the wars and conflicts that exacerbate it, sharpened this trend and focused it on Muslims and Islam but did not create it. The notion that the presence of certain groups represents an existential threat to a mythological national cohesion was present in Enoch Powell's infamous 1968 speech in which he prophesied violent consequences of non-white immigration in the UK: 'As I look ahead, I am filled with foreboding; like the Roman, I seem to see "the River Tiber foaming with much blood".' It was there in 1979 in Margaret Thatcher's sympathy with Britons who feel they are being 'swamped by an alien tide'. And it was front and centre in Jacques Chirac's 1991 *'Le bruit et l'odeur'* speech. 'How do you want a French worker who works with his wife, who earn together about 15,000 francs and who sees next to his council house a piled-up family with a father, three or four spouses and twenty children earning 50,000 francs via benefits naturally without working [...] If you add to that the noise and the smell, well, the French worker, he goes crazy.'

For these threats to gain popular traction, however, these 'others' have to be distinguished in the popular mind from other 'others'. So when black people attack other black people it is no longer crime but 'black-on-black-crime'; if a young Muslim woman is killed over a romantic relationship it is not a murder but an 'honour killing'. In a country like England that has been embroiled in virtually continuous terrorist conflict for the last forty years in Northern Ireland, the notion that there are 'home-grown' 'Muslim' bombers is supposed to represent not just a new demographic taking up armed struggle but an entirely new phenomenon. Even as the Catholic Church is embroiled in a global crisis over child sexual abuse and the Church of England is splintered in a row over gay priests, Islam and Muslims face particularly vehement demands to denounce homophobia.

The combined effect of these flawed distinctions and sweeping demonization is to unleash a series of moral panics. In 2009 in Switzerland a national referendum bans the building of minarets in a country that has only four; in 2010 70 per cent of voters in the state of Oklahoma support the banning of sharia law even though Muslims comprise less than 0.1 per cent of the population; in the Netherlands parliament seriously considered banning the burka – a garment believed to be worn by fewer than fifty women in the entire country. Disproportionate in scale and distorted in nature, these actions cannot be understood as a viable response to their named targets but rather as emblems of a broader, deeper disruption in national, racial and religious identities. At a time of diminishing national sovereignty, particularly in Europe, such campaigns help the national imagination cohere around a fixed identity even as the ability of the nation-state to actually govern itself wanes. It is a curious and paradoxical fact that as national boundaries in Europe have started to fade, the electoral appeal of nationalism has increased; fascism, and its fellow travellers, is once again a mainstream ideology in Europe, regularly polling between 5 and 15 per cent in most countries. Their success suggests that modernity, as it has been framed and presented, poses a challenge not only to Islam and that the demographic group finding it most difficult to integrate into modern society is a section of white society that feels abandoned and disoriented.

But such assaults are by no means the preserve of the far right. Many who consider themselves on the left have given liberal cover to these assaults on religious and racial minorities, ostensibly acting in defence of democracy, Enlightenment values and equal rights – particularly relating to sexual orientation and gender. Their positioning rests on two major acts of sophistry. The first is an elision between Western values and liberal values that ignores the fact that liberal values are not fully entrenched in the West and that other regions of the world also have liberal traditions. Nowhere is this clearer than with gay rights, where whatever gains do exist are recent and highly contested. In the thirty-one American states where gay marriage has been put to a popular vote it has been defeated. The only places it is legal are where it has been ushered in through the courts. Not only is gay equality not a Western value, it's not even a Californian value. The second is a desire to understand Western 'values' in abstraction from Western practice. This surge in extolling Western virtues has coincided with an illegal war that has been underpinned by both authorized and unauthorized torture and a range of other atrocities and a spike in the electoral and political currency of racism and xenophobia.

The contradictions inherent in these trends and tensions found their full expression in the existence of a gay rights chapter within the openly anti-immigrant and Islamophobic English Defence League. 'This is the symbol gay people were made to wear under Hitler,' one member told the *Guardian*, explaining the pink star he was wearing. 'Islam poses the same threat and we are here to express our opposition to that.' Unable to come up with a single, coherent new term which both encapsulates the atmosphere of fear, threat, panic, disorientation, confusion, contradiction and paradoxes and unites both far right and liberals, the opponents of this diverse, hybrid reality resurrected an old foe – 'multiculturalism'.

The beauty of multiculturalism, for its opponents, is that it can mean whatever you want it to mean so long as you don't like it. It has the added advantage of being a political orphan. Since it never had consensual support among the left – many of whom were wary of the attempt to replace anti-racism with a retreat into culture – there are few willing to give the term their full-throated endorsement. The announcement of its imminent death has concerned many not because they honoured its life but because they do not care for its assailants or the manner in which they aim to murder it. For some it clearly means the mere coexistence of 'other cultures'; for others the state promotion of 'other cultures' (although the ability to point to a time when this was ever an official policy pursued with either force or effect seems elusive); and for yet others it represents any resistance to assimilating racial, religious and ethnic cultures into national ones.

There are legitimate philosophical arguments in there somewhere. The trouble is that when applied to the specific communities they are reserved for in this specific context the term 'multiculturalism' more often than not simply becomes a proxy for 'difference'. But for all the angst invested and ink spilt about it multiculturalism is less of an ethos than a simple statement of fact. It emerges not from government edict but the lived experience of people, and at different times may be untidy, vibrant, problematic, dynamic or divisive.

The nation-state is in crisis; neoliberal globalization is in crisis; multiculturalism is simply *in situ*.

For Alvar, Jonas-Liam,
Noam, Partho, Päivi

Introduction and acknowledgements

Multiculturalism is the toxic gift that keeps on giving. As we revised this book for publication in autumn 2010, a cluster of criticisms of something called multiculturalism once again garnered various levels of publicity. They did so against a particular backdrop: the electoral gains of the Sverigedemokraterna and Geert Wilders's Partij voor de Vrijheid; Wilders's subsequent trial in Amsterdam on charges of incitement to racial hatred; the European Commission's response to the French government's Roma expulsion/repatriation policy; the ongoing discovery of the problem of the burka and niqab in ever more locations; the high-profile publication of Thilo Sarrazin's *Deutschland schafft sich ab* (2010) and his subsequent resignation from the executive board of the Deutsche Bundesbank; and, perhaps less at the centre of mainstream transnational news flow, the significant electoral advance of Freiheitliche Partei Österreichs in Vienna and projected gains for Perussuomalaiset in Finland. Odd as it may seem, for some commentators multiculturalism was directly or indirectly to blame for much of this.

Writing in the *Guardian*, and reviving a general argument first rehearsed in *New Left Review* in 1997, Slavoj Žižek (2010) proposed an explanation for this general rise in what he terms 'populist racism' by, among other things, targeting the evasions of 'liberal multiculturalism'. 'Progressive liberals', he argues, are pleased by diversity's contributions to cosmopolitan cultural capital, and schooled in a discourse of tolerance. Yet, by insisting on maintaining a sanitary cultural distance, liberal multiculturalism merely desires a 'detoxified' Other, while 'reasonably' enacting increasingly stringent, stratified and securitized immigration systems. In the UK, a themed issue of *Prospect* edited by Munira Mirza (2010) argued that if racism persisted as an issue in contemporary British society, it did so predominantly as a consequence of multiculturalism's paternalist racializing, and cultural block-thinking about the lives of 'minorities'. Finally, the German Chancellor, Angela Merkel, garnered significant publicity by declaring that multiculturalism has 'failed spectacularly' in Germany, and that attempts to build a '*multi-kulti*' society should give way to greater efforts by immigrants to integrate.

Multiculturalism, as almost everybody recognizes, is a slippery and fluid term, and it has accrued a vast range of associations and accents through decades of political, contextual and linguistic translation. It may retain a fairly useful if limited descriptive sense in post-colonial, migration societies, but it also skitters off to index normative debates, real and imagined policies, mainstream political rhetorics, consumerist desires, and resistant political appropriations. This book is not an attempt to organize this discursive messiness, nor even to systematically survey it. Instead, it is centrally concerned with the insistent sense of multiculturalism as a unitary idea, philosophy, 'failed experiment' or era. Multiculturalism has inspired a long history of backlash; however, since 11 September 2001 commentators, politicians and media coverage in a range of European and Western contexts have increasingly drawn on narratives of the 'crisis of multiculturalism' to make sense of a broad range of events and political developments, and to justify political initiatives in relation to integration, security and immigration. Yet for all this focus and sonorous rejection, multiculturalism has rarely amounted to more than a patchwork of initiatives, rhetoric and aspirations in any given context. It is this gap between the empirical realities of multiculturalism and the 'recited truths' (De Certeau 1984) of what multiculturalism is held to have been, and to have caused, which is the primary terrain of this study.

This gap can be illustrated by briefly examining Merkel's dramatic repudiation. Under pressure from the right of her party, the CDU, as it sought to siphon off populist fairy dust from Thilo Sarrazin, Merkel's lament was particularly egregious. It is not just the indecent haste with which she moved on from celebrating the youthful multiculturalism of Germany's football team in the 2010 World Cup. There is also the fact that it is not entirely clear what project or era of multiculturalism Merkel felt moved to repudiate. It is only a decade since Germany reformed its exclusionary nationality laws (a reform which made that football team possible). Following the revision of the nationality law in 2000, public discourse witnessed 'attempts by politicians of all persuasions to fill "Germanness" with new content' (Rostock and Berghann 2008: 347). The left-liberal rhetoric of *multi-kulti* – which Merkel imbued, in her speech, with material-historical form – conflicted with powerful articulations of *Leitkultur* (Pautz 2005) and the specification of *deutsche Werteordnung* (Rostock and

Berghann 2008). As Pautz has shown, some of Merkel's CDU colleagues were centrally involved in promulgating a *leitkulturedebatte*
that sought to define cultural boundaries – and hierarchies – between
'nationals and immigrants', drawing on established tropes of national
cultures endangered by the demographic challenge and confidence of
immigrant cultures in general, and Islam in particular (2005: 43–7).

Mind the gap; merely pointing out the obvious empirical lack of a
multiculturalism that failed is to miss how it functions euphemistically
in Merkel's performance. As per the convention, complex social problems and political-economic disjunctures can be blamed on 'migrants',
and the solution, in a neoliberal era, located in an increased individual
responsibility to become compatible and integrate. Merkel is only
the latest high-profile figure to engage a fictive multiculturalism as a
blunt political instrument. The range of processes of social dissolution
and varieties of anomie that multiculturalism is held responsible for
is scarcely credible. Blamed for everything from parallel societies to
gendered horror to the incubation of terrorism, the extent to which
multiculturalism was given official imprimatur, public support or
governmental form in any context is regarded as somewhat irrelevant.
As a loose assemblage of culturally pluralist sentiments, aspirations
and platitudes, or more darkly as a euphemism for lived multiculture,
it provides a mobilizing metaphor for a spectrum of political aversion
and racism that has become pronounced in western Europe.

This recited, elastic and mobile sense of multiculturalism, and its
importance in the recoding and recasting of racism today, is central to
this book. It is somewhat ironic that while multiculturalism is often
closely associated with the coded evasions of 'political correctness',
invoking the recited truths of multiculturalism depends on the same
kind of discursive strategy. In an era where the concept of race is
taboo and the charge of racism diluted, contested and inverted,
multiculturalism provides a discursive space for debating questions
of race, culture, legitimacy and belonging. Presenting it as a 'failed
experiment', and inserting it into a causal historical narrative, allows
anxieties concerning migration, globalization and the socio-political
transformations wrought by neoliberal governance to be ordered and
explained. Lamenting it as a benevolent if somewhat naive attempt
to manage the problem of difference allows for securitized migration
regimes, assimilative integrationism and neo-nationalist politics to be
presented as nothing more than rehabilitative action.

Given the multivalent dimensions of the 'multicultural backlash' over the last decade, the chapters in this book proceed by exploring different aspects and modalities of contemporary racisms, and by layering contextual discussions and a range of theoretical perspectives. Chapter 1, 'Recited truths: the contours of multicultural crisis', functions as an extended thematic, theoretical and political introduction to these dynamics, and sets out ways of thinking about 'multiculturalism' as a discursive assemblage that is produced and legitimized transnationally. Throughout the book we draw on contextual discussions and examples from a range of countries, seeking meaningful affinities and networks of exchange and meaning, while paying attention to the specificities of contexts, the pitfalls of comparative analysis, and the challenges of translation. In Chapter 1, some core theoretical ideas are explored in relation to the vociferous rejection of multiculturalism in Britain since the disturbances in northern England in the summer of 2001. The opprobrium heaped on multiculturalism after these events – and subsequently as an indirect consequence of the 'war on terror', and intensively after the London bombings of 7 July 2005 – makes Munira Mirza's arguments in *Prospect* about the current problems of multicultural policy in the UK somewhat difficult to substantiate. However, it is this very thinness which makes this second introductory example important. In a response to Mirza's essay, Gargi Bhattacharyya (2010) cut quickly to the main point:

> This is not about multiculturalism [...] what this really is, is an attack on the claim that racism exists and shapes social outcomes, and as other (contributors) point out, this is a longstanding point of political debate and struggle. The most effective method of silencing a critique of racism is to argue that racism no longer exists at all. Those claiming to suffer from its consequences must be pursuing their own selfish agendas.

A central preoccupation of this book is the ways in which the rejection of multiculturalism depends on a repudiation of racism, while being important in the reshaping of racism. Chapter 2, ' Let's talk about your culture: post-race, post-racism', engages the widely held belief that, after multiculturalism, racism no longer exists. Since the end of the Second World War and the uncovering of the crimes of the Holocaust; the scientific discrediting of biological theories of race; an often grudging recognition of the crimes of colonialism; and the end of apartheid, it has become taboo to refer to race in an openly discriminatory way. Racism, where it exists, is exceptional and aberrant, or an expression of individual pathologies. Indeed, as this chapter examines, the idea of racism is widely regarded as an 'unhelpful' accusation – needlessly inflammatory and designed to stifle debate – or as an unfair strategy deployed by minorities in competition for attention and resources.

Thus Thilo Sarrazin, the indirect trigger for Merkel's lament, was roundly criticized for discussing, in promoting *Deutschland schafft sich ab* (2010), the contention that 'all Jews share the same gene' (Grieshaber 2010). Yet his consistent contention that 'Muslim immigrants' in Europe are incapable of 'integrating', and often unwilling to, was welcomed by many as a courageous, taboo-busting utterance (regardless of how many similar, and similarly courageous, establishment contrarians have been making the same argument in syndicated newspaper columns, prime-time television shows and widely distributed books over the last decade). Chapter 2 engages in a reconsideration of theories of race and racism to show how, by effecting an ahistorical divide between ideas of (biological) 'race' and 'culture', it has become unacceptable to essentialize and scapegoat people on the basis of pseudo-science, but a refreshing and necessary form of truth-telling to do so on the basis of equally spurious understandings of culture. While the idea of 'cultural racism' is long established in sociology (Balibar and Wallerstein 1991; Stolcke 1995), this chapter examines how the conjunctural conditions of the 'war on terror', a variegated anti-immigrant politics and a range of other socio-political factors have *laundered* and relegitimized some of its core tenets, assumptions and defences.

While Žižek's general argument about the cost-free politics of liberal multiculturalism is one that is accepted in this book, what is of interest in his focus on the 'mask' of multiculturalism is the yawning gulf between his conventional mapping of multicultural politics and the changed political coordinates and discourses now assembled through it. In his somewhat sweeping summary of the European political landscape, he contends that 'There is now one predominant centrist party that stands for global capitalism, usually with a liberal cultural agenda (for example, tolerance towards abortion, gay rights, religious and ethnic minorities). Opposing this party is an increasingly strong anti-immigrant populist party which, on its fringes, is accompanied by overtly racist neofascist groups' (Žižek 2010). Aside from the varying degrees of (ir)relevance of this model to the political realities discussed in this book, two major developments are absent from this picture. First, liberalism – and the 'liberal cultural agenda' – has become a popular modality of nationalisms that are primarily grounded through attacks on the illiberalism of minority and Muslim populations, and on the 'relativist' licence multiculturalism has accorded them. Secondly, the conventional assumption that extremist ideas from the political fringes contaminate centrist politics does not describe the complex ways in which a liberal attack on multiculturalism's misplaced tolerance – on issues of liberty, expression, gender equality and sexual freedom – pervade and have been assembled across the political spectrum. Chapter 3, 'Free like me: the polyphony of liberal post-racialism', examines this pervasiveness and a number of strange political assemblages that thoroughly complicate the topography of liberalism and populism. It does this through several interlinking discussions – of 'headscarf debates' in Europe; of the racial logics of liberalism in Christian Joppke's (2009) book *Veil: Mirror of Identity*; of identity politics in the Netherlands in the aftermath of Pim Fortuyn; and of recent theories of illiberal and exclusionary liberalisms emergent in the 'war on terror' era (Tebble 2006; Triadafilopoulos 2011).

Chapter 4, 'Mediating the crisis: circuits of belief', returns in detail to the idea of recited truths to examine their transnational production and circulation. By taking the 2009 Swiss referendum on minaret construction as a central example and metaphor, it examines the ways in which mediated events are linked and indexed to each other in ways that can be made to speak of a cumulative, pan-European or Western crisis of multiculturalism. It examines why immigration and integration debates, for all their popularity and intensity, are never held to be sufficiently 'open' or 'honest'. Examining the mediation of this politics involves recognizing how the symbolic and connotative dimensions of events have become malleable political capital, but also how these dynamics are shaped and intensified by the instantaneous circuitries and networks of transnational media flow. Chapter 5, 'Good and bad diversity: the shape of neoliberal racisms', deepens the analysis of racism after multiculturalism as produced through assemblages of often disparate ideas, elements and sources. It takes as a central focus the neoliberal formation of the autonomous, self-sufficient subject, and examines the 'silencing' of race in social politics in the USA, and the post-racial logics of 'diversity politics' in European contexts that are in various states of collective self-recognition as diverse, immigration societies. It argues that under neoliberal conditions, the issue is not one of accepting or celebrating diversity, but of examining who qualifies to be recognized as 'diversity', and how questions of 'culture' and autonomy are combined in the unstated division of subjects into *good diversity* (the German football team) and *bad diversity* (the 'dis-integrated' subjects of Merkel's polemic).

Chapter 6, 'On one more condition: the politics of integration today', concludes the cumulative critique of the integrationist politics that depend on an exaggerated and stylized vision of multicultural failure to launder its racializing impacts. Departing from the argument that integration frameworks are frequently constructed to render meaningful integration impossible, the chapter examines the ways in which security, immigration and integration policies are inter-connected in systems designed to order hierarchies of good diversity, focusing on utility, 'compatibility' and autonomy. However, it is a mistake to focus solely on state action in a critique of the politics of integration. It is interesting to note that the multivalent rejection of multiculturalism traduced by Merkel involved not only conservative culturalist formations, but also civil society movements concerned that multicultural ideas were an impediment to 'teaching the "migrants" German "core values" of sexual freedom and gay friendliness' (Harita-worn and Petzen 2010). It is not only in Germany that gender and sexual politics have become inflected with an aversion to 'illiberal' forms of life, and by examining examples and cases from a range of contexts, the book concludes by examining how partial and inconsist-ent visions of already achieved equality and freedom are at the nexus of new forms of racialized exclusions being elaborated by state and civil society actors.

Given the necessarily broad theoretical, contextual and disciplinary scope of this book, and the fluid expansiveness of 'multiculturalism' and its attendant literatures and debates, it is also necessary to state some of the things this book is not. While it engages with debates in political theory, for reasons that will be abundantly clear in the analysis it does not take a normative position on multiculturalism, still less attempt to construct one. This is not to say that this is not possible, or important; Anne Phillips's (2007) *Multiculturalism without Culture*, for example, combines the forms of critical analysis favoured here with some very interesting discussions of recognition and equality. In the British context, the theorization of political multiculturalism, most obviously in the work of Bhikhu Parekh and Tariq Modood, continues to drive intensive debates. However, as our main focus is on the ways in which renditions of multiculturalism provide a space for the redrawing and laundering of contemporary racisms, a deeper engagement with this tradition, and the questions it raises about political claims-making, is beyond the scope of our analysis (see Fleras 2009 for a transnational, comparative analysis of these issues).

As a work of political and discursive analysis, we draw on a diverse range of sources, voices, examples and opinions, but, for obvious reasons of scale and scope, we do not provide a thorough overview of either the political activities and experiences of the subjects of 'crisis', or the sociocultural complexities of their lives. This relative absence should not be read as an inherent romanticization or valorization of the cultural politics and movements which emerge from these experiences and contexts. Similarly, though the anti-racist politics of this book are hardly understated, we do not attempt to offer grand plans for the necessary resistance to these formations. Other than in our critique of movements and organizations complicit in 'identity liberal' formations, we have been at pains to avoid what Lisa Duggan describes as the 'pedagogical mode' that critical writing about politics and political action can slip into. As Duggan argues, 'This common pedagogical mode seems counterproductive for political engagement, and it is too often based on incomplete knowledge of the history of the social movements being "taught"' (2003: 81). What we have instead tried to offer is a critical mapping of developments, discourses and racializing assemblages currently at play in the not-quite-post-racial present, and layered across the chapters, to offer a range of conceptual and analytical possibilities for thinking and organizing resistance.

Fittingly, for two authors with Irish backgrounds, we have accumulated many debts across Europe in the writing of this book. However, these are ones we are only too happy to acknowledge.

The editorial guidance, authorial freedom and general support provided by Tamsine O'Riordan and Jakob Horstmann at Zed Books made this book possible, and sustained our belief in it. It also benefited enormously from the detailed and insightful comments of Zed's anonymous reviewers; we hope that after all their work they are minded to read the final version, if only to receive our thanks. Ronit Lentin, Audrey Bryan and Natalie McDonnell are far from anonymous readers, but they have been as insightful, and exacting and caring, in their comments. Thanks also to Aine McDonough, who somehow made sense of the bibliographic storm we brewed over the last years. The clarity and consistency of Gary Younge's anti-racist thought has been an inspiration to both of us, and we are grateful to him for his preface, and for debating these ideas with us in a sweltering Berlin in July 2010.

We have been fortunate, particularly in the predatory climate being fostered in so many university sectors, that a broad range of scholars generously shared their work and ideas with us. For this generosity, and for the directions their ideas suggested, thanks to Rikke Andreassen, Miriyam Aouragh, Bolette Blaagaard, Carolina Sanchez Boe, Sarah Bracke, Rosi Braidotti, Jolle Demmers, Eric Fassin, Jin Haritaworn, Peter Hervik, Karina Horsti, Suvi Keskinen, Gholam Khiabany, Rebecca King O'Riain, Katya Salmi, Yasemin Shooman, Maria Stehle, Phil Triadafilopoulos and Ferruh Yilmaz.

In the same spirit, several institutions provided us with crucial support. The writing of this book was made possible by the happy coincidence of research leave granted us by the National University of Ireland, Maynooth, and Sussex University. Early on in this project, a research symposium in NUIM was given important support by Professor Ray O'Neill, vice-president for research. Contrary to natural laws, academic labour is always created and never destroyed. We are grateful to our departmental colleagues for ensuring that research leave was literally just that. The development of the ideas and analysis in this book were aided by the engagements of scholars and activists in a number of settings. For their invitations to present, and thoughtfulness in response, we are grateful to the Centre for Local Policy Studies at Edge Hill, particularly Mohammed Dhalech, CULCOM at the University of Oslo, in particular Sharam Alghasi and Thomas Hylland Eriksen, the Immigration Initiative in Trinity College Dublin, the Department of Communications at the University of Helsinki, the Diaspora, Migration and Media section of the European Communication Research Association (ECREA), Eric Fassin, Didier Fassin and Pap N'Diaye at the l'Institut de recherche interdisciplinaire sur les enjeux sociaux (IRIS) at the EHESS, Silvia Rodríguez Maeso and Marta Araujo at Centro de Estudos Sociais (CES) at the University of Coimbra, Valérie Amiraux of the Department of Sociology of the Université de Montréal, and the British Sociological Association Theory Study Group, especially Gurminder K. Bhambra. Alana wishes to thank Christophe Holzhey at the Institute for Cultural Inquiry in Berlin for hosting her as a visiting fellow during the spring of 2010, and funding a work-in-progress workshop held in July 2010.

We may take aim in this book at 'recited truths', but the standard acknowledgement that we are indebted to many, while absolving them of all responsibility for what falls between these covers, has never seemed to ring so true. So a special word of thanks to Colin Coulter, Sahar Delijani, Natalie Fenton, Joerg Forbrig, Giovanni Frazzetto, Arnika Fuhrman, Mary Gilmartin, Allan Grønbæk, Charles Husband, Kylie Jarrett, Kimmo Kallio, Andreas Karsten, Arun Kundnani, Massimo Leone, Sharmaine Lovegrove, Mark Maguire, Colm O'Cinneide, Yael Ohana, Eoin O'Mahony, Stephanie Rains, Aoife Titley, Jason Toynbee and Tobaron Waxman. These acknowledgements provide Gavan with a long-overdue opportunity to thank Michael Cronin for his academic guidance, and friendship.

Gavan would like to thank Alana for, among many, many things, making a demanding project joyful. As always, thanks to Alan and Mary Titley for their love, ideas and support. As a result of editorial over-optimism I owe the Lampinen-Titley family a proper summer holiday. I can happily add that to my gratitude to Päivi for her love, grace and sensibility, and to Jonas-Liam and Alvar for trying to accept that I'm not a fireman.

Alana would like to thank Gavan for being both exacting and challenging, and for his many trips to Brighton and Berlin, putting up with sleeping on hard floors, indeed with the occasional lack of floors. This book was written during the first year of her daughter's life, so the crisis of multiculturalism shared headspace with all the concerns that accompany a first-time parent's every waking moment. For the space and time to complete it nonetheless, Alana thanks her partner, Partho, whose unfailing support was graciously given despite the undoubted professional sacrifices entailed. This book is dedicated to Noam and Partho, her multicultural family, in love and struggle.

ONE

Recited truths: the contours of multi-cultural crisis

> Oh ye people of Europe/ GREAT injustice are committed upon deh land/ How long will we permit dem to carry on? Is Europe becoming a fascist place? The answer lies at your own gate/ and in the answer lies your fate. (Linton Kwesi Johnson, 'Reggae fi Peach')

> Much like other irritating subjects of the times – postmodernism, globalization, terrorism, among others – the very idea of multiculturalism, the ideology, disturbs out of proportion to what in fact it may be. The reality is that the world in which many people suppose they are living is actually plural: worlds – many of them, through which we pass whenever we venture out of the doors of what homes we may have. Yet, strangely, in a time like the one prevailing since the 1990s when a growing number of people began to profess the multicultural as a way of thinking about the worlds, their professions are often greeted with dismay. (Anthony Elliot and Charles Lemert, *The New Individualism* [2006: 137])

The new certainties

Multiculturalism, whatever it was, has failed. Multiculturalism, wherever it was, has imploded. Multiculturalism, whenever it was, has gifted us the pathologies that gird our new certainties.

Few people – particularly those given to regarding actually existing practices of state multiculturalism as a form of liberal nationalism, or overdetermining culturalism, or micro-colonialism, or political containment – can have guessed at the depths of its transformative power. Outlining this solid object of consternation involves more guesswork: described by Stuart Hall as a 'maddeningly spongy and imprecise discursive field', multiculturalism, as Charles W. Mills writes, is a 'conceptual grab bag' of issues relating to race, culture, and identity that 'seems to be defined simply by negation – whatever does not fit into the "traditional" political map of, say, the 1950s is stuffed in here' (2007: 89). Maddeningly spongy, but also bracingly so: an impressive spectrum of political actors and commentators hold it fully or partially responsible for an equally impressive range of cultural cleavages, social fissures and political dilemmas. The irony of multiculturalism's polysemy is that it has become a central site for coded debates about belonging, race, legitimacy and social futures in a globalized, neoliberal era.

It would be easy, given the tendency for the passing of multiculturalism to be measured out in stark, mediated death notices, to provide an illustrative pastiche of what is now a transnational genre. The fridge-magnet poetry of crisis is familiar, and easy to assemble: at five minutes to midnight the veil of multiculturalism was lifted to reveal the real suicide bomb living in seething ghettos, and so forth. So it is perhaps more interesting to see it officially represented. In January 2009, the Czech presidency of the EU unveiled *Entropa*, an art installation at the headquarters of the Council of the European Union in Brussels. Commissioned from the Czech artist Mark Czerny, it was soon swathed in the controversy it sought, as several European governments failed, as the artist put it, to show that 'Europe can laugh at itself'. In what Perry Anderson has termed Europe's contemporary climate of 'apparently illimitable narcissism' (2007), this was presumably part of the point. Yet what got obscured in the fleeting non-controversy was the political allusiveness of some of the refashioned stereotypes, and the particular dimension of narcissism they evoke. Denmark's installation cites a transnational event widely interpreted as demanding a concerted European stand for the imperilled principle of freedom of speech. The Lego construction is presented as a palimpsest of profanity, a play on the Turin Shroud, where the face of the Prophet Muhammad may or may not be superimposed on the colourful brick topography of Jutland. Keen to dampen any allusion to the 'Danish cartoon controversy' of 2005/06, the Danish government denied that this was the intention of the piece, and in so doing stayed true to their particular branch of hermeneutics. Polysemy has no place in their enlightened Europe, and much as there was then one legitimate way to read the cartoons – as a self-evident act of inclusive liberal mockery – it was important not to be wrongly free in this instance either.

The installation for the Netherlands presents a waterland finally reclaimed by the North Sea. All that survives are defiant minarets poking out from the waves, maritime navigational points for a lost civilization. This lost, plastic Holland fuses historical fears of natural erosion with more contemporary fears of racial/cultural erosion, and Czerny's creation compresses 'Eurabian' anxieties with an awareness of their transnational recognition and significance. For just as the American children's story of Hans Brinker is associated with courage in the face of natural disaster, the last decade has produced a narrative of Dutch courage in the face of cultural catastrophe. Pim Fortuyn, Theo Van Gogh, Ayaan Hirsi Ali, Rita Verdonk and Geert Wilders have attracted international attention for their resolve in shoring up the dykes against equally implacable waves of Islamification. The minarets – which in this multimedia installation actually issue a call to prayer – index their struggles to a wider transnational reality, not just of widespread protests against the construction of mosques and minarets, but to a collective reckoning with the unintended consequences of multiculturalism. For many in the Netherlands and beyond, these personalities mark out another terrain of reclamation: a post-multicultural landscape of liberal reassertiveness, cultural and elective homogeneity, and rehabilitative modes of national integration.

These plastic parodies reference key events and actors in the crisis of multiculturalism held to have unfolded over at least the last decade. A narrative of multicultural crisis has been pegged to a litany of transformative events conventionally dated to 11 September 2001, as evidence of a shared European and sometimes Western crisis, and as salutary lessons in a collective process of political reorientation. If the humanitarian and civilizing discourses of the war on terror are undergirded by a depoliticizing extraction of conflict 'from the dense lattice of geopolitical and political-economic considerations to be depicted as stark morality tales' (Seymour 2008: 215), the conventional accounting of multicultural collapse rehearses stark new certainties. Across the somewhat unsteady spectrum of left to right, through shifting and overlapping assemblages of argument and scales of evidential connection, and apropos of divergent visions of the good society traduced and the better ones to come, multiculturalism is widely regarded as a violently failed experiment. The narrative goes something like this. The 'multicultural fantasy in Europe' (Rieff 2005) valorized difference over commonality, cultural particularity over social cohesion, and an apologetic relativism at the expense of shared values and a commitment to liberty of expression, women's rights and sexual freedom. Its variously left, liberal and middle-class obsessions with self-gratifying practices of respect for cultural difference have been given spatial expression in the parallel societies, *problemområden*, ghettos, *parallelsgemeinschaften*, dish cities, *parallelsamfund* and *territoires perdus de la République* in which alien, repressive and often hostile ways of life are germinated. Each man kills the thing he loves, but only multiculturalists love that which will kill them. In what would once have been read as extremist language, it is regarded as cultural surrender; in his widely publicized book *Reflections on the Revolution in Europe: Can Europe be the same with different people in it?* Christopher Caldwell cautions that multiculturalism has derogated from the 'essence of Europe', and 'requires the sacrifice of liberties that natives once thought of as rights' (2009: 11).

There are other ways of historicizing and interpreting these sacrifices and the implicit racial compass of the natives held to have made them. This book assesses the putative crisis somewhat differently. After 9/11, and after the end of multiculturalism, delineating (national) hierarchies of belonging and of legitimate ways of being are central to political action and public culture. In this narrative, the 'failed experiment' of multiculturalism has generated unintended consequences that now require a return to the certainties it relativized and weakened. Like disappointed parents, or worldly social workers, or rueful older lovers, European nation-states promise themselves never to make the same, innocent mistakes again. The death of multiculturalism requires the rehabilitative discipline of integration, and a return to versions of the pre-experimental certainties, confidence in our values, without apologies. The scope of politics, and social futures, are held to rest on the inculcation of these shared values; values brought into relief by the identification of those who do not possess them and must be cultivated and coerced to respect them, but who constantly fail to display the will to develop them despite the density of spectacular opportunities they are offered.

Anti-racist politics has long struggled with and against multiculturalism, but the dimensions of the current conjuncture are particularly unsettling. For racialized minorities, multiculturalism – as governance, and as a broad coagulation of public values and aspirations – has, to varying degrees, made many societies nicer and fairer places to live than their historical antecedents (Fleras 2009; Hage 1998). Yet this broad acknowledgement has always been shadowed by the criticism that incremental achievement and modest gain are taken as licence to ignore and negate continuing and shifting racism in multicultural societies. For anti-racist critiques of racialized structures and patterns of power and privilege; for 'critical multiculturalist' takes on the patrician Eurocentrism of relations of recognition and tolerance; for activists protesting against the depoliticizing and culturalizing of racial injustice and inequality; for feminists, LGBT activists, youth workers and the secular left protesting against the 'micro-colonialism' of essentialized community leaders and structures of patronage: multiculturalism has, at best, provided attenuated pathways for organization and mobilization, provided the ambivalent political capital of 'recognition', and directed sporadic attention to the historical and political-economic conditions of social inequality. More often it has been seen as a mode of management and control, securing the legitimacy of the status quo through a deflection of questions of power and inequality into the relatively more malleable economy of cultural recognition. As Sneja Gunew observes, 'multiculturalism has been developed as a concept by nations and other aspirants to geopolitical cohesiveness who are trying to represent themselves as transcendentally homogenous in spite of their heterogeneity' (2004: 16). That the patrician terms of cultural recognition and the management of difference – what Arun Kundnani, in the context of the UK, terms 'the multicultural settlement' (2004: 105) – have become the depoliticized grounds for legitimate aversion is perhaps the most glaring elision of crisis talk. It is in this revisionist account, and the relational distribution of culpability between the multiculturalists and their experimental subjects, that the mainstream racism of the moment is laundered. As Martin Chanock observes,

> For a long time race and theories of racial difference held a central place in 'realistic' explanations in the West [...] it is almost too easy to contextualise such thinking and its connections with empire now, but harder to come to grips accurately with the connections in the present between the way power is distributed in the world and the growing centrality of culture as an explanatory tool. (2000: 15)

It has become even harder when the very relevance of power is obscured in neoliberal societies, and where the explanatory power of culture is structured, after '9/11', in a 'culturalist regime of truth' (Demmers and Mehendale 2010: 68). The layered ambivalence of overdetermined culturalism has long been flagged by activists, and in sociological critique (Balibar and Wallerstein 1991; Barker 1981). In a prescient passage in *Even in Sweden*, Allan Pred (2000) poses a series of questions probing the ways in which the uncritical ontological and discursive overlaps between mainstream multiculturalism and its strategic racist appropriation may serve to further produce racialized populations as subjects of problematization and regulation:

> But will these terms of discourse actually contribute to the elimina-
> tion of Sweden's widespread cultural racism or serve to perpetuate
> it? [...] will these usages, with their continued spotlighting of
> cultural distinctions and celebration of differences [...] actually now
> prevent 'culture' from masking the structures of power associated
> with conjoined production of ethnic and class inequalities, actually
> now prevent 'culture' from serving as an explanation of those
> social inequalities [...] will these current usages actually not prove
> counter-productive by further entrapping many of non-European
> and Muslim background into the language and logics of cultural
> difference, by more or less forcing them into forms of collective self-
> formation that are more than somewhat fictive, by driving them into
> the cul-de-sac of (racialized) identity politics [...] will these current
> usages somewhat prevent the occurrence of 'everyday racism' from
> being treated as if the product of spontaneous combustion rather
> than something associated with the exercise of various forms of
> power and knowledge production, with the arbitrary production of
> categorizations, with the kinds of majority-population subjectivities
> produced in the context of contemporary economic restructuring?
> (Ibid.: 280–82)

Without subscribing to the mythology of a world changed for ever on '9/11', the last decade has answered some of these questions. Multiculturalism, the failed experiment, provides a site on which the ontological parameters and political rhetorics derived from the 'new racisms' have been *laundered*. The reductive terms within which many minorities were strategically obliged to work have now become the evidence of their excess, compromised signs taken for radical wonders. The fluent mutuality of multicultural rhetoric and the confident discussion of abstract national 'models' have all too frequently been assumed to be the lived realities of multiculture. Now this multivalent, ongoing cultural *production* is rearticulated as the problematic pres-ence of a state-sponsored pre-modernity, of intolerable cocoons of atavism from which autonomous liberal individuals must be forced to metamorphose. In a context where political agency is held to be radically diminished, the new certainties of vindicated culturalism demand further attenuations, a dance-off between universalisms freed of the hard-won burden of reflexivity, and a 'relativism' fashioned as the scrapyard of political solidarities, sociological complexity and the necessity of attending to relations of power, inequality and intersectionality.

Yet this insistent rhetoric, and the new governmentality aimed at shaping culturally compatible and integrated subjects, ultimately offers up the possibilities of political critique, and that is the purpose of this book. To put it in terms of 2010's must-have risk accessory, where does the politics of crisis go when the burkas run out? For all the talk of shared values, particularized universalisms indexed in time and space to imaginative geographies of nation, Europe and the West – and to a paradoxically closed and static culture of Enlightenment – the crisis of multiculturalism is not a rejection of culturalism. It is a rejection of supposed cultural excess, and the compensatory reclamation of power over it. Minorities, as Arjun Appadurai writes,

> are the flashpoint for a series of uncertainties that mediate between everyday life and its fast shifting global backdrop. They create uncertainties about the national self and national citizenship because of their mixed status [...] their movements threaten the policing of borders [...] their lifestyles are easy ways to displace widespread tensions in society, especially in urban society. Their politics tends to be multi-focal, so they are always sources of anxiety to security states. (2006: 44–5)

In the West, where talking about racism has become taboo, displacing systemic tensions on to scapegoats is a complex undertaking. While state racisms have structural force and instrumental drive, they in turn are redacted in a broader mesh of cultural politics, social activism and trajectories of political animation. Thus multiculturalism has become the discursive space within which the contemporary politics of race finds fungible expression and plausible, multivalent vindication. The problem of multiculturalism sanctions 'crisis racism' (Balibar and Wallerstein 1991) for societies in which lived diversity cannot be effaced, in which unromantic, everyday cohabitation and banal intermixture and interaction are routine, and in which visions of cultural diversity are imbricated in late capitalist strategies and themes, urban and metropolitan imaginaries, affective and imaginative practices, and even tentative visions of the good society. Rejecting multiculturalism has become the proxy for the rejection of lived multiculture, the alibi of experimental failure justifies the ordering of *good and bad diversity*. In a neoliberal political economy of state retraction, the 'backlash' elides the fact that there was never really a lash.[1] In a transnational era of constant flow and temporary closures, where transcendental homogeneity has been, again, frayed, the crisis of multiculturalism is ultimately a myth of comforting sovereignty; *we* created this situation, and we can undo it. After multiculturalism, as Liz Fekete writes suggestively, 'in a climate of fear, hostility and suspicion, homogeneity is fast becoming western Europe's security blanket' (2009: 67–8). This is true, yet that homogeneity is not homogeneous. The unifying focus on multiculturalism may ultimately serve to illuminate the tensions and differences, despite elective affinities, that can not indefinitely be contained by 'populist' and 'progressive' dependence on specifying post-political cultural fault-lines. 'Effective thinking upon an illusory object', in Balibar's phrase, is likely to be subject to diminishing returns.

The idea that multiculturalism has run its course is an expedient one, and although it may appear new, it is merely constantly renewed. When scrambling for scapegoats replaces the search for viable alternatives, ending multiculturalism presents itself as an accomplishable goal. Competing to deliver multiculturalism's *coup de grâce* are liberals convinced of the weakness of postmodern cultural relativism, nationalists threatened by the unassimilable, progressive intellectuals for whom 'liberal multiculturalism' has weakened and divided leftist critique, and so-called race relations professionals refashioning 'diversity' and 'integration' as the new paradigms of their daily graft. Part of what makes the 'backlash' appear so unitary is the spectrum of state and non-state actors who use multiculturalism as a prism. Its refractions are intensified by the transnational circulation of the 'recited truths' of crisis, and it is to the weaving of these recitations that we now turn.

Recited truths

What has the putative failure of multiculturalism been made to mean, and what does this narrative of the recent past legitimize and sanction? Such questions are not normally answered in Dublin's evening newspapers, but the following outline of the contours of crisis provides a useful point of entry:

> Muslim immigrants bring with them cultural practices and even
> dress codes that are totally different to our Irish way of doing things.

So where do we draw the line between respecting their traditions and asking them to adapt to ours? We don't have to look very far to see that the consequences of getting this wrong could be disastrous. For 50 years the rest of Europe has followed the social policy known as 'multiculturalism', which basically means allowing separate religious communities to develop independently alongside that of their hosts. Today the evidence is overwhelming that this policy has failed. Because the countries made little or no effort to integrate their new citizens [sic], they created ghettos that became breeding grounds for violent extremists. In recent years we've seen the long-term results in the shape of race riots in France, the assassination of the controversial politician Pim Fortuyn in the Netherlands and the 7/7 bombings by British Muslims in London [...] Ireland doesn't have these problems – yet. (*Evening Herald*, 28 May 2008)

Written in response to a half-hearted 'headscarf debate', and during a period in which substantially increased and variegated migration to Ireland was subject to incessant worry over 'getting integration right' (Boucher 2008), the series of assumptions about what multiculturalism was, and what is now required to undo its pathologies, is instructive. Its circulated understanding of multiculturalism as a solid object and causal force, an understanding that picks up informational lint from European elsewheres to assemble a narrative with possible performative force for the national here, produces a ticking culture scenario – Ireland doesn't have these problems, yet. But it has Muslims. As multiculturalism's pathology, their presence signals all we need to know. They come and they bring their totally different, and specifically gendered, way of doing things. In so doing they signal perilous futures, already witnessed elsewhere, and hard choices, for it is Muslims, as the British columnist Rod Liddle put it, who 'killed multiculturalism' (2004). As multiculturalism's impossible subjects, they sit at the apex of a triangulated politics, aligned with accommodating relativists and assertive liberal-nationalists in a political geometry convinced of these axes as fixed relationships and final horizons.

That a 'policy of multiculturalism' is imaginatively dated to a period of post-war, post-colonial labour migration in western Europe, a period that has come, shorn of both its racism and the organized, internationalist opposition to it, to represent a nostalgic vision of social cohesion, is certainly erroneous. But it is also indicative of the fluidity of multiculturalism as a signifier, shifting from contested policy to the potential specification of any difference held to threaten the imperative of cultural unity and functional homogeneity. This sense of multicultural haunting is transnational, and the turbulence of its afterlife owes much to the revisionist tendencies of its obituarists:

> Multiculturalism was attacked from the right almost from its inception, and was repudiated by segments of the left for allegedly burying the inequalities of race in vague celebrations of cultural difference. It was never adopted as official policy in any part of Europe [...] in France, however, multiculturalism was rejected pretty much out of hand as at odds with republican principles; in Germany, as at odds with a predominantly ethnicized conception of citizenship; while in Italy or Spain, multiculturalism barely figured in either popular or political discourse until the last few years. In those countries most commonly cited as exemplars of multicultural policy – the UK, the Netherlands, Sweden – practices varied and were rarely codified in any explicit way. (Phillips and Sawitri 2008: 291–2)

For this reason, the Irish editorial extract is no less heuristic for being highly particular, and its importance is as an unexceptional artefact. Across both reportage and academic work it has become almost customary to establish the existence of a crisis of multiculturalism with reference to a chain of transformative events. As Vertovec and Wessendorf argue, 'since the early 2000s across Europe, the rise, ubiquity, simultaneity and convergence of arguments condemning multiculturalism has been striking' (2009: 7). These arguments are frequently instigated by and organized around 'key incidents'. Working from Paul Scheffer's article on 'The multicultural drama' (2000) in the Netherlands, their analysis extends this litany of events to include: riots in Bradford, Burnley and Oldham in 2001, 11 September 2001, David Goodhart's article 'Too diverse?' in *Prospect* magazine (2004a), the Madrid train bombings, the 2004 murder of Theo Van Gogh, the *Jyllands Posten* cartoons and extended aftermath in 2005/06, and the October 2006 *Lancashire Telegraph* article by Jack Straw, sharing his unveiled discomfort (Younge 2009: 11–12). Each event acts as an invitation to rehearse recurring crisis idioms, and these idioms could have been used to auto-generate the *Evening Herald* piece: multiculturalism is a single doctrine, which has fostered separateness and provided a haven for terrorists and reprehensible cultural practices, while stifling debate and denying problems (Vertovec and Wessendorf 2009: 13–19; see also Finney and Simpson 2009; Siapera 2009).

As a reading of recent history, Vertovec and Wessendorf are correct to argue that 'the portrayals [...] are demonstrably partial, erroneous, or false'. The editorial is also demonstrably bad journalism: the backdated 'policy of multiculturalism'; the implication that Pim Fortuyn was murdered by a violent Islamist rather than the animal rights activist Volkert Van der Graaf; a studied avoidance of how the biography of the London bomber Mohammad Sidique Khan complicated the causal significance of multiculturalism's 'parallel societies' in British public discourse (Kundnani 2007; McGhee 2008). However, these constantly circulated events are not a unified genre, and the hegemonic significance they are accorded cannot be understood solely by reference to a lack of empirical veracity. Partial and erroneous visions of multiculturalism are precisely the medium through which lived multiculture is delegitimized. Reading the crisis involves holding together both an attention to empirical elision, and the political and cultural dynamics that produce these facilitative histories.

Michel De Certeau's idea of 'recited truths' is useful here. In *The Practice of Everyday Life* (1984), he examines the assembly of such socio-political orthodoxies: 'Society has become a recited society in three senses; it is defined by stories (*récits*, the fables constituted by our advertising and informational media), by citations of stories and by the interminable recitation of stories' (ibid.: 186). Recitation involves the production of social facts through narrativizaton and repetition, facts which then appear unconstructed by anyone, and where, midst a 'forest of narrativities [...] stories have a providential and predestining function' (ibid.: 186). The image of a forest of narrativities is compelling. If multiculturalism provides a spongy referent, indexed by endless ideological manoeuvring to a spectrum of political questions, iconic events offer signposts. Recurrent assemblages explaining what these events 'mean' beat a path through the forest. Ron Eyerman, in a consideration of the murder of Theo Van Gogh, argues that occurrences become events through recitation, and

> through a dialectic of actions and interpretation. Actions occur in time and space, events unfold and take shape. An event unfolds and takes shape in the interplay between protagonists, interpreters, and audience, as sense and meaning is attributed and various interpretations compete with each other. As this meaning struggle proceeds various accounts stabilize, with perhaps one achieving some sort of

hegemony, but counter interpretations or stories may continue to
exist alongside [...] (2008: 22)

What an attention to 'some sort of hegemony' implies is that a
critical engagement must be able to apply different modes of analysis
adequate to its production, and modalities of contingent consent and
affective power. For that reason we employ several in this book. First,
the recited truths of multicultural crisis require attention for their
empirical elisions, and for the voices and counter-interpretations that
are frequently glossed over or forgotten. Over the course of the book,
analyses of discourses of multicultural crisis in different national
contexts are patterned into the themes of the chapters. They provide
examples of how particular ways of talking about multiculturalism,
allied to its idiomatic flexibility in discussions of race and ethnicity,
create an inflated sense of what multiculturalism involved. As Ralph
Grillo has argued, currents of multicultural discontent are shaped in
the gap between the 'weak multiculturalism' that has largely characterized institutional practice and the widespread critical assumption
that it is always in its 'strongest form' – that is, for many critics,
'multiculturalism is always already "unbridled"' (2007: 987). Thus,
while our primary focus is on the political uses of the unbridled
image, this must be established, to some degree, with reference to
the often tepid actualities.

In some contexts, what is understood as the nature, scope and
subject of multiculturalism is complex, in others it functions more
as a mobilizing metaphor of aversion. While France is a central site
of critique in this book, and its post-colonial social fabric could
certainly be described as 'multicultural', the term, if it features at all,
stands as a euphemism for the problems of what French republicans
refer to disparagingly as communitarianism, and for the impositions
of Anglo-American political and academic ideology (Bourdieu and
Wacquant 1999). In research, as Amiraux and Simon observe, 'in
a mimetic reflex with the republican creed, [social sciences] still
attempt to avoid the recognition of ethnic and racial minorities by
carefully closing the closet door' (2006: 208). In another key site, for
all the general association of Denmark with multicultural retreat,
the retreat is not from policy so much as from the thin membrane of
multicultural politesse. Speaking a week before the publication of the
Jyllands Posten cartoons in 2005, Brian Mikkelsen, Danish minister
for cultural affairs, illustrated the point by declaring 'war against

the multicultural ideology' because 'a medieval Muslim culture can never be as valid as Danish culture here at home [...] The struggle of culture and values has now raged for some years. And we can, I believe, note that first half is about to be won' (Klausen 2006). Lex et al. (2007) summarize the context:

> debates on the 'crisis' of multiculturalism appear slightly misplaced from a Danish academic perspective. In spite of a great deal of discursive opposition to 'multicultural ideology', which is associated with illiberalism and politically correct value relativism, no important group or constituency favours multiculturalism, if this is taken to mean a comprehensive, normatively grounded political program of accommodating cultural minority needs [...] while many policy measures are directed towards minorities in the targeting of such problems as poor labour market integration, there is also precious little in the way of multicultural policy to report. Following a standard typology, the discourses on citizenship and integration, which have prevailed since the seventies, place Denmark in the 'ethnic assimilationist' [...] corner. (Ibid.: 7)

Facts, of course, cannot simply be pared and polished to a state beyond discourse, as discourses involve 'practices that systematically form the objects of which they speak' (Foucault 2001: 49). The work of discourse, and the ways in which the idea of 'empirical multiculturalism' becomes ensnared in liquid articulations[2] of aversion to the prospect, the ideology, the obscene human supplements, and the 'facticity of multiculturalism' (Pitcher 2009), leads to a second, and more pronounced, focus of this book. This involves exploring the production and circulation of what we will also call recited truths: the circulation of beliefs about what multiculturalism was and what it did, who its subjects were and what they have become, how what happened in events over *there* seems to connect with what is happening *here*. In a recent comparative study of multicultural governance in six countries, Augie Fleras (2009) draws attention to the impact of international discourses in 'hardening European arteries' towards multiculturalism, immigration and Muslim populations (ibid.: 194–202). In many ways, his conclusion is our starting point. As Sneja Gunew argues, 'the meanings of multiculturalism are always deeply enmeshed in constructions of the local, the national, and the global' (2004: 2). Analysing meanings involves paying attention to national contexts, and the role of state power in shaping multiculturalisms and attempting to control and order migration. But it also means recognizing that under current conditions of transnational mediation and mobility, and the specific circuitry of NGOs, intergovernmental organizatons, academia, media and issue-based networks that Will Kymlicka implicates in the 'global diffusion of a political discourse of multiculturalism' (2007: 3–60), it has become a mobile signifier that cannot easily be anchored normatively or located in distinct genealogies of production.

Gunew's argument, however, means paying attention to more than the transnational dimensions of multiculturalism's fairly predictable polysemy. The question, as the *Evening Herald* extract suggests, is not just the mobility of multiculturalism as an idiom, particularly in contexts without anything approximating multicultural policy, but its properties as a mobilizing metaphor. The meanings of multiculturalism and of 'constructions of the local, the national and the global' are enmeshed in ways that position multiculturalism as a discursive space within which fundamental socio-political questions are implicated and fomented. As examinations of multicultural backlash attest, this has long been the case (Hewitt 2005). In the last decade the reach, insistence and opacity of 'multiculturalism' have prompted an interest in why and how it refracts such an array of shifting questions of race, nationhood, state, gender, class, identity and globalization (Schuster and Solomos 2001; McGhee 2008; Pitcher 2009). Our particular extension of this approach is to examine the conjunctural importance of multiculturalism in providing a site in which the politics of race can be legitimized and laundered. By tracking the ways in which iterations of multiculturalism have been used to argue for, legitimize and position new formations of the problem of difference, this book makes an argument for recovering the analytical and oppositional possibilities of race as a political category in the contemporary moment.

To speak of the politics of race and racism, of course, is to confront directly what could be seen as the primary recited truth of crisis politics. 'Race' is a fiction, and racism, when it is discussed, is largely dismissed as a fraught, accusatory moralism, or explained through an apologetics citing exceptional incidents, expressions of a classed pathology, and discriminatory expressions that 'work both ways'. In making a discussion of 'race' central to this analysis, and in insisting on its salience for understanding the variegated political trajectories and desires working through the space of multicultural crisis, we are aware that we invite a certain kind of dismissive reading, as being dabbed with the 'smell of yesteryear' in Christian Joppke's memorable phrase (2007: 16). This dismissal, whether instrumental or articulated from what Charles W. Mills argues is an agreement to misinterpret the world 'validated by white epistemic authority' (1997: 18), is precisely the odourless problem we set out to engage. As Howard Winant puts it: 'No longer unabashedly white supremacist, for the most part the world is, so to speak, abashedly white supremacist. The conflicts generated by the powerful movements for racial justice that succeeded World War II have been contained but not resolved' (2004: xiv).

The events enchained in the *Evening Herald*'s litany of recitation, their symbolic importance and their cumulative, syntagmatic logic, cannot be understood without examining the ways in which they signify racially. In relation to the 'race riots' in France, for example, Sylvie Tissot (2008) describes how the construction of social policy around the problem of *les banlieues* paradoxically infuses and defuses race as an explanatory modality, as 'the new paradigm approaches exclusion through a growing but disguised racialization of discussions of poverty, with territorial categories functioning as euphemized racial categories, as well as through the question of social ties rather than economic hardships' (ibid.: 4). With an established spatialized 'pathology', it is a short step, as Riva Kastoryano notes, to index the 2005 *émeutes* in Clichy-sous-Bois to a sensationalized instance of the 'various Islamic challenges' cultivated in territories lost to the republic (2008: 135–6).

The power of recitation is that of unrelenting focus, the constant evaluation of those 'in but not of Europe' (Hall 2003) and the insistent grafting of racial meaning to these circulating fragments of trivia. The 'race' idea, according to Paul Gilroy, remains powerful 'precisely because it supplies a foundational understanding of natural hierarchy on which a host of other supplementary social and political conflicts have come to rely. Race remains the self-evident force of nature in society' (Gilroy 2004: 9). Racial discourse cannot be dissipated like a mist exposed to the heat of empirical truth, as it is concerned with 'the fabrication of social homogeneities', in both senses of the verb (Goldberg 2009: 5). Yet the power of this racial grammar today also rests on the licence – or complacency, in Winant's terms – that stems from a consensus on being *post-race*, where race is resiliently understood solely in terms of what has been rejected; the narrow and selective terms of false biology and phenotypical classification. Thus according to the Danish writers Jens-Martin Eriksen and Frederik Stjernfelt (2010),

> 'Race' is no longer used as a valid form of identification, and all that is left is the culturalist argument. In Denmark, the Danish People's Party should be understood as being a culturalist party whose attitudes are an expression of a modern differentialism. No major political movement in Denmark or anywhere else in Europe bases its platforms on racism. Such a position is no longer held by an elite and is not represented by any but radical losers without political significance.

What is *passé* for them is *post-ness* for us. Analytically, their argument is packed with elisions and misreadings; from a discussion of 'differentialism' that does not make the link to the importance of culturalism in refocusing the differentialist 'new racisms' of popular fronts across Europe in the 1970s (Balibar and Wallerstein 1991; Barker 1981; MacMaster 2000; Stolcke 1995); to the contextual histories of 'new racism' in Denmark, tracked to the anti-asylum seeker populisms of the 1980s (Hervik 2011; Wren 2001); to the scarcely credible intellectual contention that the lack of an explicit, colour-coded racist political platform evidences the absence of racist politics in Europe. Beyond this specific analytical poverty, it evinces a wider problem, which is that the analytical possibilities of race are necessary precisely to understand the obfuscating but shifting dynamics of culturalism. Shorn of these possibilities, as Goldberg argues, 'Europe begins to exemplify what happens when no category is available to name a set of experiences that are linked in their production, or at least inflection, historically and symbolically, experientially and politically, to racial arrangements and engagements' (2009: 154). The experience of racism, and the legitimacy of resistant politics informed by those experiences, have been elided in this climate of valorized narcissism.

A critique of culturalism does not involve dismissing the significance of cultural attachments in people's lives, or of culturalization as a dimension of human subjectivity (A. Phillips 2007: 11–15). Neither does it imply an artificial divide between 'identity politics' and political economy (Duggan 2003; Fraser 2004). Rather, our focus is on the ongoing production, and uses, of static entities. Terry Eagleton argues that culture has historically involved a friction between senses of *making* and *being made* (2000: 36). Contemporary culturalisms, buoyed by a rejection of proven multicultural excess, invest enormous labour, or making, in presenting racialized others as having been made, and presenting this as the basis for political action. Thus, along a spectrum from hard and soft versions of a clash-of-civilizations logic (Huntington 1993, 1996) to the neoliberal mood music of integration as a 'two-way process', discrete ways of life are presented as under some form of threat from non-Westerners in their midst. Analysing this is further complicated by recognizing that the political capital of culturalization is embedded in a more diffuse cultural turn (Yúdice 2003). The ubiquity of 'culture' and its power are, as Levent Soysal argues, correlated: 'the more culture diffuses into everyday discourses, we observe that its potency – the degree of its use and acceptance to define, organize, manage individual and social worlds – sharply amplifies. Simply put, no domain of [personal and collective] life remains outside of or immune to culture' (2009: 5). As a consequence, highly essentialist and racialized visions of culture, indexed to a shifting vocabulary of values and ways of life, are not exceptional remnants or resistant contradictions in a socioscape permeated with the language, imagery and affective attractions of diversity. They are made and assembled in and through it.

As a consequence, this books pays ongoing attention to processes of discursive assemblage. As a dimension of this, we agree with Vertovec and Wessendorf that 'these [crisis] events seemed to provide for critics, who had long been seeking to pronounce – and to ensure – the death of multiculturalism, nails with which to seal its coffin' (2009: 12). In response to this insistent hammering, this book has a polemical intent, particularly in relation to the resistance to complexity and politics that has hugely intensified in the decades since Edward Said, in *Covering Islam*, specified the 'unquestioned assumption that Islam can be characterised limitlessly by means of a handful of recklessly general and repeatedly deployed clichés' (1991: xi). Muslims have become prosaic subjects of public debate, on which anyone can hold an opinion as to their essential compatibility, and the parameters of their permissible freedom. In opening this out, we make no claims to expertise concerning people living in Europe who self-identify as Muslims, or have Muslim backgrounds. Instead, we draw attention to the immodesty of the commentariat, and the politics of those who draw sanction from the *zeitgeist* to ignore fundamental standards of intellectual and ethical practice, and treat 'political subjectivities as expressive of a cultural and religious essence [...] [that adds] to the politically instrumental and analytically barren civilizational discourses whose resurgence has accompanied recent geopolitical conflicts' (Toscano 2010: 167).

Beyond the cohort of commentators who explicitly act as stenographers of racialized anxieties is a wider spectrum of liberal-left intellectuals who confuse their post-political sensibilities with the actual forces shaping the lives of millions. As David Edgar puts it, the apparent death of left–right divisions has moved progressive thinkers to 'posit a raft of new fault lines – liberty versus authority, secularism versus religion, free speech versus censorship, universalism versus multiculturalism, feminism versus the family – all of which are cast in forms that put the progressive middle class on one side and significant sections of the poor on the other' (2009). The development of these fault-lines is involved, but it is necessary also to appreciate how crafting them involves considerable ideological work. As Joan Wallach Scott observes in her book on the 2003/04 headscarf debates in France, the 'virtual community building' involved in a binary construction of France versus its Muslims involved ongoing homological labour, on a vision of culture that posits 'objectively discernible values and traditions that were homogenous and immutable; complexity, politics and history were absent. Culture was said to be the cause of the differences [...] this idea of culture was the effect of a very particular, historically specific political discourse' (2007: 7). As Scott argues pointedly, 'creating the reality one wants requires strong argument and the discrediting, if not silencing, of alternative points of view' (ibid.). This labour cannot be countered through Interculturalism's advocacy of better and deeper engagement, or through the frequent Cultural Studies assumption that asserting the truths of cultural hybridity and fluidity has some directly enlightening political function. Recited truths must be countered by examining them in the contexts in which they seem to make sense and are invested with significance.

As Demmers and Mehendale write in relation to the murder of Theo Van Gogh, a normative culturalism united left and right around the 'truth effect' of his death: 'Here lies the dead Dutchman, butchered like a pig by a bearded, radical Muslim. This is good and evil. This is the end of relativism and, above all, of complexity' (2010: 57). The force of these truth effects must be explained sociologically, and must account for how events serve as intimations of a cumulative coherence that is politically useful and culturally reassuring. Contemporary sociology has explored at length the relationship between neoliberal globalization, social uncertainty and anxiety, and the troubled embrace of culturalized racism. As Back and Sinha write, 'the power of the idea of cultural mortification is in its ability to evoke a system of affects, or a kind of rigged collective nervous system, that polices' (2011). Throughout the book we examine iterations of crisis in relation to how and why the idea of cultural mortification seems to resolve and compensate for so much in contemporary societies. The question remains, nevertheless: why a gathering storm around multiculturalism in a decade in which any committed philosophy and sustained political practice of multiculturalism have been all but absent?

The comforts of crisis

In a review essay on 'what is living and what is dead in multiculturalism', Geoffrey Brahm Levy (2009) notes that critiques of multiculturalism, as wilful social experimentation and as corrosive of national identity, have been around for decades. Contextual versions of the 'unfairness to Whites' discourse (Rhodes 2010) have been patterned since the 1970s as a focus for concentrating anxieties of disempowerment stemming from the socio-economic impacts of neoliberal restructuring and the general implosion of class-based politics (Hewitt 2005), the transfer of powers and borders incrementally involved in membership of the European Union (Berezin 2009), and the multiplicity of formal and informal adjustments and dilutions of state autonomy and sovereignty associated with international structures and systemic globalization (Held et al. 1999: 321–6). As Roger Hewitt (2005) documents, a multivalent backlash took shape internationally in the 1990s: in debates on equality, affirmative action and the reductively titled 'culture wars' in the USA (see also Duggan 2003); in attacks on national multicultural policy frameworks in Canada (Kymlicka 2007); in the politics of what Ghassan Hage (1998) termed 'white anxiety' and its (re)mobilizaton through Pauline Hanson's One Nation Party in Australia; and in the so-called 'cultural racism' (Stolcke 1995) that informed the political success of anti-immigration populist and far-right parties in northern and western Europe (MacMaster 2000; Fekete 2009).

So backlash is not news; the recent intensification of animus, Brahm Levy writes, results from the fact that 'with Islam and Muslims, the boundaries of the tolerable are deemed to have been stretched so far that they are now snapping back rapidly in the opposite direction' (2009: 76). As the anxieties compressed in the *Evening Herald* attest, the last decade has witnessed the naturalization of an immutable entity termed Muslims as the wedge that hinders the promise of national integration and an expansive range of normative, otherwise-achieved projects. From the obliterating fictions of imperial invasions to the right-on habitus of middle-class aversions, the racialized spectre of specifying a problematic population should be far more unsettling than it generally appears to be. That this recent history is not more unsettling owes something to the particular ways in which a crisis of multiculturalism and apparent Muslim excess have become, to a large extent, reciprocally determining. However, anti-Muslim racism in the West, for all its convergent energies, is a contingent product of differing contextual histories, subjects of aversion and situated political anxieties. It is Brahm Levy's emphasis on *deeming* which draws attention to the importance of recitation; the particular equation of multiculturalism and Muslims is always positional, but it mediates broadly comparable structural anxieties, and garners political energy from a process of transnational validation.

The allusion to the boundaries of what is deemed tolerable recalls that, in the patterning of prejudice, this is a new variation on an established inversion. In his theorizaton of crisis racism under Thatcherism and in the France of an insurgent Front national, Etienne Balibar describes how the invocation of crisis licenses the 'crossing of certain *thresholds of intolerance* [...] which are generally turned on the victims themselves and described as thresholds of tolerance' (Balibar and Wallerstein 1991: 219, italics in original). Establishing the intolerable is crucial to the exercise of racisms integral to but disavowed in national and European imaginaries (Blommaert and Verschueren 1998: 78). This preserves a hegemonic self-image of the tolerant acting intolerantly under duress: the 2004 redesignation of the wearing of the hijab in France as *intrinsically* an act of proselytization, the defence of the publication of the *Jyllands Posten* cartoons as an *inclusive* act of mockery, the objection to a Muslim cultural centre and 'inter-faith prayer space' near the former site of the World Trade Center in New York as an 'assertion of Islamic triumphalism that we should not tolerate' (see Pilkington 2010).

A seductive property of recited multiculturalism is its status as a form of unhappy tolerance. In the preface for Patrick West's *The Poverty of Multiculturalism*, Kenneth Minogue caricatures British multiculturalism as an officially enforced 'virtue of tolerance' which, while advocating parities of cultural esteem, is motivated 'less by love of others than hatred of one's own form of life' (2005: xiii). Hans

Entzinger, drawing on a Dutch national self-image of tolerance, asks 'why is it that a country that had institutionalised the acceptance of difference and that was reputed for its tolerance could shift so quickly to what is perceived as coercive and assimilationist policy?' (2006: 121). What is secured, in specifying the end of tolerance, is a set of power relations that claims tolerance as an innate majoritarian property. This crisis dialectic of tolerance and intolerance goes to the heart of multiculturalism as the will to 'transcendental homogeneity' incorporated into post-colonial and nationalist imaginaries (Gunew 2004). As Ghassan Hage argues in *White Nation* (1998):

> the coexistence of tolerance and intolerance in 'tolerant societies' was not due to the fact that tolerance was somehow not forcefully implemented. Rather it is that those who were and are asked to be tolerant remain *capable* of being intolerant, or to put it differently, that the advocacy of tolerance left people *empowered* to be intolerant. (Ibid.: 86, italics in original)

Relations of tolerance, in other words, assume the fact of control over the object of tolerance, who is 'never just present, they are positioned'. This is the other side of a politics of recognition; the tolerant gaze assumes the power to set limits, thresholds, modes through which racialized presences are recognized, contingently, as 'desirable' or 'not that undesirable' (ibid.: 90). Multicultural tolerance obfuscates the power involved in setting the limits of tolerance: 'If "racist violence" is better understood as a nationalist practice of exclusion, "tolerance", in much the same way, can be understood as a nationalist practice of inclusion. Both, however, are practices confirming an image of the White Australian as a manager of national space' (ibid.: 90–91). In this purview, the idea that Muslims have stretched the boundaries of the tolerable takes on a different aspect. 'Backlash' is patterned in multiculturalism's structures of power, and it has become a site of crisis in part because its subjects have ceased to either fit with or acquiesce to fantasies of national management, but also because 'the Muslim' has become an acute symbol of the gradual destabilization and recalibration of the fantasy of nationalist management. What has made this particularly virulent is the range of state and non-state actors that have located animating possibilities in their opposition to these 'impossible subjects' and their spiritual, moral, cultural and political certainties.

Evidently this owes much to the aftermath of '9/11', but it is not reducible to it. For those, as Malcolm Brown observes, who find it 'almost impossible to believe that Islam even existed in Western consciousness before September 11, 2001' (2006: 297), it is not difficult to uncover this patterning. Even before Huntington's 1993 essay on the 'Clash of Civilizations' in *Foreign Affairs*, Philip Schlesinger (1992) identified the multivalent ways in which Islam had 'begun to fill the void brought about by the Soviet empire's collapse', and in this mode had already suggested multiple vectors of ethno-national affirmation; as a foreign policy threat, as an internal anxiety concerning assimilation, and as a demographic scare through migration. This malleable capital became central to the so-called 'new racism' that appropriated the 'right to difference' of immigrants and minorities to recode the boundaries of the race-nation through a 'reasonable right to protect national identity and culture' (MacMaster 2000). As Neil MacMaster documents, the relative electoral gains, in the second half of the 1990s, of the radical right in Flanders, Italy, Norway and Denmark – culminating in the electoral successes of the Austrian Freedom Party and the Swiss People's Party in 1999 – were underscored by a now familiar translation of differentialist discourse into mainstream politics by parties seeking to appropriate the 'problem' message while disowning the problematic messenger (ibid.: 200–204; see also Berezin 2009, Fekete 2009). MacMaster also notes the transnational continuum established as the political specification of an external 'fundamentalist' threat fused with 'an internal Muslim danger to a European culture and identity symbolized by mosque construction, veiled women and Muslim schools' (2000: 204).

This emergence shows significant contextual variation during this period, one wider trend is noteworthy. The Muslim problem was inscribed within the 'economic chauvinism' (Gingrich and Banks 2006) formed through increased anxieties about resource competition and legitimate claims on states busy globalizing their economies and refitting labour forces to the 'flexibility' required by informational capitalism. Particularly after 1989, political reactions to increased asylum-seeking focused on a politics of unwanted numbers, eliding asylum-seeking with 'economic migration' in ways that presented 'refugee migration' as a burden on the welfare state (Crowley and Hickman 2008). Yet while the 'asylum seeker' became a racialized category of unwanted difference that collapsed the heterogeneity of those seeking asylum, anti-Muslim racism was also shaped by this effacement. In Denmark, for example, a strong public discourse constructed refugees from Muslim-majority countries as a unitary cultural threat, and family reunification programmes were politicized as a gateway to both resource drain and cultural-demographic decline (Wren 2001; Hervik 2011). Similarly, a clash-of-civilizations discourse has been an emergent pillar of the party political instrumentalization of multiculture and asylum/immigration in the Netherlands since the early 1990s (Prins 2002). However, according to Zuquette (2008), anti-Muslim racism became a 'basic ideological feature' of the European extreme right only after '9/11', as, in a more diffuse bleed, it capitalized on the mainstream culturalism of political reaction.

The events of 11 September 2001 – '9/11' – are a misleading and arbitrary point of historical transformation, yet it has become impossible to recite, or indeed analyse, the narrative of multicultural crisis without referencing them. In the selective vastness of the contemporary discursive economy, narrative, as Christian Salmon argues, is an instrument of control (2010). An instrument, but as with any hegemonic potentiality, not a guarantee; the point of 9/11 is not that it determines subsequent narratives, but that it demands some form of recalibration in the stark terms dictated by its insistent threshold of before and after. Derek Gregory captures the positional investments that stem from this when he writes of it as a moment when 'the metropolis exercised its customary privilege to inspect the rest of the world' (2004: 21). The privilege of inspection is performative, stimulating the circulation and legitimization of recited truths that attain productive and constitutive power, but inspection is as much recall as perusal, an exercise of 'the arts of memory [...] in the colonial present' (ibid.: 9). Presaging the enthusiasm of Gordon Brown and Nicolas Sarkozy for 'balanced' accounts of empire's manifest benefits and regrettable occurrences, Gregory counters: 'for what else is the war on terror other than the violent return of the colonial past, with its split geographies of "us" and "them", "civilization" and "barbarism", "Good" and "Evil"?' (ibid.: 11). Yet amnesia also begets 'new memory'. The imaginary of a resurgent threat to Western modernity and civilization, intensively mediated through a 'referential archive' of associations and images, 'creates an intertextuality which constantly weaves events as new memories crafting a new temporality to gauge and locate Islam' (Ibrahim 2007: 49). As Gregory indicates through his idea of inspection, this temporal logic was spatialized in existing power regimes and relations, and thus becomes a remembering that Yasmin Ibrahim terms *dis-orientalism*:

Since 9/11 the narrative of Islam has put the focus on Muslim communities in the West. Unlike the Islamic revolution in Iran in the late 1970s and 1980s, this 'reimagining' of Islam, narrated as posing a clear and present danger to civilization, has placed Muslim communities in the West under relentless scrutiny. The Muslim intellectual debates and responses emanating from the communities are often seen as being externalized from the conditions of modernity or its incumbent reflexivity. The constant need to respond to events associated with Islam renders immense pressure on these communities to negotiate the sustained moral and social stigmatization in narrating Islam. (Ibid.: 48)

The nebulous idea of a 'war on terror' involved *vertebrate* reaction – territorial invasion – to *cellular* formations of networked extremism (Appadurai 2006: 21–32). If amnesiac histories discard the resistant truth of the old anti-racist slogan 'we are over here because you were over there', new memory insists that 'we are over there because you are over here'. The ambit of the 'war on terror' included, from its inception, the specification and management of suspicious internal populations and dangerous transnational mobilities.[3] *Dis-orientalism* provides the temporal and spatial coordinates for recited truths, as the 'customary privilege to inspect' became focused on split geographies and 'parallel societies' within the nation. It permitted the (re)discovery of social enemies as more clearly delineated cultural ones. The 'war on terror' provided the conditions through which the equation of multiculturalism and Muslims gained significant transnational traction, patterned by a 'remarkably consistent racial politics more generally operative in the West' (Pitcher 2009: 135). There is no doubt that we would be witnessing a crisis of multiculturalism if '9/11' hadn't happened. Rather – and this is the work of narrative as an instrument of control – the events of '9/11' and after provided moments of 'ideological payout' on established modalities of anti-immigrant racism central to the rationalities of the 'market state' (Sivanandan 2003). The constant, *dis-orientalist* indexing of global events to domestic populations has had a profound impact, particularly through the performative loops of response noted by Ibrahim (2007). Symbolic events have been framed as 'I told you so' moments (Poynting and Mason 2007: 81) that strip political developments of complexity, and instead normalize the need for restorative action against the excesses of multiculture and excessive multiculturalism.

The antidote to multiculturalism, integrationism, can never be a conventionally exclusivist nationalist or racist project as it is config- ured to the needs of the 'neoliberal state located in a space of flows' (Walters 2004: 244). Immigration involves flows of human goods in and through the market state, but it is also, as Didier Bigo (2002) argues, bound up with the 'governmentality of unease'; the need to concomitantly assuage fears of risk while cultivating anxieties about threats and insecurities (see also Fortier 2008). As Peter Nyers summa- rizes, 'the most distinctive political acts today [...] involve exclusions that are enabled by employing "risk", "danger" or "insecurity" as categories' (2004: 206). In the contemporary era, where the politics of unease explicitly imbricates state security with integration governance and immigration control, the Muslim is a figure of fluid transnational- ity and potential 'disloyalty', neither entirely alien but alienating and dis-integrated, fusing the past failures of multiculturalism with the current exigencies and anxieties of immigration politics. It is not just that future 'Muslim migration' can be designated a security threat, but that the Muslim is a metonymy for undesirable non-Western migration, for bad diversity. In the terms of Ghassan Hage's economy of tolerance, Muslims have become desirably undesirable. In the par- lance of the age, immigrants are *unknown knowns*, their predictable future impact presaged in current fragmentation. Suspicious Muslim and minority populations, on the other hand, are *known unknowns*, physically co-present in parallel lives, the grudging, ambivalent recog- nition of belonging in phrases such as 'second-generation' now code for the gestation of transnational disloyalty and anomie. Junaid Rana relates this to the impact of the 'war on terror' in the USA, where 'anti-immigrant racism and Islamophobia incorporate the Muslim into the US racial formation in several social and cultural groups to become a singular threat: the Muslim' (2007: 159).

In an evident sense, this refreshes Balibar's (Balibar and Wallerstein 1991) notion of the 'immigrant' subject of crisis racism, as a category including 'not all foreigners and not only foreigners'. What differenti- ates 'the immigrant' from 'the idea of the Muslim' (Goldberg 2009) is a particular form of *cultural capital* that recurs throughout the examples considered in this book. As Didier Fassin (2005) argues, European space was held before, but intensively after '9/11', to be menaced at the national level by terrorist attacks, and to be experi- encing intolerable demands on the welfare state and sovereign borders. Since '9/11', he argues, a third dimension of menace has become more pronounced: 'Although difficult to name, as it is masked by cultural or religious, sometimes ethnic description, it can be characterized more bluntly as a racial security: it has to do with the protection of a European, Christian and white civilization against Third World, Muslim or black populations' (2008: 228). The mainstreaming of a civilizational menace, in these terms, does not reference anything as banal as the tautologies of the 'clash of civilizations' (Huntington 1993). The point is not one of blanket animus, but of the suffusion and legitimization of the ontologies of 'cultural racism' in filtering and grading good and bad diversity in a security–culture nexus. In the final part of this chapter, some of these general, introductory themes are examined in the context of the British retreat from a long unsettled multiculturalism.

The recited truths of (British) multiculturalism: a rough guide

Species of blowback In late August 2010 an event called We Are Bradford was organized in response to a planned march by the English Defence League (EDL) in the city. Flagged as a 'celebration of unity and our multicultural society', the protest was mobilized to reclaim the streets from the far-right movement, but was of heightened symbolic importance because of the location. As a *Guardian* investigation during the summer of 2010 uncovered, the EDL planned to hold rallies in 'racially sensitive areas' such as Tower Hamlets in London, but focused on Bradford as 'the big one' (Taylor 2010). Bradford was the big one because the EDL's ostensible protests against the 'spread of militant Islam' provided cover for an attempt to unsettle and agitate in a city consistently associated with the summer of 2001, when far-right attacks on British Asian communities in Oldham in May resulted in riots which spread to Leeds, Burnley and eventually, in July, to Bradford. In the general media narrative, the EDL is held to have emerged in reaction to a demonstration in Luton in 2009, by a small Islamist group, during a homecoming parade for British soldiers. As Richard Seymour has documented, although the EDL protests that it is not anti-Muslim, but merely opposed to the threat of sharia law, it has close ties with the British National Party and established neo-Nazi and far-right groups in the UK and Europe (Seymour 2010).[4] In the *Guardian* investigation, among the many unguarded thoughts offered to the undercover journalist was the observation, before a march in Bolton, that 'It's going to be a good 'un today [...] we're going to get to twat some Paki, I can feel it' (Taylor 2010). In a response to the *Guardian* article, which took offence at the parallel drawn between the 'multiracial EDL' and the fascist, whites-only National Front primarily active in the 1970s and 1980s, the EDL argued:

> It is quite obvious that they are incapable of countering the EDL's argument that spread of sharia norms in the United Kingdon is a very dangerous and divisive development that runs counter [*sic*] the basic principles of equal opportunities. Why should women be second class citizens? Why should non-Muslims be third class citizens? Why should there be no equality before the law? Why should homosexuals be brutally oppressed? Why should we abandon our most basic liberty of freedom of expression?[5]

The EDL are the street shadow of the National Front, but the argument above is a product of a decade of recited truths, an almost genealogical rehearsal of the suturing of liberal goals and rhetoric to an exclusionary, laundered culturalism. And much like the anti-Muslim horrorism[6] of Geert Wilders in the Netherlands, their repertoire, while structured by the neo-racist, Powellite desire to not be seen as 'racialist', has bled as much from the 'establishment' to the radical margins as in the other, conventional direction. The EDL's adoption of a values-based, anti-Islamic discourse has been facilitated by the problem of multiculturalism functioning in mainstream discourse as a euphemism for 'the Muslim problem' (Ghannoushi 2006). The hegemonic intent of 'new racism' (MacMaster 2000) has always entailed a politically reflexive search for legitimacy and tactical avoidance of stigmatizaton, and the force of mainstream coverage and political riffing on risky asylum seekers and immoderate Muslims has provided a space of 'legitimacy construction' for the British National Party (Goodwin 2007: 248). The EDL has also insinuated itself into legitimized aversions, and their response to the *Guardian* rehearses a politics self-consciously situated in what Jin Haritaworn terms the 'post 9-11 gender regime' (2008).

In recent discussions of '"feminist" ethics as a new racism' (Pitcher 2009: 128–34) and the 're-gendering of "the Muslim problem"' (McGhee 2008: 95–9), attention has been focused on the symbolic importance of Jack Straw's instigation, following an article in the *Lancashire Evening Telegraph* in October 2006, of a debate on the niqab. Arguing from a stated 'commitment to equal rights for Muslim communities and an equal concern about adverse developments about

parallel communities', Straw described the veil as 'a visible statement
of separation and difference' (quoted in ibid.: 96). Straw's intervention illustrates a number of dimensions in the layered specification
by New Labour of a Muslim Problem. By positioning the veil as an
embodiment of the discourse of parallel societies that developed
after the summer of 2001, he re-energized the culturalist diagnosis
amplified from the Cantle Report into the riots, where 'by targeting
multiculturalism as the enemy of community cohesion much of the
cost of the transition to postindustrialism is laid at the feet of new and
settled migrant communities' (Crowley and Hickman 2008: 1232). By
situating veiled women as a priori denied equal rights, Straw explicitly
sutured a discourse of inherent cultural hierarchy to the problem
of parallelism. This is the gender regime specified by Haritaworn;
a regime that, in locating anti-feminist practices and homophobia
as resistant characteristics of racialized groups, has become central
to unfolding and prolonging the Muslim problem over time, while
locating a liberal progressive telos in the articulation of integrationist
nationalisms.

Concomitantly, it is difficult to imagine the force of these progressive alibis for adaptive racialization without the symbolic circuitry
of the war on terror. From the start of the invasion of Afghanistan,
the image of what President Bush called 'women of cover' became a
central trope of the justification of war (Stabile and Kumar 2005). The
particularly evocative semiotics of a war on patriarchy provided a key
dimension of the human rights narrative of what Costas Douzinas has
termed 'military humanitarianism', a politics dependent on imagery
of distant suffering, predicated on the post-ideological guarantee of
rights, but ultimately consistent with a 'historical pattern in which
all high morality comes from the west as a civilising agent against
lower forms of civilisation in the rest of the world' (2007: 21). A
reflexive defence against this argument, however, is ready built into
the moral justification of bombing for rights. A critique of imperialism, during this period, was received as an inflated expression of
the relativism that cultivated multiculturalism's difficult subjects.
Just as Straw should not be misinterpreted for simply attempting to
champion equality, the argument goes, neither should the legitimacy
of humanitarian claims for military action be taken for anything other
than a moral position. As Wendy Brown writes, tolerance is 'a crucial
analytic hinge between the constitution of abject domestic subjects
and barbarous global ones, between liberalism and the justification

of its imperial and colonial adventures' (2006: 8). Straw's intervention focused on the domestically and internationally *intolerable*. Given moral force by the performative act of confronting the taboo of bad diversity, it laundered the specification of cultural hierarchy by appropriating struggles for liberation strategically detached from their historical interconnections with antiracism (Cooper 2004).

It is the cumulative effect of this laundering which informs the rhetorical cannibalism of the EDL, and which accounts for the disorienting political coordinates of racism in Britain. As Gary Younge wrote, in relation to Jack Straw's positioning as an anti-racist champion in a BBC *Question Time* debate with Nick Griffin, leader of the British National Party, in October 2009, 'The BNP [...] is merely the most vile electoral expression of our degraded racial discourse and political sclerosis. Under such circumstances setting Straw – and the rest of the political class – against Griffin is simply putting the cause against the symptom without any suggestion of an antidote' (2009). To understand this, and the circulation of tropes of crisis, it is necessary to situate them in the largely *post-multicultural* politics in which multiculturalism has become a source of anxiety. While the death of multiculturalism cannot be accurately dated, Paul Gilroy dismisses any sense of it as 'active ideology' since the abolition of the Greater London Council in 1986 (2004). Kundnani, in several accounts (2002, 2004, 2007), draws attention to different perspectives on the nature and duration of the 'multicultural settlement'. Multiculturalist policies were a response to the coalitions that arose across the West in the 1970s around what can variously be named diversity, identity or anti-racist politics. Providing 'cultural solutions to cultural problems' would, it was hoped, have the effect of dampening the autonomous movements of second-generation 'migrants' contesting state racism, labour market exclusion and their status as unwanted guests of the nation.

The containment of anti-racist politics in the UK involved, on the one hand, the Race Relations Act of 1976 – which Kundnani describes as limited in effect by the motility of racist practices – and on the other, policies designed to recognize and celebrate minority cultures. The Scarman Inquiry, which followed the Brixton uprisings of 1981, recognized the problem of 'disproportionate and indiscriminate policing' but refused any suggestion of institutional racism, blaming the 'riots' on the weak culture[7] of African-Caribbeans in the UK and advocating a 'multicultural solution' to problems of unemployment, poor education and ill health (Bourne 2001; Gilroy 1987). As Imogen Tyler has recently argued, the anxiety caused by the 1981 Nationality Act – which created 'aliens' and second-class citizens within the state by removing the right to citizenship of Commonwealth subjects – fuelled the riots but was rarely connected to them in public discourse (2010: 63–4). In the face of the reformulation of 'imperial racism' (ibid.), the micro-colonial structures of 'town hall multiculturalism' were always variously regarded as limited, unasked for and, in anti-racist terms, depoliticizing. As Avtar Brah summarizes, 'the confrontation was generally perceived as an opposition between the woolly liberalism of multiculturalism and the Left radicalism of anti-racism' (1996: 230). The irony of the turn against multiculturalism in the era of the 'war on terror' is that the established government conduit of ready-made communities has been extended to include 'faith communities', which can similarly be cajoled and supported into bringing difficult populations into line. Thus, over time, these structures have engendered

> the erosion of anti-racism and the emergence, in its place, of a highly compromised politics of communal identity, in which unrepresentative community organizations lobby for state favours through the promotion of their own inward-looking sense of victimizaton, while at the grassroots level, the demand for organizations that can mobilize, support and empower communities goes largely unmet. (Kundnani 2007: 183)

The consequences of this constraining essentialism are well known: playing into the differentialist terrain of new racism, fostering a sense of community competition and white disadvantage, and marginalizing a spectrum of disempowered or nonconformist 'members' of the community. However, the focus of activist critique, for example the tradition of the Institute of Race Relations from which Kundnani writes, was to assess the impact of multicultural containment on the lived, political realities of racism in Britain. After multiculturalism, their assessment of community politics and cultural essentialism has become somewhat mainstream, but it is predominantly conflated with the actual lives of multiculture's subjects, and taken as evidence of the problem of too much culture of the wrong kind, a fragmented, risky mosaic that requires the glue of the shared values of Britishness. What is left of multiculturalism in Britain is broadly represented by the struggle in Bradford in 2010. Mobilized as a commonplace in anti-racist action is 'our multicultural society', the lived diversity that Stuart Hall locates in a 'species multicultural drift in Britain' (Hall and Back 2009), or what Gilroy terms the 'conviviality' of urban life (2004: xi). On the other hand, and assimilated to the EDL's repertoire, is the recited truth of multiculturalism, the 'governance image' amplified during the past decade of war as a mode of rationalizing the exercise of political and sociocultural power (McGhee 2008: 6–7).

The long unsettled settlement The recent history of multicultural politics in Britain has been the subject of several fine critical analyses of late, and it is not our intention here to provide a rough guide to their detailed work (Kundnani 2007; Finney and Simpson 2009; McGhee 2008; Pitcher 2009; A. Phillips 2007). Considerations of multiculturalism in Britain recur in the book; in what follows we focus on particular dimensions of this history to open out some of our introductory contentions on multiculturalism as a laundering, discursive space. As a consequence of intense political contestation, a pronounced dimension of recent British public discourse is a clear, reflexive sense of multiculturalism's overt status as a straw dummy, or 'grab bag' in which a mass of socio-political disjunctures and 'social bads' can be stuffed. As Derek McGhee argues, the debates on multiculturalism following the riots of 2001 became, after the terrorist attacks of 7 July 2005, an 'open hostility to the concept of multiculturalism [… that] is, on examination, an exercise in avoiding using the term "multiculturalism" rather than moving away from the principles of multiculturalism altogether' (2008: 85). While the latent principles of multiculturalism have been more than offset by the range of securitarian measures, civil rights restrictions and human rights abuses aimed at the internal threat of the 'Muslim community' (Brittain 2009; see also McGhee 2008: 11–81), the gap identified by McGhee is critical in understanding why multiculturalism became a compressed site for multiple trajectories of conflict.

As Ben Pitcher has perceptively argued, 'the London bombings are symbolic of a new reality of multicultural Britain, a multiculturalism that is best thought of not as moral, but as structural, not a nice idea but a social reality, and a necessary consideration in future state practice' (2009: 161). In other words, the debate about multiculturalism and its culpability 'for promoting segregation and integration, legitimizing moral relativism and inculcating a culture of victimhood that creates expectations of entitlement and special treatment' (Lerman 2010) is not mainly or even tangentially about the consequences of long-diluted state practices. What Pitcher suggests is that for all the lip-service paid, in Britain as elsewhere, to the idea of being a multicultural society, it is only because of the particular, conjunctural conditions of the last decade, where lived diversity has evaded and transgressed the shapes designed for its management, that a dawning sense of actual, irreducible multiculture has once again become a pressing subject of state practice. Therefore 'the relative permanency of this multicultural politics means we need to recognize that it is substantially independent of whatever currency the specific term "multiculturalism" might have at any particular point in time' (Pitcher 2009: 164). Axiomatically, a guiding image of failed multiculturalism is integral to generating the upgraded forms of 'transcendental homogeneity' required to supersede multiculturalism's degraded powers of containment.

The conventional narrative starting point for the problem of multi-cultural dis-integration involves the 'urban disorders' or, gleefully, 'race riots' (Burnett 2007) in northern England in the summer of 2001, and the unstable specification of the problem of social and/or community cohesion (Worley 2005). Although there were parallels between these events and 'uprisings' past, most famously Brixton and Toxteth in 1981, Kundnani points out important differences. The violence of the 'Asian' (mainly Pakistani and Bangladeshi) third generation

> was ad hoc, improvised and haphazard. It was no longer the organised community self-defence of 1981 [...] And whereas the 1981 and 1985 uprisings against the police in Brixton, Handsworth, Tottenham and Toxteth had been the violence of a community united – black and white – in their anger at the 'heavy manners' of the police, the fires this time were lit by the youths of communities falling apart from within, as well as from without; youths whose violence was, therefore, all the more desperate. It was the violence of communities fragmented by colour lines, class lines and police lines. It was the violence of hopelessness. It was the violence of the violated. (2001)

Kundnani's point is that, beyond the provocative actions of organ-ized racist groups, the violence combusted in a social context politely discussed as one of 'post-industrial decline' or, more forcefully, as the localized experience of 'de-industrializaton, the destruction of the welfare state, privatization, marketizaton and immiseration' (Gilroy 2004). Crowley and Hickman draw attention to how these conditions are immanent in the neoliberal transubstantiation of social cohesion into community cohesion, thus 'laying the difficulties of modern life at the door of race relations and failed assimilation' (2008). The comforts of racialized intelligibility were apparent in media coverage that condemned the violent extremists of the National Front and Combat 18 as un-British, but sought insight in the communal tendencies of young Asian men towards criminality and Muslim recidivism (Burnett 2004). The riots resulted in the establishment of four independent inquiries and one inter-ministerial group reporting on the events (Pitcher 2009). Of the four, the report written by local government official Ted Cantle, for a national review team, provided the main basis for a significant government policy shift towards 'community cohesion' (Burnett 2007: 115–16).

The vision of community cohesion, in turn, marks the emergence of integration discourses explicitly predicated on the failure of multiculturalism, and instigates a lingering tendency to reduce the politics of race to the problem of community (Pitcher 2009). Cantle concluded that the riots could be put down to a 'depth of polarization' around segregated communities living 'a series of parallel lives'. This led to the formulation of the idea of 'community cohesion' as a means of increasing 'interaction, integration, shared space and shared values' between 'Asians' and 'whites' on either side of the cultural fence that divided the towns (Burnett 2007: 116). According to Virinder S. Kalra, this 'comically simple' diagnosis of segregation could in turn be reduced to a diagnosis of how 'these people do not live together and therefore this is the reason they do not get on and riot' (2002: 25). By emphasizing the geographical – Asians mainly populate the run-down town centres while whites live on housing estates[8] – and the cultural separation between groups, the Cantle Report was held to ignore the post-industrial patterns of 'white flight', the active presence of the far right and fears of harassment, and the transformation of modern relations between economy and society bundled into the idea of post-industrialism (for an overview, see McGhee 2008: 54–5). While the report tends towards a sense of the 'Asian community' as self-segregating, the 'white community' fared no better. Concluding that the 'host community' also had to change, the Cantle Report presented an elitist picture of local whites 'as lacking in moral fibre' (Burnett 2007: 118).

Of interest to our wider argument are the dimensions of culturalism contoured in the wake of the Cantle Report. The idea of community cohesion sanctions a certain kind of nostalgia for what Crowley and Hickman term a 'racialized, patriarchal industrial capitalism' (2008) – that is, for a post-war period in which social, class-based spatial segregation was routine, and in which 'Commonwealth racism' was unvarnished.[9] The language of community, and its indexical relation to culture, works in interlocking ways. In one sense, in the nostalgic accent, it proposes an idealized and pre-political response to social fragmentation (Outhwaite 2005: 32), inflected with a 'covert lament for irreversible sociological changes from Middle England' (Pathak 2007: 263). The language of community was also inflected with a particular kind of post-racial sense,[10] allowing public policy actors to discuss problem populations through known-in-common coordinates, but without having to specifically name and engage them (Worley 2005: 487). However, as a modality of social engineering that proposes thematics for affective investment, as a 'mode of action on actions' (Miller and Rose 2008: 8), 'community cohesion' emerges as one technology among many put to work in fostering social cohesion on the terrain of culture as a 'resource for both sociopolitical and economic amelioration' (Yúdice 2003: 9). As we examine in Chapter 5, the rush of state-sanctioned visions of how subjects should conduct themselves, in essence a series of directives on appropriate relations between subjectivity, citizenship and culture, has led to a burgeoning interest in sociology in Britain in the relation between the crisis of multiculturalism and broader transitions to neoliberal governmentality (Fortier 2010; Pitcher 2009). The specification of a cultural problem demands a primarily cultural answer, and it is this configuration which, as Kalra argued at the time, reframes community cohesion as an opportunity to 'responsibilize' difficult subjects:

> And so now it becomes clearer why segregation has become so important. Where other major policy changes are bounded by and require legislation, and so are difficult to achieve, blaming the communities for self-segregating is easy, blaming young people for being angry, blaming Asian Muslims for being too different. Pointing the finger in this way means there is no restriction on what can be done, because it is not the government or institutions that needs to do the doing. (2002)

This lack of restriction has been used cynically, but also writing at the time, Back et al. (2002) situated it structurally in New Labour's uncertainty about the relationship between lived multiculture and a national polity 'in an era of intense economic globalization, European integration and geopolitical uncertainty' (ibid.: 453). For all the semiosis of 'Cool Britannia', what they termed New Labour's 'white heart' could conceive of the problem of integration only in quieted, racial terms. The dis-integrating associations that emerged in and after the Cantle Report between immigration, diversity and segregation cemented a tremulous new sense of the social bad, a complex of disturbances embodied by the 'immigrant', and replacing a sense of the civic value of living with difference with an anxious mobilization around *coping* with difference (Fortier 2010). The Cantle Report is bound up in the unfurling specification of thresholds of tolerance that came to focus intensely on the compatibility and loyalty of British Muslims to an articulation of Britishness that, in appropriating a tolerant multiculturalism to its benevolent shelter, can produce it to secure the post-racial foundation of its exclusionary actions. The laundered problematic, as it first appeared, is that 'in a multicultural country there must be a clear political will to reach a consensus on what level of "difference" is accepted and which differences are acceptable' (Cantle 2005, cited in Burnett 2007: 116). Cantle can be threaded into a consensus developing under New Labour, specifically after the specification of 'institutional racism' in the London Metropolitan Police in the Macpherson Report,[11] that race relations had gone too far. David Blunkett's dismissal, for example, of the Lawrence Inquiry as evidence of the British being insufficiently 'proud of what we've got'[12] presaged his condemnation, as Home Secretary, of the weaknesses of 'cultural difference and moral relativism' (Blunkett 2001, cited in Kundnani 2002).

Ameliorative pride in Britishness was envisaged through a form of 'civic nationalism', in which multicultural diversity was united in loyalty to principles of political citizenship and democracy that were derived, tautologically, from the cultural content of Britishness. Following 9/11, and proceeding through a series of official projects for encompassing the problem of transnational disloyalty in a context of transnational war, the problem of cohesion and citizenship became explicitly connected to security and diasporic disloyalty. After '7/7' it organized the 'Muslim question' along a slide-rule from 'allegiance to evilization' (McGhee 2008: 29). It is important to recognize the ways in which a range of questions to do with immigration, foreign policy and the future of society came to be articulated through a softly racialized lens of Britishness. There is an apparent novelty, frequently cited as *proof* of the objectively given dimensions of multicultural collapse, in the overlapping inscriptions of a progressive nationalism within this rubric from 'left and right'. It is for this reason that David Goodhart's 2004 article for *Prospect* magazine, 'The discomfort of strangers', appears in the litany of key events.[13]

Goodhart's far from original argument[14] placed particular stress on the problem of ethnic diversity among the multiple fissures of postmodern anomie. The erosion of a common culture, and the felt legitimacy of reciprocal care required for a progressive vision of the welfare state, are threatened by diversity because 'if values become more diverse, if lifestyles become more differentiated, then it becomes more difficult to sustain the legitimacy of a universal risk-pooling welfare state. People ask: "Why should I pay for them when they are doing things that I wouldn't do?"' (Goodhart 2004a). Goodhart is careful to stress that diversity is not merely a question of ethnicity, but more a question of values, and, ambiguously, 'norms'. However, because ethnicity is the most visible of diversities, it is the most politically sensitive, and it also 'overshadows' the others; 'Changes in the ethnic composition of a city or neighbourhood can come to stand for the wider changes of modern life' (ibid.). But visibility only serves to remind 'us' that 'they' are strangers. And this, for Goodhart, is a bad thing because 'it is important that we feel that most people have made the same effort to be self-supporting and will not take advantage. We need to be reassured that strangers, especially those from other countries, have the same idea of reciprocity as we do' (ibid.). In absorbing cultural racism's emphasis on ideas of problematic proximity and inexorable tension, Goodhart sutured the securitized politics of migration to a newly acceptable form of nationalism, and simply branded it 'progressive'. In so doing, we can see the trace of a wider 'new realism' (Prins 2002) discourse that regards the prime obstacle to progressive politics as the excessive erection of guilt taboos on the conflated field of multiculturalism, race and immigration. As Goodhart remarked in an interview tellingly entitled 'Is this man the left's Enoch Powell?', immigration is 'an area where you can say entirely common-sensical things and be met with irrational, paranoid outbursts from otherwise sensible people'.[15]

Despite the strange makeover accorded to Powell over the last years,[16] Pathik Pathak is correct to argue that accusations of racism against Goodhart are wide of the mark, not least because they simplify the ways in which, as we examine in Chapter 3, emergent articulations of liberalism as nationalism depend on the certainties of a post-racial terrain. Instead, what is identified is the problem of too much culture as a constitutive dimension of just enough culture, or, as Pathak observes, 'he sanctions a sovereign form of community – nationalism – and stigmatizes all others' (2007: 262). This liberal conceit is possible only if the attenuated terms of the multicultural settlement are understood ontologically. As Pathak argues, community, after 2001, had become a 'covert slur', a 'politically distinctive way of behaving' whereby for liberal nationalists 'when you're identified as belonging to a community you cease to be a citizen' (ibid.: 263). In Britain at war, this community was increasingly understood as a securitized, transnational continuum, and was specified in these terms by liberal proponents of the wars in Afghanistan and Iraq. In positioning 'Islamo-fascism' as a pressing existential threat, influential actors in that class fraction of the British media that Seymour calls 'the belligerati' (2008: 234) drew increasingly explicit connections between the need to discipline immoderate populations at home, to secure borders against risky migrants and transnational agitation, and to oppose Islamic 'totalitarianism' on its benighted terrains.

Ultimately, however, Goodhart's highly mediated work stands here as an exemplary instance of the ways in which immigration, diversity, post-industrial 'segregation' and an inchoate anxiety concerning structural shifts in the market state (Sivanandan 2003) were bundled into a culturalist diagnostic and prescribed the broadly ameliorative state of integration. In their important rebuttal of a wide variety of evidential distortions and lacunae in the racialized interpretation of statistical and empirical evidence, Finney and Simpson delineate a 'litany of myths' assembled from this conflation; 'Immigrants are a burden, taking jobs and resources, living piled together in segregated areas; segregation prevents integration, clashed with British culture, heightens tension and breeds violence' (2009: 162). Although Trevor Phillips, head of the then Commission for Racial Equality, critiqued Goodhart as a 'liberal Powellite', the title of Finney and Simpson's book, *'Sleepwalking into Segregation'?*, is taken from one of many widely circulated warnings by Phillips that multiculturalism had patterned forms of segregation that were being exacerbated by immigration and the splintering of any common social imaginary of commonality and allegiance.

Finney and Simpson take Phillips to task as a 'leading myth-maker' whose 'cavalier attitude' to statistics had extracted a dramatic recitation of 'white flight' from a 'general movement from inner cities of all ethnic origins' (ibid.: 165). In focusing on the complex flows of population movement in Bradford's wards and how the 'picture of growth, dispersal and mixing seen in Bradford is common across Britain' (ibid.: 129–33), Finney and Simpson's patient, empirical rebuttal of recited truths illustrates Paul Gilroy's contention, in relation to the debate surrounding Goodhart's intervention, that 'it's just easier to go along with the traditional script that makes Britain's perennial, organic crisis primarily intelligible as a matter of race and nation' (2004).

We take up the further instalments in this script as they unfurl post-'7/7' subsequently. The next chapter examines the contemporary workings of race as a central political idea that makes social life intelligible; we begin with the assumption that race-making is no longer a part of the script.

TWO

Let's talk about your culture: post-race, post-racism

Nas @43 where have I mentioned the word 'genetics' or the word 'race'? My problem is with Somali culture not Somali genes. (Cauldron, 21 August 2009 at 11.41 a.m.)[1]

Introduction: 'race is irrelevant, but all is race'

One of the certainties, after multiculturalism, is that racism no longer exists. Prejudice and discrimination exist, but they are cultural in origin, not racial. Race is associated with the biological and the genetic, and most commonly with the outward signifier of skin colour. Since the end of the Second World War, the uncovering of the crimes of the Holocaust, a limited reckoning with the crimes of colonialism, and the global impact of the end of apartheid, it has become taboo to refer to race in a discriminatory manner. Indeed, racism is often regarded as the trump card in the pack of political correctness, played to stifle honest opinion on sensitive subjects. In the managerial drift of political discourse, it is regarded as an 'unhelpful' idea (Joppke 2009). In 1995, at the cusp of the electoral resurgence of the radical right in Europe, the Council of Europe organized, in and through extensive networks of NGOs and youth movements, a campaign against racism, anti-Semitism, xenophobia and intolerance. Noting that 'the struggle still goes on', in 2006 it organized a follow-up campaign for diversity, participation and human rights. The stated rationale was that there is no need to oppose racism when being for diversity amounts to the same, and provides a more positive message. So we have established, in theory, that we belong to a single, human, race. So why doesn't racism, helpfully, just go away?

Racism persists because there has been no serious effort made to challenge the interconnections between the idea of race and the institutions and structures of the modern nation-state. Race has been semantically conquered, but it remains deeply ingrained in the political imaginaries, structures and practices of 'the West'. This self-evident force, and what Ann Stoler calls the 'motility' of race-thinking, combines powerfully with the certainties of being after race in the contemporary politics of securitized migration and hierarchies of belonging (Stoler 1997). It is these certainties which allowed Michael McDowell, the Irish minister for justice, to portray a citizenship referendum in 2004 – which changed the constitutional basis of citizenship from *jus solis* to *jus sanguinis*, and which was justified politically by accusations of Third World 'citizenship tourism' – as a post-racial third way: 'I simply won't allow the proposal to be hijacked by those who wish to further a racist agenda; but equally I will be harsh in my criticism of those on the other end of the political spectrum who claim to detect racism in any action, however rational, fair-minded or soundly based, that affects immigration or citizenship policy' (2004).

As against this position, a dominant view holds that racism still exists but that it is now cultural in nature (Stolcke 1995; Taguieff et al. 1991). Emerging from the discursive appropriations of the far right in Europe since the 1970s, it is the cultural norms, values, traditions and lifestyles of outsiders which are now held to be problematic, rather than physiognomy. In the so-called 'differentialist turn' racism became a regrettable but natural result of too much uncomfortable proximity through immigration. To quote from the Austrian Freedom Party's bespoke diversity policy: 'the *awareness* of the special *qualities* of one's own people is inseparably linked to the willingness to *respect what is special about other peoples*' (1997, italics in original). In theory, the limited mutability accorded the idea of culture allows for the assimilation or acceptable transformation of the problem of difference, potentially bringing an end to discrimination and intolerance. An obvious problem with this is that it presumes that this would actually be the case; however, historical evidence from the case of assimilated German Jewry shows that racism can be exacerbated by the threat of the margins infiltrating the centre (Bauman 1991). The tendency, for example, to describe people of North African heritage in France as *les immigrés* and worse[2] regardless of their citizenship of the republic, often for several generations, signals the enduring nature of colonial relations and the impossibility of being regarded as integrated (Khiari 2006, 2009). As Anne Phillips notes, 'that the discourse employs the language of culture rather than race does not ensure its innocence' (2007: 56). Presaging the discussions of assertive liberalism to come, we could add that the contemporary appeal to 'shared values' presents a similar ambivalence.

The assumption that culturalism, or ethnocentrism, has replaced racism presents a second problem, centrally explored in this chapter. Race and culture have always been intertwined, or, as Robert Young puts it, 'the racial was always cultural' (1995: 28). Unfolding how this modality of race-thinking has become unremarkable, and is particularly resurgent in contemporary Europe, is a central motivation of this book. A useful point of entry is one of its most successful Anglo-American manifestations in recent years.

Reflections on reflections: can Europe be racialized with cultural people in it?

Racism, the blogosphere tells us, is stupid, but Islamophobia is common sense. This post-race maxim has been given coffee-table form by Christopher Caldwell in his 2009 book *Reflections on the Revolution in Europe: Can Europe be the same with different people in it?* It is a mark of the normalization of the 'Muslim problem', as well as the author's position in elite media networks, that Caldwell appeared on several flagship television and radio programmes in the UK to explain his thesis. Martin Woollacott in the *Guardian* warns against dismissing Caldwell's book as 'rightwing rubbish', as his 'columns in the *Financial Times* frequently dispense a sharp common sense that many liberals find salutary, although not all might say so'.[3] Caldwell's diagnosis is certainly sharp: 'If you understand how immigration, Islam and native European culture interact in any Western European country, you can predict roughly how they will interact in any other' (ibid.: 19). This prediction is based less on sociological than ideological certainty, as Caldwell's genre of urbane post-racial alarmism has established roots in particular reactionary paradigms. In an essay on the increasing ideological and figurative influence of 'Eurabian' theses post-9/11, Matt Carr argues that:

> the growing pessimism regarding Europe's imminent cultural and political subjugation by Islam is no longer limited to the marginal fascist fringe. On the contrary, the consensus regarding Eurabia spans a surprisingly wide spectrum of opinion, which includes French nouveaux philosophes, 'hard liberals' such as *The Daily Mail* columnist Melanie Phillips, acclaimed historians such as Niall Ferguson [...] and the interlocking network of conservative thinktanks in the US that have helped shape the ideological framework of the 'war on terror'. (2006: 2)

In a subsequent review of Caldwell, Carr notes that while he displays a 'lackadaisical attitude towards factual accuracy', his success rests on avoiding what Alberto Toscano calls 'raving with reason' (2010), and shaping an authorial voice as a 'puzzled and concerned observer of the European predicament, driven only by a willingness to consider all angles of a serious debate that others are ignoring' (Carr 2009). For all this studied bemusement, the central tropes in Caldwell's work allow us to read him through an older paradigm. Racism, in his argument, is a fig leaf that hides the truth of Europe as a 'civilization in decline' as a direct result of unassimilable Muslim immigration (ibid.: 284). A narrative of decline and decadence has become a central culturalist idiom of the radical right in Europe over the last decade (Zuquette 2008), but it also resonates strongly with the imaginaries of modern anti-Semitism.

In his writing, Caldwell is consistently attuned to the 'accusation' of racism, insisting on the far from stable lexicon of culture, ethnicity and religion. Discussing Spain's policy of 'ethnic filtering' – preferring Latin American migrants on grounds of compatibility – he writes that '[I]t is not racist. Spain is less concerned that its immigrants be white than they have similarities of worldview with the people already established there, starting with knowing what the inside of a church looks like' (2009: 52). While this indicator of integration might not be regarded as the most unifying in a cursory reading of twentieth-century Spanish history, discourses of compatibility do not depend on veracity, but on suggestion and affect. Nonetheless, the example has a central point, which is to insist on racism as being tied to skin colour and phenotype, a flat reduction that positions any other grounds for discrimination as not-racism, and thus relative to it. For any act of violence or exclusion to be considered 'racist', it must be provable that the victim was passive, and did not possess any attribute nor be open to any ascribed difference beyond a dark(er) skin colour. As soon as the victim can be found to be involved in practices or possessed of cultural attributes that set her apart from dominant society, or that she was in any way not passive, the violence and exclusion are something other than racism. This 'something other', in the discourse of Caldwell and his co-civilizationists, is the space of mere common sense. Cultures are incompatible, races, officially, do not exist. Hence neither does racism.

The fact that Caldwell feels compelled to continually deny the racism of his argument demonstrates his tacit acceptance of the trace

race leaves in his writing. Setting his arguments concerning the un-assimilable Muslim in a historical context reveals the inadequacy of the simple separation of race and culture betrayed in this trace. Caldwell's interpretation of the 'problem' of Islam for Europe mirrors the obsession of twentieth-century anti-Semites in several ways. His characterization of Muslims as 'dominat[ing] or v[ying] for domination of certain European cities' (ibid.: 96) closely mirrors early twentieth-century European attitudes to Jews. Seen as a 'race within the race', Jews were the objects of both hatred and fascination (Arendt 1966). In an era when, to quote British prime minister Benjamin Disraeli, 'race was all', Jews were seen as a race apart. Although their caricatured physical attributes were used to demonize them, Jews were despised whether or not they could actually be told apart from their Gentile neighbours. In Germany, where Jews were for the main part assimilated, they were hated for the very fact of their invisibility, seen to be able to move like an unseen force, all the more damaging for the fact of being able to go unnoticed. Most often physically indistinguishable, the problem with Jews was with their culture, which was depicted as utterly alien to that of the countries in which they lived. These cultural attributes were racialized, seen as encompassing everything for which the Jews stood. As Joseph Roth wrote in the second edition of *The Wandering Jews* in 1937, some assimilated German Jews projected anti-Semitism on to the obvious difference of 'Jews from the East' and most

> German Jews regarded themselves, despite an abundance of clearly threatening evidence of anti-Semitism, as perfectly good Germans; on High Holy Days, at most, they thought of themselves as Jewish Germans. They took great pains to take no account of latent anti-Semitism or to overlook it altogether. In the case of many or even most Western Jews, they attempted to replace the lost or diluted faith of their fathers with a willful blindness, which I describe as a superstitious belief in progress. (2001: 122)

Among Eurabianists who circulate factoids and fragments of Arabic to signify considered knowledge, the idea of *taqiyya* in the Koran – the permission to deny faith heretically under extreme duress – is taken as a commandment of everyday deception, as a framework within which to see through the dissembling of 'moderate' Muslims, to understand anything as its opposite, a reworking, in other words, of the 'Jewish attribute' of deception in modern anti-Semitic propaganda (Shooman and Spielhaus 2010: 213–16). More prosaically, the constant reduction and amplification of people, regardless of religiosity, nationality, context, attachments, politics and experience, to a homogenized transnational population, to the 'idea of the Muslim', performs the work of race, shaping and naturalizing the 'groupings it identifies in its own name' (Goldberg 1993: 81).

Early twentieth-century anti-Semitism, and contemporary anti-Muslim racism, naturalize unassimilable groupings as the embodiments of complex, socio-political problems. Racism, as Allan Pred observes, involves a 'metonymical magic' whereby the few become the many become the one of the problematic population (2000: 63). Writing in the *Financial Times* days after the attempted murder of the Danish cartoonist Kurt Westergaard in January 2010, Caldwell rehearses a complementary indexical magic, whereby headscarves and minarets become symbols of an essentially terroristic telos. On the slippery slope to Islamicization, any signifier of difference can be linked to others in syntagmatic chains that obscure contextual political struggles and considerations:

> Political violence is aimed at promoting a cause – in this case,
> special consideration for Islam. If a country cannot stop the violence
> directly, then the public will demand that it stop the violence indi-
> rectly, by thwarting the cause the violence serves. The rise of Geert
> Wilders's party in the Netherlands, the referendum to ban minarets
> in Switzerland, the proposed ban on burkas in France – these are
> all desperate measures to declare that Islam is not the first religion
> of Europe. 'This is a war,' the mainstream French weekly *L'Express*
> editorialised in the wake of the attempt on Mr Westergaard's life.
> 'To flee this conflict would be to buy tranquillity today at an exorbi-
> tant price in blood tomorrow.' It concluded: 'Banning every kind of
> full-body cover [the burka] in our public spaces is a necessity.' This is
> not the non-sequitur it appears to be. (Caldwell 2009)

In this ticking-culture scenario, it is not surprising that Caldwell dedicates special attention to the fact that 'many Muslim neighbourhoods have turned into ghettoes, with customs, rules, and institutions of their own' (ibid.: 99). As an authoritative source, he turns to *The Spectator* journalist Rod Liddle, who was widely criticized in 2007 for misinterpreting statistics while claiming that the 'overwhelming majority of street crime, knife crime, gun crime, robbery and crimes of sexual violence in London' are perpetrated by 'young men from the African-Caribbean community' (Seymour 2010). In this instance Liddle states that there is 'a string of towns and cities from Rennes in the South, through Lille, Brussels, Antwerp, Zeebrugge, Bremen to Aarhus in Denmark in the far north, where the Muslim population approaches or exceeds twenty per cent (and in some cases constitutes a majority)'. As Finney and Simpson have shown in the UK, these demographic anxieties and spatial fixations may not hold up to statistical or sociological inquiry,[4] but the idea of 'Minority White Cities' provides a powerful trope of multicultural anxiety (2009: 142). Furthermore, the enormous complexities involved in 'ethnic' census or any form of official quantitative data collection in France are ignored (Amiraux and Simon 2006).

Nevertheless, on this evidential basis Caldwell claims that 'ethnic colonies' in European cities – a standard white backlash trope at play in the idea of reverse colonialism; he also discusses population 'beachheads' – have become European-free zones where 'violence has kept native Europeans out [...] as effectively as an electric fence' (2009). A recent special edition of the *Journal of Ethnic and Migration Studies* provides a series of empirical studies challenging precisely the consistent link made between 'the integration of minority ethnic groups and their residential segregation', pointing to significant variations between neighbourhoods in the same cities, depending on 'variations in the local economy, housing market conditions or local politics, which help to cast migrants as deserving or undeserving competitors for housing, jobs or welfare resources' (Bolt et al. 2010: 182). Arguing that racialized hierarchies of acceptability organize majority perceptions of populations in place, they point out that Jewish migrants at the turn of the last century were 'constructed as an "alien race": they were socially and spatially excluded and their segregation was viewed as problematic' (ibid.).

This inversion of the ghetto, from a space of enclosure to one of supposed self-segregation (Stehle 2006), evokes Jews as the 'nation within the nation'. Muslim transnational disloyalty, arising from their inability to transcend the language and traditions[5] of their 'countries of origin', or stoked by overriding transnational affiliations, mirrors fears about Jews' lack of allegiance in the pre-war period. The traditional anti-Semitic view sees Jews as a nation apart whose true allegiance is always kept for their co-religionists. In *The Origins of Totalitarianism* (1966), Hannah Arendt distinguished between Judaism and Jewishness. Assimilated Jews, especially the urbanized and educated among them, wished to be seen as members of the nation. While it was easy to erase one's Judaism by converting or relinquishing a Jewish way of life, the totalizing effect of racism ensured that the essence of Jewishness could never be erased. Jews were therefore marginalized as either 'pariahs' or 'parvenus', or if they maintained their traditions, they became 'untouchables'. Yet if they embraced the nation and forgot Judaism they were seen as mere impostors; as Roth remarked of Jewish military deaths on all sides of the First World War, they were 'reproached for dying without enthusiasm' (2001: 20).

So too it appears for Muslims today. In 2009 a report funded by George Soros and conducted by Gallup 'found that on average 78% of Muslims identified themselves as British'[6] – compared to just 50 per cent of the public – and that 82 per cent said they were loyal to the UK, a pattern common across Europe (Seymour 2010). While Seymour reminds us that such modes of declaration must be seen in the political context that sanctions such pointed questioning and its reflexive responses (ibid.), Caldwell presents an unremitting image of Muslims demographically, politically, culturally and ideologically overwhelming the countries in which they live. Yet it is an unremitting image composed of snippets from which totalities are conjured. The problem is one of 'dis-assimilation' (2009: 108) evidenced by 'protests over the serving of non-halal meat in school cafeterias' in Denmark (ibid.: 109) and the fact that 'Turkish was still the language of the cafés, mosques and hairdressers of Neufeld, near Duisberg – even for German-born young people' (ibid.).

The problem of the ideological reluctance of sociological data, and of the 'naive' and 'Panglossian' insistence of many researchers on social complexity, is overcome not only through a reliance on recited truths, but also through totalizing appeals to the animating forces of an 'adversary culture'. This is particularly controlling among a constituency called Muslim youth, animated by a transnationalism that drives them to reject their 'host nation' and which renders them 'furious partisans of the Arab cause in Iraq, Afghanistan and Palestine'. It is telling that when Caldwell links to the politics of transnational solidarities, he does so by configuring political action as an expression of cultural drive. The culturalization of politics, as Wendy Brown summarizes, proceeds on the basis that 'every culture has a tangible essence that defines it and then explains politics as a consequence of that essence' (2006: 20). The meta-effect is depoliticization, which 'involves removing a political phenomenon from comprehension of its historical emergence and from a recognition of the powers that produce and contour it. No matter its particular form and mechanics, depoliticization always eschews power and history in the representation of its subject' (ibid.: 15). While this culturalization, as Brown notes, is flecked with the conceit that culture rules them, while we rule ourselves and enjoy culture fruitfully (ibid.), the tectonic dramas of Caldwell's *Weltanschauung* make clear that all references to what he interchangeably refers to as 'natives' and 'Europeans' versus 'immigrants' and 'Muslims' should be read within an overtly neoconservative geopolitics:

> Imagine that the West, at the height of the Cold War, had received a mass inflow of immigrants from Communist countries who were ambivalent about which side they supported. Something similar is taking place now. European countries have lately been at war with Muslim forces in Iraq, Afghanistan, the Balkans, and Africa: and this is leaving aside countries of European culture, such as the United States and Israel, that are fighting similar battles. (2009: 132)

The full force of race-thinking is illustrated by Caldwell's omission of the diverse millions that marched and organized in Europe and the United States against the invasions of Afghanistan and Iraq, motivated by political traditions that cannot easily be disassociated from something called European culture. 'With us or against us': it is not possible, apparently, to mobilize against Western imperialism and transnational complicities and investments in the repressive Arab and Muslim state regimes, while *also* rejecting political Islam's responses and violence. Yet in the cross-hairs of culturalism, problems have no source other than those that are held to embody them. This reduction, as we discuss subsequently, is essential to the political assemblages of neoliberalism: in many western European countries, socio-political anxieties are focused less on the 'unsuccessful implementation of the equality specified in the European democratic model' than on culturalist diagnoses of civil unrest and the securitarian challenge of 'static collectivist cultures' (Boukhars 2009: 297–8).

This is at its most pronounced when Caldwell stumbles into the dense field of political mobilization and research emerging from the *émeutes* in Paris and other urban areas of France in October 2005. As noted in Chapter 1, the 'race riots' in France are a key recited event. As an idiom of crisis or point of political comparison, they were influential in focusing political attention on spatial evidence of dis-cohesion, as an element of the intense focus on integration in other European countries during this period (Stehle 2006; Koff and Duprez 2009). Riots erupted in Clichy-sous-Bois (Seine-St-Denis) in protest at the deaths of Zyed Benna and Bouna Traoré, who were electrocuted when hiding in an electricity substation from police interested in performing a 'routine identity check'. These events were intensively interpreted and contested in France, and internationally; the insistence of Caldwell's racial subtext is evident in the selectivity with which he sutures recited truths to a framework of culturalist closure. Dismissive of ideas of 'official racism, or some form of exclusion' (2009: 113), Caldwell argues that the rallying cry of '*Nique la France*' (ibid.: 117) should not be understood as 'the result of social unfairness or native racism' (ibid.). Instead, he ploughs the furrow prepared by the sound-bites of the *nouveaux philosophes* when rallying in defence of the then interior minister Nicolas Sarkozy's inflammatory description of the rioters as *racaille* (scum). Describing them variously as 'nihilism' and an 'anti-Republican pogrom', Alain Finkielkraut was most explicit in characterizing the events as a 'revolt with an ethno-religious character [...] these are very violent declarations of hate for France' (quoted in Murray 2006: 43). Caldwell layers his impressionistic methodology on this narrative, noting that 'Islam seemed important to the rioters' (2009: 115) as 'in Clichy, there were shouts of Allah Akbar!' (ibid.). The atavism of Muslim culture is attacking France, and thus Europe, from the inside: 'neighbourhood nationalism' – allegiance to the transnationalized locality rather than to France – was a sign, according to Caldwell, of 'tribal identities' (ibid.: 119).

This can charitably be described, to adapt Stephen Colbert's phrase, as recited truthiness;[7] as the introduction to a comparative research project on the riots makes clear, 'while the media (and certain politicians) framed the riots as "a threat to the French Republic", this position could hardly be further from the truth. At no time did the rioters stake any claims to ethnic or religious rights. Moreover, the ethnic composition of those participating in the riots varied greatly' (Koff and Duprez 2009: 727). The Institute of Race Relations also emphasized the popularity, at the time, of 'theories that explain urban unrest in terms of cultural deficit' (Cleary 2006: 2). However, subsequent research has emphasized the disorienting and unsettling impact of the urban revolts on mythologies of republicanism, particularly the tendency, owing to the racialized status of the participants, to read the riots as challenges to the republic. 'In the postcolonial period', as Paul Silverstein argues, 'the multiracial banlieues have become the colonial space against which new French national imaginaries are formulated' (2004: 6). Following the riots, Silverstein and Tetreault have more explicitly compared the *banlieues* to the 'colonial dual cities' of French-occupied North Africa, where populations with immigrant backgrounds are corralled in a 'state of immobile apartheid, at a perpetual distance from urban, bourgeois centres' (2006). This spatialization is of keen imaginative importance, as it also signals the perpetual distance of the post-colonial, and specifically Muslim, population, and thus allows the 'integration problem' to be explained as a cultural problem, without reference to sustained and structured inequality.[8]

Republican rhetoric refuses racial and cultural distinctions, but it requires the problematic difference of the *banlieues*, it needs their inhabitants to remain *outside*, as a stabilizing force for the shape of hegemonic identity (Grewal 2007). As several commentators have pointed out, for all the discussion of 'integration' that followed the riots, much of the debate proceeded as if this had little or nothing to do with France proper; the 'problem' of the *banlieues* was somehow external to French society and the conduct of democracy, and did not require much reflection on the nature of the society that the failed integrants were being asked to demonstrate loyalty to (Bouteldja 2009; Koff and Duprez 2009; de Laforcade 2006). Within the circuitry of crisis, the *émeutes* were also interpreted through their proximity to the attacks in London in July 2005. The understanding of the riots as an expression of *communautarisme* allowed for the confirmation, in failure, of the superiority of republican ideology to British *multiculturalisme* (Murray 2006). However, this also renders vulnerable the paradox of acknowledging racial stratification and segregation while denying the effect of racialization on everyday life; 'the Republican model creates the beast but dares not speak its name' (Silverman 2007: 635). Thus a contrary, and consistent, position in public debate also read the riots in terms of an enactment of and demand for citizenship, where rioters were not so much rejecting the republic but protesting their lack of access to and inclusion in it, as well as protesting against the 'unrepublican' nature of populist demonization by significant players in French politics (Koff and Duprez 2009: 728).

Nevertheless, this direct mode of contesting ossified iterations of the republic fails to account for the colonial ontology discussed by Silverstein (2004). In other words, the dangerous particularity of the rioters, held to either efface or seek entry to the universal promise of citizenship, elides the cultural racism that universalizes the nation and national identity through these antagonistic relations. As Max Silverman puts it, 'the republican model disavows its own role in racializing self and other, and [...] presents itself as the neutral opponent of all particular identities in the public sphere' (2007: 634). The impact of the riots made it more difficult to burnish this neutrality, and to maintain unquestioned the reciprocal slippage between the putative universalism of republicanism and the ethnocentric elucidation of a specifically national identity (Balibar and Wallerstein 1991). As Geoffrey de Laforcade observed, the riots concentrated a cumulative questioning of a 'hollow shell of republican universalism', and

> opened a decisive breach in the ability of the univocal discourse
> of republicanism to exclude the grievances of the colonized. The
> casting of French history as a narrative encompassing its global and
> regional dimensions, rather than as a spatially confined genealogy
> of hexagonal territory and institutions, showed signs of gaining
> momentum in the public debate. (2006: 230)

In extracting a narrative of culturalist threat from this lattice of political contestation, Caldwell demonstrates that his interest in the *banlieues* is merely that of a micro-spatial metaphor for the macro-scale vision of European decline. This is why it is easier for Caldwell to make the spatial racial in precisely the terms critiqued by Tissot (2008); multifaceted problems to do with post-industrialism, consequent unemployment, discriminatory public policy, housing crises and bad urban planning are translated into mobile crisis idioms such as 'space of sharia' (Caldwell 2009: 108), 'self-segregation' (ibid.: 104) and 'lawless zones' (ibid.: 102).

His association of crime and violence with immigrants, and Muslims in particular, mirrors the nineteenth- and twentieth-century views of Jews as violent Bolsheviks and anarchists. Like Muslims who are involved in crime, or indeed terrorism, a minority of Jews were involved in anarchist movements and some used violence to further their cause. However, anti-Semitism or anti-Muslim racism comes into play through the patient application of metonymical magic, whereby these activities become characteristics of 'communities' that then threaten society. In a dismissive analysis of how an abstract 'terrorism' has been placed upon 'a pedestal as the greatest threat to Western Civilization', Tony Judt (2008) points out that the various violent organizations active in the second half of the twentieth century in Europe were not confronted as 'European extremism', but rather as political movements that shared forms of action, not ideological content. To raise political violence into a 'moral category, an ideological abstraction and a global foe', he argues, is to prefer an ahistorical civilizationism and the comforts of 'our way of life' to the work of informed historical and socio-political analysis (ibid.: 17–19).

This analytical preference for world historical threat makes clear that what drives Caldwell's analysis is a fear of 'decadence', a neo-conservative narrative that positions European multiculturalism as a domesticated expression of a supposed European preference in international affairs for diplomacy and the rule of international law. 'Preferring moral and cultural explanations to political ones, however, neo-cons attribute European dissension to a softening of the continent's moral fibre, to burgeoning anti-Americanism, and, as the ultimate cause of both, to the growing importance of Islam on the continent' (Mazower 2009). Immigration, for Caldwell, corrodes European civilization from the inside, and Islam has 'broken [...] a good many of the European customs, received ideas, and state structures with which it has come in contact' (Caldwell 2009: 11). This decadence, of course, is haunted by an older one; the modern anti-Semitism that attempted to find 'reasons' for its hatred of the Jews but, in fact, was ultimately concerned with the uneasy feeling that the presence of Jews signified. Their cosmopolitanism, their lack of allegiance, their strange customs, and so on, were capable of eating away at Europe from the inside.

The mirroring of the *fin-de-siècle* European unease in this *début-de-siècle* offering is clear in Caldwell's outright rejection of the contribution of immigration. Although on the face of things, he remarks in conclusion, a multilingual migrant sneaker salesman in Denmark may appear to bode well for the future of Europe, European civilization is suffering because 'it is missing some hard-to-define factor' (ibid.: 284). In contrast to the 'insecure, malleable, relativistic culture' of Europe, migrants, and Muslims in particular, are 'anchored, confident, and strengthened by common doctrines' (ibid.: 286). As a consequence, he concludes, they will devour their tolerant yet anxious hosts. It was precisely this combination of hatred and envy, or hatred caused by envy, which defined the Judaeophilia that Arendt describes as being the obsession of early twentieth-century Europe. It is the culture of immigrants, like that of the Jews before them, which is seen as natural, inherent and homogeneous, and potent enough to destroy the stylized and often fictive ways of life held to have existed before their arrival:

> Europeans know more about Arabic calligraphy and kente cloth because they know less about Montaigne and Goethe. If the spread of Pakistani cuisine is the single greatest improvement in British public life over the past half-century, it is also worth noting that the bombs used for the failed London transport attacks of July 21, 2005, were made from a mix of hydrogen peroxide and chapatti flour. Immigration is not enhancing or validating European culture; it is supplanting it. (Ibid.: 17)

To paraphrase Caldwell, these are the non-sequiturs they appear to be; they make sense only if the ambivalence of *Islamophilia*, and the underlying grammar of race-thinking, are made evident. If, for Disraeli, race was all, for Caldwell it seems that 'race is irrelevant, but all is race' (Goldberg 1993: 6).

The apparatus of race

No race, no power, new problems Reading Caldwell against the backdrop of modern anti-Semitism reveals the artificial nature of the separation made between racial and cultural arguments for distinguishing between human groups. A language of culture and values has almost completely supplanted one of race, but the effects of such a language, couched though it often is in relativist terms, produces racial dividends: division, hierarchy, exclusion. Simply replacing the concept of race with culture is not yet an option. In the current conjuncture, the separation made between racial and cultural arguments about immigration, Islam or multiculturalism is as dangerous as it is artificial. On the one hand it descends from the supreme effort made to expunge race from the politically correct lexicon, and to elevate culture in its place as a means of conceptualizing difference. On the other hand, it is not difficult to see how race and culture work in the same way when applied as a means of formulating the problem posed by Otherness in society. The formal distinction made between race and culture is that the former is immutable while the latter can change. The generalizing conflations and homogenizing stereotypes derived from culture belie this distinction, and reveal how race thinking can equally be applied to the contemporary fixation with 'culture'. This is what Stuart Hall (1997) means when he describes race as a 'floating signifier': rather than being an objective category, race has come over time to signify a host of *differences*, or ways of distinguishing between human beings. Cultural attributes, just as much as physical ones, can come to be associated with particular groups of people, interpreted as fixed and unchangeable, effecting a racialization put to justificatory work in and through hierarchies and structures of power. Commentators such as Caldwell, and the many others considered in this book, may or may not be ignorant of the substantial literature on race and racialization (cf. Appiah and Gutmann 1996; Gilroy 1987, 2000; Winant 2004; Hall 1997; Goldberg 2002, 2009; Mills 1997), but central to contouring the debate on multicultural crisis is their perpetuation of the resilient commonsense distinction between race (biology) and culture.

Without such a straightforward, structuring distinction, warnings about the dangers of 'too much diversity' take on a different tenor. Yet when predicated on an elision of the arbitrariness of the race–culture divide, culture talk, and the stream of critical observations merely flowing from one cultural island to another, cannot be racist. Put this way it is difficult to find fault with such a position. Whatever we take culture to be, there are elements in all ways of life that may attract, alienate, fascinate, bore or repel. There is nothing racist per se in these mundane processes of interpretation and evaluation, a fact deliberately overlooked when multiculturalism is constructed as an authoritarian form of relativism that detects racism in any form of ethical, political and inter-subjective engagement. This also holds for the recited mantra that 'multiculturalists' excuse gender-based or sexual violence on the basis of a 'cultural defence'. The problem is the metonymical magic of inflation and homogenization, when all members of a perceived group are associated with – or asked to loudly dissociate themselves from – the practices of some. The 'problem' of multiculturalism cannot be conceptualized without these forms of abstraction and reification, operations central to race-thinking.

What the problem of multiculturalism allows, however, with its etiolated relations of cultural recognition and pedagogical histories of failure, is a further misrepresentation of the power relations and hierarchies that multiculturalism emerged from. The irony of rhetorics of 'all cultures are equal' is that, after the manifest failure of the putative experiment, there is a widely held contention that this has been proved to be false. Approaching all cultures as equal – in the sense of equivalence, not equality – and hence equally open to criticism, posits a disabling relativism as *the* key ethical and political challenge for diverse societies. However, these equivalences, as much as the cultural abstractions lined up against each other, are racially ordered. To criticize 'white European culture' as imperialist is not the same as claiming that all migrants are wife-beaters, or homophobes. The first contention, however furiously it is debated, makes little impact on the everyday lives of whites occupying hegemonic and relatively privileged social positions. The second, as well as overdetermining gender-based violence as cultural (A. Phillips 2007), has cumulative political power, requiring everyone ascribed to those groups to negotiate it in some form, and leading to the further demonization of large groups of people already diminished in power vis-à-vis the majority in the societies in which they live. It is for this reason that multiculturalism has always been politicized as a form of unfairness, or reverse discrimination, or even reverse racism, as its culturalized predicates and programmatic solutions lend themselves to the denial of largely persistent power relations. When power and history are reduced and traduced, 'an ontological naturalness or essentialism almost inevitably takes up residence in our understandings and explanations' (W. Brown 2006: 15). It is these resident understandings which allow whites in Europe, North America and Australia to fixate on fears of 'illiberal minorities' as near-existential threats. In the face of this race is explanatory in a way culture is not, and it suggests that the certainties and recited truths of multicultural crisis are one of the central ways in which racist discourse is constructed today.

An illustrative dimension of the eschewal of power is the pointed inversion of the idea of minorities as 'victims'. According to Jan Fleischhauer, an editor of *Der Spiegel* and author of *Unter Linken* ('Among Leftists') (2009), 'the victim is the spiritual food of leftists, they can ignite and invent themselves with it again and again, pointing out real and perceived discriminations'.[9] Contrary to this, critical politics has consistently unsettled the designation of victims, seeing it as a potentially reductive category that can obscure contextual histories and people's agency, experience and opinions. However, this projection makes sense only if questions of power and equality are regarded as being, if not solved, then tangential. Extending a previous example is useful in this regard. In his account of tribalist conflagration in the suburbs of Paris, Caldwell approvingly describes Alain Finkielkraut as choosing 'to see the rioters as historical actors rather than as victims of a callous society' (2009: 116). What this interesting appropriation of political vocabulary does, of course, is to extract the rioters from history, celebrating their agency only insofar as it can be taken as evidence of the illusory nature of the oppression being resisted.

A little more familiarity with Finkielkraut and the *nouveaux philosophes* as 'historical actors' suggests a different reading of this backhanded tribute to youth empowerment. In their perceived struggle against the dangers of 'communitarianism' and creeping multiculturalism, the actions and collectivized identities of minorities are held to violate the universal principles of French republicanism. For the French *nouveaux philosophes*, a revisionist mitigation of the crimes and legacies of French colonialism in Algeria is a central ideological pillar of this struggle, a project of disavowal that in and of itself confirms David Silverstein's theorization of France and Algeria as a space of 'transpolitics' (2004). To take an apposite example from 2005, an appeal was signed by, among others, Finkielkraut, Pierre-André Taguieff and Bernard Kouchner protesting against what they called *les ratonnades anti-blancs* (anti-white racist attacks). They referred to attacks on white students by black youths, assumed to be *casseurs* from the *banlieues*, during demonstrations by high-school students. The appeal read:

> [H]igh school student demonstrations have become, for some, the pretext for what we may call 'anti-white *ratonnades*'. The students, often alone, are thrown to the ground, beaten, robbed and their aggressors affirm with a smile that it is 'because they are French'. This is a new appeal because we do not wish to accept this and because, for us, David, Kader and Sebastien have the same right to dignity.[10]

The choice of words is important on two counts. First, the term *ratonnades* is not arbitrary. It comes from *raton*, a highly pejorative word in French slang to denote an Algerian. *Ratonnades* refer specifically to organized paramilitary violence against North Africans, living in the post-war immigrant *bidonvilles* formed on the outskirts of industrial cities, during the 1950s and 1960s in the context of the Algerian war of independence. The use of the word in this context achieves a number of ideological effects. It deflates the seriousness and specificity of colonialist crimes by inflating the localized violence of young black men towards white students through a suggestion of equivalence. The casual implication is that the imperial violence experienced by North Africans under French colonialism is as trivial as these individually painful yet mundane urban occurrences. The simplistic invocation of reverse racism is sufficiently problematic, recalling the smug dinner parties of post-colonial memory and forgetting explored in Michael Haneke's *Caché* (2005). However, the full import is dependent on the pluralist tableau of David (the Jew), Kader (the Arab) and Sebastien (the French boy). By equalizing all three as victims of a general intolerance, the signatories of the appeal put histories and structures of racism and anti-Semitism on a par with the essentially random and sporadic violence of blacks against whites. The structural discrimination, racial ordering and repertoires of aversion of anti-Semitism, post-colonial racism and anti-immigrant populism are, at the stroke of intellectual signatures, reduced to the stylized pluralism of a Benetton ad.

The propagation of a post-colonial idea of anti-white racism is not new among the *nouveaux philosophes* (Murray 2006: 34). Yet the violence of its inverted iconography over the few years is in major part a consequence of the breaching of the terms of republicanism by anti-colonial discourse, as previously described by de Laforcade (2006). In 2007, for example, the spokesperson for the Mouvement des indigènes de la République, Houria Bouteldja, during a discussion on a popular TV chat show, insisted on the need to educate the white French population about the history of racism and colonialism. She used the term *'souschien'*, an ironic neologism that makes reference to the category *'Français de souche'*, first employed by Front national leader Jean-Marie Le Pen in 1979 and later taken up by French demographers to refer to 'indigenous' (white) French people, thus distinguishing them from the black and Arab population. Although her use of the term was accepted at face value at the time, Alain Finkielkraut, in his role as a leading *'enragé* of the Republic' (Jallon and Mounier 1999), chose to add a hyphen to render the word as *'sous-chien'*, or 'sub-dog' (mongrel), and accused Bouteldja of anti-French or anti-white racism (Confiant 2008).[11] Finkielkraut's provocative repunctuation was widely regarded as a disingenuous act, but it nevertheless provided another recited truth for those, among them the 'republican' magazine *Marianne*, keen to demonstrate how France's post-colonial citizens had been allowed too much leeway. The French interior minister, Brice Hortefeux, who knew well 'that Houria Bouteldja was being ironic' (ibid.), was one of the first to take up Finkielkraut's call to arms, leading Raphael Confiant to remind us that

What is at stake here is the right of French people of non-European origin to open their mouths, the right to bandy words about or make puns like any other French person or not. And here, the reply is delivered by the very same Hortefeux in another newspaper. He declared that foreigners that France 'welcomes, hosts and feeds do not have the right to insult French people'. (Ibid.)

This is precisely the disavowed racialization – 'the foreigners that we feed' – that Bouteldja and countless other formal citizens of the French republic are mobilizing against. Three years later, in May 2010, Bouteldja was summoned before the courts on charges of anti-French racism, the result of a case prepared against her by the General Alliance against Racism and for the Respect of French and Christian Identity (AGRIF).[12] That the AGRIF emerged from agents of the Vichy regime and the murderous OAS in Algeria, and has strong contemporary links to the Front national, illustrates the centrality of 'anti-white racism' to a right–left consensus premised on the threat posed by a rising movement of autonomous anti-racist intellectuals. Neither is the timing of Bouteldja's interpellation innocent or coincidental, as it comes shortly after the formation of the Parti des indigènes de la république (PIR) in February 2010, a 'decolonial' party established with the aim of contesting the next round of French elections. More generally, however, this case points to a structuring irony of the contemporary politics of difference; being able to prosecute something touted as anti-French racism depends on a now hegemonic view of Western societies as *post-racial*.

An era of post-racialism The idea of post-racialism describes an era – the one in which we currently live – in which talking about racism has become increasingly difficult, not only because of its culturalization, but because of its pastness. Howard Winant has discussed what he calls a 'renewed racial complacency', shaped by the fact that governmental action on anti-discrimination laws, restricted programmes of immigrant naturalization – and state acceptance of the 'internationalization of multiculturalism' (Kymlicka 2007: 27–60) – have made contemporary states 'far more difficult targets for protest than were their intransigent predecessors' (Winant 2004: xv). Beyond complacency, it is also a question of silence. David Goldberg (2010: 90) argues that 'racial terror and death have been aided by neoliberalizing conditions by the quieting, even the evaporation, of an *explicit* racial register in state-making'. While Goldberg is right to point to something unique in the contemporary evisceration of racism, the silence about race is not completely new. Despite the efforts of anti-colonialists, Black Panthers, radical anti-racists and critical scholars to retain the meaningfulness of race to confronting the lived experience of racism (Fanon 1986; Hall 1997) there has been a progressive silencing of race, and consequently of racism, during the second half of the twentieth century and race's fall from political grace. The triumphalism accompanying the end of the well-known totems of overt organized racism – the official end of slavery, and later the collapse of colonialism, Jim Crow segregation, apartheid, not to mention the demise of the Nazi regime – meant that the persistence of more covert, shifting everyday racism (Essed 1991) within state structures and institutions was frequently effaced.

The political denial of race and racism through a mobilization of the language of culture requires further elaboration here, as this essentially semantic shift has gradually led to an inability to openly engage with race, its roots in modern European political thought, and its pernicious and persistent consequences for individual lives. As previously noted, despite the mobilization of culture in lieu of race, the two have never been easily distinguishable. In his discussion of Goldberg's *The Threat of Race* (2009), Peter Wade (2010) picks up on the tentative definition of race offered by the author: 'Race has to do – it has always has to do – more complexly with the set of views, dispositions, and predilections concerning culture, or more accurately of culture tied to colour, of being tied to body, of "blood" to behaviour' (Goldberg 2009: 175). Wade notes that Goldberg's linking of nature and culture is crucial because 'it highlights that the whole apparatus of race (racial categorizations, racial concepts, racisms) has always been as much about culture as it has about nature, that race has always been shifting between these two domains' (Wade 2010: 45). Foundational to modernity's forms of ordering and classification was a drive to ontologically separate nature from culture (see Bhambra 2007). Yet race exemplifies how this has never been possible. Race naturalizes and classifies the cultural attributes of human groups, ordering those deemed to be inferior and superior on the basis of those seen as capable of mastering nature, and those incapable of emerging from a state of nature (Mills 1997: 41–53).

Paradoxically, racism naturalizes this very separation by positing the immutability of a racial hierarchy. By this token, whites were deemed *naturally* superior because of their ability to control nature and thus progress. Racism, itself a cultural product of the specific world historical conditions of European modernity (Bauman 1989, 1991), is an example of how 'science', purportedly invested in delineating the divide between nature and culture, has been incorporated in political projects for which the epistemological clarity of such divisions is essentially unimportant. Racism has always been theorized in relation to, and on the basis of, the perceived behavioural and cultural characteristics of human groups. The historical attachment of these characteristics to real or imagined physical traits enables the belief that race is concerned with phenotypical difference alone, held to be the signifier of genetic variation par excellence. Yet we do not have to stray far for evidence of how myriad other distinguishing characteristics signify in and through categorical hierarchies. The tendency to racialize hijab-wearing Muslim women, for example, to see the woman as the veil, is evidence of the fact that cultural tropes can just as easily serve as racial signifiers as skin colour (see Chapter 3).[13]

The interpenetration of race and culture raises the question as to why 'race' remains important in the theorization of racism. Is culture, lightened of the baggage of 'race' and holding out the promise of mutability, hybridity and change, not simply a better term? At stake here are the ways in which the terms mutually reinforce each other even as culture is preferred as a more politically neutral term. Although there was every good reason to reject 'race' in the aftermath of the Holocaust and in respect of the crimes of slavery and enforced racial segregation and hierarchy, a result of this was also to make it increasingly difficult to speak about racism, which persists beyond race's 'never again' moments. Race, as Charles W. Mills writes, '*is sociopolitical rather than biological, but it is nonetheless real*' (1997: 126, italics in original). Rejecting bogus science is not the same as rejecting the structuring 'commonsense' assumptions about immutable differences between groups of humans. Despite the efforts of anti-racists, and even the institutionalization of programmes to tackle racial disadvantage by governments across the West, the origins of racial thought, indissociable from the reciprocity of race and nation in the structures of the modern nation-state, the histories of capitalism, imperialism, and of modernity itself, have never been fully confronted (cf. Arendt 1966; Bauman 1989; Balibar and Wallerstein 1991; Hannaford 1996; Goldberg 2002, Mills 1997). What characterizes the rejection of racism today is what Goldberg (2009: 10) calls *anti-*

racialism: 'to take a stand [...] against a concept, a name, a category, categorizing [which] does not itself involve standing [up] against [a set of] conditions of being or living'. *Anti-racism*, in contrast, *does* mean standing up to those conditions. In extreme circumstances, it is 'the risk of death' in the name of refusing the 'imposition and constraint, [...] the devaluation and attendant humiliation' (ibid.) caused by being raced. For Goldberg, 'there is clearly no evidence of antiracialism ever commanding that sort of risk' (ibid.).

The ascent of culture The elevation of culture, as an official concept for encapsulating human difference, parallels the demise of race and must be understood in relation to the specific institutional and political histories associated with repudiating race. A lexicon for difference, drawing on ideas of ethnicity, origins and heritage, was proposed by anthropologists including Claude Lévi-Strauss and institutionalized by structures such as UNESCO (Lentin 2004). Lévi-Strauss's 1960 book *Race et Histoire*, commissioned by UNESCO, was particularly influential, becoming required reading for French schoolchildren (Lévi-Strauss and Eribon 1991 [1988]). Against the common misconception of his position as a *tiersmondiste*, the aim of his book was to 'defend those little peoples who wish to remain faithful to their traditional way of life, outside the conflicts that divide the modern world' (ibid.: 213). However, Lévi-Strauss's belief in the importance of a relativistic approach in order to preserve the specificity of non-dominant cultures in what we now think of as an era of globalization was dampened by his pessimism: Soon, he claimed, 'we will awake from the dream that equality and brotherhood will one day rule among men without compromising their diversity' (Lévi-Strauss 1979 [1975]: 461).

Although Lévi-Strauss is often taken to be emblematic of the 'UNESCO Tradition' (Barker 1981), Hylland Eriksen points out that his 'perspective on culture and intergroup relations is unhelpful as a theoretical matrix for the UNESCO' (2001). The need for compromise among the members of the UNESCO panel led to the production of a much more general statement. While the scientists who contributed to the Statement on Race and Racial Prejudice[14] denied the scientific utility of the concept of race, they failed to take into account the close foundational relationship between race and culture in the construction of racist notions, a fact pointed out by Lévi-Strauss himself when he remarked that, rather than culture producing races, 'race – or that which one generally means by this term – is one of several functions of culture' (Lévi-Strauss 1979 [1975]: 446). Insisting on the need to undo the potency of race, the UNESCO panel recommended that ethnicity be used instead as a more accurate descriptor of difference, allowing differences in the level of progress attained by various ethnic groups across the world to be explained in relativistic terms:

> Current biological knowledge does not permit us to impute cultural achievements to differences in genetic potential. Differences in the achievements of different peoples should be attributed solely to their cultural history. The peoples of the world today appear to possess equal biological potentialities for attaining any level of civilization. (UNESCO 1968: 270)

In the political context of a world reeling from the devastation of war and the revelations of the Holocaust, and a fractious international order struggling with millions of displaced persons, this statement remains remarkable. Yet as a mode of political prescription, it has an enormously ambivalent legacy. Erasing racial languages does little to excise the striation of racial thought in structures of power. Developmental differences may not be genetic, for example, but understood as cultural differences; the explanation is just as naturalizing, and colonially complicit, as overt recourse to race itself. Making 'race' taboo *also* extinguished the taboo associated with assigning groups to categories along a biologically determined racial hierarchy. Culture's potential for adaptation and mutability promises that these categories need not be eternally fixed. Yet that if they were to shift, this would most likely require the willingness of the group itself to change the cultural practices that deny it access to progress. This is the limited sense of agency proscribed by Finkielkraut for the youth of the *banlieues*: detached from structures of power, and sixty years after the start of the process of decolonization and the official end of the 'civilizing mission', the political fixation of the times still involves the promise of integration for those who transcend their cultural limitations. Finkielkraut has made this argument consistently; in *The Undoing of Thought* (1988) he applies it to the UNESCO settlement: 'the United Nations, founded to propagate the universalist ideals of Enlightened Europe, now speaks on behalf of every ethnic prejudice, believing that peoples, nations and cultures have rights which outweigh the rights of man. The "multicultural" lobby dismisses the liberal values of Europe as "racist", while championing the narrow chauvinism of every minority culture' (ibid.: 138).

Thomas Hylland Eriksen has noted how Finkielkraut's critique replaces the imposition of one homogeneity (culture) with that of another, an 'unreformed Enlightenment position', and that 'it is between these extremes that contemporary politics must manoeuvre' (2001: 145). The construction of these extremes presages the culturalist liberalism, discussed in the next chapter, that now posits a similar totality in lieu of multicultural parochialism. Finkielkraut's attack on what he saw as another *tiersmondiste* front draws out how the UNESCO approach profiled the development of essentialist multiculturalisms that, although established in response to racism, frequently compounded it by institutionalizing the volatile economy of cultural relativism. It is certainly laudable to claim, as Lévi-Strauss did, that cultural relativism states 'that there is no criterion that enables one to make an absolute judgment as to how one culture is superior to another' (1991: 147–8). Yet as the ideological hinge for policies ostensibly implemented to tackle racial discrimination, cultural relativism does little to explain why such discrimination exists. It cannot provide an adequate explanation of the inequalities produced on a global scale by European imperialism, nor of those produced more recently in post-colonial, post-immigration societies in which the racialized continue to be the targets of both institutionalized discrimination and popular scapegoating, and where, as Arun Kundnani argues, 'racisms are no longer domestically driven but take their impetus from an attempt to legitimize a deeply divided global order' (2007: 4). It is the processes in which such inequalities are produced and naturalized, rather than mere cultural variation, which are accountable for the different 'level[s] of civilization' (UNESCO 1968) of various populations. The problem with cultural relativism is not the sentiments that produced it. As with multiculturalism itself, the intention was to negate racial thinking, oppose it on scientific grounds, and provide an alternative, non-hierarchical, framework for thinking about human variation. However, cultural relativists, while working to deny race, did not follow through the implications of this denial for ethical and epistemological frameworks predicated on the European right to study 'other cultures', and the types of knowledge organized through the classificatory practices of relativist frameworks:

> At least part of the impetus for multiculturalism was the need to challenge dismissive and disparaging stereotypes of people from minority cultural groups, to contest the hierarchy of 'us' and 'them'.

But insofar as it starts from the unquestioned 'fact' of cultural difference, multiculturalism tends to call up its own stereotypes, categorizing people in ways that simplify differences, emphasize typical features, and suggest defining features for each cultural group. This intentionally promotes a view of individuals from minority and non-Western cultural groups as guided by different norms and values and inadvertently fuels a perception of them as driven by illiberal and undemocratic ones. (A. Phillips 2007: 31)

It was never clear who the 'saris, samosas and steel bands' (Anthias and Yuval-Davis 1992) of multicultural recognition were for, but it was certainly obvious that, for those whom they were officially supposed to benefit, they could not replace palpable empowerment and the redressing of racism. In response to the renewed success of the extreme right in Europe in the 1980s and 1990s, the theorists of a new cultural racism (Taguieff et al. 1991; Stolcke 1995) claimed that it had replaced the old biological variant. It was proposed that what made this 'neo-racism' (Balibar and Wallerstein 1991) different to racism as conventionally understood was its ostensible repudiation of racial hierarchy in favour of appropriating the idea of a 'right to difference'. Different cultural groups should be kept 'separate but equal', as each cultural group has its 'natural' home. Neil MacMaster provides an interesting account of the elaboration of the 'new racism' in the 1970s among far-right intellectual circles such as the Salisbury Group in the UK, and the network of *Nouvelle Droite* journalists, intellectuals and career fascists gathered around the Club de l'Horloge and Groupement de recherche et d'études pour la civilisation européenne in France (2000: 193–205). These networks, MacMaster emphasizes, were engaged in a hegemonic project to reshape the terms of racial exclusion in and through a cultural discourse laden with affective resonance and 'commonsense' differentialism. As Barker explored in his classic text, *The New Racism* (1981), the racism that emerged in 1970s Britain was constructed through a rejection of immigration, building on the momentum captured by Enoch Powell and his infamous 1968 'Rivers of Blood' speech.

In Barker's analysis, what he calls the 'argument from genuine fears' of the population regarding immigration, the commonsense notion that immigration is unfair to the everyman, is linked to the defence of a 'way of life' against 'alien invasion'. The defence of a culture is inextricable from the fears deemed to have been expressed by its members because 'the very existence of fears about damage to the unity of the nation is proof that the unity of the nation is being threatened' (1981: 17). Because immigrants are said to threaten national unity by being unable or unwilling to assimilate into the British way of life, the whole meaning of racial prejudice is inverted. Racism now becomes the very refusal of immigrants to adopt the national lifestyle of their host country. According to this unfolding theory, it becomes natural for the ordinary person to want to defend herself by protesting against the rise in immigration. This reformulation of racist discourse strips it of its very racism by purposefully refusing any proposition of racial hierarchy that would characterize immigrants as the members of inferior 'races'. Rather, the argument is that any national group would react similarly to such inflows of immigrants and that the neo-racist theory is therefore universally resonant. The control of immigration is postulated as a kindness to foreigners themselves, who 'too have natural homes' (ibid.: 21). In this way, racism becomes a commonsense argument based on the natural tendency of human beings all over the world to form exclusive groups. The new racism is, thus, a theory of

> pseudo-biological culturalism. Nations on this view are not built out of politics and economics, but out of human nature. It is in our biology, our instincts, to defend our way of life, traditions and customs against outsiders – not because they are inferior, but because they are part of different cultures. This is a non-rational process; and none the worse for it. For we are soaked in, made up out of, our traditions and our culture. (Ibid.: 23–4)

While, for Barker, new racism was very much an invention and hegemonic project of the Conservative right wing, in contrast, for French *politologue* Pierre-André Taguieff (Taguieff et al. 1991), it was anti-racism, built on the principles of cultural relativism, which was directly responsible for the electoral success of the Front national in France in the 1980s. The Front national, which developed in the 1970s from the shards of French fascist groups active in the Algerian war, had no difficulties adopting a 'differentialism' that spoke of the incompatibility of Berber and Arab 'immigrants' from Algeria and agitating for their repatriation to what had, until very recently, been an integral territory of the Republic. Noting the appropriation of the very discourse upon which the anti-racist milieu relied, Taguieff criticized 'the incapacity of the organised anti-racist milieus, by means of coherent counter-arguments, to face up to this new ideological situation in which symbolic racism artfully absorbs certain traditionally anti-racist principles' (ibid.: 54).

This targeting of *tiersmondiste* anti-racists as responsible for providing the conditions for the far-right inversions of cultural relativism is inaccurate: quite apart from the mainstream success of the New Right's hegemonic strategies in the era of the Thatcher and Mitterrand governments (Barker 1981; MacMaster 2000), the elevation of culture was not initiated by anti-colonialists promoting a pragmatic politics of *négritude*, but by Western elites embarrassed by race and eager to sequester it as a historical exception. The account of who was responsible for a culturally relativist view of social relations is not merely a matter of record: the belief that multiculturalism was demanded or imposed by minorities animated by demands for *cultural recognition* has become, as the quote from Finkielkraut's attack on the UN demonstrates, a central tenet of anti-multicultural critique, and the loaded ballast for a determined swing to an unreflective and idealized liberalism. Multiculturalism has been variously and contextually understood *as* anti-racism (as an adequate critical politics), as accompanying anti-racism (cultural valorization complementing more radical political demands) or as a diversion from anti-racism (Mills 2007; see also Lentin 2004). Charles W. Mills has argued that from the standpoint of anti-racist politics, Charles Taylor's canonical 'Politics of Recognition' (1992) is an example of how the radical intent of anti-racism has been traduced through *mis*recognition. Taylor conflates recognition as a question of equal personhood (racial justice) with recognition of distinct (cultural/other) identity. Following Blum (1994), Mills notes that Taylor's argument is little concerned with anti-racism, but rather, ultimately, with equality of distinctiveness:

> To the extent that racism is intimately tied up with the denial of people's humanity, the denial of equal personhood, an anti-racist politics will need to be centred on issues of racial justice and the demanding of an end to the color-coding of nominally universalist, but in reality racialised, Western values of equality and inclusion. The 'distinctiveness' cited will be not so much that of different cultures as that of systematically differential treatment. (2007: 97)

This conflation is inscribed in the backlash against multiculturalism without a lash, and in the idea of an 'experiment' that, having been forced on sceptical societies by 'ethnic minorities', requires a return to any one of a number of overlapping and competing imaginaries of elective homogeneity. The rise of culture goes in parallel with the demise of race. However, it is not accompanied by a decrease in *racism*. What the concept of culture as a replacement for race now provides is the opportunity to speak out against multiculture while avoiding the charge of racism. The persistence of racism in the lives of millions is denigrated through a reading of the plastic and broadly gratifying rhetorics of cultural celebration and appreciation as the empirical proof of substantive change. The fictive equivalences of cultural relativism provide a language for specifying the problem of difference when race is taboo, as Caldwell so ably demonstrates.

In providing this language, of course, it has also made the work of anti-racism far more complex. Because the language of race and racism has been abandoned for that of different but equal cultures, the terms of the debate fail to incorporate not just the ways lives in globalized contexts are lived beyond these static constructions, but the experience of racism and the struggle for equality and justice that anti-racism involves. One of the most salutary dimensions of the post-racial era is the way in which the experience of racism, the right of the racialized to define and oppose racism on their own terms, has simply been dismissed. This is evident, for example, in the way in which the phrase 'playing the race card', originally used as a criticism of politicians injecting racial animus into social affairs for popular gain, is now more often intended as a criticism of people of colour, held to be injecting victimology into otherwise neutral proceedings for their own individual or communal gain.

In the next sections we explore the rejection of multiculturalism in relation to the idea of post-racialism. Post-racialism informs a variegated set of oppositions to the demand for equality by those still considered to be outsiders and their right, as equals, to mobilize against racist oppression. Opposition to multiculturalism is profoundly animated by a sense that they are taking up too much space, claiming more than their fair share, congregating in ways that have 'gone too far', fraying a common social fabric and its cohering cultural weave. In other words, minorities are held to have exceeded the limited forms of autonomy that multiculturalism was designed to impose, and to have complicated the 'transcendental homogeneity' (Gunew 2004) that multiculturalism was shaped to project. In the space of post-racialism, however, there is significant competition among different visions of transcendental homogeneity. In the next chapter, we engage the legacy of 'new racisms' in the assertive liberalism of contemporary Europe. The remainder of this chapter focuses on the globally mediated example of post-racial politics in the contemporary United States.

The fault-lines of post-racialism

And the libs, of course, say that minorities cannot be racists because they don't have the power to implement their racism. Well, those days are gone, because reverse racists certainly do have the power to implement their power. Obama is the greatest living example of a reverse racist, and now he's appointed one.[15]

Since the election of Barack Obama as president, the argument that the United States is over race and/or beyond racism has been repeated in a variety of fora. The summer of 2009 alone produced several high-profile examples of post-racialism in action, the consequences of which, in particular the backlash against Obama and the formation of the Tea Party Movement,[16] are profound for US society and politics. The three stories below each point to how the debate over whether race is still an issue is – owing to the very fact that it is posed at all – proof of the extent to which rac*ism* remains integral to US life notwithstanding Obama's ascent to power. The first of these stories is the Birther Movement, a group of influential right-wingers[17] claiming that Obama has no right to be US president because he is not a 'natural-born citizen'. Despite evidence to the contrary, supplied by the State of Hawaii, that Obama *was* born there, the Birthers claim that he was in fact born in Kenya. Although there is no support for such claims, the movement has led to eleven Republican congressmen signing a 'Birther Bill' that would demand a birth certificate from all future US presidents. Twenty-eight per cent of US Americans believe that Obama was not born in the USA while 30 per cent are unsure.[18] Furthermore, a Pew Research poll conducted in 2010 found that one in five Americans believe that Obama is Muslim. The poll was taken before Obama offered indirect support for the faith centre – referred to on Conservative blogs such as that of the Center for Security Policy as a 'Sharia beachhead'[19] – by affirming the right to religious freedom. Although the 'mosque' is to be built two blocks from the site of the World Trade Center, opponents capitalized on the feeling that, according to Sarah Palin, 'to build a mosque at Ground Zero is a stab in the heart of the families of the innocent victims of those horrific attacks'.[20]

The second event of the race-laden summer of 2009 concerns the election of Sonia Sotomayor to the US Supreme Court, the first Hispanic woman ever to accede to the post and Obama's first nomination to the body. Ms Sotomayor invoked right-wing scorn and centrist 'concerns' over a 2001 lecture she gave in which she claimed that 'I would hope that a wise Latina woman with the richness of her experiences would more often than not reach a better conclusion than a white male who hasn't lived that life.' The statement merely notes Sotomayor's reflection, unremarkable in social science, that complete objectivity is a fallacy, and that it is worth thinking through the ways lived experience can provide reflexive insight when thinking about what happens in society. Nevertheless, Sotomayor's opponents detected double standards in the case of her nomination because, in their view, her statement was nothing short of racism. According to Newt Gingrich, 'imagine a judicial nominee said "my experience as a white man makes me better than a [L]atina woman." [N]ew racism is no better than old racism.' Gingrich's formulation, like the inversion of the *ratonnades anti-blancs*, does not just imply that Sotomayor's statement was on a par with white racism, it suggests that it has replaced it. At work here are the most basic dimensions of critiques of raced and gendered neutrality; it is hard to conceive of a white official being pilloried in public for a tendency to identify more closely with the concerns of a white defendant, simply because to do so is the unquestioned norm. Nevertheless, the 'new racism' Sotomayor has been accused of embodying was framed by 'shock jock' Rush Limbaugh through a predictable iconography of historical oppression: 'whites [are] becoming "the new oppressed minority" [with] Republicans [...] going along with it by "moving to the back of the bus" and obliging by drinking only out of designated water fountains."'[21]

The third incident is the arrest of Harvard professor Henry Louis 'Skip' Gates at his home by a policeman investigating an assumption that Gates was attempting to break into his own home. The police were alerted by a neighbour upon seeing Gates and a taxi driver attempting to resolve the problem of Gates's mislaid keys. When the arresting officer, Sergeant Crowley, came to investigate he was reassured by Gates that he was indeed the homeowner. The exact interchange between the two is unclear, although Gates clearly reprimanded Crowley. What is known is that Gates was officially arrested for 'disturbing the peace'. The notion that the sergeant was in any sense under threat from the five-foot-five disabled professor has been called into question. It is more likely that Gates was arrested for what used to be known as being 'uppity'.[22] Obama weighed in on the case, initially calling Crowley 'stupid' but later retracting this and inviting both men to the White House for a chat over beer.

Each of these three events is emblematic of the current status of race in the USA. The election of Obama and other landmarks, not least the nomination of Sotomayor and the fact that there *are* top Harvard professors who are black, is taken by many to mean that race – as a barrier to achievement – has been overcome. However, the fact that race still appears to take up so much space in the collective consciousness of a purportedly post-racial society is evidence of the fact that, as the blogger Chris Hallquist put it, 'a post-racial country would not be obsessing over a presidential candidate's alleged post-racialness. America is not so much post-racial as getting-over-the-subject-but-not-quite-there-racial.'[23] The obsession with race itself produces post-racialism. The 'post' in post-race sidesteps the fact that, for advocates of post-racialism, it is racelessness (Goldberg 2002) which is actually being invoked. To be post something is at least to acknowledge its past significance. However, the central conviction of post-racialism is the denial of the salience of race in the lived experience of the racialized. For, broadly speaking, the liberal left, racism was certainly a historical fact, but it was something 'the left' didn't do, and is not complicit in. This is not only an anti-sociological denial of the historical and contiguous realities of white privilege,[24] in some contexts it is a central plank of the rejection of multiculturalism as a misguided product of white liberal guilt (see Bruckner 2010).

For the US right wing, on the other hand, racism was never really systemic, and lingers primarily in the subjectivity of those who claimed to have experienced it, and is thus relative. It is this which allows figures in the USA who have proclaimed post-racialism, such as Dinesh D'Souza, to reject the importance of race in the production and reproduction of inequalities to a lack of honest engagement with 'group differences'. Thus, in D'Souza's widely discussed *The End of Racism* (1995), endemic problems in 'African American culture' legitimize 'rational discrimination', such as the association of young black men with crime and rape. Rehearsing an argument that has subsequently proved influential in debates in Europe, D'Souza constructs affirmative action and 'multiculturalism' as a liberal politics of guilt (cf. Joppke 2009; Bruckner 2010) that is, in effect, the prime remaining racism, as it is 'aimed at camouflaging the embarrassing reality of black failure to meet merit standards of academic achievement and economic performance' (1995: xiii–xiv). In a detailed rebuttal of his critics in the preface to the second edition of the book, D'Souza is at pains to position his work as anti-racist. However, in locating racism as a rational (white) response to threat and risk, the prime obstacle to a 'race-neutral society' is the pathologies of 'black culture',[25] which go unconfronted and tolerated, but which must be overcome within black culture in order for the majority to overcome the rational foundations of their aversion:

> I believe the book's effect to be profoundly antiracist, because it identifies the strongest contemporary force that supports and defends white racism and offers a concrete strategy to deal with it. In my view, nothing perpetuates white hostility to blacks today more than the scandalous pathologies of the African American underclass. These pathologies reinforce racism by giving it an empirical foundation, a foundation in experience. The best way to address these pathologies is not through a public pretense that nothing distinguishes the African American underclass from the rest of society [...] but through bold and realistic enterprise to identify the entrenched behavioral problems and work to change them. (Ibid.: xxx)

Reading opposing arguments thus, D'Souza elides what is really at stake; not the claim that 'nothing distinguishes' them, but the grounds on which distinguishing arguments are made, i.e. an insistence on a social-structural analysis as against the segregationist culturalism that marks the idea of 'pathology'. Yet this mode of explanation is the outcome of a telos of 'race neutrality'. In the United States, Martin Luther King's dream that his 'four little children will one day live in a nation where they will not be judged by the colour of their skin, but by the content of their character' is often taken literally. King was not advocating a colour-blind approach to race but the civil rights movement's message continues to be misinterpreted as doing so. Refusing to see the colour of someone's skin is not the same as working towards a day when it will be truly unimportant. *Contra* this, racelessness interprets colour blindness as being 'blind to *people of colour*' (Goldberg 2002: 223). Declaring society post-race is to ignore that, in actual fact, racelessness applies only to white people who see themselves as existing outside the racial framework. White is interpreted as being race neutral while everyone else 'has race'. Richard Dyer makes this clear when he points out that, while it is common for whites to point out the 'blackness' or 'Chineseness' of non-whites, 'we don't mention the whiteness of the white people we know' (Dyer 1997: 22). Racelessness is thus equated with racial neutrality, which in turn is interpreted as whiteness.

Whiteness then becomes the default according to which all else is set. However, this makes racism almost impossible to overcome. The logical conclusion of the argument that, in order to end racism, everyone should simply be seen as racially neutral is that everyone should be seen as white. The problem with doing this often goes unrealized even by the most well-meaning of white liberals who, as Dyer – following bell hooks (1992) – points out, become enraged when their whiteness is pointed out. Emphasizing whiteness is not what whites find enraging per se – 'many non-white societies have their own versions of the same concept' (Hewitt 2005: 7). The problem with pointing whiteness out to those who pride themselves on their anti-racism is that in Western societies, what is in fact being pointed out is white people's privilege. It thus undermines white liberals' 'deep emotional investment in the myth of "sameness", even as their actions reflect the primacy of whiteness as a sign informing who they are and how they think' (hooks 1992: 167). However much we may like skin colour not to matter, real differences between people do exist (Hall 1997) and race-thinking has created a status quo according to which negative attributes are associated with non-white and non-Western signifiers; the accretion of cultural meaning that D'Souza invests with the status of instrumental rationality. Therefore, merely proceeding as if we were all white not only cannot contribute to transforming racism but in fact perpetuates it, as whites react against those claiming the spaces of privilege once reserved for them:

> Nonwhites then find that race is paradoxically, both everywhere and nowhere, structuring their lives but not formally recognized in political/moral theory. But in a racially structured polity, the only people who can find it psychologically possible to deny the centrality of race are those who are racially privileged, for whom race is invisible precisely because the world is structured around them. (Mills 1997: 76)

In fact, spaces of limited privilege have become open to non-whites in the United States (and to a much lesser extent in other Western countries) owing only to the efforts of activists to reverse racial discrimination. With some success, civil rights legislation in the United States has outlawed the blatant discriminations of the Jim Crow era and allowed many of those formerly excluded on the basis of their race to access institutions from which they were previously denied entry. Only a handful among them – the Obamas and the Sotomayors – have acceded to real power, but metonymical magic works here also, as their symbolic status can also be contested through the established reversals of backlash politics, which situate 'black advantage' as an overwrought product of the social engineering of liberal elites, and which historically reacts against 'the *possibility* of whites having to compete with blacks on legal, occupational, educational, and/or residential grounds where white advantage would be diminished if not nullified' (Hewitt 2005: 5–6, italics in original). The furore over Obama's 'back to school' address in September 2009 exemplifies the tenacious motility of this position. As an optional possibility for schools, Obama planned a motivating message for schoolchildren, promoting an unremarkable set of meritocratic goals motivating children to work hard so 'they can compete in the global economy for good jobs and live rewarding and productive lives as American citizens'.[26] Obama's right to address the nation's schoolchildren was questioned by people such as one-time Republican presidential hopeful Gary Bauer, who called the speech 'an unprecedented use of power', or Oklahoma state senator Steve Russell, who said, 'this is something you'd expect to see in North Korea or in Saddam Hussein's Iraq'.[27]

The precise degree of racial animus present in the hostility to Obama is a disputed question in political analysis, yet the cloud of floating signifiers that position him as a 'socialist' or a 'Muslim' betray the wiring of race-thinking more clearly than attempts to find overt expressions of hostility to his blackness. Obama is made to embody a political divisiveness that transcends routine partisanship. For people like Bauer and Russell, or TV host Glenn Beck and other commentators, the problem with Obama's election to the US presidency or Sotomayor's nomination to the Senate is that they are claiming positions that are ultimately not seen as theirs for the taking. Thus framing his every political gesture as proof of his 'foreignness' and 'radical politics' serves to recall and underscore his more radical alterity; race, as Stuart Hall observes, works here as the *signifier* for his coded bundle of illegitimacies. The corollary of the threat of race, in Obama's case, is the promise of its irrelevance. Thus conservative opponents of affirmative action, including prominent African-Americans such as Ward Connerly, consider Obama as another embodied proof, this time for the irrelevance of anti-meritocratic politics. As Connerly remarked in the run-up to the 2008 US presidential election, 'the presidential candidacy of Sen. Barack Obama is testimony that America is about ready to end the consideration of race in American life. In effect, he is the symbol of the American people "overcoming" race.'[28]

Backlash politics unfold established repertoires of 'common sense' through the rhythms of recited truths and mediated events that seem to exemplify the problem, and it is this which makes the critical task of unsettling hidden, normative assumptions so cyclically problematic. The counter-critique to portrayals of affirmative action as unegalitarian, because it purportedly elevates gender and ethnicity over merit, is well established. Those who reject it do not consider their own identities and privileges as in any way contributing to their social position and status; instead they take the 'status quo of differential racial entitlement as normatively legitimate' (Mills 1997: 40). Yet, as Mills argues, 'by treating the present as a somehow neutral baseline, with its given configuration of wealth, property, social standing, and psychological willingness to sacrifice', each new event becomes evidence of having done enough, or having gone too far. Those who objected to Sotomayor's appointment because they saw her as the Latina candidate rather than being both Latina and, crucially, the candidate with the most 'judicial experience [of] anyone confirmed for the court in seventy years' (Younge 2010a: 58) would undoubtedly object to anyone reducing them to the fact of being, for the most part, white and male. Yet the current post-racial moment allows the laundering and recycling of the assumed racial neutrality of their positions. After race, racialized configurations of power and opportunity function as discrete structures. Thus post-racial logic, rather than undermining racial privilege, compounds the sense of entitlement that is definitive of racisms, both past and present.

Post-racialism has, therefore, to be understood in terms of the threat contained in the promise of post-race – because it is nevertheless an ideal that must be upheld – for those for whom it entails the loss of historically accumulated power. Thus to invoke racelessness or recommend integration is not really to press for a future without racism or with full equality for all. It is rather to say that these differences do not matter long before race has ceased to have lived significance for the great majority of racialized people. Calling time on race before its salience as a 'political system of exclusion and differential privilege' (Mills 1997: 131) has been transformed is the main expression of racism in our times.

THREE

Free like me: the polyphony of liberal post-racialism

From evil to relativism

James Tully uses Stanley Cavell's analysis of Ibsen's *A Doll's House* to pose a question central to this chapter:

> Nora is trying to say something that is important to her, but the dominant language in which Thorvold listens and responds misrepresents the way she says it, what she is saying, and her understanding of the intersubjective practice in which she speaks. Thorvold takes it as a matter of course that a marriage is a dollhouse, and he recognises, interacts with, and responds to the problems Nora raises always already as if she were a doll, with the limited range of possible conduct this form of subjectivity entails. As a result, Thorvold fails to secure uptake of her speech act as a 'claim of reason', and so a democratic dialogue over the justice of the oppressive relations between them (which compose their practice of marriage) is disqualified from the outset. She is deprived of a voice in her political world. The first question for political philosophy today is, therefore, 'How do we attend to the strange multiplicity of political voices and activities without distorting or disqualifying them in the very way we approach them?' (2002: 537)

In the current discussion, the idea of disavowed claims to reason conjures with contemporary liberal obsessions concerning Muslim dress. Liberalism, as Davina Cooper notes, has confronted multiculturalism by focusing on 'that which is different', locating cultural harm in minority practices, and thus flagging up 'the distinctive rather than the commonplace, practices, groups and identities rather than institutions and systems, and the conduct of minority, rather than majority constituencies' (2004: 192). Over the last years this focus has become acute, and in many contexts the hijab, and more recently the niqab and burka, have become nodal signifiers for significant lines of multicultural discontent, standing for the theocratic and patriarchal submission or oppression of women; as manifestations of parallel communities and weak integration; as an assault on the secular nature of public institutions and, in some instances, public space; and perhaps above all, as a relativist affront to the exceptional cultures of gender equality which have prospered in the West. As such, they have become centrally incorporated into liberal criticism of multiculturalism's reductionist and essentialist culturalism. If the previous chapter examined the ways in which the post-racial consensus allows for the marking out of culturalism on a terrain stripped of power, this chapter examines how forms of liberal discourse currently mark themselves out as transcending this terrain, as restoring universal certainties in the face of particularist excess. As the Danish writers Jens-Martin Eriksen and Frederik Stjernfelt argue, in a telling reference to enlightenment, 'there is scarcely a more important task in contemporary politics and political philosophy than giving full consideration to developing universal enlightenment and with the greatest possible force turning against both the prevailing right and leftwing forms of culturalism and their enslavement of the individual in his or her own "culture"' (2010).

In one sense, the shape of this debate is intensely familiar. The disagreements between liberalism and forms of 'communitarianism' are historically well mapped (Etzioni 1993), and the latent character of the liberal public sphere has been a central site of critical engagement (Durham Peters 2005). Over the last decades of the twentieth century, liberalism's socio-political adequacy was subject to sustained foundational critique, driven by feminist, queer and multicultural theorists contesting the questions of power, domination and substantive barriers to equality concealed in the alleged universality of citizenship and the putative neutrality of law, political structures and constitutional rights (for an overview, see O'Cinneide 2004). As Laden and Owen summarize, 'The idea that cultural diversity may require adopting differential treatment as a means of producing equality has generated some of the most strident debates between liberals and those who criticize liberalism's capacity to address issues of cultural diversity adequately' (2007: 10). As against this, in the canon of mainstream political theory on multiculturalism, the idea that the multicultural principle of recognition (Taylor 1994) has weakened the reach of universality and perverted the emancipatory possibilities of liberalism is also established. This critique is frequently rehearsed with reference to Brian Barry's *Culture and Equality* (2001). Barry's suspicion of multiculturalism is at least twofold. In locating significant political lacks within liberalism, multiculturalism undermines the principles of equal treatment and equal opportunity that are minorities' best recourse to overcoming discrimination. It follows from this relativization that the rights of women, children and various non-conformists within 'ethnic minority communities' are also rendered more vulnerable, through a system that recognizes communitarian group rights above those of the individual.

A marked vulnerability of these debates within political theory is the lingering insistence on modular cultures tailored to the templates of theoretical development, rather than reflexive engagement built from political practices (Laden and Owen 2007: 12–21; A. Phillips 2007: 19–21). In this vein, Pathik Pathak has argued – in a reading of Barry's critique of Bhikhu Parekh's *Rethinking Multiculturalism* (2000) – that Barry's criticism of the communitarianism in multiculturalism is made possible chiefly by exaggerating its distance from liberalism (2008: 126). Pathak shares the scepticism of anti-racist campaigners as to the conservative political aspirations of the 'mild doses' of recognition advocated in the accepted house philosophies of multiculturalism. The problem, in his reading, is also twofold: it leads to the conflation of philosophical multiculturalism with the deliberately attenuated culturalism of political practice, suggesting that the contemporary crisis has, in some way, been philosophically sanctioned. Equally, it places multiculturalism as something other than liberalism rather than as a debate conducted within divergent readings of the liberal tradition (Gray 2000), positioning specific iterations of liberalism as the default point of return. Thus Barry's accusation that Parekh agitates for a 'policy that will splinter Britain into communal division' elides the stress Parekh places on the dialogical relationship between liberalism and multiculturalism, where society 'is committed to both liberalism and multiculturalism, privileges neither, and moderates the logic of one by that of the other' (Parekh 2000: 340). As Pathak concludes, 'exalting multiculturalism as a fully grown ideology is to demand too much of a relatively limited set of political ideals. What Barry willfully overlooks is that Parekh does not disavow liberal values themselves but understandably contests the presumption of liberal superiority to other "operative public values"' (2008: 126).

Multiculturalism addresses liberal *exceptionalism*, not liberalism itself, and Pathak's reading of Parekh brings out the latter's desire to primarily temper liberal hubris, as 'liberal societies have a higher propensity to illiberalism because they absolutise their own values' (2008: 127).

While we agree with Pathak's theoretical contention that 'the merits of liberal society are precisely its tolerance and inclusivity, not an authoritarian will to autonomy, individualism and self-creation' (ibid.), our focus here is on the licence provided to untempered hubris by prevailing diagnostics of multicultural crisis. In other words, how has this propensity to illiberalism, absolutism and authoritarian will to autonomy become a key exclusionary feature of the post-racial political landscape? The debates on headscarves illustrate how, rather than deconstructing the culturalist ontology of multiculturalism, contemporary liberalisms have simply reified its forms to project their own shapes. Like Thorvold, European liberalism has doll-housed Muslim women, failing to note how a fixation on veils and other 'extreme' forms of dress positions the veil as the defining feature of subjectivity and as a racialized signifier of civilizational hierarchy. Addressing this does not require recourse to an equivalent doll house in the sociologically empty signifier of the veil as automatically oppositional, or anti-imperialist, or as a radically hybrid symbol. In-depth studies of veiling practices refute precisely these instrumental polarities; as Emma Tarlo argues in her study of 'radical sartorial activism' among female Hizb' ut-Tahrir activists in London, dominant stereotypes may not always be rejected but rather accorded a generative capacity 'as a rich creative source out of which to build counter-stereotypes of the Western woman' (2005). Moreover, the 'veil debates' of the last decade are shaped in particular political contexts, in and through different historical and constitutional relationships between organized religion and the state, and in these contexts the 'veil' has been suffused with different meanings and subject to different forms of policy measures.

For all that, shifting constructions of the veil are inscribed in an increasingly dominant political template, whereby the liberal state and a broad spectrum of public commentators insist on the legitimacy of varieties of constraint, prohibition and compulsory enculturation in order to protect dominant liberal norms and values against illiberal forms of life. In keeping with the semiosis of reverse racism, the veil is constructed as a 'challenge' to otherwise neutral and accommodating norms, and it is a challenge that is at once overdetermined as such, but also underdetermined, capable of being invested with ever more intolerable dimensions. The objectification of women who veil or cover, and the fluid appropriation of the veil to anti-Muslim racism, has served largely to obscure the ways in which the veil is contested and coded in different contexts by Muslim women activists (Afshar 2008). As Lettinga and Andreassen argue in their European survey of recent debates, the veil has become an uneven site of compressed political struggle, where 'the nationalizing of gender equality – as an integrated part of a hegemonic national culture that is being threatened by the culturally "other" – results in exclusionary and racialized understandings of gender equality and of the national community' (2008).

In Fatemeh Fakhraie's 'An open letter to white, non-Muslim feminists', she writes: 'I notice a lot of condescension and arrogance when you talk to us or about us. Let me be clear: you do not know more about us than we know about ourselves, our religion, our cultures, our families, or the forces that shape our lives. You do not know what's best for us more than we do' (2009). But liberalism *does* know better. Anything else is relativism, and it is in this turn that a multiplicity of political voices and activities are distorted and disqualified in the very way they are approached. 'Liberal ideology at its most generic', Wendy Brown writes, 'always already eschews power and history in its articulation and comprehension of the social and the subject' (2006: 18). Liberalism today does not just eschew power; it over-accumulates it. It does so through the specification of threat – to social cohesion, gender equality and unsettled imaginaries of secular/Christian societies – and through foundational acts of ontological dispossession. The capacity to make a 'claim to reason' is made contingent on particular forms of recognition, forms that disqualify, as nothing more than false consciousness or the ventriloquism of tacit communal pressure, the multiplicity of contextual debates, interpretations, political commitments, relations to faith, intersubjective relations and fashions that are negotiated through varieties of veiling *practices* (Tarlo 2010; Kiliç et al. 2008). With the soldering of what Sirma Bilge terms the normative interpretative framework of '*equality-and-sexual-freedoms*' to the repertoire of core value clashes, the veiled Muslim woman is held to merely express the internalization of oppression, oppressions which are understood within bounded cultural forms, and outside of grids of social and historical power. Their lives stand as stark sociological exceptions: as Anne Phillips argues, conceiving of subjects as constrained by gender and class, but also capable of autonomous action even in relation to those constraints, is relatively uncontroversial, yet 'in the debates around multiculturalism, to allow for the *relevance* of culture without making culture a *determinant* of action' is to relapse into a hapless relativism (2007: 130–31, italics in original).

It is this determinism, and the relations of patronage it sanctions, which returns these debates to the problem of post-racialism. As Hylland Eriksen warned in his reading of Finkielkraut, convinced of cultural prisons, liberalism has erected a polarized terminus of culturalist rationality while denying that any meaningful politics can take place in the interstitial space. Like Thorvold, an assertive liberalism so in thrall to its progressive intent cannot but co-opt, flatten and objectify its newly adopted constituency. The assumption that gender equality is a property of a 'community' of white European secularism; that those in but not of Europe are always already excluded from this state of being, and lack the capacities to define and organize their own liberations; the ways in which this sneaks liberalism into civilizational discourse, and vice versa (W. Brown 2006: 8); the unmistakable resonance of histories of a 'raced incapacity for rationality' (Mills 1997: 59) in this will to make (in)dependent; recourse to state discipline and coercion in addressing 'alien values'; none of this can easily be dissociated from racializing processes.

The purpose of this chapter is to open out some of the ways in which discourses of liberalism shape racialized exclusion in a post-racial socioscape. Tully's questions invite this exploration, but it is important to digress and note how they do not lead directly to it. The question 'How do we attend to the strange multiplicity of political voices and activities without distorting or disqualifying them in the very way we approach them?' applies equally to what we have thus far called liberalism. The contemporary specification of the problem of difference depends heavily on a language of rights, freedom, equality and moral and individual autonomy. Frequently, however, these are articulated simply as axes of differential value, mutually opposed cultural attributes that are easily assembled and incorporated into varieties of political practice. As Phil Triadafilopoulos (2011) argues in a rich theorization of what he terms 'Schmittian liberalism', it remains necessary to distinguish between the self-consciously liberal rejection of multiculturalism, and the piggybacking appropriations of manifestly xenophobic political actors. Noting the rise of 'civic integrationism', he argues that these initiatives cannot be considered outside of the public elaboration, by politicians, journalists, academics and 'aspirant public intellectuals', of a 'sharply antagonistic discourse designating putatively clear and inviolable boundaries of liberal-democratic conduct' (ibid.).

Schmittian liberalism, in this formulation, justifies a sharp differentiation of 'friends and enemies' based on asserting a non-negotiable set of core liberal values, and advocates the use of coercive state power to protect the open society from illiberal forms of life. It has an existentialist drive, or at least justification, in that it insists on civilizational self-identification in putatively ideological terms. Huntington's search for stability through the stabilizing polarity of conflict – 'for people seeking identity and reinventing ethnicity, enemies are essential' (1996: 20) – has been given more explicit contours by the 'clarity' engendered by the events of 9/11 and after, and it is this imperative for political community which returns the analysis to the political thought of Carl Schmitt, and his contention that 'a politically conscious people is thus "homogenous" in some sense, that is, it is united around a common set of characteristics [...] arrived at through engagement in "genuine" politics' (Triadafilopoulos 2011). Whether in the arguments of commentators such as Christopher Caldwell, politicians such as Pim Fortuyn or in the policies of many European governments, assimilating compatible immigrants and excluding dangerous ones forms part of a converging state apparatus of *integration* that justifies 'illiberal' action in existential terms.

In his critique, Triadafilopoulos rightly argues that simply approaching the exclusions of Schmittian liberalism as conventional state racism cannot account for the concomitant acceptance of the social reality of plural and diverse societies, and is thus indicative of how 'debates no longer revolve around *whether* to include immigrants, but rather over *how* integration ought to be pursued' (ibid., italics in original). Furthermore, such an account cannot run together the discursive piracy of the born-again feminists and queer activists of the radical right with arguments made in defence of genuinely held liberal goals, by 'actors with impeccable liberal credentials' (ibid.). For that reason, the most effective riposte to the Schmittian turn is not a counter-normative one, but a pragmatic critique; the demand for societal homogeneity, even if in the medium of values rather than race, cannot coercively cultivate belonging and integration (ibid.).

There are a number of issues that emerge from this. The most foundational, the relationship of liberalism to race and racism, is discussed subsequently. The nature of racist practice is also relevant here. To simply 'label' these positions racist is certainly reductive, both because it is a pointless form of categorization, always already placed in the force field of anti-racialism, and also because it provides no critical insight into this 'peculiar development' in liberal practice. Nevertheless, it does not follow from this that such positions are not complicit in racism, as racism is a question of practices, not intent, and has to be 'comprehended in terms of its consequences, not as a matter of intentions or beliefs' (Winant 2004: 135). Schmittian liberalism may appeal to core principles,[1] but it informs and justifies the selective differentialism, civic stratification and 'new hierarchies of belonging' (Back and Sinha 2011) that permeate state racisms in Europe.

In terms of the broader development of liberal polyphony, discourse is not a reliable basis on which to map this strange multiplicity of voices. What, beyond forms of habitus, differentiates the philosopher Andre Glucksmann's observations that 'the veil is a terrorist operation' and that it is 'stained with blood' (Scott 2007: 84, 158), from the philosopher Bernard-Henri Lévy's description of it as an invitation to rape (Seymour 2008: 13), from the German feminist Alice Schwarzer's comparison of the patriarchal compulsion to wear the hijab to the national-socialist insistence on Jews wearing the yellow star, from Søren Krarup, the *éminence grise* of the Danish People's Party, comparing it to a swastika (Andreassen 2010), from the 'populist' Geert Wilders's proposal for a 'head rag tax'? This medley illustrates how the prevalent division of life into liberal and illiberal forms involves a double collapse. Insisting on the heterogeneity of 'Muslims' must concomitantly involve unfolding, and attempting to account for, the vast range of voices laying claim to liberal sureties and patronage of illiberal subjects. This post-multicultural liberalism hosts a spectrum of political practices, projects of political (re)animation and modes of racialization that require differentiated forms of analysis.

We commence this examination with three readings. In the first, we engage with Christian Joppke's book *Veil: Mirror of Identity* (2009) and provide a reading of how liberal theory's problematic relationship with critical race and post-colonial thought and activism is set to one side by the licence of being after the 'failed experiment'. The critical gap between idealized invocations of French republicanism, and the socio-political grounds on which it is contested by the racialized of the republic, allows us to draw out some of the key modalities of liberal anti-racialism. In the second, we focus on the contextual, political production of resurgent liberal certainties, through a focus on the recited truths of multicultural backlash in the Netherlands, and the mainstream liberal antipathy shaped by the politics of Pim Fortuyn. Finally, we discuss whether understanding this polyphony is a question, ultimately, of categorizing different forms and practices, or of attempting to identify the ideological work of these new certainties. To this end, we suggest that the relationship of the new liberal assertiveness to the 'new racism' paradigm requires more attention, particularly in the reworking of incompatibility in moral rather than spatio-cultural terms.

In the mirror, through the looking glass

In *Veil: Mirror of Identity* (2009), Christian Joppke examines controversies concerning the Muslim headscarf in three different countries, and posits it as a mirror of identity 'which forces the French, the British and the Germans to see who they are and to rethink the kinds of societies and public institutions they want to have' (ibid.: x). Mirrors are not innocent metaphors, as both Lacan and Snow White would advise. We *gaze* into mirrors and choose to focus on a particular object. We accept the arbitrary relations of what is within and without the frame. Gazing in this mirror involves a deliberate decision to look for insight in this place, from this object, and through a structured relation that cannot but yield polarized and polarizing likenesses. Across Europe, the veil, broadly understood, has become the focus of an objectifying gaze, not only as a piece of cloth but as a *body* of women, signifying cultural, religious and ethnic differences cultivated by the failures of multi-culturalism (Rosenberger and Sauer 2006). While the metaphor of the mirror plays out in different ways in Joppke's analysis, it is important to unsettle it as a naturalized metaphor of reflection, and instead to draw attention to the idea of the veil as a floating signifier, *sought out* for interpretation, and problematized, mediated and made to stand for a range of problems.

While our focus here is on Joppke's defence of the prohibitive approach of the French republic, his study is comparative, and involves a detailed discussion of sub-federal *Länder* laws in Germany concerning dress for public schoolteachers in 2004 and 2005 (see also Rottmann and Marx Ferree 2008) and the question of school participation and the *jilbab* and *niqab* in the UK (see also Tarlo 2005). In essentially awarding Germany a third-place finish, as a consequence of its explicitly 'Christian-occidental' institutional exclusion of Islam (2009: 125–6), Joppke situates the debate on veils squarely in terms of contrasting liberal approaches, with liberalism 'constitutive of all the attempts at national self-definition that have been made in Europe's great debate surrounding Muslim integration' (ibid.: 25). This framing extends beyond his triptych of illustrations. Across western Europe, the veil is implicated in a meta-discourse of national-ized liberalism versus Muslim illiberalism. As Kiliç, Saharso and Sauer document, beyond this discursive commonality, actual state practices vary enormously. A prohibitive approach, in France, Turkey and some federal states in Germany enacts a ban on all forms of Muslim head covering in public institutions. A selective approach has tended to focus on 'extreme' covering such as the frequently conflated niqab and burka, where restrictions are in operation in Finland, Sweden and the Netherlands. Finally, a non-restrictive approach tends to apply in Denmark, the UK, Greece and Austria (2008: 397–9).

State approaches are shaped by established state–Church relations and consequent traditions of religious liberty, and more recently by anti-discrimination legislation. The complexity of the politicization of the veil is captured by its anomalous or exceptional status in some contexts; in the contrast between its symbolic overdetermination in the public sphere and constitutional/legislative defence in others; and the contrast between legal protection and context-specific bans and forms of harassment in many countries. In the Netherlands, the headscarf is protected by anti-discrimination legislation as well as conceived of as an expression of religious freedom within a general understanding of pillarized Dutch secularism. However, the intense political focus on the failure of multicultural 'accommodation' has positioned the veil as a symbol of the backwardness that must be relinquished in a context where 'Dutch society has [...] become the norm of civilization and universal equality' (Lettinga 2009: 260). In Austria the institutional accommodation of Islam within the Austro-Hungarian Empire, fol-lowing the annexation of Bosnia Herzegovina in 1908, established a tradition of viewing the headscarf as an expression of religious liberty. This accommodation appears exceptional given the ethno-cultural basis of Austrian citizenship, the general restrictiveness of immigra-tion and citizenship regimes, and the electoral evidence of significant racist sympathies in society in Austria (Gresch et al. 2008, see also Karner 2007). This resolute legal protection is in marked contrast to the incorporation of images from elsewhere into mainstream debates

– what Gresch et al. term 'the politics of non-issues' – with the veil increasingly framed as 'alien to our values' both by the populist right's expansion of over-foreignerization (*Überfremdung*) discourses to the problem of Islam, and as a symbol of unsatisfactory integration by some voices of the centre-left (Gresch et al. 2008: 425–7).

Attention to how 'veil' debates travel and are specified in place is important, not least because it draws attention to what is subsumed in the innocent proceduralism of liberalism's language of 'accommodation' (or, as Joppke puts it, 'the work that liberalism does in the reception of the headscarf'). In other words, veils are accommodated until they are politicized as requiring accommodation, and this frequently happens through circuits of recited truths that index and draw legitimacy from elsewhere. Following the 2003 report of the Stasi Commission on the wearing of 'ostentatious religious symbols' in France, francophone politicians in Belgium sought an analogous ban in public institutions in defence of equality and state neutrality (Coene and Longman 2008: 304). Given the complex cultural and multilevel institutional arrangements of Belgian politics, the debate on the hijab latched extensively, but far from fully, on to regional affinities with French republican ideals and Dutch tenets of religious accommodation (Jacobs 2004; Mielants 2006). In an analysis of the resulting debate, which resulted in a rejection of any such general legislation, Coene and Longman show how schools, local government and private employers in Brussels, francophone Belgium and Flanders nevertheless introduced their own context-specific prohibitions (2008: 304–8).

In *Le Voile médiatique* (2005) Pierre Tévanien draws attention to how public debate in France frequently conflated the *foulard* (the hijab) with *voile* (veil), connoting an ominous sense of full veiling and indexing the contested *foulard* to a dramatized rift between – gendered – forms of civilization. In the atmosphere of pronounced public racism that has dominated Danish politics in the last decade, the 'veil' has similarly functioned as a conflated cipher. It is afforded constitutional protection as an expression of religious liberty, but provides a fecund site for recited truths concerning Danish culture, gender equality and sexual liberty (Siim and Skjeie 2008; Lettinga and Andreassen 2008). Rikke Andreassen points to the absurdity of a public debate in 2007 on a proposed ban on burka-wearing women working in daycare centres, and of burka-wearing in schools, despite the near-total social absence of the burka, and no registered cases of niqab wearers in the public employ or seeking entry to the schools in question (2010).

After the attacks of July 2005 in London, the conflated veil began to circulate through public discourse in the UK, attracting a level of mediated aversion at odds with the lack of any legislative restriction on wearing any form of veil in public institutions. As Sevgi Kiliç has argued, following the intervention of Jack Straw in 2006, the niqab in particular came to embody the parallel societies and lives ostensibly fostered by multiculturalism (Kiliç et al. 2008).

This brief review of a complex terrain is necessary if only to insist on the ways in which the veil has been incorporated into political constellations and vested with *dis-orientalist* accents, processes of racialization that are not only entirely absent, but actively discounted in Christian Joppke's account of the 'Islamic headscarf' as the principal 'affront to liberal self-definition' in Europe (2009: 2). The construction of the headscarf as politically problematic in these terms is principally associated with France. The French debate of 2003/04 must be related to its antecedents in 1989 and 1994, yet without seeing this as a cumulative confrontation with an increasing or homogeneous 'challenge' (Scott 2007: 21).[2] In France, the veil, as a mediating symbol, has come to stand not only for incommensurable infra-national loyalties unfolded across lines of gender and culture, but also for a politics of immigration centred on the problem of second-generation 'immigrant youth' in the symbolically freighted *banlieues* (Khiari 2006). Scott (2007) identifies the timing and gradual harshening of approaches to the headscarf with the desire of the political mainstream, particularly the RPR/UMP (Rassemblement pour la République/Union pour un mouvement populaire), to both contain and translate the racist platforms of Le Pen's Front national:

> In 1989 the expulsions at Creil followed Le Pen's strong showing in the presidential election the year before; Bayrou's ministerial circular and the sixty-nine expulsions in 1994 followed the National Front's winning seats in the European parliament; and Chirac's law came shortly after he defeated Le Pen in the second round of the presidential election of 2002. In each case, the fear of Le Pen's party pushed more moderate parties farther to the right. (Ibid.: 38)

The force of Scott's point is this: the debates surrounding the eventual implementation of a law banning 'ostentatious' signs of religious affiliation took place in the aftermath of an election in which 16.86 per cent of the electorate had voted for a fascist party. In contrast, a consideration of this well-known backdrop to racial conflict in France is absent from Joppke's discussion. This is because, for Joppke, the Muslim headscarf is not so much a question for the sociological analysis of political struggle as an instrumental illustration of *the* classical liberal problem: 'the toleration of the intolerant' (2009: 117). Joppke's threshold of tolerance is a fundament, as it situates Islam as ultimately incompatible with liberal democracy. In endorsing this clash, in these terms, Joppke's analysis exemplifies three important dimensions of post-racial analysis. First, in attenuating the manifold lines of contestation seared in liberalism's shiny surfaces, this analysis has no interest in the ways in which race attenuates liberalism, closing off the promise of the 'individual' to the racialized. Secondly, the contextual histories from which these critical race interrogations have derived are also absent, as histories of colonialism, post-coloniality and racism are explicitly dismissed in the debates surrounding Muslims in Europe. Thirdly, and as a consequence of this historical closure, a dense sociological literature on the 'veil', which pays attention to the lived experiences and social conditions in France of those who wear it, is deemed irrelevant (cf. Chouder et al. 2008; Amiraux 2001; Amir-Moazami 2007).

Veil revisits the drama of French debates to reconsider theoretical debates about liberal ideas of the good life. More specifically, the book aims to reconcile headscarf bans '*à la française*' with liberalism, contending that 'prohibiting the headscarf in the name of republicanism is [...] within the ambit of liberalism' (Joppke 2009: ix). The argument proceeds from a broad mapping of French and British approaches on to John Gray's specification of liberalism's two faces; 'that of a modus vivendi for reconciling many ways of life; and that of a way of life in itself' (ibid.: ix). Britain is held to broadly represent the first variant of liberalism, while France represents the second. French republicanism, understood as liberalism as a way of life lived 'autonomously and rationally' (ibid.), is thus consistent with the banning of the headscarf, and so too is the classical British position of live and let live. Joppke compares the situation facing veiled women in both countries, arguing that, while in France 'liberalism risks [a] turn to its repressive opposite', in Britain 'liberalism encourages illiberal extremism' (ibid.). Joppke recognizes that today 'liberalism does the "exclusionary" work which, at an earlier time, had been done by racism or nationalism' (ibid.: 2),[3] yet he justifies the importance of such exclusion in the face of 'the affront to liberal self-definition for which the Islamic headscarf stands today above all' (ibid.).

It is worth opening out Gray's distinction a little further in this regard. Tolerance is historically one face of liberalism, committed not to 'relativism', but to tolerance as a processual dimension of dealing with 'things that were judged to be bad or false' as a means to rational consensus on the best life for all (2000: 2–33). Accordingly, it is the 'manifest imperfection of human reason that underpinned the ideal of toleration as a means to consensus. The hope of a rational consensus on values supports the liberal philosophies that prevail today. Yet the idea that the persistence of many ways of life is a mark of imperfection has little to support it' (ibid.: 3). Gray's wider argument is built on this point. The second face of liberalism is that of modus vivendi, an understanding of tolerance not as an ideal of rational consensus but as recognition of the fact that humans will always live life differently:

> For the predominant ideal of liberal toleration, the best life may be unattainable, but it is the same for all. From a standpoint of modus vivendi, no kind of life can be the best for everyone. The human good is too diverse to be realized in any life. Our inherited ideal of toleration accepts with regret the fact that there are many ways of life. If we adopt modus vivendi as our ideal we will welcome it. (Ibid.: 5)

Arguably, these two faces form another mirror. What is perceived as a given affront to liberal self-definition could also be approached through the hint of political neurosis inherent in Gray's mirroring of affront as regret at *imperfection*. While Gray's discussion remains steadfastly within the realm of political philosophy, framing minority lives as a mark of imperfection maps on to the 'anxiety of incompleteness' latent in the national project, and unsettled by the mobilities and uncertainties of globalization (Appadurai 2006: 6–18). Thus the two faces of abstract liberalism also suggest two ways of reading the problem of the veil: as a discrete, intrinsic challenge, or as a symbol in 'an emerging repertoire of efforts to produce previously unrequired levels of certainty about social identity, values, survival and dignity' (ibid: 7). By opting for the parameters of the discrete challenge, Joppke enacts a series of analytical exclusions that are ultimately choices necessary to the conduct of liberal exposition. The foundational move is to admit of liberalism's exclusionary work while positioning it as having transcended exclusionary formations of racism and nationalism. Yet to take seriously the scholarship on the modern nation-state and the shifting yet reciprocal determination of 'race' and nation (Balibar and Wallerstein 1991) involves insisting on the historical imbrication of liberalism in these formations. The idea of reasoned liberal exclusion, after racism, is possible only if the relationship between racism and universalism is overlooked.

Balibar connects racism to the idea of the universal human subject through its ability to define the 'frontiers of an ideal humanity' (ibid.: 61). Race, as Charles W. Mills argues, 'is in no way an "afterthought", a "deviation" from ostensibly raceless Western ideals, but rather a central shaping constituent of those ideals' (1997: 14). Political theory, in Mills's critique, has played a particular role in failing to question the 'appropriateness of concepts that *derace* the polity, denying its actual racial structure' (ibid.: 95). Despite the centrality of race and racism to the majority of the world's population in the modern period, and the massive political tapestry of anti-colonial and anti-racist movements through which resistance has been organized and theorized, little or nothing of this appears within the 'bleached weave of the standard First World political philosophy text' (ibid.: 124). The salient aspect of Mills's critique is the question of choice. In the light of decades of research and thinking on universalism, racial structure and the political struggle against it, it is a scholarly choice to work with 'an *idealizing* abstraction that abstracts away from the crucial realities of the racial polity' (ibid.: 76, italics in original). The glaring omission of France's racially charged electoral politics at work in the veil debates is a symptom of this, but the consequences of abstraction run deeper.

Somewhat ironically, while the veil is figured as a symbol of religious incompatibility with the secular state, its challenge is initially fixed as that of a wider political gesture that 'seems to carry a broadly anti-western meaning' (ibid.: 4). Joppke draws on a 'monumental study of Islam' by Hans Küng – a Catholic theologian who has described Islam as having 'special problems with modernity'[4] – in which he calls the veil a 'symbol of religious-political conviction [...] for Islam and against the secular state' (Küng 2004: 738, cited in Joppke 2009: 4). Focusing on this meaning leads him to ask whether, if the veil is associated with a rejection of Western lifestyles, it is 'so far-fetched if [...] a French president [Jacques Chirac] perceived the Islamic headscarf as a kind of "aggression"?' (ibid.). That is, having established the ontological determinacy of the symbol, and the symbolic position of the wearers, the only perspective that demands consideration is that of the head of state, who operates beyond any such cultural positionality. Raised to the ideal, hijab-wearing women are reduced, in this account, to silence, an oversight, which in this instance has sociological affinity with the contours of mainstream national debate in France.

Against this, Chouder et al. (2008), in *Les Filles voilées parlent*, gather the absented accounts of headscarf-wearing women and girls. Taking up Chirac's denotation of the headscarf as an aggression, Malika Latrèche notes that aggression is in fact often turned against those who wear the headscarf. Despite the real 'risk of being aggressed', she remarks, '[m]y fear of being aggressed is hidden behind another, stronger, fear: the fear of being seen as "the" submissive veiled woman, illiterate, reserved, who is good for nothing but cooking or making one baby after another and who does not go out or speak except under her husband's control'. Tackling the exclusion of 'voices' can easily lead to an unreflective fetish for the 'voice' of authenticity. The drive of this collection is different; the majority of testimonies disrupt the neatly delineated, idealized collision between the automated subjects of Islam and the hermetic principles of French republicanism.[5] For example, Mona, who experienced discrimination for substituting a bandana for the hijab during her *baccalauréat*, nevertheless expresses the desire to become a teacher: 'I know the law of 1880 that imposes religious neutrality on school teachers, and I completely agree with it' (ibid.: 39).

The Les mots sont importants collective points out that opposing the 2004 law does not imply negating the foundational laws of 1880, 1882 and 1886 which institutionalized French secularism by ensuring the separation of Church and state (2003). In contrast to the original laws, which obliged institutional, rather than individual, neutrality, the 2004 law 'is not aimed at secularizing institutions, but at excluding individuals by denying them a fundamental right, one of the most important achievements of the struggle for *laicité*: the right of everyone to an education'.[6] The 1989 Conseil d'État ruling on the headscarf concluded that there was no principled clash between wearing the headscarf and the conduct of a secular educational system, and that this pertained as long as the symbols were not ostentatious, or used to further 'acts of pressure, of provocation, of proselytism or of propaganda challenging the dignity or liberty of the student or other members of the educational community' (quoted in Silverstein 2004: 140). However, the report of the Stasi Commission in December

2003, enacted in law in March 2004, understood all 'conspicuous' signs of religious affiliation as *inherently* proselytizing. It is this semiotic manoeuvre which provides dominant public discourse in France, which Joppke appears to assimilate, with the certainties that obscure the paradoxical rejection of the principles of secularism that the ban on the headscarf entails. In light of this, as Tévanien remarks, it was vital to collect the testimonies of the 'defeated' for whom 'the watchwords "ban on ostentatious symbols" or "neutrality of public space" were neither synonyms for "a reaffirmation of *laïcité*" nor for "emancipation" or "promoting living together", but simply, prosaically, humiliations, exclusions, insults or even aggressions' (Chouder et al. 2008: 15).

Those empowered to tolerate may or may not do so; the tolerated, and the intolerable, endure (Hage 1998). The disjuncture between the rhetoric of 'excluding to include' and the additional accretion of the headscarf to the lexicon of racialization and humiliation draws attention to the fragile containment of racism in Joppke's argument. In effect, his rejection of racism is based on a recurring dismissal of Joan Wallach Scott's (2007) view that 'a colonial view of Muslims as "lesser people" undergirds French aversion to the headscarf' (ibid.: 108). Nevertheless, he relies almost exclusively on the foil of Scott's work, without engaging the work of French academics and activists, Muslims, people of colour and anti-racists, who provide ample data and analysis to substantiate Scott's argument (Khiari 2006, 2009; Fassin and Fassin 2006; Ndiaye 2008; Tévanien 2005; Amiraux 2010). By compounding the silence of the veiled with the silence of those critically invested in French society, Joppke illustrates Sadri Khiari's claim that: 'blacks, Arabs, Muslims. Present in France for a short while or for a long time. "First, second, third generation ..." French. Non-French. We who do not exist [... are not] meant to exist' (Khiari 2009: 9). Khiari links the refusal to acknowledge the political existence of the racialized to the refusal to acknowledge their existence *tout court* because, following Abdelmalak Sayad, 'to exist is to exist politically' (ibid.).

It is here that liberalism's attenuated vision of the social and the post-racial elision of the experience of racism are most in tune. Having established the irrational subject, liberalism is not required to engage in the messy 'reverse-racism' equivalences discussed in the previous chapter. Attention to the testimonies of veiled women cannot but reveal the racism laundered by the headscarf ban, where the legal restriction of the headscarf in public institutions sanctioned wider expressions of aversion from overzealous teachers or members of the public[7] (Chouder et al. 2008). Rejecting the interpretation of the veil as a symbol of women's oppression, Fatima (twenty) asks,

> If my veil is a 'symbol of oppression', should I come to the conclusion that I oppress myself? [...] In my view, the real cause of this law is racism. A racism that is gravely underestimated. In this country there are prejudices about religion, dress, skin colour, and even between social classes: when you live in a marginal neighbourhood, even if you are of French origin, you are put in the same box as blacks and Arabs. (Ibid.: 53)

Joppke's boxes are big ones. He upholds Samuel Huntington's (1996: 217) claim that 'the underlying problem for the West is not Islamic fundamentalism. It is Islam.' Islam is 'structurally fundamentalist' (Joppke 2009: 111), thus there can be no European variant of Islam because it constructs itself in opposition to other nations as 'an alternative type of nationality which claims jurisdiction over all aspects of human activities' (Shavit 2007: 6, cited in Joppke 2009: 113). Islamic doctrine envelops the lives of Muslims in Europe, a determinism which supports a particular diagnosis of the problem of integration. Eschewing sociological accounts of the barriers to integration faced by the descendants of post-colonial Muslim migrants in France and Britain or of *gästarbeiter* in Germany (Abbas 2005; Geisser 2003; Silverstein 2004; Poynting and Mason 2007); which examine the contextual adaptations and integration of these migrants over generations (Husain and O'Brien 2000; Werbner 2005a); and which interrogate practices of identification and the 'making Muslim' of suspicious populations over time (Bleich 2009), Joppke's Muslims are bound by their faith to respect the local law only insofar as they are contractually obliged to, but with a view to transforming this once in a demographic majority. This Caldwellian turn is evidenced by dismissing Joan Scott's contention that the headscarf ban was motivated 'by the (questionable) view that "one could not be both Muslim and French"' (Scott 2007: 135, cited in Joppke 2009: 112), and citing the Egyptian Muslim Brotherhood imam Yusuf al-Qaradawi, who is banned from entering both the USA and the UK, and who rejects the possibility of having a hyphenated European-Muslim identity. Basing his contention on Qaradawi, Joppke describes Muslims as being duty-bound by their religious leaders to be united – hence opposed, in his reading, to the dominant culture – not assimilate and proselytize:

While western political elites worry about the Muslims' 'dual loyalty', this is no issue for Muslim jurists, for whom western nation-states are 'mere social mechanisms enabling Muslims to practice Islam to its fullness' (Qaradawi, cited in Shavit 207: 3). Expected to implode from their inner spiritual void, if not be destroyed by the wrath of God for their 'idolatrous barbarism' (Buruma and Margalit 2004: 12), western nation-states are simply no serious competitor to the spiritually strong, global Muslim nation. (Joppke 2009: 113)

There is also a basic sociological duty to examine whether theological prescription walks in straight lines. Qaradawi's totalizing explanation is preferred over an engagement with the lived 'contradictions' of a figure such as the self-professed *Islamogauchiste* Hanane, a headscarf-wearing member of the Ligue communiste révolutionnaire, who argues that 'I wear the veil because I submit to a God – and I take complete responsibility for this submission – but that means that I am not subjected to anyone else [...] if anyone wants to dictate my behaviour, I send them packing!' (Chouder et al. 2008). Similarly, the continual *production* of the alien Islamic subject through sociopolitical process is absent. As the Muslim feminist Zahra Ali details, in discussing how the work of her organization, Al Houda, is restricted to the undeclared multicultural terrain of the republic:

So basically when it's about mosques, there is no problem, our contribution is sought. But when it's not strictly related to community or religious issues, when it's about social or political issues, all the stuff related to 'being fully-fledged female citizens', at that level, everything we do or ask for is perceived as provocative and extreme, as propaganda or as proselytizing. (Bouteldja 2009)

By ignoring embodied, political actors in favour of an asocial theory of theological automation, and elevating religious rationales over approaches adequate to multidimensional phenomena, this argument performs the conventional reification of a heterogeneous population of Muslims in France. It denies the importance of intersectionality to theorizing feminist emancipation, an importance, as Bilge argues, that is traduced in accounts that bind, a priori, the meaning of the veil to a 'teleology of emancipation, whether feminist or anti-imperialist' (2010). Welcome to the doll's house; Joppke explicitly places the veil ban as securing liberation through a 'lexical ordering' in which discrimination is tackled secondarily. In effect, however, discrimination is not important in the argument. In describing the subsequent establishment of HALDE,[8] the organ to combat discrimination, as being 'driven by guilt' (2009: 109), Joppke echoes the most recent expression of *nouveau philosophe* regret at the imperfection of many ways of life, Pascal Bruckner's *The Tyranny of Guilt* (2010). The need to redress discrimination seems unnecessary when the liberal struggle involves two equivalent entities, something called liberalism and something called Islam. Conceiving of Muslims as social beings is unnecessary because Islam does not view the individual as autonomous, a perspective that 'cannot but clash with the liberal view' (Joppke 2009: 110). 'It is unhelpful', Joppke cautions, 'to deny this clash of principles under the label of "racism"' (ibid.).

This admonition cuts to the core of liberal post-racialism: unhelpful, precisely, for whom? Joppke's methodological approach involves ignoring the 'decisive breach' in the univocal discourse of republicanism discussed by de Laforcade (2006: 230). This is not limited to the idealization of the headscarf, but is more fundamentally expressed in the idealization – or sacralization in Balibar's (Balibar and Wallerstein 1991) terms – of the republic. The liberal state stands outside the historical production of intertwining, particularist and universalist iterations of Frenchness, but also, crucially, beyond the task set by Silverstein in his anthropological history of *Algeria in France* (2004), where he maintains that it is necessary to re-examine 'genealogically the French national imaginary of republican universalism as a historical product of colonialism, to show how its definitions of "nation", "nationality" and "citizenship" are themselves historically linked to a series of ongoing exclusions of particular people and cultural features' (ibid.: 32–3).

This genealogy extends into the present, for colonial relationships of domination endure. In *Pour une politique de la racaille* (2006), Sadri Khiari regards the label 'scum' (*racaille*) as produced in and through the colonial relationship and its reproduction in the contemporary management of the racialized population in France, still regarded as *immigrés* and thus dissociable from the past of France and of its former colonies, Algeria in particular. The Mouvement de l'immigration et des banlieues (MIB) made this clear in its denouncement of the handling of the *banlieues* as 'colonial management'. For Khiari, the notion of post-colonialism unveils the persistence of both a colonial mindset and a continuity of practices; however,

Postcolonialism does not mean the identical perpetuation of these colonial relationships, no more than it is insufficient for referring to the importation to the Metropole of modes of management put in place in the territories formerly occupied by France [...] Postcolonialism also means the invention of new forms of ethnic discrimination applied to postcolonial 'immigrant' populations and generalized, at least in part, to other sectors of the population [...] Postcolonial means the intermeshing of these forms of domination with other relationships of oppression and exploitation. (Ibid.: 20–21)

Joppke's inattention to the post-colonial exemplifies the post-racialism of his approach. The French position is not 'an attitude of exclusion or racism, as some have argued, but of setting clear and equal terms of integration' (2009: 125). Thus if Islam is a threat to 'liberal Europe', racism exists only in the reverse threat of Muslims to their 'host' countries. Paradoxically perhaps, the racism experienced by the women interviewed by Chouder et al. (2008) does not induce them to reject the universalism of the *République*. For example, Houda:

The message I would like to address to the French society is one of hope: whether you are black, frizzy, yellow, white, whether you are called Paul, Jacques, Zoubida, Amina, Claire or Mohamed, we are all human beings, we live in the same country, and we all have something to offer each other, culturally, as human beings, religiously. We are here to help each other, to hold each other's hands in order to enrich our country and offer a better future to our children and to our society. (Ibid.: 155)

Liberals also address all human beings, while wearing universalism as a badge of transcendent identity, because, to paraphrase Du Bois, they have never been forced to wear any other. The racial hand of liberalism is hidden while extended for a greeting between putative equals. Denied voice and experience, extracted from grids of socio-economic disadvantage and living histories of racialized power, minorities are required to submit to forms of top-down 'civic integrationism' that may require open societies to 'violate some of their own liberal precepts' (Joppke 2009: xi). Final paradoxes emerge here. By advocating unequal treatment to cultivate liberal subjects, Joppke admits that the liberal individual is a *status earned through recognition.* In other words, it is the particularist creation of European political thought within given conditions, not least the structuring opposition to the 'irrationality' of the non-European world (Hesse 2007; Mills 1997). Given the evidence of *what is not recognized* in contemporary France, why should this structuring opposition be trusted to work out differently, this time? The Thorvold moment becomes clearer when we consider how Joppke argues that French Muslims have for the most part 'understood and accepted' the 'setting of clear and equal terms of integration'. This should raise the question as to why, then, there was such a profound need to establish Muslims as fundamentally opposed to liberalism throughout the book, but the answer is more likely to be found in the metaphor of reflection. It is liberalism, Narcissus-like, which is gazing in the fairground mirror, but whether the distortions are grotesque or flattering depends on who is doing the staring.

Liberal populism, and populist liberalism

Europe's prime multicultural experiment Writing in the *New Yorker* in 2006, Jane Kramer concludes a dark assessment of the failures of 'The Dutch Model' by evoking the frisson of the ghetto and European decline:

> Friends who a few years earlier would walk you through a neighborhood like the Baarsjes, with its shrouded women and its state-funded Islamic school and its defiantly secretive mosque, and call this a 'multicultural success' or a 'model of tolerance', have begun to suspect that that peculiarly Dutch myth of a democracy integrated but not assimilated might be not only a contradiction in terms but a dangerous fiction. But, like everybody else in Europe, they have no adequate answer to the question, What now?

During the course of the article, and apropos a brief dismissal of 'Amsterdam's born-again Marxists, many of them Muslim students', Kramer 'asked a Moroccan feminist-cum-radical activist named Miriyam Aouragh for her opinion', only to dismiss it. In a public reply, Aouragh and Anouk de Koning noted that they had offered Kramer the chance to meet and discuss with community workers and organizers in Amsterdam, but that she preferred instead to rely on 'high profile voices that present a mind-set of "alloctones" as caught up in a false consciousness of tribal-religious loyalty'.[9] Kramer, they argued, was content to replicate a generic narrative of multicultural

weakness and cultural conflict. Any discussion of entrenched discrimination, everyday racism and the concerted political targeting of
migrant-descended citizens was actively discounted. Yet while Kramer
quickly dismissed 'racism' as the language of political obsolescence,
even within the parameters of her confident liberalism, others are not
so sure. The political scientist Bert van den Brink steers far closer to
Aouragh in his analysis of the 'crisis of civic integrity' that followed
the murder of Theo Van Gogh, which involved 'a worrying breakdown of civic competence among politicians, intellectuals, journalists,
columnists and "ordinary" citizens' that translated the problem of
Islamic terrorism into the problem of Muslim 'immigrants' in general
(2007: 350).

The Netherlands commands its own sub-narrative of the 'rise
and fall of multiculturalism' (Entzinger 2003). Widely held to have
'pursued Europe's most prominent and proudly exhibited multiculturalism policy', since the early years of the new millennium the
state has pursued a programme of civic integration characterized by a
panoply of compulsory measures aimed at instilling dominant Dutch,
and liberal, values and norms (Joppke 2007: 5–8). A consequence of
the turn to assimilative integration has been to magnify academic
differences on the nature, extent, coherence and impact of Dutch
multiculturalism. Most historical accounts note the pre-9/11 retreat
from what Koopmans et al. call 'the most overt European experiment
in multiculturalism' (2005: 428). However, there remains a level of
intense disagreement as to what was retreated from. As Augie Fleras
summarizes,

> Reactions to the status of multiculturalism have varied: for some
> Holland was a reluctant multiculturalism at best [...] it was never
> committed to the principles of multiculturalism except by default
> or as expediency. For others, by supporting the distinctiveness and
> coexistence of racial and ethnic minorities, it symbolized a classic
> multicultural governance. (2009: 149)

Despite the scale and complexity of flows of post-colonial migration and post-war *gästarbeiter*, no explicit government policy existed
in relation to the integration of people viewed either as temporary
labour[10] or as being 'naturally inclined' towards Dutch society (Entzinger 2003; Fleras 2009). Thus most accounts of multicultural
elaboration converge, and significantly diverge, on the implications
of the 'Memorandum Minorities Policy' *(Nota Minderhedenbeleid)*

adopted in 1983. Explicitly recognizing that migrant labourers were here to stay, the policy combined a programme of citizenship and naturalization; welfare measures in housing, education and employment; anti-discrimination legislation and public subsidy for cultural expression (Penninx 2005). Anne Phillips captures a widespread sense of its significance when she describes it as marking the Netherlands as 'Europe's most explicitly multicultural regime, committed to addressing socioeconomic advantage, but also recognizing the right of minority groups to retain and develop their cultural and religious identities, and representing this as an enrichment of the whole society' (2007: 7). Taken as a package of measures and as symbolic action, the emergent policy of the 1980s has a clear sense of the obstacles to equality and participation faced by migrant subjects. In Jane Kramer's postcard of fear and loathing, the policy is described as a 'singularly shortsighted document, but at the time it was considered a beacon of multicultural correctness' (2006). The shortsightedness, however, may have more to do with assuming that policy is future reality in an Ikea flat-pack. In a limited elaboration, some lines of disagreement concerning the subsequent engineering of multiculturalism can be mentioned here.

The first is the extent to which Dutch government policy has ever meaningfully been something called multiculturalism. Maarten Vink (2007) provides an account that challenges both the tendency to see multiculturalism as developing from the institutionalized pluralism and tolerance of religious-communal pillarization (*verzuiling*), and of viewing these policy developments as multiculturalism per se. Policy references to multiculturalism in the 1980s were descriptive of social change, not indicators of normative commitment, and thus these measures were never intended as anything other than transitive dimensions of *integration*: 'there was never any serious discussion of an unequivocal right for newcomers to express their identities from an assumed symmetry of cultures. The 1983 Memorandum discarded outright such a relativist notion of cultural equality: "It [integration] is a confrontation between unequal partners. The majority culture is after all anchored in Dutch society"' (ibid.: 345).

While there is no contesting the development, as elsewhere, of a pervasive rhetoric of cultural diversity and mutual tolerance, support for 'ethnic community' organizations, and the informal aggregation of group-specific programmes, particularly in education, what is cast as a prehistory of flourishing multiculturalism is better read as a stage in the elaboration of an integrationist project in which multi-culturalism is a dimension of an ideology of national unity (Fleras 2009). Of course, such clarifications also map on to the substantive disagreements as to what constitutes 'multiculturalism'. Yet given that what is at stake is an established contention that something called multiculturalism is culpable for socio-economic stagnation, cultural conflict and layered anomie, the main vector of clarification concerns the second line of disagreement: the establishment of these causal links. An assessment of this terrain is provided by Ellie Vasta in her consideration of the shift from 'ethnic minority to ethnic majority policy' (2007). Welfare-related integration programmes of the 1980s were criticized for not delivering outcomes on 'labour market integra-tion', and from the early 1990s a mainstream rhetoric of implacable differentialism was progressively suffused with a moralized assessment of migrant failure to integrate (Prins 2002). This discursive shift is congruent with a demonstrable 'ideological shift [in the early 1990s] from support for group needs to promoting individual identity. Even if there is agreement that there has been strong multiculturalism for the past ten years, officially this is not the case' (Vasta 2007: 733).

From 1994's Integration Policy, the approach has been informed by convictions concerning the problem of cultural difference, the im-perative of fashioning autonomous individuals through ameliorative culturalization, and an institutional/ideological redefinition of inte-gration as a 'law and order affair' (Entzinger 2003: 9). Vasta's review of recent research points to the weak development and delivery of early 'multicultural' policies despite the overt commitment to fostering equality and limited recognition. Based on Duyvendak et al. (2005), she suggests that there is no empirical evidence that 'Dutch integration policy failed because the Dutch have been too tolerant of cultural and religious difference' (2007: 733; see also Fleras 2009: 156–9). Faced with the pervasive banality of multicultural rhetoric and patchy policy correlatives, Vasta counters: 'how can a society that perceives itself as "liberal" demand conformity, while blaming immigrants for not integrating and using coercive measures to secure integration? How can a "tolerant" society claim that certain religions and cultures are backward? In addition, how can such a society continue to show such high levels of structural marginalization?' (2007: 727).

Multiculturalism, such as it was, has always existed alongside, and frequently obscured, the structural marginalization and institutional racism experienced by *allochtonen* (non-natives) (ibid.: 727–32).

Racism is held not to exist in the Netherlands, because it is held with particular force, post-*Shoah*, to have been expunged, lingering only in exceptional incidents and individual pathologies. Hondius (2009) situates this elision in the context of the 'hardly digested' realities of colonial and post-colonial history, where downplaying these constitutive formations further underlines the 'anti-racist norm [...] that says that racial difference does not matter'. Consequently, she argues for recognizing a lineage of colonial paternalism extending through multiculturalism and integrationism as contemporary forms of hierarchical ordering. In an influential study, Essed and Nimako (2006) dissect the 'symbolic assassination' of critical race engagements within public discourse on integration and within dominant paradigms of knowledge production. Organized through assimilation and integration paradigms, 'research is largely about ethnic minorities – invariably called *allochtonen*, the Dutch word for non-natives or *aliens*; about their migration and their degree (or lack) of economic, social and political integration in the Netherlands' (ibid.: 286). Research into the historical and structural dimensions of racism was frequently dismissed as a fad imported from the obviously racialized contexts of the UK and USA, as a direct assault on 'the uniquely Dutch character trait of tolerance', or as a form of political correctness. As part of the 1990s shift towards the intensive problematization of the un-integrated and dis-integrating 'migrant', recurring idioms of racism-mitigation have bled from research to broader discourse: a natural hostility to 'foreigners' that cannot be racist as it is not expressed in terms of white superiority; the exceptional absence of racism in Dutch society; the reluctance to evaluate statements or actions in terms of racism; a defence of Dutch tolerance against the subjective contestations of ethnic minorities and the exaggerations of anti-racists; a self-victimization that sees mainstream (white) society as imprisoned by its own tolerance and kindness (ibid.: 298–303).

The denial of racism removes both the specificities of racialized experience, and the possibility to protest in terms adequate to the valences of systemic exclusion: 'it is not that the Dutch do not deal with discrimination [...] the problem is that racism is taken out of the equation. Ethnic minorities, whether black, Moroccan or Muslim, experience racialization, a process that is normalized and hence rendered invisible to the native Dutch' (Vasta 2007: 732). The recited truths of multiculturalism assume an integral role in the dynamics of racism, as they create a sense of expectation that the subjects of multiculturalism are actually or even disproportionately benefiting from its experimental largesse. Yet as 'they' remain visibly mired in unemployment and apparently taking refuge in isolationist, regressive cultures, the only possible explanation is their refusal to benefit, and to integrate. The failure of the experiment stratifies the undeclared dynamics of racialization, for after multiculturalism, asserting the house rules should not be confused with racism. The boundary is marked by their irredentism and 'our' past excess – there can be no more apologies, no more opportunities to 'abuse our multicultural love' (Ahmed 2008).

The new realism The Netherlands provides a powerful example of what Sara Ahmed (ibid.) has theorized as the anti-performativity of multiculturalism – utterances that do not bring into being what they name. Under these conditions, 'multiculturalism is a fantasy which conceals forms of racism, violence and inequality as if the organization/nation can now say, how can you experience racism when we are committed to diversity?' (ibid.). Paul Scheffer's (2000) frequently cited essay on 'The multicultural drama', in the conservative quality paper *NRC Handelsblad*, provides a heuristic example. The essay is frequently understood as an elaborated version of the 'prisoners of kindness and tolerance' discourse. Yet several readings draw attention to its affinities with materialist anti-racist concerns, with the widening poverty and mobility gap between *allochtonen* and *autochtonous* and with the governmental and elite indifference couched in ideals of multicultural tolerance (van Bruinessen 2006; Prins 2002). As Essed and Nimako point out, the rupture in Scheffer's argument, as in David Goodhart's (2004a), is that 'rather than writing about emancipation, antiracism and transformative change in society, Scheffer's solution was different; fix the ethnic minorities in order to enable them to live up to the culturally more advanced level of Dutch norms and values' (2006: 305).

This is based on the assumption that multiculturalism damaged both minorities and society. In the presumed absence of solidarity, and in the presence of dangerous levels of structured inequality, cohesion can purportedly only be forged in the affirmation of national identity. The problem, in the Netherlands as elsewhere, is that the ongoing production of a contingent but sufficient homogeneity is not only troubled by the 'unassimilable' cultural difference and transversal attachments of diasporic minoritized populations, but by the wider conditions of globalization these populations are made to stand in for (Appadurai 2006). Pim Fortuyn's politics emerged in this conjunctural space, conventionally linking the 'failure to integrate' of the *allochtonen* and government failure to manage immigration to render 'immigrants' an affective proxy for the transformative globalization of Dutch society:

> The political situation in which Fortuyn emerged as a formidable contender was one where the ruling parties had lost credibility in dealing with both the most important domestic issue, immigration, and the most important international issue, Holland's superior moral standing among the nations. Moreover, the ruling parties had run out of steam in managing the economic downturn and political instability that affected the world economy. Even voters who were not especially attracted to Fortuyn's message felt that a fundamental change was needed, and Fortuyn seemed to have the charisma to bring this about. The attacks on the United States on September 11, 2001, seemed further to confirm Fortuyn's message that the world had changed and that fearsome Muslim terrorists were ready to attack Western civilization. To respond to these new challenges, one needed new leaders, and Fortuyn seemed to fit the bill. (Van der Veer 2006: 117)

In his account of Fortuyn's significance, Christopher Caldwell situates him in a land of oppressive official multiculturalism, where his rise is narrated through his 'sudden decision' to run for office in the months after '9/11'. The immense popularity of his taboo-busting discussions of Islam as a 'life-threatening culture' and the need for immigration control proved that 'Holland's entire multicultural order was being propped up by taboos, not consent, and that most Dutch natives felt immigrants were using Dutch tolerance to take them for a ride' (2009: 254). Caldwell presents Fortuyn through the populist trope of the leader as reluctantly political, stirred less by will to power than by dutiful response to urgent political need (Mudde 2004). Yet Fortuyn had long been active politically, journeying right, and was well known for his writing, in the weekly *Elsevier*, on Islam and its incompatibility with the advanced Dutch nation. Intensely mediated after 9/11, he recited a set of positions patterned by a 'cultural line of critique [that] goes back to 1991 when Frits Bolkestein, then leader of the liberal party VVD, publicly questioned the compatibility of Islamic and Western values' (Vink 2007: 338; see also Prins 2002).

The lineage to Bolkestein is significant, as his 1991 intervention 'in defence of European civilizations and its core values' is held to mark the deliberate and largely unprecedented party politicization of migration, through an influential specification of incompatible values that has become near-hegemonic (Bonjour 2005; van Bruinessen 2006).

On the basis of this, Colin Crouch is right to regard Fortuyn as 'both an example of post-democracy and a kind of attempted response to it', appealing to the socio-political dislocation and thin allegiances of the electorate with the force of charismatic personality, and the ephemeral ballast of an 'appeal to identity based on hostility to immigrants' (Crouch 2004: 28). However, this appeal is more complex than mere hostility. Demmers and Mehendale (2010) argue that the neoliberal collapse of left and right into a technocratic consensus on political economy foregrounded migration/integration as a space of political differentiation, leading to what they term a 'cultural-nationalist bidding war' in which Fortuyn refined the role of anti-Muslim racism in both explaining and responding to social uncertainty. The 1990s involved the gradual 'becoming Muslim' of different minority populations, a familiar collectivization that in this instance bore little relation to the relatively low levels of religious observance among Turks and Moroccans, but which coalesced around the seeming consolidation of 'failed' asylum seekers in a Muslim 'underclass' shared with second- and third-generation Moroccans and Turks, and produced through shifting connotations of criminality, resistant isolationist traditionalism, and security and radicalization (van der Veer 2006: 116–17; Essed and Nimako 2006: 229–30).

This *dis-orientalist* becoming is pivotal to the discourse of 'new realism' as a populist form of common sense: the realism to speak the truth to politically correct evasion, to the stagnant, complacent consensus of the 'left' elite, to articulate the discontent and anxieties felt by 'ordinary people' concerning a loss of national identity and sovereignty through immigration and, in particular, 'Islamization' (Prins 2002: 12–13). The cultural capital of undesirability is relevant here; 'Islamization' also signalled a discursive shift away from uneasy questions of class and race to a well-patterned cultural conflict that 'made xenophobia socially acceptable to segments of the middle class' (van Bruinessen 2006: 9). The easy incorporation of Muslims, as the *ur-migrant*, into a populist structure of meaning does not in any sense guarantee 'popular' investment in a politics of the folk devil, and tells even less about situated negotiations and resistance to this politics in social life (Mepschen 2009a). Nevertheless, the political impact of Fortuyn is consistently regarded as a transformative 'truth event' that shifted public policy and political culture radically in the direction of a disciplining *Leitkultur*:

> the so-called Fortuyn-revolt of 2002 transformed the Netherlands from a relatively tolerant and relaxed country to a nation that called for repression, tough measures and neo-patriotism [...] while intellectuals emphasized the need for the reinvention of a Dutch canon, and also questioned the value of cultural diversity and the loyalty of the Muslim population to Dutch society. (Prins and Saharso 2008: 379)

Integral to this neo-patriotism is the liberal discourse of inclusionary exclusion that has suffused European public cultures, providing malleable possibilities for the ongoing cultural labour of imagined communities.

Liberal populism, and populist liberalism In a consideration ofGeert Wilder's *Fitna*, Jolle Demmers (2009) remarks on the sense of anti-climax on its release, speculating that the film represented simply 'an exaggeration of what is already considered almost uncontested'. Its impact, such as it was, is better understood in structural rather than relational or representational terms, as a footnote to 'the rise of xenophobia as part of a larger process of a mostly market-controlled reclaiming of symbolic forms of collectiveness in an increasingly atomized society' (Demmers and Mehendale 2010: 54). Situating Wilders in this way recalls how Appadurai, in elaborating his 'fear of small numbers', briefly distinguished between two Europes; 'the world of inclusion and multiculturalism in one set of European societies and the anxious xenophobia of what we may call Pim Fortuyn's Europe' (2006: 8). While this distinction is not central to Appadurai's argument, approaching these two Europes less in terms of actual territorial states, more in terms of the assemblages generated and under neoliberal conditions, is instructive.

Appadurai's argument departs from the recognition that the foundational idea of a 'national ethnos', regardless of public or institutional commitments to tolerance or multiculturalism, harbours both an insistent vestige of particular 'ethnic genius', and an 'anxiety of incompleteness' concerning the legitimacy and place of minorities in the nation-state (ibid.: 4–13). Incompleteness is magnified and transformed by new orders of social uncertainty relating both to the material uncertainties of individual relations to the state – in what Hage terms the 'non-nurturing social reality of neo-liberal policy' (2003: 43) – and to the visible transformations of migration and multivalent transnationalization. Logics of uncertainty and incompleteness can combine in large-scale mobilization and violence, but globally Appadurai points to a 'repertoire of efforts' to stabilize sociocultural identities (ibid). Yet a corollary of this uncertainty is the difficulty of imagining the 'unsullied national whole' in societies of immigration and 'banal cosmopolitanism' (Beck 2006), and in societies where informational capitalism implies that 'difference rather than homogenization infuses the prevailing logic of accumulation' (Yúdice 2003: 28). The mobilization of national identity and neo-patriotism, under such conditions, requires the elaboration of 'new technologies of the neonational self' for making and remaking the boundaries of legitimacy and identity (Gilroy 2004: 28). It is in these terms that Paul Mepschen (2009a) makes a compelling argument for understanding Fortuyn's appeal in terms of how specific iterations of liberal freedoms, gender and sexuality combine in anti-Muslim racism. Mepschen argues that the contemporary work of elaborating national identity involves investing it with desirability as a 'sexy and authentic cultural option'. Fortuyn understood this politics of imagination:

> Fortuyn combined a personal, almost erotic, political aesthetic and charisma with neonationalist and Islamophobic political ideas and fulfilled a deep desire for belonging, meaning, direction, a closed and clear identity, and an ever more strictly defined definition of 'the other'. Fortuyn wanted to embody the modern, free, tolerant, Dutch nation and did so by liberating the sexual norms and the aesthetics of part of the international and Dutch gay male community from the gay ghetto and bringing them into the Dutch public domain. As an essential part of this political discourse, Muslims were represented by Fortuyn as the exact opposites of the free, liberal, modern Dutch person. (Ibid.)

The symbolic importance of Fortuyn's 'open' homosexuality is often misunderstood. Caldwell produces his sexuality as the empirical proof of his non-racism, balancing ledger entries in an account of one-dimensional man: 'Fortuyn was not a racist, and his colorful repartee about the Moroccan men he had slept with was adequate to place him above the suspicion of being one' (2009: 254). All of this is to miss the role of 'counter-patriarchy' as a technology of the neo-national self. In *The Power of Identity* (2004 [1997]), Manuel Castells's account of the post-industrial decline of the 'legitimizing identity' of modern institutions and mobilizing political ideologies, contemporary political struggle involves intense contest over cultural codes, compelling actors to become 'symbol mobilizers'. Central to this symbolic struggle are two forms of identity practice; 'resistance identities' – where meaning is reinscribed through defensive identities formed on collective resistance and exclusionary practices – and 'project identities', including the counter-patriarchal movements of feminism and queer, where social actors, 'on the basis of whatever cultural materials are available to them, build a new identity that redefines their position in society and, by so doing, seek the transformation of the overall social structure' (ibid.: 8). Castells hypothesizes that new project identities are unlikely to emerge from 'former identities of civil society in the industrial era' but may emerge from resistance identities 'in continuity with the values of communal resistance to dominant interests enacted by global flows of capital, power and information' (ibid.: 422).

Fortuyn represents a specific iteration of a politics that inhabits the hollows of 'progressive' politics, rearticulating resistance identities of nativist hierarchy and assimilationist integration as liberal project identities. It is this mediated, populist dimension of liberalism which is neglected by Christian Joppke in his discussion of near-generic 'repetitions of the self-same creed of liberal democracy' occurring in nation-building in pluralistic and individualized societies (2009: 120–21). That liberal collective self-descriptions appear more 'exchangeable' does not mean they are not, in fact, particularized. Among the new certainties of post-multiculturalism is the idea that 'identity politics' is something they do, and indulged to dangerous excess. The new integrationism shaped in response to this assessment is also assuredly identity politics, but it is an identity politics that is predicated on transcendent claims to the common good of cohesion, and on inscribing the cultural codes of counter-patriarchy in the core values of the enlightened nation. By identifying a static body of Muslims as the vanguard of repressive patriarchy, Fortuyn expanded the repertoire of essential differentiation, and racialized the historical interpellation of tolerance with Dutch *autochtony*. As Paul Mepschen argues, sexuality as 'a breaker of a clash of civilizations discourse' was important in providing a language and imaginary to articulate the integral quality of national identity, and in 'providing a grounding for the reinvention of Dutch national identity as post-religious, tolerant, modern and (neo)liberal' (2009b). The figure of the autonomous homosexual, standing not only in stark contrast with, but in starker danger from, the 'Muslim colonized by scripture', invites an opposition predicated on 'a powerful conviction that religious and racial communities are more homophobic than white mainstream queer communities are racist' (Puar 2007: 15).

The proposal that homophobia is alien to Western democracies, and an intolerable property of the alien, does not depend on liberal convictions any more than Fortuyn's colonized sexual alibis evidence his anti-racism. As code, sexuality is a flexible idiom. Van der Veer notes that a central repulsion of the patriarchal Muslim is its status as the 'left behind' of Dutch Calvinism, that 'for the Dutch, Muslims stand for theft of enjoyment. Their strict sexual morals remind the Dutch too much of what they have recently left behind' (2006: 19). More importantly, the fluidity of symbolic mobilization combines modern conceits of national and European superiority and tolerance with the codes of anti-racialism, a repertoire that has provided extensive *populist* possibilities and assemblages. Populism, as several theorists recognize, is a slippery and fractious concept, principally because of what Taggart terms its 'empty heart' as an ideology without commitment to key values (2000: 2–7). It is this sense of populism as a political dimension that Benjamin Arditi captures in his idea of populism as an 'internal periphery of democratic politics' (2008: 49–53). Populism can be approached as a 'mode of representation', alert and responsive in the ways in which it reduces the complexity of issues; deploys styles or modes of persuasion; promises inclusion and intervention; employs a deliberately vague sense of 'the people'; and, in political parties, shapes the leader as a condensing 'symbolic device' (ibid.: 60–71).

Western Europe has experienced a 'populist zeitgeist' since the mid-1990s (Mudde 2004). The post-industrial de-alignment of voters; the post-Cold War loss of democracy's arch-enemy; the actual and perceived threat of globalization; the mediated 'transparency' of political life; and the fiction of the 'primacy of politics' over the political economy have seen the mainstreaming of populist strategies and repertoires across the conventional political spectrum. Populism, according to Mudde, is moralistic and a 'thin-centred ideology', in that its empty heart can easily incorporate and refashion disparate ideological elements and issues along a crucial central distinction 'that considers society to be ultimately separated into two homogenous and antagonistic groups, the "pure people" versus the "corrupt elite", and which argues that politics should be an expression of the *volonté générale* [general will] of the people' (ibid.: 543). The 'failed experiment' of multiculturalism is a refinement of the central antagonism of populism, where the perception of elite distance is magnified by the distaste of 'the people' for the imposition of political correctness. Invocations of 'the people' are always hazy and radically contingent; stated bluntly, the 'cultural capital' of multivalent Muslim intolerableness is its cross-demographic appeal. Populism's empty heart pumps expansive codes of belonging into the public sphere, capitalizing on the refraction of all that is intolerable about the Muslim Other to offer a spectrum of legitimations for assembling and reviving the national.

Conceptualizing populism as a mode of representation helps explain why the much-vaunted contradiction in populist right and conservative politics, between moral conservatism and 'saving our gays', is no such thing. Contradiction is predicated on the expectation of consistency. As Taggart argues, the populist idealization of the people invariably situates them in an idealized landscape, and in so doing 'populism excludes elements it sees as alien, corrupt or debased, and works on a distinction between the things which are wholesome and those which are not' (2000: 3). Threatened by the intolerable, the gay citizen is contingently welcome in the heartland and rendered tolerable at least in this modality of distinction, and in this constellation of appropriated codes. Thus recited rhetorics of sexual freedom and equality provide a pliable justification for reactionary xenophobia (Fassin 2010). Similarly, Puar's theorization of 'homonationalism' identifies 'Islamophobia in the global North' as a key political modality whereby 'homonormative and queer gay men can enact forms of national, racial or other belongings by contributing to a collective vilification of Muslims' (2007: 21). Mepschen emphasizes the political cost of this symbolic incorporation for queer politics, for in being assimilated to the symbolic economy of nationalism, in being suffused through the cultural circuitry that rewires the resistant as the project, the 'tolerated gay' also reproduces a dominant order where sexuality is a tolerable dimension of 'a self who in every other way reproduces an ideal of a national citizen' (2009a). The sexualization of this ideal has minimal impact on the heteronormative order, but sexuality provides a diffuse, affective sense of being on the right side of modernity, and substantiates a 'reinvented Dutch nationalism [...] of which the moral universe of liberal secularism and an ideology of neoliberal subjectivity [are ...] the characteristic elements' (ibid.).

Yet this is not quite the last word on 'liberty'. Fortuyn's depiction of Islam as a 'backward religion' that has 'not gone through the laundro-mat of humanism and enlightenment' was increasingly deployed in asserting a constitutive counterpoint for the 'moral superiority of post-traditionalist, modern and individualistic lifestyles' (van den Brink 2007: 356). Van den Brink traces what he terms an 'aggressive form of secular humanism' in the subsequent politics of Ayaan Hirsi Ali and Theo Van Gogh, an assertive liberalism that claimed such a comprehensive definition of the 'good' that anything deviant from invocations of personal autonomy automatically resides in the realm of unreason (ibid.: 356–8). The pervasive specification of Muslim and non-Western Others as the pre-modern – who can be saved – and the anti-modern, who must be policed and externalized (Mamdani 2005: 18), is modulated across contemporary Western contexts and institutionalized in the new politics of integration, particularly in the Netherlands[11] and the Nordic states, where a discourse of gender equality is central to modern national self-images (Keskinen 2010). This is further discussed in Chapter 6; the remainder of this chapter turns to a coda on illiberal liberalism.

The polyphony of 'identity liberalism'

According to Adam James Tebble (2006), a discourse of 'identity liberalism' has emerged in explicit opposition to multiculturalism, advocating a national culture of shared values, compulsory forms of immigrant assimilation and the duty of the state to protect lib-eral national culture, up to and including, as Fortuyn argued, the exclusion of non-liberal forms of life in the interests of democracy. Identity liberalism, for Tebble, is frequently a form or component of right-wing nationalism. The crucial distinction is that its claim to distinctiveness is based not on a singular national ethnos threatened by incompatible cultures, but instead on a vision of the defence of liberal principles and ways of life – the national identity of liberal polities – against illiberal forces, and against the threat of bad diver-sity to both the liberal polity and the individual rights of encultured minorities. Thus for identity liberals, 'multiculturalism as a response to diversity does not represent the equalization of cultural expression but rather the death of the very culture that permitted multicultural-ism in the first place' (ibid.: 481). Writing in the aftermath of the London bombings in 2005, Irshad Manji makes a central identity liberal argument:

> As Westerners bow down before multiculturalism, we anesthetize ourselves into believing that anything goes. We see our readiness to accommodate as a strength [...] Radical Muslims, on the other hand, see our inclusive instincts as a form of corruption that makes us soft and rudderless [...] Paradoxically, then, the more we accommodate to placate, the more their contempt for our 'weakness' grows. An ultimate paradox may be that in order to defend our diversity, we'll need to be less tolerant. (2005)

As with Triadafilopoulos's idea of 'Schmittian liberalism', what is striking is the sheer range of practices that conceivably qualify as 'identity liberalism', and the array of contexts in which its basic formulations now supplement and modify entrenched ideologies. As Zuquette observes in a study of the rapid establishment post-'9/11' of anti-Muslim racism as the basic ideological feature of the European extreme right, 'the extent or degree to which [...] the extreme right has influenced the establishment (mainstreaming of its positions) and/or was influenced by a favourable anti-Muslim environment' is unclear (2008: 337). The force, shape and permeability of identity liberalism in the post-multicultural era suggests a continuity absent from Tebble's depiction of it as a 'progressive identity-based normative discourse' claimed in defence of a nationalist politics of assimilation (2006). In our reading, the assemblages of 'identity liberalism' have a contiguous relationship to the 'new racism' discussed in the previous chapter. Racisms have always combined principles of inferiorization and dif-ferentiation (Werbner 2005b). While predicated on latent assumptions of hierarchy, 'new racism' could not make such explicit claims, and instead mapped the new imaginary of an 'equality of cultures'. In Balibar's account, this political ingestion destabilized 'traditional anti-racist defences' through a series of 'turn-about effects', the most fundamental of which was to argue that racist conduct can be explained, if not excused, by the natural, defensive reactions of incompatible cultures brought into inadvisable proximity through immigration (Balibar and Wallerstein 1991: 21–4).

We would propose here that the logic of 'identity liberalism' also depends on a turn-about effect, an effect laundered by the constant recitation of epochal clarity. Identity liberalism maintains the assumption of incompatibility underpinning the 'right to difference', but, mediated by the truth effects of transformative events and the liberal imperialism of the colonial present, it does so in the name of newly legitimized hierarchy. For Balibar, the 'new racism' was a 'second-position racism, which presents itself as having drawn the lessons from the conflict between racism and anti-racism, as a politically operational theory of the causes of social aggression' (ibid.: 22). The prime lesson was the necessity of cultural distances. After multiculturalism, identity liberalism derives legitimacy from pointing at the purported experimental failure to respect these realities of cultural distance. However, the imaginary of natural cultural distance here is not spatial quarantine, as identity liberalism is produced within the realities of immigration societies that have, to recall Hall's phrase, undergone some form of 'multicultural species drift' (Hall and Back 2009). Instead it is a failure of assimilation, of the inculcation of values and elective homogeneity on which social cohesion is held to depend.

The identity liberal position draws on an emaciated idea of liberalism's transcendent commitment to the good life for all, but holding out the progressive promise of inclusion does not dilute an ideology of differentialism. The very act of liberal identification requires illiberal others, and this has become the constitutive Other in the mirror, the irrational, threatening figure who is required to shed attributes which are frequently projected and inferred. Race, Angela Mitropoulos argues, now 'marks the boundary of that which is considered to not be amenable to will; that which lies beyond or without will, that which is deemed as being neither responsive to liberalism's "good will" nor capable of assuming its inclination' (2008: 1). Identity liberalism does not racialize on the basis of the insurmountability of cultural difference, it does so on the basis of the perceived refusal to surmount it, to become free like me, to free oneself, to remain a mark of imperfection.

However, as the next chapter examines, the mediated conditions within which the politics of crisis are shaped ultimately make it difficult to theorize the polyphony, contingency and opportunism of these discursive liberal formations in categorical terms. This is why the mirror cannot do metaphorical justice to these processes of identity clarification. A more appropriate metaphor was offered when Theo Van Gogh and Ayaan Hirsi Ali inscribed and projected

Koranic verses on to the bodies of Muslim women in *Submission*. The Muslim post-multiculturalism is not a mirror, but a palimpsest. There is no unitary Clash of Civilizations; instead the Muslim is a partner in many anxious binaries, and as the last decade in particular has shown, there is almost no end, if you forget hard enough, to what can be reanimated in contradistinction to their difference.

FOUR

Mediating the crisis: circuits of belief

Mediated minarets

On 29 November 2009, the Swiss electorate voted by a majority of 57.5 per cent for a constitutional amendment to ban the construction of minarets. The referendum was organized by the Swiss People's Party (SPP) and the Federal Democratic Union. At the time of the vote four minarets existed in the country, prohibited by environmental legislation from broadcasting a call to prayer. Nevertheless, this new cultural precondition is necessary, according to Ulrich Schlüer, a SPP MP, to prevent a particular kind of domino effect: 'The fear is great that the minarets will be followed by the calls to prayer of the muezzin [...] sharia is gaining in importance in Switzerland and in Europe. That means honour killings, forced marriages, circumcision, wearing the burka, ignoring school rules, and even stoning' (Traynor 2009). The Yes vote was widely regarded as a shock; having been opposed by most political parties, it was held to be an attack on freedom of religion, to damage Switzerland's image as a peaceful, multicultural country, and to bring the tradition of direct democracy into conflict with obligations under international law (Solioz 2009).

Commenting on the pan-European coverage of the referendum, Nilüfer Göle notes how 'the debate on the minarets in particular, and the visibility of Islam in general, generates transnational dynamics and assemblages of disparate elements' (2010). Transnational dynamics permeated debate in the Swiss public sphere, though the disparate elements are given coherence in the narrative of crisis. Following a published opinion by the Swiss Federal Commission against Racism that a key SVP poster – portraying a woman in a burka foregrounded against a Swiss flag forested by minarets[1] – 'defamed Switzerland's peaceful Muslim community' Basle and Lausanne banned the posters (while Zurich did not). Inevitably, replacement posters indexed the offending graphic to the *Jyllands Posten* cartoons, and thus to another key dimension of Muslim illiberalism: '*Censure! Raison de plus de dire* Oui *à l'interdiction des minarets.*' These assemblages were not limited to Swiss debate. President Sarkozy linked the minaret vote to his ongoing initiative, the Great Debate on National Identity, cautioning against criticism of the Swiss electorate by contending that '*Les peuples d'Europe sont accueillants, sont tolérants, c'est dans leur nature et dans leur culture*' (2009).

What Göle terms transnational assemblages have clear affinities with the idea of recited truths, and this accelerated weave of references, and appeal to a convergent crisis by understanding *here* through *there*, arguably positions the minaret referendum as a new addition to the open-ended litany compiled by Vertovec and Wessendorf (2009). The minaret debate is woven through this chapter as a heuristic device, providing a focus for the implicit weight given in this book to the mediation of multicultural crisis. The immediacy with which the minaret became a lightning conductor for complicit and resistant connections requires a discussion of how 'new, fast, intense and potentially less controllable media realities' (Eide et al. 2008) shape a crisis politics organized and narrated through symbolic events. Unfolding this implicit attention analytically requires some parameters, however, as far too frequently the banal truth of media power results in a dependence on reading, and reading from, representations, or on an undifferentiated appeal to 'the media' as some form of world spirit. In this vein, as Hesmondhalgh and Toynbee put it, 'the world is considered to be a product of representation, with the media then being the central means of that representation, or else the media is treated as obscurers of the real world' (2008: 12).

The politics of multiculturalism has, for obvious reasons, centrally involved a critical, constructivist focus on questions of representation: on denaturalizing signifying practices, historicizing and interrogating dominant repertoires and stereotypes, tracking the ideological insinuations of 'everyday' coverage, foregrounding and contesting images of the collective and the transgressive, deconstructing Eurocentrism, and so forth. If the work of race involves the manufacture of homogeneities (Goldberg 2009: 5), then critical work on representation never ceases to be important. Nevertheless, and to simplify somewhat, an impatience with the academic popularity of deconstructions of *Self and Other* has been marked by a critique of approaches that see the social primarily as a matter of representation (Hesmondhalgh and Toynbee 2008: 110), the political as a struggle over the 'indeterminacy' of racial discourse (Kundnani 2007: 51), and the binary of 'self and other' outside of material conditions, including the material conditions of mediation that render questions of inattention, absent others and non-signification important.[2] The politics of representation needs to be continually folded into a more complex understanding of symbolic labour and symbolic power, for as the discussions that have preceded this suggest, the struggle over codes, symbols, images – always central to the ongoing production of 'imagined communities' – is a key site for the elaboration and prolongation of 'crisis'. However, the task is not just to deconstruct these representations, but to examine them by examining media *in* society, in and through transnational flows and dynamics, and in the complex grids of power, causality and reflexivity that bind media actors within, while acting upon, socio-political relations.

Attention to the collapse of politics into media has, since 9/11,[3] been accompanied by a renewed interest in ideas of the image and the spectacle (Debord 1992 [1967]) and what Régis Debray terms the 'videosphere', or more germanely to this analysis, 'the civilization of the index' (1993: 31). For the Retort Collective, 9/11 involved an assault on the spectacle, a form of image death that demanded a response in terms of symbolic power as well as political power. The recitations of this symbolic power, the burka indexed to bomb power, have become pronounced dimensions of the compressed, mediatized market space within which the conductors of crisis have taken shape. The flows and assemblage at play move through these principal arteries, but the capillary action must also be accounted for. Roger Silverstone's (2007) discussion of the 'space of appearance' provides a guiding idea for this task. Silverstone offers a description of the *mediapolis* as an imagined, singular space of mediation that is fragmented, uneven and functionally infinite, but which nevertheless allows for a way of thinking about a deterritorialized, social environment within which mediated communication is formative. The mediapolis, he argues, is 'late modernity's space of appearance, both in the sense of where *the world appears*, and in the sense of *appearance as such* constituting that world' (ibid.: 27, italics in original). Presented in such brevity, the idea sounds rather ethereal. Yet the veil, the 'idea of the Muslim', the recited truths of dis-integration – they can only be given sense within it. As a research project (Fekete 2008) on the integration debate in several European countries concluded, the single most pervasive 'effect' of mediation is to endlessly frame and index local issues to international events. The instantaneous coverage of events, and the incessant indexing of events and 'issues' to proximate maps of local issues and actors, and to the index stream of 'slippery slopes', winds the loop of dis-orientalism (Ibrahim 2007) ever tighter.

In this chapter, we approach these assemblages by integrating theories of mediation to the analytical frameworks of culturalization and post-racism. As Sonia Livingstone (2009) points out, to speak of a mediated phenomenon is to do more than make banal reference to the penetration and ubiquity of media work. This banality is not un-important; it is banal in the sense that everyday life in the overdeveloped world is suffused with mediated representations, a suffusion which is accorded varying, and contested, degrees of ontological significance (De Zengotita 2005). The conduct of politics, similarly, is not just unthinkable beyond mediation, it has been profoundly transformed[4] by the shifting political economy of news and entertainment media within the wider transition to neoliberal state formations (Castells 2004 [1997]; Crouch 2004; A. Davis 2007; Hallin 2008; Negrine 2008; Dean 2009). Rather, Livingstone's point is to draw attention to how mediation makes a claim that the phenomenon in question is 'trans-formed, reconstituted, by contemporary processes of mediation' (2009: 2). The purpose of this chapter, then, is to identify mediated logics that are instrumental in producing, sustaining and acting upon the problem of multiculture. This involves building on the focus in Chapter 1 on discursive repertoires, recitations and idioms, on the focus in subsequent chapters on the socio-political conditions in which they attain traction, and pre-empting the discussion in the next chapter on the importance of symbolic events to neoliberal governance.

Mediated events are important because they are also *mediating* events, invested with truth effects, hailed and contested in order to perform political work and to secure particular understandings of the 'problems we face'. This chapter proceeds by first examining the work of spectacles of multicultural failure. As the example of the minarets referendum suggests, the litany of transformative events organized under the sign of crisis is well into its second phase; the spectacular acts of violence between 2001 and 2005 have long given way to organized spectacles of prohibition, provocation or precondi-tion, which single out problematic populations in order to reconfirm dimensions of their cultural incompatibility or dis-integratedness. Yet these events must be made to mean, they must compete within a con-text that Nick Couldry describes as that of '"continuous spectacle" [...] the intertextual and temporal intensity by which contemporary media spectacle creates, or appears to create, a "media world" for our attention' (2008: 162). Following on from this, we examine the idea of circuits of belief (Cronin 2004) as a way of thinking about the diffuseness of culturalist frameworks and explanations in a contemporary media economy characterized by speed, 'creative cannibalisation' and de-specialization (Fenton 2009).

From integration debates to integration events

The diminishing returns of honesty and openness In its very inception, the minaret referendum was conceived of and calibrated as a media event, emerging from a wider search for a point of symbolic controversy. As Tariq Ramadan reported, targeting traditional methods of animal slaughter had been initially proposed, until the potential implications of this for the Swiss Jewish population were realized (Ramadan 2009). At one level, this suggests that direct democracy is far from immune to post-democracy's dependence on marketing and targeted demographic appeals (Crouch 2004). Yet it is also a form of symbolic refinement that is made possible by the spectrum of codes available for mobilization around the problem of multiculture, and the strategic calibration this allows the radical right. In his study of the shifting anti-immigration discourse of the Swiss radical right, Damir Skenderovic notes that the comparatively early development of anti-immigration movements since the 1960s in Switzerland has instigated a durable but malleable discursive framework of *Überfremdung* or 'over-foreignization' (2007: 156–68). The term involves a historical sense of guest-worker overpopulation – central to the French Swiss equivalent, *surpopulation étrangère* – with an increasingly dominant accent of cultural penetration and threat (Bolaffi et al. 2003: 320). In common with the temporal shifts in social enemies across Europe, the 1980s saw asylum seekers become the main focus of threat, with the radical right amending the established idea of cultural threat through the differentialist codes of 'cultural racism' (Skenderovic 2007: 169–71). By the 1990s, with the rise and significant electoral successes of the SVP, 'Alpine racism' in general began to focus on the particular incapabilities of Muslims to integrate culturally and respect Swiss and Austrian societies. The system of direct democracy, Skenderovic argues, provided an 'institutional opportunity structure' for the radical right, allowing them to propose, adapt and oppose policies related to immigration and integration, to keep the 'issue' simmering on the political agenda, and at base to forge a strategy whereby 'referendums on issues related to immigration are often less about specific policy changes than the expression of a general disapproval of immigration and a resentment towards immigrants, asylum-seekers and foreign residents' (ibid.: 174). Between 1970 and 2002, Swiss radical right parties initiated nine referenda based on motions explicitly resisting over-foreignization through status and citizenship restrictions, and through immigration control.

The minaret referendum clearly stands in this tradition, but its carefully calibrated choice of mobilizing symbol is guided by the accretion of multiple lines of political conflict to the general funnelling of anti-immigrant sentiment. Much like the unwitting metaphor of projection in Van Gogh and Hirsi Ali's *Submission*, the instability of Europe's iconographic obsessions is such that they also suggest the grounds for critique. The minaret emerged as a lightning conductor for disparate political energies beyond the populist opportunism of the Swiss right. While the opportunity structure of direct democracy is largely particular to Switzerland, it is also possible to read the minaret referendum as a particular kind of crisis event, and one shaped by the demands of competition for attention and space in an era of 'continuous event' (Couldry 2008). During the same period, the French *grand débat sur l'identité nationale* was interpreted, by government, as resulting in a popular desire to return authoritatively to the problem of the burka. In part as a result, proposed burka bans were formulated, amplified or dusted off in other countries. The next chapter discusses the flickering obsession with the burka in terms of governmentality events, particularly this key move from integration debate to prohibitive integration event in France. In advance of that, these initiatives need to be considered as mediated, and mediating, events that refine the political dynamics of debate.

The immigration debate, and its conjoined twin, the integration debate, is a fairly common genre. Across national contexts, they share a common paradox: always ongoing, they are never *really* happening. The politics of such debates involves filling imaginary silences; perhaps in response to a particular incident, very often in response to a piece of research about migrant and minority lives, or even more frequently in counter-response to an elite utterance, politicians and varying public figures 'call' for a real debate. In the information age, as Thomas Hylland Eriksen argues, densities of news and informational flow provoke an experience of speed and abundance whereby the 'next moment kills the present' (2001). Ritual debates are subject to this curtailment through compression, but are further structured by an immanent frustration; they are never really happening because they are always already a prelude to a more open, more honest, more mature version of themselves. There are many reasons why 'migration/integration debates' are never felt to be satisfactorily open, most obviously because they are screens for the projection of profound and emotionally involving questions about social and national futures. The dynamics of crisis racism are ultimately ambivalent: the racial category and political proxy of the 'immigrant' allow for the temporary compression of conjunctural anxieties, yet they never fully capture or reduce these anxieties, and cannot provide political possibilities, beyond the fantastical, for their resolution.

The perpetuation of frustration inherent in the 'call' for debate draws attention to immigration/integration debates as a political form. The colloquial reach of the term 'spin' indicates, however roughly, a widespread awareness of the deep, transformative penetration of mediated logics and modes of communications management in political affairs. As Castells notes, 'the fact that politics has to be framed in the language of electronically based media has profound consequences for the characteristics, organization and goals of political processes, political actors and political institutions' (2000: 507). While the impact and consequences of these changes for democratic participation are contested, Aeron Davis – in an account that is critical of mechanistic, linear accounts of manipulation and management – nevertheless contends that 'both elite-mass media management and mediated, inter-elite competition are contributors to power imbalances and inequalities in society' (2007: 55).

In the case of immigration/integration debates, however, the pervasive logics of mediatization and political management are airbrushed for an idea of debate that retains a normative, modern sense of being constituted by and expressing public reason. The act of calling for a debate is to call for the attention of fellow citizens, and as Peter Singer summarizes, to invite them to engage in 'a kind of public conversation about issues of common concern, with a decision-procedure for reaching temporary closure on these issues when the time for action has come' (2004). It is not necessary to attempt to summarize here the various critiques to which the idea of reasoned, unifying public debate has been subjected (see Durham Peters 2005). Rather, the question is one of the insistent traces of modern expectation attached to broadly postmodern arrangements. The disparity between the affect and effect of debate, between the form of a politics of representation and the myth of a resultant politics of intervention, is a disparity that maps on to Wendy Brown's account of the 'residues of old-fashioned democracy inside the legitimation project of neoliberalism' (2005: 49).

At one level this is the populist gamble; the 'illusory object' demands the reciprocal fiction that the artificially cosseted 'issue' of immigrants can be solved. Yet public opinion, malleable, fictive resource though it is, has little or no substantive influence on migration policy (Jordan and Düvell 2003). The structural necessity and relative ungovernability of global movements of labour, and the role of powerful capitalist interests in shaping the flexible, stratifying 'migration management regimes' discussed in Chapter 6, are rarely fully admitted in discussion. They disturb the affiliated fictions of redemptive acts of sovereignty and residual assumptions about the deliberative and decisive role of debate. In this latter fiction, media are expressive of public opinion, facilitate its expression to power, and thus enhance decision-making and accountability. Debating immigration thus becomes a tacit and risky admission of disempowerment in the form of a ritual of empowerment – it becomes, as Jordan and Düvell argue, a site that 'connotes all the unresolved issues of membership in present-day societies' (ibid.: 62). That such a debate is never fulfilled, and never fulfilling, is the point at which the frustrated trace of democratic expectation masks a deliberate procedure of neoliberal governance.[5]

Migration/integration debates as a technology of governance, rather than as a relation to government, are theorized by Ghassan Hage in his reading of multicultural backlash in Australia (1998). The success of Howardism in 1990s Australia, according to Greenfield and Williams, was to blend 'economic fundamentalism, assimilationist social agendas, the steady privatisation of capital and risk, and nostalgic politics' (2001: 32). In Hage's reading, migration debates provided a cultural form capable of containing and exploiting the contradictions of early Howardism, where the frequency of public debates stood in stark contrast to the implacable global-labour integrationism of federal policy. Disconnected from expressive and representative fallacies, debates can be read as anthropological rituals providing a 'white governmental buzz': the fantasy not only of control over incoming 'numbers', but of 'governmental belonging' and reassurance as to the undisturbed centrality of white Australians to the destiny of the nation (1998: 240–43). In being asked to pronounce on the future, an implicit hierarchical right to comment on the present is also being invoked:

immigration debates and opinion polls are an invitation to judge those who have already immigrated, as well as those who are about to immigrate. Not only is this facilitated through the use of the word 'migrant', whose meaning slides freely between the two categories, but also, and inescapably, to pronounce a judgement on the value of migration is to pronounce a judgement on the value of the contribution of existing Third-World looking Australians to the country's development. It is in the conditions created by all these discursive effects that a White immigration speak flourishes – a language operating in itself as a technology of problematisation and marginalisation: 'they should come' and 'they shouldn't', 'they have contributed' and 'they haven't', 'there are too many' and 'there aren't enough' [...] it is on such fertile ground that the White nation fantasy seasonally rejuvenated itself and tried to keep the multicultural real at bay. In this sense, the immigration debate became the main form in which the dialectic of inclusion and exclusion was ritualised and institutionalised in Australia. (Ibid.: 242)

It is clear from the jaded posturing of calls for 'honesty, maturity and openness'[6] that debate as a 'technology of problematization' still retains purchase. In the multicultural crisis era, however, it has reduced viability as a technology of governance. Governmental buzz, like any buzz, fades and diminishes unless the 'kick' intensifies. The prerequisite of ritual remains, but the form of the spectacle adapts. Immigration and integration events have evolved from the limitations of debate: as mediated and mediating phenomena, they attempt to draw on the dynamics of neoliberal governance, and to provide a node of temporary fixation in the flow of 'continuous spectacle' (Couldry 2008). By way of developing this argument, it is useful to consider Jodi Dean's analysis of communicative capitalism and 'democracy that speaks without listening' (2009). Dean reformulates the expressive fallacy in the lingering modern sense of debate through a discussion of the morphing of *message* into *contribution*. A message is defined by an assumption of use value, whether in linear theories of communication – a message depends on being received – or in deliberative theories of democratic communication, where 'understanding is a necessary part of the communicative exchange' (ibid.: 27). Under the conditions of informational abundance and networked hyper-participation that Dean terms *communicative capitalism*, messages are instead defined by their exchange value, by their 'contribution to a larger pool, flow, or circulation of content' (ibid.). Communicative access and participation in the circulation of opinion is an organizing myth of the network society, and a 'contemporary ideological formation of communicative capitalism [that] fetishizes speech, opinion and participation' (ibid.: 17). A hegemonic democratic rhetoric is sustained in the face of globalized neoliberalism, in part, by an overarching misrecognition of ritual as process – that is, exchange value as use value. The event has an ephemeral centrifugal effect, attracting mediating energies and inviting linkage, framing, narrativization:

> Media circulate and extend information about an issue or event, amplifying its affect and seemingly its significance. The amplification draws in more media, more commentary and opinion, more parody and comic relief, more attachment to communicative capitalism's information and entertainment networks such that the knot of feedback and enjoyment itself operates as (and in place of) the political issue or event. (Ibid.: 32)

Symbolic politics thrives in this environment, and the politics of immigration/integration debates involves two specific inflections. Populism as a mode of representation (Arditi 2008), and the mediatized dynamics of government, involve a reflex of overt responsiveness that raises the bar for 'governmental buzz'. Bluntly put, the simulation of national management through debate is increasingly accompanied by the performance of national management through symbolic event. Within the terrain of multicultural crisis, where the problem of difference has been flagged, soldered to and circulated through a matrix of issues and series of transformative events, it demands ever-increasing spectacle. Given the core political focus on cultural excess and dis-integration, governance involves being seen to discipline excess and to insist on integration. It must be seen to restore, through acting on what Emmanuel Terray (2004), in the context of French headscarf debates in 2003/04, termed the 'fictive substitute', some form of mediated relation between deliberation and action.

Genres of event In the loosest sense of the term, several genres exist within this intensification of symbolic politics. Events often present themselves opportunistically; they must be hailed and constructed as such. During the 1990s, as asylum-seeking lost its fragile legitimacy, and multilevel policies of asylum deterrence were developed (Fekete 2009: 20–42), instructive spectacles were required to manifest their complex punitive implications. Perhaps the most notorious instance was the decision of the Howard government in Australia to deny the Norwegian freighter, the *Tampa*, which had rescued refugees in the Indian Ocean, permission to land, rerouting it instead to a detention camp on the island of Nauru. Occurring during a federal election campaign in 2001, the demonization of asylum seekers, despite the limited numbers seeking asylum in Australia, was a strategic veil on the Howard government's expansion of labour immigration through stratified modes of entry (Kuhn 2009: 58–60). The political decision to refuse landing, and to stage political drama through the real-time narrative of impending, unclean contact, was consistently explained in terms of 'sending a clear message' (Poynting and Mason 2007: 79).

If the Howard government lied, two months after the *Tampa* affair, about refugees aboard a sinking fishing trawler threatening to throw their children overboard unless they were allowed entry to Australia, the Irish government justified a 2004 referendum, reversing the *jus solis* basis for citizenship in favour of *jus sanguinis*, as necessary to prevent 'citizenship tourism'.[7] In a series of pronouncements by politicians, migrant mothers were held to be deliberately arriving to have babies in Ireland to gain Irish citizenship for their children and residency rights for themselves, and despite being publicly contradicted by the relevant professional body, the minister for justice consistently maintained that the referendum had been requested by the directors of the maternity hospitals. The referendum, as a symbolic event, was an instructive fusion of technocratic depoliticization – just 'closing a legal loophole' – and populist technology. Held just before the accession of ten new countries to the EU and an anticipated period of substantial labour mobility, the referendum facilitated a period of anti-immigrant racism focused on the 'bogus', the 'illegal' and the disposable – that is, on racialized immigrants held to be a problematic, unproductive population flow, in contrast to the useful, circular migratory mobilities of Polish and other eastern European workers (Lentin 2007; Gilmartin and Mills 2008).

These spectacles work as border events, enactments of 'domopolitics' (Walters 2004) that secure the home against bad flows. Yet it is more usual that asylum seekers are subjected to regimes of inattention (Crary 1999), to practices less concerned with the problem of cultural difference than the problem of obscuring human similarity (Hage 2003). The 'bogus' asylum seeker is a friend to populism and media spectacularization everywhere; however, the predominant politics is one of non-representation; the burdensome and the unproductive are rendered invisible, prevented, at their first encounter with the mobile matrix of border controls, from becoming a subject of troubled multiculture.[8] As Michel Agier has argued, the systems devised for the punitive impoverishment and warehousing of asylum seekers in an extraterritorial 'grey zone' of camps, detention centres and 'security vestibules' works to signify through absence, to silence race, and also to racialize:

> this 'out-of-the-way-place' where they end up [...] becomes the most obvious and stable basis for their identity [...] their isolation seems to empirically create an attitude of xenophobia against them ('if they're isolated, it must be for a good reason') that, in turn, tends to morally 'criminalize' them, thus making it easier to accept their confinement. (2009: 41)

Far more prominent is the symbolic politics of integration; events organized to provide specific evidence of bad multiculture and the ways in which it can and should be acted upon. The minaret referendum, in this aspect, was designed to become a focus of disparate assemblage. The minaret, as an icon in political posters,[9] served to visualize the cultural penetration of *Überfremdung*, leaching the irony from Czerny's sunken, Islamified lowlands and appearing, imposed and imposingly out of scalar proportion, on wholesome, heartland images of Swiss villages. Yet it was also represented penetrating the heart of the flag, or nation, as a 'bayonet' of militant Islam and as a phallus, pointing at the future pan-ethnic extension of the current repression of Muslim women. As a report in *Der Spiegel* noted, the strategy of the campaign paid relatively little attention to the substantive issue, but instead to cultivating an indexical logic: the constant linking and invitation, through the instability of symbolic mobilization, to debates within feminism,[10] secularism and liberalism that have accreted to and been reanimated by the prism of Islam in Europe (von Rohr 2009). The efficiency of this strategy is not dissipated by its transparency, as once the overdetermined issue of the minaret is indexed to widely rehearsed conflicts within mainstream feminism, or the shape of public space and the limits of secularism, the effect is to ultimately obscure these figurative dynamics through a kind of political literalism; we know it is a proxy, but having taken note, we cannot shirk the 'issue'.

The point here is not to obviate normative debate, but to examine its susceptibility to the assimilative logics of mediated politics. Hänggli and Kriesi, in a study of issue-framing in a 2002 Swiss referendum on asylum law, argue that referendum campaigns are intrinsically contests of substantive framing, involving the need to clarify a mode of understanding and to oppose it to competing modes, while limiting 'trespass' (2010). The logic of an integration event reverses this; indexical strategies involve encouraging 'trespass', broadening the frame, playing, as discussed in relation to Pim Fortuyn, with expansive codes and encouraging refraction across a terrain bounded only by the search for the limits of Western values. Indexical logics organize the assemblages wrought from the repertoires of association produced by multicultural crisis and its symbolic events. The 'slippery slope' to Islamicization is a syntagmatic variant, allowing any one sign to be linked back and forth in a narrative of surrender. *Fitna*, Geert Wilders's cinematic attempt to once again warn the Netherlands of the dangers of Islam, is instructive here, as its form can be understood only within this logic of mediation. *Fitna* is superficially a montage, but one shorn of the form's dialectical relations, interspersing quotations from the Koran with evidence of anti-Semitic, homophobic, patriarchal, anti-democratic and anti-Western violence. The one-hand-clapping dialectic of *Fitna*'s montage is a quality captured in Rosi Braidotti's reading of *Fitna* as a coercive performance of freedom of expression, an elaborated form of the hyper-realistic frankness for its own sake identified by Prins (2002) in the discourse of 'new realism':

> As spectators in a pornographic script, we are positioned in such ways that we cannot answer back to the images that we are exposed to. We can either agree or disagree, but there is no other room for dialogue or for engagement: we are actually being spoken to, lectured to – we are being told what we should do – sexually, culturally, or in the case of 'Fitna' – politically. Populist ultra-nationalist pornographic horror is the paternalistic and authoritarian master's voice telling us what to do. [...] Representations construct the author's subjectivity as the viewpoint of the dominant majority and impose his paranoid fantasies on the rest of us. Whether the instruction in question concerns sex, or race, or politics – the structure of representation is exactly the same: a sado-masochistic scenario with us as the captive, that is to say involuntary audience, of a master's fantasies and desires. (2009)

This formal preclusion of dialogic engagement is shaped by the

logics of communicative capitalism. In other words, *Fitna* was promoted as a message – Geert Wilders has an important message for
the West – but its political function was as a contribution, Geert
Wilders *speaks*. According to de Vries, it was manifestly clear that
Fitna was intended to feed and feed upon 'the anger or feelings of
white middle class Dutch about things they cannot control or explain,
presented as the problem of immigration and integration of Muslims
to Dutch society' (2010: 65–6). Yet as Demmers argues, the eventual
release of *Fitna* online in April 2008 was anticlimactic in a society
where it represented an 'exaggeration of what is already considered
almost uncontested. It is a continuation of Van Gogh's "goat fuckers"
and Fortuyn's "Islam is a backward culture" tune' (2009: 3). The
message of *Fitna* was not its Powerpoint recitation of the totalitarian
threat, but its form as a mediating event; it indexes an anxious socio-
political 'desire to shout' to the legitimizing idiom of 'freedom of
expression' (de Vries 2010). A core purpose of *Fitna* was to act as a
hypertext, recalling Fortuyn's taboo-busting and Van Gogh and Hirsi
Ali's *Submission*, and interpolating Wilders in a mediated pantheon
of champions of free expression. In cultivating this lineage, *Fitna* was
intended to act as a collective event, of the genre where: 'Individual
events in such chains normally refer to prior events, composing them
into a more or less cohesive narrative of transformation, as well as
constructing a collective memory of the past and promoting visions
of what is to come' (Mihelj 2008: 481).

Freedom of expression functions as a mobilizing vector of crisis
because it has been folded into the indexical logic of communicative capitalism, while mediating an important liberal threshold of
tolerance. Prins captures this in arguing that Fortuyn's success was
based on turning 'new realism into [...] a kind of hyperrealism.
Frankness was no longer practiced for the sake of truth, but for
its own sake' (Prins 2002: 13). *Fitna* does not need to be seen to be
believed; formally it functions as a mediated minaret, encouraging
trespass, intertextuality and the accretion of meaning to the film as
an event more than as a text. Wilders actively sought to construct the
film as a freedom-of-speech roadshow, seeking the kinds of prohibition and censorship required to stimulate a sluggish mobilization of
transnational symbolic legitimacy. His invitation to screen the film
in the British House of Lords in February 2009, and his subsequent
refusal of entry as 'a threat to social cohesion', provided this to some
degree, and the film was subsequently presented there without his

attendance. While he promoted the film, Wilders was already touting a sequel for release after the June 2010 Dutch elections.[11] For all this conventional cinematic promotion, in analysing how *Fitna* 'tailgates' the *Jyllands Posten* controversy by opening with Kurt Westergaard's image of the turban-shaped bomb,[12] Bolette Blaagaard (2010) illustrates how *Fitna* was less a conventional film than a cut 'n' mixed YouTube video response, a fan video made to pay homage to and link with venerated artefacts, and structured as a viral phenomenon.[13] With its frequent cutaways to the *Jyllands Posten* cartoons and its spectral tributes to *Submission*, *Fitna* auditioned as a symbolic event for multiple publics, offering the connotative hooks for its narrative placement. The problem for such audition events is that the dynamics of communicative capitalism also dissipate them; the narrative must be constantly secured in relation to its preferred texture for different audiences.

The Swiss minaret ban, on the other hand, was rapidly adopted as a point of transnational mobilization by networks of the European far right, particularly through the 'internationalist' platform 'Cities Against Islamization', formed by the Vlaams Belang in Belgium in 2008. In February 2010 plans to build a minaret on an existing mosque in Völklingen in Germany were used as a point of mobilization, channelled through a far-right party called Pro-NWR (North-Rhine Westphalia) that had been instrumental in organizing a campaign against a mosque in Cologne in 2008, and which received support and investment from Vlaams Belang and the Austrian Freedom party (FPÖ).[14] Subsequently, the Pro-NWR hosted a 'pan-European' conference in Gelsenkirchen in March 2010 looking for an EU-wide minaret ban by replicating the opportunity structure of Swiss referenda in the direct democracy provisions of the Lisbon Treaty. While the future of any such initiative is unclear, the lack of any action emerging from this conference confirms not only the cyclical difficulties encountered by the populist right in transnational mobilization (Mudde 2004), but also that the opportunity structure is not just constitutional. The metaphor of the minaret as a lightning conductor involves more than just figurative fancy; its currency as an event depends on the broad mobilization of codes and political trespass, and this would seem to be dissipated by becoming an 'issue' more exclusively identified with far-right movements. Moreover, the shaping of an event is not significantly determined by the communicative action of its masters' voices. This suggests the need to include other modes and circuits of mediation, and a discussion of the 'Danish cartoon' affair opens some of these out.

Something rotten, etc., etc. John Durham Peters (2005) maintains that freedom of speech has a recursive character, whereby the substantive issue at stake is frequently subsumed to meta-debates about the remit and stature of the principle itself. Organized around this abstraction is a 'threefold cast of characters' beginning with the protagonist who breaks a taboo in pursuit of freedom, who is subsequently supported by principled defenders of the open society, and both of whom triangulate with the subject who has taken offence. In the contemporary West, Muslims are cast as this intolerant apex, and thus positioned, 'end up being treated as deficient in comparison with the evident open-mindedness of those who tolerate transgression' (ibid.: 276). Durham Peters makes the basic rogation now demanded of critical analysis, which is that this structure of analysis does not justify reactionary violence nor traduce the ideals of a radically open democratic public sphere. Instead, it draws attention to how 'the global liberal public sphere rarely has operated this way' (ibid.). Insinuating *Fitna* into this structure of conflict, for example, was essential to its status as an event; the recursive character of freedom of speech has provided, like the enaction of democratic will through referendum, an opportunity structure for racist action. Mediated politics allows forms of 'identity liberalism' to propose their politics as standing for something else, as relating to audition events and symbolic fractures that involve or provoke others in raising 'their claims to the status of a universal' (Dean 2009: 16).

As the circulation of referents in the previous cases attest, the template for these freedom-of-speech events is the *Jyllands Posten* cartoon crisis that principally unfolded in 2005/06, but whose aftershocks, subplots and out-takes continued into 2010.[15] The publication, on 30 September 2005, of twelve cartoons of the Prophet Muhammad by different cartoonists slowly suffused through global networks of communication and mobilization into an international political crisis for the Danish state. Narrated as an editorial decision to draw attention to the effects of self-censorship derived from the pervasive relativism of multiculturalism (Klausen 2006), the cartoons 'event' has been primarily constructed as a freedom-of-speech issue, and the limits or lack thereof in relation to religious and cultural sensitivites (Amirthalingam 2007). The cartoons were republished in several countries, sparking off a dizzying set of sub-dramas and fusions (see Hervik et al. 2008: 29–38) with intensive debate between newspapers and media outlets as to their institutional relationship to the recursive principle in socio-national contexts (Strömbäck et al. 2008; Craft and Waisbord 2008). While Durham Peters's triangulation is not intended to exhaust the positionalities at play in the intensive circuits of interpretation and remediation at work in the 'crisis', it is an enormously useful starting point for thinking about how a set of antagonisms etched in the hegemonic cultural racism of Danish politics came to be raised to the status of universal.

This raising is related to, but not simply a matter of, the globalization of the cartoons crisis. As Hervik et al. demonstrate, narrating the event is complicated by the categorical, political act of declaring a national or international narrative starting point, such as the commissioning or publication of the cartoons, or the refusal of the Danish prime minister Anders Fog Rasmussen to meet with eleven ambassadors from Muslim-majority nations. And as recent Nordic media research contests, narratives of the cartoon crisis that are oriented towards explaining their globalized significance frequently neglect the political history of *Jyllands Posten*, from its European fascist sympathies in the first half of the twentieth century (Brun and Hersh 2008) to a pronounced 'right wing anti-Islamic history' in recent years (Hervik et al. 2008: 32). This history, in turn, is infrequently contextualized in the recent history of Danish neo-nationalism (Hervik 2011; Wren 2001). That history is clearly beyond the scope of this book; however, it is impossible to understand the gestation and mediation of the cartoons crisis without recognizing how the idea of 'cultural racism' as a hegemonic project, seeking points of influence and dissemination within media and networks of influence (MacMaster 2000), has been a pronounced feature of the cartoon crisis's gestation (Yilmaz 2011).

Karen Wren (2001) has traced the strong emergence of a culturally racist discourse to the relationship between distinct phases of Muslim immigration and asylum-seeking in Denmark between the 1970s and 1990s, and the changing political economy following the 1973 oil crisis, and subsequent economic restructuring (see also Hervik 2011; Brun and Hersh 2008). 'Egalitarian-liberal' Danish nationalism, tied to the welfare state as a 'system of mutual symbolic recognition', placed a high degree of emphasis on solidarity understood in terms of cultural homogeneity (Lex et al. 2007: 5–8). It is in the context of perceived alien disruption of this compact that Gingrich theorizes the development of interlocking forms of negative political affect, instrumental in the rise of far-right parties in the affluent societies of north and west Europe. Economic chauvinism, 'this wealth is ours and we do not want to share it with anybody', cannot be understood without the affective creep of cultural pessimism: 'what will happen to our small country in this changing world of Europe-wide and global developments' (Gingrich and Banks 2006: 37–8).

While Muslims have become the endless wellspring of cultural pessimism, the sense of almost generic Muslim invasion (Miles 1989) that emerged in western Europe in relation to disparate guest-worker and asylum-seeking populations has been dated to the early 1980s in Denmark (Yilmaz 2011). Ferruh Yilmaz (2006), in a discourse analysis of press coverage in the 1980s, has shown how calculated interventions through *Jyllands Posten*, particularly by Søren Krarup, a Lutheran priest and later ideologue of the Danish People's Party, shifted public debate towards a hegemonic culturalist framework within which the established modality of speaking truth to taboos and speaking up for the silenced majority reduced the threshold for racist speech in the public sphere. However, while ideologues such as Krarup were socially conservative and concerned with cultural homogeneity, there is also an embedded and complex articulation of cultural racism with and through gender politics in Denmark. The emphasis on economic independence and equal political presence in the 'traditional gender equality agenda' in Denmark has led to a longer history of tensions concerning the co-option of feminism to nationalist formations. The specification of Danish qualities of gender equality, as against the practices of patriarchal ethnic minorities, is marked out as a 'gender political field of its own' (Langvasbråten 2008: 46; see also Siim and Skjeie 2008). Wren stresses the impact of these tensions on the space for anti-racist politics in Denmark in the 1990s:

> To an outsider it appears that racism is everywhere, particularly in the media, but evidence has shown that this is a direct result of extremely clever marketing of xenophobic viewpoints by a relatively small but very active group of people who had a free rein in the press due to the absence of any sophisticated co-ordinated anti-racist opposition from the political left. This vacuum has been created by the involvement of the political left in a discourse which has constructed ethnic minorities, and in particular Muslim culture, as oppressive

to women, thereby constituting a 'threat' to a society where gender equality is regarded as an important social and political achievement. (2001: 158)

The election of a liberal-conservative government in 2001, dependent on parliamentary support from the Danish People's Party, had a dramatic impact on anti-immigration politics, as did the involvement of Denmark in the coalition of the willing involved in invading Iraq in 2003 (Brun and Hersh 2008). Several studies demonstrate how the political rise of the DPP was inseparable from the supporting editorial line of the main tabloid newspapers over an extended period of time (Hervik 2008, 2011; Brun and Hersh 2008). In particular, the repoliticization of media actors through a discourse of 'values-based' journalism that placed an emphasis on strong opinion lines, and in some instances campaigning on anti-immigration issues, provides the context for the *Jyllands Posten* cartoon event (Eide et al. 2008). The cartoons, as Ellen Brun and Jacques Hersh point out, were intended as an escalation in this 'values-based' campaigning, as 'their publication was a clarion call to the media to overcome their restraint and participate actively in the mobilization of opinion against the Muslim population. In other words, this attack was intended to influence the political culture of the Danes in the direction of Islamophobia' (2008). The specific character of the cartoons as a cumulative act of provocation is frequently lost in accounts of the affair, and the irony that a newspaper with a partisan history of this nature has become, if not a global symbol, then at least a global focus of freedom-of-speech debates is not lost on several Danish analysts (e.g. Klausen 2006). We focus here on a key consequence of this, which is how the recursive relation to freedom of speech is easily grafted on to a 'clash of civilizations' framework of understanding.

One way of illustrating how this localized event was laundered is to examine the different ways in which it is held to have been globalized. In an interview, Jörn Mikkelsen, editor-in-chief of *Jyllands Posten*, remembers seeing a short report on the AP press wire in December 2005, detailing a small protest against the cartoons in Kashmir; 'we laughed about it in the editorial department, but later [...] I started to have a queasy feeling. How did they find out about this? Who reads *Jyllands Posten* in Kashmir?' (Broder 2010). What Mikkelsen is pointing to is the significance of diasporic and transnational networks of circulation and animation, whereby the 'Islamic world' mobilized, with apparent violence,[16] in an assault on a Danish expression of core Western values. As Hervik summarizes, the 'collective memory' of the cartoons crisis is primarily as a free speech issue:

> The debate in Danish news is marred by this repeated assertion that 'freedom of speech is a Danish freedom' and foreign events such as demonstrations [...] are not examples of freedom of expression. The moral anger of some Danes is tremendous when it comes to the foreign reactions, but when it comes to the cartoon publications, the right to publish is the first thing evoked. Hence, the debate suggests that the free speech response is not much more than a reflection of the powerful, hegemonic dichotomization of a positive 'us' and a negative 'them' in Danish society. (Hervik 2008: 70)

The gradual reporting of how *Jyllands Posten* had, in 2003, refused to publish cartoons of Jesus because they would 'provoke an outcry' (Klausen 2006; Younge 2010a) drew attention to the fairly predictable inconsistencies that surface in these kinds of events. However, Hervik's point draws attention to more than hypocrisy; it suggests an important culturalized formation of the event: they have diasporic ties, we have mobilizing values. As Flemming Rose, the culture editor of *Jyllands Posten* who commissioned the cartoons, points out, international mobilization in support of the paper was merely the triangulated expression of principle, whereas criticism simply

> unmasked unpleasant realities about Europe's failed experiment with multiculturalism. It's time for the Old Continent to face facts and make some profound changes in its outlook on immigration, integration and the coming Muslim demographic surge. After decades of appeasement and political correctness, combined with growing fear of a radical minority prepared to commit serious violence, Europe's moment of truth is here. Europe today finds itself trapped in a posture of moral relativism that is undermining its liberal values. An unholy three-cornered alliance between Middle Eastern dictators, radical imams who live in Europe and Europe's traditional left wing is establishing a politics of victimology. (2006)

The mobilization of a global defence of the cartoons in the terms indicated by Rose also depended on 'diasporic ties', but ones forged instead through 'liberal fundamentalism' (Kunelius and Alhassan 2008). That is, long-standing and quickly activated circuitries involving neoconservative think tanks and connections in the USA and elsewhere in Europe (Brun and Hersh 2008; Hervik 2008). In Hervik's study of the cartoon spin campaigns in Denmark, he examines the gradual evolution over the course of 2006 of a dominant framework of 'freedom of speech', and the intensive location of it, by government, as a Danish and Western property under threat. Hervik pays specific attention to the interconnections between Flemming Rose and a range of other well-known and usually former far-left Danish columnists, writers and politicians networked through a semi-secret society called the Giordano Bruno Society. Dedicated to a totalizing anti-Muslim politics, they are in turn connected to Daniel Pipes and other influential neoconservative commentators and think tanks across the Atlantic (2008: 70–74). As Hervik rightly notes, an inbuilt resistance to neat 'conspiracy theory'-style explanations overlooks the scale of influence possible in a relatively small country, and also the reflexive impact of an insistent transnational framing of these issues in universalist terms as one of Western free speech by a 'network of actors reaching from Jyllands-Posten to the neo-conservative radical right wing in the USA' (ibid.: 72).

Given the polysemy of the cartoons and their fluid movement, incorporation, framing and interpretations across contexts, no dominant framework can be applied to their reading (Klausen 2009). Nevertheless, Ferruh Yilmaz argues that very little attention has been paid to how the recursive dimension of freedom of speech – and the demands this makes on media operating within broadly liberal traditions to flag a position in the debate – naturalizes the 'timeless ontological categories' of Muslims and the West. He adds a fourth position to Durham Peters's triangulation of free-speech dramas, which involves those broadly understanding of Muslim protests and who argue for increased sensitivity, respect for diversity or the need for greater tolerance and understanding. In so doing, they effect a further 'hegemonic displacement' by raising the claims of anti-Muslim racism to the status of the universal, and by compounding the abstraction of the crisis from recent Danish history by treating the global diffusionism in civilizational terms:

> To bring back politics into the center of discourse, we need to ask much simpler questions: who initiates these crises around Muslims and Islam? What are their politics, and what are the socio-political implications of these crises? A discussion of such questions will reveal that there are certain political and ideological sources that

push certain issues onto the agenda and force us to be drawn into principle discussions about those issues rather than the politics of the debate. (2011)

Recited truths, circuits of belief

Writing in the *Jerusalem Post* ten days after the referendum, Daniel Pipes drew on an extensive series of online polls to situate the minaret affair as a potential turning point in 'European resistance to Islamicization': 49,000 readers of *Le Figaro*, 24,000 readers of *L'Express* and 29,000 readers of *Der Spiegel*, among others, had rejected the construction of minarets by jubilant percentages.[17] The questions posed by the polls inhabited a spectrum from faithful domestication of the Swiss question to such variations as the construction of mosques, anxiety concerning 'Islamicization', and the process of immigrant integration. While Pipes admits of a certain lack of scientific veracity in the polls, he regards this mobility as more significant than the referendum ban itself, though he clearly does not understand that what makes this mobility possible is the fragmentation and transnationalization of the reading 'public'. These polls are conventional instances of the domestication of news, and the poll form has become ubiquitous as part of the reformation of newspapers as multimedia news platforms. The mechanical rotation of the minaret 'issue' through this form says as much about the generic nature of 'interactivity' as it does about any frisson of Eurabianist expectation. Nevertheless, the instantaneous circuitries of news are clearly significant to an analysis of recited truths, as they invite an ongoing indexing and *dis-orientalist* framing of issues and events.

Mainstream news is analysed in particular media and political systems and grids of financial, technological and institutional possibility and constraint (Hallin and Mancini 2004), complicated by new media convergences and transnational integration (Fenton 2009). Even in a limited account, it is necessary to avoid reducing the discussion of news to deterministic theoretical structures read from a political-economic base or model of ideological dissemination (Cottle and Rai 2006). Nevertheless, some basic dimensions are important to establish a way of thinking about how issues travel and how recitation works in communicative terms. A not unexpected irony of the digital proliferation of news platforms has involved a certain homogenization of mainstream news content and news agendas. Natalie Fenton argues that the main online news sites are heavily reliant on foreign news reports from dominant news agencies, and that a consequence of the sheer availability of news has led to journalists drawing heavily on other news producers as their sources, or for their material (2009: 9–11). In turn, this referential networking and repurposing of news must be related to the neoliberal restructuring of news production over the last decades (Hallin 2008). This has involved the imperative of increasing the flow of news in a continuous real-time news environment, where 'stories' are never complete but roll on and piggyback on related stories and sources. The drive to cost efficiency and the migration of advertising to online platforms is held to have led to a certain deskilling and flexibilization of journalists, limiting original news gathering and investigative reporting and recasting many journalists as workers involved in informational 'cannibalization', filling more space at increasing speed (Witschge et al. 2010). While no one vector of production can be elevated above others, particularly given contextual and institutional differences in this picture (Örnebring 2009), the consequences of these changes for the democratic and public functions of journalism have come under scrutiny.[18]

For the purposes of this argument, this media environment provides the conditions[19] for the increased circulation of recited truths, as culturalist modes of explanation are reified in and through these changes in the ecology of news. We draw here on Anne M. Cronin's idea, in *Advertising Myths: The strange half-lives of images and commodities* (2004), of 'circuits of belief'. In cautioning against an abstracted category of advertising which is then incorporated into normative debates about capitalism, or read as a genealogy of the social, Cronin argues that advertising must be understood in terms of a complex circulation of beliefs as to what it is and what it does, and which 'operate in multiple registers including popular enjoyment and critique, academic analysis, advertising agencies' own rhetoric about advertising, and regulatory and self-regulatory bodies' (ibid.: 2). Circuits of belief involve 'invested understandings' that come to shape the engagement of different bodies and actors with advertising, which in turn constitute it as a social institution. The suggestive idea of circuits of belief allows us to make a speculative argument[20] about the mediation of crisis. In conditions of continuous, instantaneous and remediated news, invested understandings about the current terrain of crisis become more dependent on culturalist explanations that provide resilient and transferable frameworks of knowledge.

This dependence emphasizes the laundered grammar of differential-ism, but even more elemental is the 'tendency to call on culture when faced with anything we cannot otherwise understand' (A. Phillips 2007: 46). Phillips' argument rejects critiques of culturalization that seek to replace it with other modalities of determinism, and her argument is not primarily concerned with the ideological uses of cul-ture. Instead culturalization produces forms of functionally adequate knowledge, produced in institutional and socio-political relations of power that circumscribe the possibilities for sticky counter-narratives and explanations. Embedded in practices and routines, it may involve 'regarding arbitrarily defined populations as uniform natural units' (Pred 2000: 77), but equally importantly, as the occlusion of 'plausible noncultural accounts' and multiple lines of investigation (A. Phillips 2007: 45–8). Circuits of belief, in the current era, are driven by elective affinities between culturalized repertoires, and the indexical logics of informational production shaped by speed and increased contiguity with the events being mediated (Lash 2002: 3). Here, for example, is the respected columnist Anne Applebaum a week after the referendum, pressed into explaining Switzerland for the impeccably liberal readership of *Slate*:

> there is very little evidence that separatist, politically extreme Islam is growing rapidly in Switzerland. However the Swiss read news-papers, and they watch television. And in recent years, separatist politically extreme forms of Islam have indeed emerged in every European country with a large Muslim population. Britain, France, Germany, the Netherlands, Denmark and Sweden have seen court cases and scandals concerning forced marriage, female circumcision, and honor killings. There have also been terrorist incidents: think of the London transportation bombings, the Spanish train bombs, the murder of Dutch film director Theo Van Gogh. Remember that the 9/11 pilots came from Hamburg [...] as grotesquely unfair as a refer-endum to ban minarets may have been to hundreds of thousands of ordinary well-integrated Muslims, I've no doubt that the Swiss voted in favor primarily because they don't have much Islamic extremism – and they don't want any either. (2009)

As journalism this is possessed of a radical poverty, but as an artefact of recitation it has the purity of a haiku; Applebaum empties her associative archive fully on to the desk and arranges the fragments in the shape of Swiss society. In other words, while this reportage evidently depends on the transposable cipher of the 'idea of the Muslim' (Goldberg 2009), it equally depends on interchangeable chunks of Western modernity. Organized in a recitational framework, they are available to *make sense* of each emergent *issue*, and thus obscure the continual accretion of these invested understandings to a vision of crisis. Ayaan Hirsi Ali explained the vote in the *Christian Science Monitor*, also a week later, by juxtaposing a disapproving and blinkered cosmopolitan class concerned at the Yes vote with those who reject political Islam because 'they are in touch with Muslims on a local level. They have been asked to accept Muslim immigrants as neighbors, classmates, colleagues – they are what Americans would refer to as Main Street' (2009). The problem with this is not just the sociological fantasy of Main Street, and its location in the complex socio-geography of a federal country, but the more empirical fact that voting in the referendum broke down along highly complex lines. According to data from the Swiss Federal Statistics Office, in large cities the Yes vote achieved only 38.6 per cent, 50.7 per cent in mid-sized urban centres, and was at its highest, 68.3 per cent, in '*communes agricoles et agraires-mixte*'.[21] In other words, if the voting patterns present any units of data for 'informational stacking' (Eriksen 2001), it is that the people who are predominantly *not* in touch with Muslims and immigrants on a local level voted to ban minaret construction. Hirsi Ali's misreading is clearly framed by her post-racial orthodoxy – and one raised to global significance during the *Jyllands Posten* cartoon affair – that the vote was 'for tolerance and inclusion'. Also of interest here is the circuitry of belief. In claiming, on several occasions, to speak for 'ordinary working class voters' Ali transposes the precise social formation rehearsed in the Dutch new realism discourse (Prins 2002) on to an entirely imaginary Switzerland.

The circulation of cultural beliefs is ideological, involving the forms of discursive labour discussed in Chapter 1, but it is also produced within the constraints and dynamics of transnational knowledge production. The presence of Muslims, as a transnationally legitimized object of problematization, orders and scripts the analysis of vastly different national contexts, which in turn contributes to occluding these histories of production, to their becoming social (Ahmed 2004). Because the foundational shapes of culturalist frameworks are broadly shared and understood, they provide conduits for the explanations of *here* in terms of *there*; transposable knowledge frameworks that

Bourdieu (1998) associates with the mediating requirements of 'fast-thinking', and which Mathew Hyland captures in this topical parody:

First a fact is invoked that lays claim to the utmost moral gravity (the diaspora of Oriental bombs in Western metropolises being the obvious but by no means the only example), followed by some observations on the dis-integration of cultural behaviour (preferably a fusion of anecdote and dislocated statistics as in: 'only x per cent of Muslims born here think of themselves as British, and in parts of town nobody speaks English'). The necessary causal relation between one set of phenomena and the other is presumed to be too obvious for statement, and the Expert moves straight on to consider what, in particular, should be done in order *to induce self-identification with 'society' among culturally dis-integrated subjects.* (2006: 4, italics in original)

To illustrate this, further, we turn to a specific discussion of ghetto imaginaries as idioms of multicultural crisis.

Petri-dish cities Maria Stehle's (2006) study of how narratives of Europe are produced through 'ghetto spaces' compares coverage in *Der Speigel* of 'emerging ghettos' of guest workers in the 1970s and of 'ghettos' in Berlin in 2005. While 1970s discussions were framed in terms of fear of 'Harlem-symptoms', following the riots in Paris in 2005, Kreuzberg and other areas of Berlin became objects of anxious reportage, conceiving of predominantly migrant areas as 'internal borderlands' where similar violence may be inevitable (ibid.: 50–54). Stehle's tremulous counterpoints of Harlem, then Paris, re-call Wacquant's analysis of the 'topographic lexicon' through which marginal spaces are mediated in relation to each other, such that perception 'contributes powerfully to fabricating reality' (2008: 1). Symbolized by Harlem, 'America's dark ghetto' was held in Europe – but particularly in France in the 1970s and 1980s – as a model and metaphor for urban degeneration and 'lawless zones'. Similarities in 'ethnically-marked populations', and a generally comparative diagnosis of post-industrial decline, crime and unemployment, collapsed the differences in internal diversity and generative political-economic specificities of the *banlieue* and the ghetto as 'two disparate socio-spatial formations' (ibid.: 135–60). As Wacquant has argued in relation to the circulated, 'territorial stigma' of the ghetto, it is a 'racial formation that spawns a society-wide web of material and symbolic associations between colour, place and a host of negatively valued social properties' (1993, quoted in Pred 2000: 128). Stehle's analysis examines how the *banlieue* has replaced the black ghetto as a free-floating signifier that offers a more intensely culturalized explanation, projecting a uneasy coherence on to disparate, raced spaces:

> The attempts to ghettoize what is not supposed to be European reveals a series of paradoxical structures that are crucial for the emergence of new racisms: Europe is defined via the space that should not exist, the space of failed 'integration' and the 'other' space where rights and freedoms need to be restricted. The European ghetto is both feared and needed; it shows both the importance and the impossibility of 'integration'; it is the location of the threat to Europe and the space where the 'other' needs to be restricted and violence needs to be contained. (Stehle 2006: 62)

The 'ghetto' demonstrates the formation of multicultural crisis narratives in the transnational space of appearance. The 'ghetto', the constitutive outside, inside, condenses manifold, post-colonial fears of those possessed of tenuous spatial legitimacy in the imaginative terrain of the nation-state. From the fearful minority-white cities and parallel lives of British discourse to the brilliant metaphor – in a study of Australian media discourses on race, terrorism and immigration – of Poynting et al.'s *Bin Laden in the Suburbs* (2004), the real and perceived spatial concentration of communities provides another palimpsest on to which racial anxieties can be projected. In keeping with Wacquant's observation, this unceasing *reproduction* becomes performative in space and productive of space, where the problem of territory becomes the problem of people. As Allan Pred observes in discussing the *problemömraden* of areas such as Rinkeby in Stockholm and Rosengård in Malmö, 'any one of these names has generally come to serve as a stand in for all of them' through repeated metaphoric and metonymic usage (2000: 127–9). This production is mutable, as the circulation of anxieties finds temporary form in spatial imaginaries that are transnationally derived but particularized in place. These spaces materialize, of course, the Muslim problem, but they also spatialize the problem of will, the resistant unwillingness to integrate.

The idea of the *dish city*, for example, emerged in French political discourse during the civil war in Algeria, crystallizing fears of ideological doctrination flowing unchecked through satellite television

(Hargreaves and McKinney 1997: 94). In a synergy of cultural racism and a lingering assumption from mass society theories of communication, the material possibility of transnational media audiencehood becomes a cipher for the hypodermic delivery of problematic ideologies. In *Murder in Amsterdam*, Ian Buruma shows how the image of the 'dish city' functions as a social fact while accreting multiple registers and traces of stigma; a friend of Theo Van Gogh describes the dish cities as having grown into 'hotbeds of religious bigotry' yet also becoming like 'the South Bronx' (2006: 54–5). As Haritaworn and Petzen trace (2010) in their discussion of the 'Muslim homophobia drama' in Germany in the 2000s, 'unsafe' urban spaces were mapped on to the post-9/11 gender regime and linked in gay activism to the tremulous image of risky spaces in other European cities. Ambiguous, violent incidents in Berlin's Kreuzberg and Neukölln in 2008 were taken up in a mediated moral panic, as local iterations of the emerging, transposable script of atavistic, globalized Muslim homophobia, an 'existential struggle between queer lovers and fearsome Others' (ibid.).

These repertoires instance the capillary action of racialization, and the intensified, post-9/11 production of *dis-orientalist* communities and spaces within established post-colonial and immigration societies. Yet as the Irish newspaper article referenced in the introduction suggests, circuits of belief are tapped and redirected in societies where the force of explaining the new and the strange *here* provides a particular explanatory currency for evidence from *there*. In the anxious modality of the newspaper editorial, the only way to explain a fleeting, limited confusion over the status of a headscarf in a school was by indexing it to markers in the space of appearance. A similar form of analysis can be extended to Finland. In the space of no more than the last two years, public life in Finland has witnessed a particular discursive formation around the idea of immigration scepticism (*maahanmuuttokriittinen*), and the emergence of self-proclaimed immigration sceptics (Keskinen et al. 2009). The arguments made under this label are unexceptional renderings of established recitations; that multiculturalism is hegemonic, and that honest, sceptical debate is being trammelled through political correctness, personified by the idiom of the *kukkahattutäti*, the flower-hatted aunty who stands for moralistic middle-class preachiness on difference and tolerance. What has given this loose formation of bloggers, right-wing politicians, journalists and academics gathered through particular nodal online fora such as *Homma* a degree of influence is their success at positioning a multicultural consensus as the 'imagined centre' of public discourse (Couldry 2008).

A number of factors converge in this moment. In parliamentary politics, the steady rise of the True Finns party (*Perussuomalaiset*) since the mid-2000s on a populist anti-immigration, anti-EU platform has led to actors within the centrist parties looking to position themselves in relation to the True Finns' appeal. A general centrist orientation on economic policy in the context of the global downturn has also led, in the build-up to the 2011 parliamentary elections, to the increased emphasis on immigration and integration as wedge issues, prompting all parties to seek publicity for their particular platform (Spongenberg 2010). Karina Horsti has pointed to the ways in which changes in the field of journalism have created particularly suitable conditions for the sudden rise of the 'immigration issue'. Journalism in Finland has also shifted towards more clearly politicized and debate/opinion-oriented formats, and Horsti links this in part to the shifts in orientation that emerge from digital convergence and the inclusion of 'interactive' possibilities, particularly moderated and unmoderated spaces to provide comments after opinion and news articles online (2010). Increasingly, these debates are remediated and linked through social networking sites in ways that encourage flash conversion on certain sites of debate, and the main newspapers' online sites tend to be moderated in ways that allow formulations and opinions that would not appear 'above the line' (ibid.).

These dynamics work within the dynamics of communicative capitalism (Dean 2009), but important differences emerge when the relations between use and exchange are translated into this particular national and linguistic context. In the absence of qualitative research into such a recent phenomenon, it is possible to contingently theorize these developments. In a study of media governmentality and the coverage of Pauline Hanson in Australia, David Nolan has shown how Hanson's explicitly populist appropriation of the 'ordinary people' benefited from journalism's 'particular representative affinity' with an imaginary of the ordinary reader, rendering its expressive fallacy vulnerable to the legitimation of new forms of racist 'common sense' (2003). In the Finnish context, the prominence attained by immigration sceptics owes much to a similar fallacy, where their translation of anti-elitist recited truths has been included in the interests of 'balanced' debate, an established weakness of the liberal public sphere that has been amplified precisely by the noise and endless circuits of exchange of contemporary communication. The virulent nature of online debate in Finland has recently led to several prosecutions for hate speech;[22] however, a far more consequential development is the reconversion of exchange value into relative use value through mainstream journalistic practice. The integration of blogosphere agitation into the abstract spectrum of balance has given it back its use value, and disproportionate access, coverage and potential influence as a result. The clearest example of this was in February 2010, when the monthly review of the main national paper, *Helsingin Sanomat*, conducted an interview with the immigration minister Astrid Thors after requesting the main network of sceptics, the online *Homma* forum, to provide the questions for the interview (Nousianinen 2010). The article allowed questions to be posed from the anonymity of user-names, and gave no sense as to why these particular questions, and the assumptions embedded in them, should be preferred over, say, a mixed forum involving contributors to *Homma* but also a broader range of questions from migrants to Finland, anti-racist groups and wider civil society.

As elsewhere, a consequence of this has been to expose the culturalist repertoire of middle-class multiculturalism (Hage 2003) to the strategic inversions of cultural racism. As Essed and Nimako discerned in relation to opponents of Pim Fortuyn, the post-racial tendency to counter this repertoire in moral rather than political terms is exposed and instrumentalized (2006: 308). This vulnerability is increased by the integration of the Finnish blogosphere into Swedish and Danish right-wing networks, where these arguments and debates have been honed over a far longer period of time, and can be translated into mainstream Finnish public discourse with more toxic effect. The recited truths of elsewhere are circulated through this confluence and have become stable points of reference in mainstream debate. This is a very recent development; Suvi Keskinen has demonstrated how media coverage of 'honour-related violence' in Sweden, particularly following the murder of Fadime Sahindal in 2002, tended to place Finland as a 'lucky bystander', drawing attention to a range of important social differences and tending to discuss them in the context of Swedish society (2009: 263). This is in marked contrast to the tendency to now imagine Sweden, in particular, as a future laboratory of multicultural discontent; Finland doesn't have these problems, yet. A major article published in *Helsingin Sanomat*'s Sunday Debate column entitled 'Time running out on immigrant integration' in

September 2009 provides an illustrative example. Ilkka Salmi, head of Supo, the state security police, and Jorma Vuorio, director of the Finnish Immigration Service, drew attention to relative increases in asylum seekers from Iraq and Somalia being 'driven to Finland [...] by the tighter immigration policies of our neighbouring countries, and by the good level of Finnish social welfare'. In a securitarian formulation discussed in Chapter 6 in terms of 'domopolitics' (Walters 2004), Salmi and Vuorio argue:

> From the point of view of security officials, there are risks inherent to a strong increase in immigration, which could lead to serious problems for security. Risk factors include increases in crime, gang formation, violence and disturbances of the peace. Such events have been seen in Europe – in Sweden and France, for instance [...] according to the prevailing opinion of Europan security officials, another danger in immigration is the infiltration of terrorists into the flows of immigrants [...] in certain suburbs of Helsinki and Turku, the proportion of foreigners in the population has risen as high as 30 percent. According to some studies, such a large concentration of immigrants can lead to uncontrolled ethnic isolation of the communities. (2009)

In this ticking-culture scenario, where 'the window of opportunity will only remain open for a few years', these state officials weave a picture of potential unrest and a slippery slope to radicalization solely on the basis of unreferenced studies from elsewhere, an undifferentiated picture of foreigners in suburbs, overwritten with the powerful affect of 'events in Sweden' indexing images of violence and unrest in the Rosengård area of Malmö. Admitting that the security police knew of no individuals involved in terrorism in Finland, at no point is anything of sociological specificity to Finland actually referenced. Instead their arguments are, like *Fitna*, a cut 'n' mix from circuits of belief, laying out a future, dis-integrated vision of increased racism, tensions and violence between natives and immigrants, illiteracy, large families and 'the disappearance of the values that are a part of democracy' (ibid.). In other words, these state officials can imagine areas and inhabitants of their own society only through the space of appearance, through a transnational, imaginative geography of fear. Inserted into mobile culturalist frameworks of knowing, idioms of crisis become plausible units of knowledge, futures that can be acted upon in the here and now.

Coda: on critics

Writing on the coverage of the Algerian civil war in France, Pierre Bourdieu drew attention to the ways in which the efforts of the many who worked with Algerian refugees to counter one-sided media narratives of the war, and to understand and explain the complex reality as a moment in attempting to 'reinstate respect for the complexity of the world' (1999: 91), would periodically witness how their efforts could be undone instantly by media comment. Implicitly taking aim at Bernard-Henri Lévy, Bourdieu argues:

> The negative intellectual has done his job: who could want to express solidarity with mass murderers and rapists – especially when they are a people who are described, without historical justification, as 'madmen of Islam', enveloped under the abominated name of Islamicism, the quintessence of all Oriental fanaticism, designed to give racist contempt the impeccable alibi of ethical and secular legitimacy? To pose the problem in such terms, you don't need to be a great intellectual. And yet that is how the originator of this crude operation of symbolic policing, which is the absolute antithesis of everything that defines the intellectual – freedom with respect to those in power, the critique of received ideas, the demolition of simplistic either-ors, respect for the complexity of problems – has come to be consecrated by journalists as an intellectual in the full sense of the word. (Ibid.: 92)

The narrative of multicultural crisis is grafted and circulated by negative intellectuals who have found a civilizational justification for simplistic dichotomies, and whose symbolic policing has been girded by the 'existentialist threat' of the post-9/11 era (Triadafilopoulos 2011; Tebble 2006). While Bourdieu's critical assessment provides a faithful map of the contemporary negative intellectual terrain, the circuitries of communicative capitalism ensure that a significant range of overlapping and hybridizing genres have come to prominence. Matt Carr has traced what he brackets as *Eurabian* discourse – derived from the work of Bat Ye'or on the secret agreement between left-wing European politicians and Arab governments for the 'Islamicization' of Europe – fixated on narratives of decadence (see Chapter 2) and the looming demographic catastrophe of European civilization. Multiculturalism figures in Eurabian scenarios as an explicit manifestation of affluent softness and, in some versions, civilizational self-hatred, a softness that can only be rectified through the forms of moral clarity associated with the 'war on terror' and an explicit commitment to universalizing universalism. Thus multicultural accommodation of all sorts is tantamount to *dhimmitude,* or an acceptance of subject status (Carr 2006: 3).

As discussed in relation to Christopher Caldwell, the explicitly conspiratorial vision of Eurabianists such as Mark Steyn and Melanie Phillips is not shared by many writers who have emerged in what Richard Seymour (2008) calls the liberal 'belligerati' of the war-on-terror era, but their stark dichotomous appeals to religious/secular, enlightened/unenlightened amount to a similar dependence on a simplistic schism of values and given hierarchies of life. Andrew Anthony, in his post-7/7 coming-to-political-wisdom book *The Fallout: How a Guilty Liberal Lost His Innocence* (2008), argues that British culture has historically valued 'certain rights, liberties, responsibilities, protections and opportunities' while 'many traditional cultures in the Third World' value 'petty corruption, sexism, homophobia, tribalism and patriarchal authoritarianism' (ibid.: 123–4, quoted in Kundnani 2011). As Arun Kundnani points out, Anthony cites two examples for this world historical sweep – voting fraud in Birmingham and rigged exams in an Indian university – but the empirical argument is less important than drawing

> battle lines in his liberal version of the clash of civilisations: on the one side, the western Enlightenment and, on the other, what he calls the 'Endarkenment' of the Islamic world. The Arab world, says Anthony, suffers from a 'lack of intellectual curiosity' and 'self-willed ignorance' (p. 234). Its cultural failure to produce rational, independent thinking implies that western liberals must not shy away from imposing their own superior values. (Ibid.)

The idiom of Enlightenment has become a euphemism for civilization, but is also put to work in totalizing ways. The problem for those who strap on the pith helmet of the Enlightenment warrior only to calcify radical, critical thought in the name of defending the present is not only the obvious denial of emancipatory visions in the contemporary political moment (Toscano 2010: 99; see also Hind 2007). It is, as Toscano argues, 'the ideological comfort of fighting on the side of the powerful while presenting oneself as a member of a beleaguered and courageous minority' (2010: 100; see also Hind 2007, Titley 2007). Here there is another irony, as this appeal to enlightenment depends on precisely the same reverse victimology

associated, in Chapter 3, with the 'new racism' and the communicative structures of populism. In the populist mobilization, intellectual
elites are held to disdain the capacities of ordinary people, with their
experimental imposition of multiculturalism being among their most
self-serving gestures. In the 'Enlightenment' paradigm, actors who are
invested in these structures of mediated privilege redirect anti-elitist
discourse through a class fractional battle, positioning opponents as
the 'delusional left' who refuse to recognize the scale of the threat,
and thus endanger a whole way of life.

This strategy is not just restricted to the *nouveaux philosophes*
and fractional battles of British journalism. The immigration sceptic
paradigm in Finland was given significant publicity and credibility
with the publication of *Länsimaiden tuho* (*The Decline of the Western
Nations*, 2009) by a Russian Studies professor, Timo Vihavainen,
whose loose assemblage of established *récits* benefited from their
translation into Finnish by a figure with significant cultural capital.
Yet in arguing that immigration is Western cultural suicide and that
Islam is an aggressive culture ready to exploit Western narcissism
and relativism, Vihavainen also wrote himself out of the conventional
identity liberalism script by drawing explicit parallels between multicultural relativism and 'feminism and women's studies' as forms of
contemporary communist-style ideology, deflecting criticism through
political correctness. The circulation of ideas of taboo and political correctness allows the publication of such totalizing analyses to
also audition as minor truth events, as iterations that finally, again,
challenge the cosy consensus. In 2006 Karen Jespersen, a former
Social Democrat government minister – remembered for attempting
to have asylum seekers confined on islands in Copenhagen harbour
during the 1990s – and Ralph Pittelkow, a former government adviser
and columnist for *Jyllands Posten*, published a best-selling book,
Islamists and Naivists (*Islamisten en näivisten*). They argued that
the cartoons affair laid bare the naivety of those who could not see
that the controversy was fundamentally about the replacement of
freedom of speech with sharia. In their presentation of self and the
book, Jespersen and Pittelkow frequently refer to their radical youth
and history in left-wing politics to insert themselves in a 'mugged
by reality' genre that plays well in media narratives of how the left
and right are now in consensus on the problem of multiculturalism.
Both, however, are prominent members of the Giordano Bruno society
and its transatlantic networks (Hervik 2008: 71). More broadly, this

recited truth of left-wing awakening and maturity rarely explores the historical relationship between the anti-Stalinist left of the past and neoconservative formations of the past decade (Seymour 2008).

As artefacts intimately shaped by communicative capitalism's flows of exchange, to audition as events, such books are aso required to intensify the buzz. Jespersen and Pittelkow's contribution has been to issue their wake-up call in relation to Islamism as a movement comparable to Nazism and communism, an idiom of crisis usually restricted to the blogosphere or to more obviously Eurabian literature. In his angry lament for the absence of historical sense in an 'age of forgetting', Tony Judt (2008) reserves particular fire for those who yoke together disparate political contexts to detect skirmishes in a new, global Good Fight, providing a sense of clarity, surety and purpose comparable to the anti-fascism of the Second World War and the liberal opposition to international communism: 'Once again, they assert, things are clear. The world is ideologically divided; and – as before – we must take our stand on the issue of the age. Long nostalgic for the comforting verities of a simpler time, today's liberal intellectuals have at least discovered a sense of purpose: they are at war with "Islamo-fascism"' (ibid.: 386). Judt's dismissive swipe at nostalgic certainties is certainly adequate to the intellectual content of these contributions, but it also opens up a way of understanding them within the logics of mediation, and the performative attraction of certainty. Put another way, how can we account for the contribution of negative intellectuals dedicated, in Bourdieu's terms, to *disrespect* for the complexity of the world?

The range of clefts specified in this genre have clear affinities with the 'with us or against us' rhetoric of George W. Bush in the aftermath of '9/11', a Manichaeanism explored by Jodi Dean in her consideration of the idiom of 'evil' in US politics. Discussing George W. Bush's specification of the axis of evil in his 2002 State of the Union address, Dean asks 'what could hold this unstable train of signification together? How is such a monstrous, bizarre moral geography even comprehensible?' (2009: 95). Dean is not convinced by explanations for the appearance of evil that reach for the mantra that 11 September 2001 changed everything, as the idea that liberal America had lost its moral compass has long been cultivated in the 'culture wars' against relativism. Similarly, the apparent explanatory power of religion in public life in the USA, and the biographical spotlight of Bush's born-again Christianity, fails to account for how religious language 'inhabits the political register in multiple, changing and inconsistent ways' (ibid.: 98). Instead, Dean argues, evil does not function as a master signifier but as a demonstration of resolve that depends on ambiguous invocation:

> when 'everybody knows' what evil is, when its meaning is clear and seemingly widely accepted, then its use in a presidential speech describes an object. Yet when 'evil' is amorphous and unclear, its appearance in a presidential speech says something not about an object but about the (dogmatic) conviction and resolve of the subject willing to name evil. (Ibid.: 101)

The expression of absolute certainty is less about the object of signification than the projected quality of the signifying subject, the performance of intensely held and registered convictions and beliefs. As a consequence, evil becomes ontological; a shifting, mutating potentiality you will know by the certainty of its opponents, who are licensed to regard explanation, analysis and reason as the failure of certainty, but 'at worst, they are hosts for pernicious evil, a mutant form of liberalism or leftism in which evil hides' (ibid.: 121). In the shifting discursive terrain of identity liberalism and its polyphonic derivations, 'relativism' plays the same role as evil, a category, as per Hylland Eriksen's critique of Finkielkraut (see Chapter 2), where anything beyond ritual invocations of the universal can be consigned. The post '9/11' discursive context has allowed any lingering engagements with postmodern critiques of ethics, and post-colonial contestations of power and knowledge, to be dismissed as so much decadent introspection. The attack on amorphous relativism extends from global contestations of the liberal humanitarian intentions of imperial wars to the local insistence on the complexity of lived multiculture. Laundered in the availability of comforting verities, the negative intellectuals of the moment depend on an expansive category of relativism as an alibi for their dependence on transferable culturalist frameworks of knowledge. When we know – in the clarifying processes of Schmittian liberalism (Triadafilopoulos 2011) – who we are, and who they are, and who some of them can become, then a more demanding 'respect for the complexity of problems' (Bourdieu 1999) does not inhibit communicative transactions in the frames most favoured by 'fast thinkers'. Instead, for these students of the Enlightenment, it sanctions the recitation of values *as* knowledge. This is ultimately why the rather tired self-positioning in relation to taboos and political

correctness persists. Just as when evil is amorphous, the contrarian-
ism of the moment depends on the diffuse polysemy of 'relativism'
and 'political correctness' as a signification that, above all, displays
resolve, courage and clear-sightedness, the conviction of the subject
willing to name it. Thus for all the appeals to the universal, it would
seem that the mediated logic of the negative intellectual is primarily
about self-positioning in the space of appearance.

FIVE

Good and bad diversity: the shape of neoliberal racisms

Neoliberalism was constructed in and through cultural and identity politics and cannot be undone by a movement without the constituencies and analyses that respond directly to that fact. Nor will it be possible to build a new social movement that might be strong, creative and diverse enough to engage the work of reinventing global politics for the new millennium as long as cultural and identity issues are separated, analytically and organizationally, from the political economy in which they are embedded. (Duggan 2003: 3)

Introduction: pragmatic, elastic, ubiquitous

In July 2010, Ricardo Dominguez, an associate professor in the Visual Arts Department of the University of California, San Diego, was threatened with the loss of his academic tenure.[1] Dominguez was originally granted tenure in 2006 for his work on the interstices of art and new media, specifically his controversial electronic civil disobedience work. In the late 1990s, through his performance-art-cum-activist organization, Electronic Disturbance Theatre (EDT), he set up Virtual Sit-In technology, which was used in a series of anti-government online protests and in collaboration with the Zapatistas in 1994. He has continued working in this vein, at the BANG (Bits, Atoms, Neurons and Genes) Lab at the California Institute for Telecommunications and Information Technology, Calit2.[2] He was investigated by police and faced the potential loss of his university tenure for coordinating a virtual sit-in of the website of the University of California Office of the President, as part of a general wave of protests organized on 4 March 2010 against the increasing attacks on education in the state.[3] Although protests against the marketization of university education have become widespread,[4] it appears that Dominguez's more serious crime was an invention – the Transborder Immigrant Tool – that embarrassed the university authorities. The tool, a cracked cellphone with a built-in compass, tells the user where to 'find water left by the Border Angels, where to find Quaker help centers that will wrap your feet, how far you are from the highway – things to make the application really benefit individuals who are crossing the border'.[5] True to its primary identification as a piece of art, the tool also welcomes its users to the USA with poetry 'read by' the phone. The petition to defend Dominguez makes it clear that his involvement in the Virtual Sit-In was a mere excuse for ending the Transborder Immigrant Tool project. This was despite the fact that 'there were never plans to mass-produce the device, and there have been no reported uses by border-crossers. The project was about the political perceptions, possibilities, and reactions that could be generated by technology. This doesn't make the gesture any less tangible. Perceptions are tangible, reactions even more so.'[6]

That the tool was restricted to a symbolic utility which could not actually halt the three to four hundred deaths that occur annually during attempted border crossings[7] between Mexico and the USA did little to mitigate the hostile reaction. Following an op-ed piece by a California congressman, Duncan Hunter, in November 2009, the Transborder Immigrant Tool became the target of significant media attention leading to the university establishing an audit of the project in January 2010. In calling for funding to be removed from the project, Hunter argued that 'given the immense problems we already face with drug smuggling, violence and illegal immigration, this is an irresponsible use of technology that would only compound existing security challenges'.[8] Hunter's ostensible attention is to questions of security, an elastic construct that has come to encompass a continuum of internal and external threats (Aradau 2008) and the incorporation of migration to the 'hegemony of risk' (Nyers 2004: 206). Yet to read this solely through the fish-eye of the securitarian lens would be to miss the concomitant managerialism of Hunter's protest against such 'irresponsibility' in the face of 'challenges'. Hunter's protest is intensely political – it is, after all, opposition to subversive action – but its terms deny the political nature of Dominguez's work and what it represents. It precludes the political by siphoning all ideology from the antagonism, proposing instead the signature pragmatism of neoliberal discourse. Hunter's terms obscure the very conditions in which subversive action has become, as Dominguez's work attests, politically necessary.

The impact of neoliberalism is woven through this study, from the insistence on how structural problems and waning capacities to

address them have been reclaimed through the specification and discipline of cultural threats; to the multivalent depoliticization and
culturalization of social, political and *cultural* life; to the recited
impact of consumerist discourses and practices of multiculturalism
on the perception of experimental excess; to the dissolution and
strange resolutions of questions of power; to the affinities between
culturalized knowledge and media forms in the working of circuits
of belief. This chapter involves a more concentrated exploration of
neoliberal racial formations and assemblages.

Analysing contamination

David Harvey argues that 'we can [...] interpret neoliberalization
[as a political-economic formation] either as a utopian project to
realize a theoretical design for the reorganization of international
capitalism or as a political project to re-establish the conditions for
capital accumulation and to restore the power of economic elites [...]
the second of these objectives has in practice dominated' (2005: 19).
While the global economic crisis from 2008 has been widely hailed
as signalling the end of a neoliberal consensus, this is not the same
as declaring an 'end' to the forms of *governmentality* propagated
by this political project. According to Wendy Brown, 'neoliberalism
entails the erosion of oppositional political, moral, or subjective
claims located *outside* capitalist rationality yet inside liberal democratic society, that is, the erosion of institutions, venues, and values
organized by nonmarket rationalities in democracies' (2005: 45).
Neoliberalism occupies the shell of liberalism, using the rhetorics
of liberal democracy while turning liberalism 'in the direction of
liberality rather than *liberty*' (ibid.: 39). In so doing, it values only an
individualist, economic rationality and not only rejects contestation,
but denies the validity of the normative basis of such contestations.
This dominant articulation through a hegemonic liberal democratic
vocabulary makes neoliberal ideology a slippery object of analysis, as
it runs the risk of becoming a 'totalising device'. Neoliberalism functions as a contaminable discourse, striated in and articulated in conjunction with different political logics (Phelan 2009). As Breda Gray
notes, in an examination of neoliberal integration policy, 'although
policies directed at migrants cannot be made fully intelligible by
reference to a neo-liberal logic (Lippert, 1998), the pervasiveness of
this logic demands constant vigilance in order that other logics are
not appropriated to neo-liberal ends' (Gray 2006: 123).

It is precisely these processes of appropriation, of organizing neo-liberal rationalities through established normative terms and universal claims, which are explored in Wendy Brown's influential account (2005). She characterizes neoliberalism as follows. First, political life is reduced to economics and everything, including individual action, is judged according to its profitability and 'rationality'. Secondly, a state's success is judged solely in terms of economic growth. It must therefore *'think and behave like a market actor* across all of its functions, including law' (ibid.: 42, emphasis in original). Thirdly, market rationality extends to the individual; we are all expected to be entrepreneurial. Individual morality is thus judged according to 'our capacity for "self care"' (ibid.). Everyone is expected to have full personal responsibility over her actions in all spheres of life, at risk of a consequent loss of rights for a life mismanaged, or the failure to 'navigate impediments to prosperity' (ibid.). Despite the increasing structural constraints over individuals, neoliberal governmentality paradoxically constructs 'free' subjects who, because rational action is cast as an achievable, guiding norm, police themselves according to 'a rational assessment of the costs and benefits of certain acts' (ibid.: 43). Citizenship is thus reduced to one's success in this endeavour, leading us, as Brown puts it, to be controlled *through our freedom.*

Under such conditions, what Tony Judt (2008) has termed the 'prophylactic' dimension of modern Western states – ensuring public goods and at least 'basic standards' of material welfare and opportunity – can be dismantled in the cause of freedom. The privatization of its former functions leads not to the dismantling of state power, but towards the 'radical reconstruction of the state into an authoritarian tool' for the protection of capitalist interests and mobilities (Dean 2009: 9). In tandem with this emphasis on risk and security, neoliberalism involves the construction of adaptive forms of governmentality. Individuals are invited to police their own legitimacy by actively demonstrating that they are no burden on a public that, depending on the national context, has been unsettled, diluted or eviscerated. The residue of the notion of liberty in the shell of liberalism allows the elevation and naturalization of a dominant ideology of individual autonomy, and a hollowed simulacrum of liberal democracy where government's 'role is less to ensure public goods and solve collective problems than to address the personal issues of subjects' (ibid.: 11).

An idea of 'responsibility', for example, is now keenly associated with facilitating the shrinking state, and as the Dominguez case illustrates, opposing public support for anything that is 'irresponsible' or properly private (in the sense of not being in the interest of the market). Of course, this example draws attention to the strange equivocation between what is considered private under neoliberalism, and what is considered (too) political. In the context of the United States, Lisa Duggan (2003) shows how right-wing opposition to the civil rights movement, and to the advances towards greater equality made by feminism and gay rights activism, became congruous with the neoliberal demise of the public, understood as a space for non-market collective action. In the 1980s the second-wave feminist idea of 'the personal as political' was co-opted by the right in arguing that abortion and gay marriage were political, and hence public, issues. However, the right's politicization of these issues was designed to privatize and confine these 'issues' to the shadowy realms of the home, the back room and the backstreet, and to delegitimize them in the public sphere.

Duggan develops this central paradox by showing how conservative politics, over a significant period of time following the New Deal and the gradual post-war instigation of some form of welfare state in the USA, focused on 'reprivatizing as much of the common life of the nation as possible' (ibid.: 8). This reprivatization depended on a ideologically constricted remit for freedom, excluding those whose private relations conflicted with the hegemony of acceptable norms embodied by 'the procreative, intraracially married' (ibid.), and shaping the well-worn conservative advocacy of more state control over intimate life and less over the economy and civil society (Hewitt 2005). However, as Duggan points out, the fact that some advances had been made towards greater legislative equality in the two decades preceding the 1980s meant that the right came to understand reprivatization as being blocked by 'liberals' aligned with the state, which was then framed as a 'bad, coercive, intrusive force against freedom' (ibid.). The particular contribution of neoliberal ideology in the 1990s was to square the antagonism between rights-based activism and the cultural backlash it unleashed by suffusing conservative critiques of state interventionism with 'old' liberalism. The so-called 'third way' was based on a 'leaner, meaner government (fewer social services, more "law and order"), a state-supported but "privatized" economy, an invigorated and socially responsible civil society, and a moralized family with gendered marriage at its centre' (Duggan 2003: 10). The implications of this for the racialized poor, in particular, were to become all too obvious in the United States most strikingly, but also in Europe, where the privatization of liberalism is key to understanding the contemporary attack on multiculturalism.

Racy: racial neoliberalism and the privatization of race

Neoliberalism, as definitive of global state formations since the mid-1970s (Goldberg 2009), does not merely exist; it has to be constantly constructed in reaction to the forces that resist it or merely fail to be appropriately acquiescent subjects. This clash, between the ordering forces of neoliberalism and those unwilling or unable to become, for example, 'integrated citizens', throws the racial dimensions of neoliberalism into sharp relief. The 'forces of unruliness' (ibid.: 334) that obstruct neoliberalism's spatial or governmental imperatives – both 'rogue' states or 'undisciplined' individuals including welfare dependants, criminalized black youth and 'illegals' on foreign territory – are often racially defined. They can thus be disciplined according to the lesser status accorded to them by their place in the racial hierarchy. As several commentators have argued, following Giorgio Agamben (1998, 2005), such individuals are, or can be, reduced to 'bare life' – taken to exist outside juridical law – and thus expendable according to a 'state of exception' that justifies mistreatment, imprisonment or even death (Gregory 2004). The explosion in post-'9/11' legal revisionism and extrajudicial procedures has created networked states of exception, within which it is necessary and possible to 'restrict, restrain, or disappear' those existing – or subsisting – outside of particular understandings of sovereignty (Asad 2010) or categories of legitimacy.

The securitarian response to '9/11' is built on a 'parallel security state' erected in and between the United States and the European Union since the end of the Cold War (Fekete 2009). The surveillance and control technologies currently targeting Muslim populations are built on structures of exclusion erected for asylum seekers and 'illegal' immigrants (McGhee 2008; Fekete 2009). These security innovations have augmented and themed the securitization of migration, a process that incorporates modern forms of border control into 'an assemblage of systems to filter mobility, separate the good from the bad; systems that make use of new technologies that promise secure identities, and systems that couple security and migration together with visions of integration' (Maguire and Murphy 2009: 7). The border is everywhere, and because, as A. Sivanandan reminds us, the subjects of xeno-racism wear their passports on their faces, the border follows them. The amalgamated threat of the 'illegal' immigrant, terrorist and cultural recalcitrant is related both discursively and through particular policies to those considered 'in but not of' the nation-state: its racialized others. As the Cette France Là collective (2009) points out, those who committed the attacks on New York, Madrid and London were, whatever else they also were, '*issus de l'immigration*' and identified as the eternal enemy within, no matter how well they may have been integrated according to conventional social and biographical indicators.[9] It is precisely this specification of a hazy, compound threat which allows analysis to approach the war on terror (foreign and domestic), the roll-back of equality legislation, the delegitimization of asylum seekers and the managerial stratification of migration through a lens that privileges what David Goldberg (2009) explicitly refers to as 'racial neoliberalism'. As Duggan remarks, neoliberalism

> organizes material and political life *in terms of* race, gender, and sexuality as well as economic class and nationality, or ethnicity and religion. But the categories through which Liberalism (and thus also neoliberalism) classifies human activity and relationships *actively obscure* the connections among these organising terms. (2003: 3, emphasis in original)

Understanding racism in a neoliberal age requires making sense of this double move, towards the privatization of both the *doing* of race and the experience of racism, on the one hand, and of their further disconnection from intersecting modalities of discrimination and strategies of resistance, on the other. In the next chapter we turn to the interlocking securitarian, culturalist and utilitarian rationalities of emerging 'integrationist' regimes, revealing how they are consistent with the working of neoliberal states in a globalized era. Here, we examine the effects of the privatization of race on the domestic sphere – on those already 'here' – relating the mechanisms of discipline and punishment that order the lives of the poor and racialized. Focusing on the emptying out of the social under neoliberalism explains how what appear to be progressive claims about transcending personal barriers to achievement serve principally to obscure the maintenance of a racially structured status quo. In the context of the USA, the coexistence of punitive regimes of control ordering racialized lives – in particular those of poor blacks and Latinos – with public commitments to transracial diversity (Winant 1997) is evidence, not of a conflict at the heart of social policy, but of the occlusion of race from the public sphere. In Chapter 2, we discussed how post-racialism undergirds contemporary racism by effectively silencing the hold race continues to have on ordinary lives. The post-racial idea is not unique to the contemporary era but has been intrinsic to how racial formations have, since abolitionism at least, had their own denial built into them (Goldberg 2002). Post-racialism is thus a useful means for making sense of the turn against multiculturalism; the denial of the significance of race to the lived experience of the racialized mirrors the flattening out of multiculture as a tangible, inhabited dimension of people's lives. To the extent that it can be used to describe something of their experience, occluding it also means foreshortening people's capacity for self-description. In part, understanding racial neoliberalism is bound to the understanding of how post-racialism plays out in political terms. What happens when the denial of the capacity to describe one's own condition is made a basis for policy?

In the context of the contemporary United States, Howard Winant argues that it is impossible to apply the same explanations of racism that pertained prior to the civil rights era of the 1960s and 1970s. Since that time,

> US society has undergone a substantial modification of the pre-
> viously far more rigid lines of exclusion and segregation, permitting
> real mobility for more favoured sectors (that is, certain class-based
> segments) of racially defined minority groups. This period has also
> witnessed the substantial diversification of the North American
> population, in the aftermath of the 1965 reform of immigration
> laws. Panethnic phenomena have increased among Asians, Latinos
> and Native Americans, reconstituting the US racial panorama in a
> multipolar (as opposed to the old bipolar) direction. Racial identity
> has been problematized (at least somewhat) for whites – a fact
> which has its dangers but also reflects progress – and the movements
> to which the black struggle gave initial impetus, notably feminism
> and gay liberation in their many forms, have developed to the point
> where a whole range of cross-cutting subjectivities and tensions (as
> well as new alliances) have been framed. (Winant 1998: 759)

Despite this, Winant insists that what he describes as a hegemonic 'new right' vision opposes itself to these gains, rearticulating 'the demands for equality and justice made by the black movement and its allies in a conservative discourse of individualism, competition and *laissez-faire*' (ibid.). The conflict between a lived reality of multi-culturalism, coupled with the real gains of the civil rights movement in the United States, and what is essentially the rejection of these facts by a new right that fears the loss of white privilege (Goldberg 2009), leads to confusion over how to define racism today (Winant 1998). Racial neoliberalism capitalizes on this confusion. To lend some clarity, Winant insists that there are no timeless absolutes in defining racism. Rather, it should be seen 'as a property of certain political projects that link the representation and organization of race – that engage in the "work" of racial formation.[10] Such an approach focuses on the "work" essentialism does for domination, and the "need" domination displays to essentialize the subordinated' (ibid.: 761). The focus on 'work' and 'need' draws out the functionality of racism, its expediency in given contexts and times and with regard to particular populations.

Privatizing racism Neoliberal approaches to race take it for granted that capital in the USA since the 1960s has been colour blind (Winant 1997). Neoliberals are thus deeply invested in the commitment to post-racialism, not only as an ideal but as an already achieved reality, because capitalism, it is held, gains no advantages in reproducing racisms. Racial discrimination, therefore, cannot be said to be responsible for the greater deprivation experienced by people of colour, disparities which many neoliberals admit, but which are attributed to a host of other, racially inflected, reasons for individual under-achievement. Under neoliberalism, 'it is not just that the personal is the political. The personal is the only politics there is' (Comaroff and Comaroff 2000: 305). Anyone who *feels* that she is the victim of racism has also to look to her responsibility; by the same token, any residual racism is a matter of 'personal "taste"' (Robbins 2004: 3). In the individualizing logic of neoliberalism, history, politics and the state are increasingly written out of any analysis of disadvantage generally, and racialized disadvantage particularly. The focus on capital as a social corrector, rather than as a participant in the perpetuation of discrimination, inequality and poverty, is based on a denial of the reciprocal relationship between the state and neoliberal capital (W. Brown 2005). In this, the hegemony in the United States is far more pronounced than elsewhere; if the markets and rational economic behaviour fail to correct racial discrimination, it is the individual's inability to make the best of things which is to blame.

Under neoliberalism race is essentially privatized, in the sense of being silenced or made invisible. When racism is understood as an irrational attribute or behaviour, it has diminished purchase in a social vision that places rational and autonomous actors centre stage. Concomitantly, because of the dilution of collective action, in part in favour of these individualized rationalities, the anti-racist politics that formerly drew attention to issues of race and racism are sidelined (Duggan 2003), making it more and more difficult to develop responsive strategies to make visible and oppose this privatizing move. Under these conditions, state resources are increasingly directed towards 'novel arrangements of demographic management', including the detailed regulation of the presence and mobility of 'migrants' (Goldberg 2009: 333), the policing of welfare dependants racialized as such (D.-A. Davis 2007; Schram et al. 2008), and the mass incarceration of 'people from poor, immigrant, and racially marginalized communities' (Davis 1998). Racial formation in the United States exemplifies how the state is not rendered redundant under neoliberalism, as was claimed by some analysts during the heyday of globalization theory (Ohmae 1995). Instead, it is engaged in 'an intensification of some of its core features', in particular the intrusive and repressive functions of surveillance and control (Comaroff, cited in Goldberg 2009; Dean 2009). In the absence of structural critique and the possibilities of race as a political analytics, the fact that it is most often the racialized 'unruly populations' which are subject to the greatest sanctions is scarcely politicized beyond the work of dedicated activists (Goldberg 2009: 334).[11]

State repression under neoliberalism is managerial: a necessary corrective to the individual failure to be or become autonomous. Existent racism is suffused in neoliberal contexts but is compounded by the invisibility of power, and the refusal of the kinds of socio-political analysis that would unveil neoliberalism as a racial formation. Neoliberalism is never seen as a 'particular set of interests and political interventions, but as a kind of nonpolitics', inviting the difficulties of opposing a contaminable formation that merely presents 'a way of being reasonable, and of promoting universally desirable forms of economic expansion and democratic government around the globe' (Duggan 2003: 10). Contemporary racial neoliberalism as it plays out in the United States is thus a complex and slippery formation. It is not merely laissez-faire, nor is it a straightforward project of domination. Neoliberal governance has no ideological intent with regard to race.

While there are certainly clear overlaps between neoliberalism and neoconservatism with regard to the maintenance of white privilege in the USA (ibid.), neoliberalism does not invest ideologically in racism, be it the overt racism of the far or new right or the colour-blind consensus favoured by neoconservatives (Winant 1997, 1998). State neoliberalism governmentalizes, but it does not always do so in consistent terms, borrowing instead from a range of discourses, histories and practices. Thus, racialized populations are both subject to greater discipline and control while being spoken about in terms that borrow from the language of civil rights and identity politics.

Neoliberal conditions therefore coexist with a legal apparatus that, thanks to the advances of civil rights, makes it difficult for the state to explicitly condone or practise racial discrimination. Moreover, overt discrimination undermines the fundaments of universalist merit-ocracy embedded in the shorthand of the 'American Dream' but also in the individualized promise of neoliberalism. Therefore, as David Goldberg points out, the role of the state is limited with regards to 'privatized [...] racial expression' (2009: 335). Nevertheless, the partially successful redressing of structural racial discrimination has created its own backlash. Affirmative action legislation in the USA from the 1970s led to the state becoming the biggest single employer of African-Americans. Accordingly, the neoconservative perception of the state's stance on race was that black people are either employees of the state owing to affirmative action programmes, or 'on welfare'. The neoconservative 'fear of a black state' linked to 'concern about the impending impotence of whiteness' (ibid.: 337) finds a response in neoliberalism, which, by privileging the privatization of state func-tions, plays a role in restructuring the state 'to support the privatizing of race' (ibid.). This is achieved in practice by 'absolving the govern-ment from its role in the intervention and management of racial disparities' (D.-A. Davis 2007: 349). So, while it may be impossible to alter the racial make-up of public service, it *is* possible both to reduce the size of the state – as neoliberalism dictates globally – and roll back welfare: 'Further racial discrimination can be resolved simply by having citizens enter the workforce' (ibid.).

The instigation of 'welfare-to-work' programmes is a major feature of the transformation of the role of the state from one of protection to one of control. There has been a 'paternalist turn' in the USA that 'expresses a loss of faith in the belief that market incentives, state supports and social-group norms can be sufficient on their own to move the poor toward full societal incorporation' (Schram et al. 2008: 18). However, because neoliberalism envisages a role for the market in transforming, rather than opposing, the state, paternalism does not entail a direct relationship between the state and the poor (ibid.). The outsourcing of an increasing number of state functions is consistent both with the imperative to reduce the size of the public sector, and with making the management of dependent populations more efficient. As Schram et al. note, in their study of Temporary Assistance for Needy Families (TANF) programmes in Florida, the service is run by 'for-profit providers' who are submitted to 'performance measurement for holding contracted agencies accountable' for getting recipients off welfare and into work (ibid.: 21). As a result, the contracting out of social welfare and criminal justice to private contractors in the United States makes it more likely that punitive measures will be used to 'get results' (D.-A. Davis 2007; Schram et al. 2008).[12] While welfare reform along neoliberal lines in the United States officially focuses on poverty reduction, the 'racial indexing' of black and Latino populations that it assimilates barely needs remarking upon. Echoing the mediated logics discussed in the last chapter, Dana-Ain Davis uses the concept of 'indexicality' to describe the ways in which race, though unspoken, is implicit in the ways that African-Americans, in particular, are thought about and thus treated. The lexical significance of 'Welfare' or 'Quota' Queens, for example, is an immediately understandable reference to the presumed perpetual dependency of (undeserving) blacks on the state. There is no possibility of mistaking these terms as making reference to whites; poor white people are simply never held up in this way as 'exemplary models' (D.-A. Davis 2007: 356).[13] As Davis discusses, the decrease in white welfare recipients and the concomitant increase in blacks and Latinos receiving TANF between 1992 and 2001 is rarely discussed in terms of the 'racial consequence of welfare reform' (ibid.: 353).[14] However, if the privatization of welfare programmes is taken together with what Davis refers to as 'muted racializing and racism' – the 'barely audible and covert vehicles through which racial discourse, tension and hierarchies are framed' (ibid.: 351) – the racial consequences become very clear.

Because welfare providers are under pressure to perform in a competitive environment, they rely on hegemonic racial precepts to ensure performance. In their Florida study, Schram et al. (2008) observed that blacks were more likely to be sanctioned than white

TANF recipients, and that this was especially the case when the workforce region was behind on its performance rankings. Getting people into work, as Davis remarks, was not the only aim of welfare reform, 'it was also about moving people toward middle class behaviour' (D.-A. Davis 2007: 355). As a virtual impossibility for many of the highly marginalized and racialized people targeted by TANF, this becomes a basis upon which to submit them to more punitive sanctions, relegating swathes of the citizenry to the realm of the hopelessly, eternally dependent. This status in turn undergirds claims as to the drain placed on the taxpayer – construed as white, middle-class and law-abiding as opposed to black, poor and criminal – by the recalcitrant racialized subject. The sanctions inherent in US welfare programmes perversely compound poverty by most often being applied to the most financially vulnerable (Schram et al. 2008: 32). The system allows the state to become 'invasively repressive' in the lives of the mainly racialized poor (Goldberg 2009: 335), despite the neoliberal promise of the state's retreat. In fact, under neo-liberalism, 'deregulating libertarianism has turned out to apply only in the realm of the economic, playing up the fears of insecurity by playing down welfarist convictions regarding social security' (ibid.). In other words, if the neoliberal state's function is to ensure citizens' security, rather than their welfare, it must protect the desirables from the undesirables by either locking them up – 70 per cent of the US prison population is of colour (Davis 1998) – or locking them out in the case of migrants, or failing both, submitting them to increasingly punitive measures that drive a deeper wedge between 'us' and 'them'. For Henry Giroux, the societal consequences are profound:

> As safety nets and social services are being hollowed out and communities crumble and give way to individualized, one-man archipelagos, it is increasingly difficult to struggle as a collectivity, to act in concert against a state that fails to meet the basic needs of its citizens or to maintain the social investments that provide life-sustaining services. (2006)

This is what Giroux describes as the 'politics of disposability', where 'entire populations expelled from the benefits of the market-place [… are] reified as products without any value and […] disposed of' (ibid.). In addition to the consolidation of racialized poverty by punitive welfare systems, the growth of a privatized 'prison-industrial complex' – in which the USA is the world leader – has created a situation in which prisons have become industrial actors for which 'bodies destined for profitable punishment' have to be 'delivered up' (Davis 1998). Disposable lives are contained by actual or metaphorical prisons to protect a privatized and exclusionary vision of 'America' that Goldberg exemplifies with the slogan of the anti-immigration vigilante Minute Men: 'This is America, get off my property' (2009: 336). For Giroux, as for Goldberg and others, most poignantly Spike Lee in his film *When the Levees Broke* (2006), the full force of disposability was exposed during the Hurricane Katrina disaster of 2005. During the storm, 'the economically secure drove out of town, checked into hotels and called their insurance companies. The 120,000 people in New Orleans without cars, who depended on the state to organize their evacuation, waited for help that did not arrive, making desperate SOS signs or rafts out of their refrigerator doors' (Klein 2007: 408). The mainly black bodies that washed up, bloated and decomposing as the rains over New Orleans subsided, 'revealed a modality of state terrorism marked less by an overt form of white racism than by a highly mediated displacement of race as a central concept for understanding both Katrina and its place in the broader history of US racism' (Giroux 2006). In other words, for most people, Hurricane Katrina, while undoubtedly a tragic disaster during which poor African-Americans suffered disproportionately, was not *about* race. But the negation of the relevance of race is precisely the act that reveals the extent of its centrality.

In *The Shock Doctrine*, Naomi Klein (2007) recounts her visit to New Orleans, part of which was still under water, in the second week of September 2005. She was involved in a car accident during which no one was seriously hurt, but she was nevertheless brought to hospital. Klein contrasted her experience at Ochsner Hospital with Charity Hospital, 'New Orleans' primary public emergency room', where, during the storm, 'staff had struggled without power to keep patients alive' (ibid.: 407). Questioning a young doctor at Ochsner about the disaster, Klein was struck by his answer: '"I wasn't on duty, thank God. I live outside the city"' (ibid.). Reflecting on the disparity between these conditions of wartime emergency medicine and the 'spa-like' treatment she received, Klein understands them as 'the embodiment of the culture that had made the horrors of Hurricane Katrina possible, the culture that left New Orleans' poorest residents to drown' (ibid.: 408). Thus despite the embarrassment and even outrage expressed about the aftermath of Katrina by staunch neoconservatives, the aftermath also represented a market opportunity. Among many examples of legitimized profiteering, Klein reveals how Kenyon, the private company brought in to retrieve dead bodies, dictated that

> Emergency workers and local volunteers were forbidden to step in to help because handling the bodies impinged on Kenyon's commercial territory. The company charged the state $12,500 a victim, and it has since been accused of failing to properly label many bodies. For almost a year after the flood, decayed corpses were still being discovered in attics. (Ibid.: 411)

Klein, Giroux and Goldberg all draw parallels between Katrina and 'that "other" gulf crisis in the Middle East' (Giroux 2006): the war in Iraq. Washed-up black bodies and 'Iraqis forced to assume the additional indignity of a dog leash' (ibid.) have to be understood together: 'Post-Katrina New Orleans, in short, is simply Iraq come home' (Goldberg 2009: 89). While Klein fails to make the explicit point that Katrina and Iraq are exemplary of what Goldberg calls 'enduring occupations' both at home and abroad, and of how these are fundamentally and profoundly raced, Giroux is uncompromising: the politics of disposability, the latest manifestation of which was Katrina, has 'deep roots in the segregated South' (ibid.). But unlike the situation in the South – which may have been segregated, but in which blacks lived whether or not whites liked the fact – the privatized rebuilding of New Orleans is turning it into a gentrified city with fewer black people in it. As Goldberg details, 82 per cent of the disaster loan applications received by the Small Business Administration have been refused; 'the loans that have been approved have gone exclusively to wealthier and whiter neighbourhoods' (2009: 90). Predominantly black neighbourhoods, such as the Lower Ninth Ward, which suffered the brunt of the storm, as well as black schools and hospitals in unofficially segregated New Orleans, are simply not being (fully) rebuilt. As Goldberg remarks, this is 'neither mistake nor oversight. Its destruction by Katrina and its burial by FEMA were as surely the outcome of neoliberal privatization as its neglected condition was a product of the redlining of the segregating racial state' (ibid.: 91).

The real mark of disposability is the fact that the privatized, profitable whitening of New Orleans goes unseen by a majority for whom the election of Barack Obama, as we discussed in Chapter 2, is proof of the end of race. However, as David Goldberg notes, we have entered a neo-neoliberal era – a 'hyper-extenuation of the neo-liberal' (ibid.: 363) – in which the invisibility of human disposability is par for the course. Under these conditions, there is 'unrestricted flow, implacability and irreplaceability at one end, hyper-visibility, invisibility, and unplaceability at the other' (ibid.). The racialized are either nowhere, and thus insignificant and ultimately disposable, or irritatingly everywhere and thus requiring management. It is this balance between disposability and management which structures racial neoliberalism. Yet the individualization and privatization of race must be understood in concert with the specifications of good and bad diversity in the messy, minimal realities of lived multiculture.

The promise, and problem of diversity

Commenting on a headscarf 'controversy' in Norway, Thomas Hylland Eriksen draws attention to how 'economically profitable and morally harmless' diversity has been sequestered from differences that unsettle the modes of individualism immanent in neoliberal rationality. 'In this perspective', he argues, 'it is no wonder that immigrants were praised in the 1970s, when the collectivist ideology of social democracy still held sway in Scandinavia, for their strong family solidarity; while in the new century, they are criticised for it since it impedes personal freedom' (2006: 34). A concerted turn to an institutional and governmental rubric of diversity has accompanied the slow death of multiculturalism; nonetheless, the relation between difference and diversity is an established critical concern. Homi Bhabha (1990), for example, captures the drive of a central critique when he argues that the construction of cultural diversity brings about the containment of cultural difference within a logic of tolerant universalism, in which difference is elided as a relation of power that demands a response in transformative, political terms. The current critique is similarly concerned with difference and power, but the ascent of diversity as a ubiquitous mode of affirming and celebrating difference changes the nature of the containment. As we have argued elsewhere, where there is 'diversity', there must, despite its expansive compass, also be that which is *not* diversity (Lentin and Titley 2008). This assertion acts as a starting point for analysing the *politics of diversity*, a politics that has become centrally important to marking out the terrain of racialization under neoliberalism,[15] foregrounding the diverse subject who is autonomous, non-conflictual and oriented to the 'responsibilization' that 'gives a particular character to the contemporary politics of life in advanced liberal democracies' (Rose 2006: 4).

Diversity, as a form of governmentality involved in specifying and acting upon forms of 'good' and 'bad' diversity in (post-) multicultural societies, is prevalent in the European Union, where diversity is publicly and officially celebrated yet where not everybody qualifies to be recognized as the right kind of diverse subject. In the European shift to the privatization of race, the shifting border between good diversity, requiring celebration and cultivation, and bad diversity, diverse matter recognized as out of place, is central to understanding a particularly influential inflection of anti-racialism. How can there be racism when the official commitment to diversity is so manifest, and so mediated? Hylland Eriksen's example illustrates a conflation central to the politics of diversity. Diversity, like the headscarf, which expresses the problem of will or wrong freedom, is *bad diversity*. It cannot be celebrated as a detachable, diverse *good*, it belongs to the resistant, risky, communitarianism of the multicultural past. Yet the specification of bad diversity is bound up in the ongoing articulation of the common, national, transcendent values that mark 'us' out as different. Bad diversity, in other words, is integral to the reworking of multiculturalist ontology after the failed experiment. The next chapter examines how the fantasy of integration is central to the stratification and control of migrants and racialized populations in contemporary Europe. First we analyse the production of good and bad diversity, and examine how culturalization has become increasingly central to neoliberal governmentality (Fortier 2010).

Love diversity, hate racism In the slow news days of summer 2010, President Nicolas Sarkozy of France provided good copy by launching a three-pronged attack: on burka-wearing women, 'criminal' immigrants, and Roma. According to the French Interior Ministry, approximately 1,900 women – or 0.1 per cent of the French Muslim population – wear the burka. As a quizzical editorial in *Le Monde* put it, 'we find it difficult to believe that *laïcité*, the cardinal value of the Republic, would be endangered by this ultra-minoritarian practice' (23 December 2009). During the period from March to May 2010, a proposed ban on full face veils was proposed by a parliamentary committee, voted for in a non-binding resolution in parliament – as 'an affront to the nation's values of dignity and equality' – approved in cabinet in May, and voted for by the lower house of the French parliament in July 2010. The sheer force of colonial ontology is inscribed in the familiar, recited justifications of the proposed ban. Echoing the emotional censorship of the Danish cartoons debate, Sarkozy urged that 'Nobody should feel hurt or stigmatised. I'm thinking in particular of our Muslim compatriots, who have their place in the Republic and should feel respected.' Outlining the range of punishments for veiled women and their oppressors – a €150 fine or citizenship lessons for the veiled, a year in jail and a €15,000 fine for the veiler – the justice minister, Michele Alliot-Marie, noted that 'as we see it, these women are victims. It would be ideal if these sanctions didn't have to be imposed on them.'

Hot on the heels of the ban, Sarkozy delivered a speech to police at the prefecture in Grenoble during which he made an explicit link, for the first time in his presidency, between immigration and crime and delinquency. In the speech which followed the fatal shooting in the town of a gang member by police during an armed robbery, Sarkozy declared that, 'It should be possible to take French nationality away from anybody of foreign origin who voluntarily causes the death of a police officer, a gendarme or anyone representing a public authority [...] acquiring French nationality should not be automatic upon reaching the age of majority for a delinquent minor.'[16] Following these declarations – which, if made law, would necessitate the rewriting of the French constitution[17] – Sarkozy's France went viral when hundreds of thousands of people watched and circulated an amateur film of Franco-African women and their babies being manhandled by CRS riot police during a sit-in concerning housing rights in the Parisian *cité* La Courneuve.[18] Not to be deterred, Sarkozy further refined his attack on 'foreigners' by ordering the expulsion of all illegal encampments of Roma, Gypsies and travellers. Sarkozy's clampdown on European citizens was defended by a discourse that establishes an opposition between crime and integration.[19] Defending Sarkozy's stance, France's Europe minister, Pierre Lellouche, remarked, 'very few of the people coming here try to integrate, to fit in, and huge numbers of minors are involved in drug trafficking networks'.[20] This polemic has been echoed by politicians in Italy, Sweden[21] and Germany, and led French politicians to advocate revoking the right to freedom of movement for Roma citizens of the EU, and to attempt to organize a special ministerial conference for invited countries, including Canada, as it 'currently has a number of specific problems with the EU and Roma coming from the Czech Republic and Hungary' (Philips 2010).

These ideas are thus far consistent with the structures of racial neoliberalism, as well as congruous with the historical construction of the Roma as an unassimilable presence and expendable human population.[22] The framing of 'delinquents' as foreign impostors on French soil is entirely congruous with the post-colonial marginalization and disempowerment of racialized French citizens that, as Silverstein has argued, makes a 'mockery of republican ideologies of sociocultural integration' (2004: 6). It also exemplifies how racial neoliberalism draws on a shifting spectrum of old and new targets of racial stigmatization, mobilizing not just conventional, national insider/outsider distinctions, but increasingly the boundaries between the rational, self-managing citizen-subject and the wilful, dependent, resource-heavy subject.[23] Sarkozy's panoply of disciplinary actions suggests that those who 'fail' to integrate impact on the public good, with particular consequences for cohesion, liberty and women's rights. His government calls not merely for the need to discipline the unruly in society to ensure security, but also 'our' greater happiness. The 'our' here not only includes those historically considered insiders, the '*français de souche*'; it purportedly extends to all those upon whom the light of legitimacy is shone. Who is and who is not considered legitimate can shift over time; the almost mechanical, cyclical focus on the Roma suggests they will never accede to this status, they will never become *diverse*. Yet in the societies in question in this study, there is an ongoing attempt to broaden the compass of who 'we' are in post-colonial, post-immigration societies. There is, therefore, an apparent contradiction between the naked state racism faced by migrants, asylum seekers, Roma and the descendants of immigrants across the West, and a concomitant commitment to the struggle against discrimination and for 'diversity'. As French historian Esther Benbassa remarks, the principal effect of creating, in practice, a two-tiered citizenship, one for those considered really French, the other for those always to be considered 'foreign', is that 'French people born to foreign parents will feel more and more foreign, will have more and more resentment for France, and the "pure" French will discriminate at whim, with the benediction of the President, *while at the same time considering themselves non-racist*, yet authorised to see some of their compatriots as inferior' (2010, emphasis added).

A particularity of racism in a neoliberal age is captured in Benbassa's observation that the consideration of some members of the population as inferior can easily coexist with the belief in 'our' own non-racism. The example of Sarkozy's France, in this regard, is not unique. It proves a particularly interesting example because despite the mesh of initiatives instigated in 2009/10, unique among French presidents, Sarkozy has declared his commitment to the struggle against discrimination and for diversity in France, thus unsettling core republican mythologies by admitting that meritocracy is not colour blind. Sarkozy is the first French president to have included women of colour – Rachida Dati, Fadéla Amara and Rama Yade – in his government, and not only in the usual remit of ministries of equality, youth or integration. He has also committed to institutionalizing diversity policies, in employment practices, for example, by establishing a committee to examine means to alter the French constitution towards that end. Nevertheless, as Badiou has argued, Sarkozy also governs through 'negative affect', that is, through the restless specification of 'fear of foreigners, of workers, of the people, of youngsters from the *banlieues*, Muslims, black Africans'; 2009: 9. The Cette France Là collective of activists and researchers, established in 2008 to provide 'counter-expertise' to the politicization of immigration during the Sarkozy presidency, organizes this litany of fear in terms of the move towards 'phobic democracy' in France (2009: 418). The neoliberal project, they argue, works towards instituting entrepreneurial self-governance through an assault on the idea of social welfare, focusing on projecting a good society cohered through individualized self-esteem and collective prosperity. Whereas previous phases targeted trade unions, civil servants and the unemployed, phobic democracy involves an ambivalent focus on immigrants: 'While being brandished as living proof of an openness to the world, reconciling economic pragmatism with anti-discrimination activism, they are also stigmatized as the incarnation of abusive behaviour that, by being a burden on the public purse, are responsible for turning the host nation against globalization' (ibid.).

This ambivalence towards migrants, as well as towards non-white citizens more generally, can be made sense of in terms of the role envisaged for cultural diversity under neoliberalism.

Diversity politics, and the politics of diversity The contemporary emphasis on culture as the cohering force of integration, and the concomitant valorization of diversity, may initially appear contradictory.

In general terms, diversity has become what Yudhishthir Raj Isar terms a 'normative meta-narrative' widely deployed 'with a view to supporting the 'right to be different' of many different categories of individuals/groups placed in some ways outside dominant social and cultural norms, hence including disabled people, gays and lesbians, women, as well as the poor and the elderly' (2006: 373). That this normative and inclusive sense of diversity has deep affinities with the 'new spirit of capitalism' (Boltanski and Chiapello 2005) is widely recognized.[24] However, our primary concern here is the fact that diversity is predominantly used as a euphemism for racial and ethnic difference (Ahmed et al. 2006). Diversity provides an upgraded discourse and policy framework for the problem of difference, after multiculturalism. As Ahmed (2008) notes, multiculturalism, formerly a happy object, has come to be a source of social anxiety which can only be happy again if recalibrated around integration. Diversity has come to increasingly 'triangulate' this unhappy relationship, yet, like multiculturalism, it is discursively unstable, flitting between descriptions of social fact, institutional desire and subjective identities. To structure this discussion, we need to contingently distinguish between *diversity politics* and the *politics of diversity*. Diversity politics, according to Davina Cooper (2004: 5), must be seen as the product of the interlacing of a range of political and analytical projects:

> [It] is a broad, discursive space that emerged out of the very particular social, cultural and political conditions of the 1980s and 1990s – namely, the dismantling of the Soviet Union and of the communist regimes of eastern Europe, the upsurge of neo-liberal ideology, the backlash against radical feminism, the expansion of lesbian and gay politics, including the birth of Queer, and the struggles around multiculturalism and anti-racism. Intellectually, diversity politics sits at the confluence of several currents that include liberalism, communitarianism, poststructuralism, post-Marxism, post-colonialism and queer. In the twenty-first century, the politics of diversity continue to exert a powerful influence on progressive and radical thinking in the West. (Ibid.: 5)

This broad space of diversity politics, while porous and shifting, coalesces around some key critical and political concerns. Diversity politics eschews liberal notions of tolerance, and resituates minority identities and practices in the public sphere independent of the contingencies of benevolent recognition. Radical strands of diversity

politics are informed by critiques of patriarchy, racialization, heteronormativity and ablism, and in working for social justice, insist on
the structuring influence of power geometries of class, gender and
ethno-racial categorization. These aspects of diversity politics are
crucial, Cooper argues, as what she terms 'thin and hesitant processes
of differentiation' lead to confusion over what registers as diversity
in this broad discursive space. Diversity politics regards two kinds of
diversity as problematic: power imbalances and practices considered
as harmful. It is useful to consider these two problems in terms of the
elaboration of the argument concerning post-racialism. The problem
of power in diversity politics maps on to the critique of culturalism in
Chapter 2, as it involves the 'collective self-interpellation of seemingly
powerful groups through discourses of vulnerability' (ibid.: 6) – for
example, conservative religious groups, far-right movements, smokers
and increasingly a spoken-for 'white majority' apparently left behind
by multiculturalism. Excluding anti-racism from multiculturalism has
led to the translation of affective unease into a politics of vulnerability.
The neat imaginary of more or less equal communities living side
by side structures a backlash, in which the gradual disempowerment
of communities in the market state can be explained through the
conventional focus on favouritism and multicultural clientelism. It
is the collapse of even thin and hesitant processes of differentiation
which underpins the varying claims of reverse racism, victimhood
and cultural neglect that are now scattered across the terrain of
post-multiculturalism.

As a consequence, diversity politics must engage with claims of
marginalized difference through a consideration of material, political
and symbolic relations of dominance, but also through an ethical
critique of 'legitimately different ways of being' (Weeks 1995: 11,
in Cooper 2004: 7). This arises because, as Chapter 3 shows, a key
threat to diversity politics is the liberal obsession with the distinctive practices of minorities. By locating cultural harm hermetically,
and outside of the power geometries of patriarchy, race and class,
diversity politics is skewed towards the 'problem' of minority culture and away from a structural and intersectional critique of the
problem of social (il)legitimacy (Cooper 2004: 191–3). The central
problematic of diversity politics, in Cooper's analysis, is not the
valorization of difference but establishing the stratified relations of
differences to social legitimacy and individual possibility, and to a
complex understanding of freedom composed of three dimensions

that overlap and unsettle each other. First, diversity politics values a broadly liberal emphasis on freedom from oppression, which would, in the example of the problem of the headscarf, emphasize the need to struggle for meaningful agency against the state, the community and the family. Leaving aside the racializing assemblages within which headscarves are made to mean, this idealized commitment to negative freedom cannot account for, and is rarely interested in, the other vectors of freedom that Cooper elucidates. The second positive freedom, i.e. an attention to asymmetrical structures and relations of power, privilege, advantage and ethno-cultural capital, has a tense and intensely contested relationship with negative freedom. Nevertheless, this tension is absent, for example, in the logic of a 'lexical ordering of headscarf first, discrimination second' defended by Christian Joppke (2009) in his discussion of French state practice. In other words, if the focus is less on the 'affront' of the headscarf and instead on the putative liberation of the irrational subject, it is simply not clear what form her freedom is meant to take while this lexical ordering is unfolded. Thirdly, freedom is also a form of practice, and such practices

> may include transgressions; they may also include expressions of self-discipline and mastery. While the latter entails forms of conduct, they are principally concerned with an inner sense of self: specifically, the ways in which, through our actions, including through processes of denial and giving ourselves to a cause, community or faith, we perceive ourselves as free. (Cooper 2004: 25)

The idea of freedom as practice, and as a subjective understanding of freedom given form through practices always already understood, in the liberal hegemony, as unfree, recalls the problematic of the doll's house – of race as a failure of will – discussed in Chapter 3. The ways in which liberal procedures disavow the political process of *making* something problematic is discussed by Cooper, in calling for attention to 'the institutionalized, systemic processes through which differences arise and are made to speak' (ibid.: 194). The processes through which differences are made speak are pivotal in appending an idea of the 'politics of diversity' to Cooper's lucid framework. The 'politics of diversity' is a blunt distinction intended to focus the ways in which diversity provides a mode of talking about difference, and of managing difference, while avoiding the intersectional political demands of diversity politics. In societies where multiculturalism has failed, but multiculture lives, diversity provides a gently unifying, cost-free form of political commitment attuned to the mediated imaginaries of consumer societies. Images and celebrations of 'diversity' are congruent with the 'aesthetic cosmopolitanism' (Urry 2003) of globalized consumerism which sources and refracts images and symbols of diversity with eager promiscuity, and which is increasingly important in shaping the habitus of the nation as a site for investment flows under informational capitalism. In Australia, for example, the Howard government was instrumental both in dismantling state investment in multicultural community structures and diminishing it as a 'national narrative'. Concomitantly, as Fleras demonstrates, a governmental theme of 'productive diversity' – 'All Australians benefit from the social and economic dividends of a productive diversity' – became central to the 'marketing of multicultural differences and an orderly multicultural governance [...] as core assets to enhance Australia's economic advantage in a global market economy' (2009: 121).

This cost-free sense is made possible only by the anti-racialist turn; diversity unites us, both in our diversity, and in the positive energy of being for diversity, as opposed to the surly negativism of being against racism. The 2006/07 European youth campaign referenced at the start of Chapter 2 illustrates some of the orthodox positions that being for diversity generates: 'The celebration of diversity, as an added value, is crucial today in a Europe which is a diverse continent. Learning more about each other is an enriching experience that usually leads someone to a greater sensitivity and understanding of others. That is why diversity is essential to ensure Europe's cohesion' (EYF 2006). The *politics of diversity* – the institutional and broadly managerial deployment of diversity as a dimension of integration governance – contaminates the space of diversity politics. It recognizes an array of differences in society, but in knitting them into a tableau of plurality it robs difference of its critical significance. Diversity is given as a state of harmony, yet this disguises how 'diversity is the managerial view of the field of differences to be harmonized, controlled and made to fit into a coherent (i.e. national) whole by the (nation) state' (Ang and St Louis 2005: 96).

In being deployed as its successor, the turn to diversity effects a second order depoliticization of multiculturalism.[25] Multiculturalism was a means of redirecting action against racism away from an analysis of structures of domination and exclusion grounded in capitalism and imperialism. Nevertheless, the term itself, for all its indeterminacy and co-option, cannot be fully stripped of political significance, or constrained to the limited dimensions of the political that culturalist approaches reproduce. Shohat and Stam (2003: 8) argue that 'the *multi* in multiculturalism brings with it the idea of a constitutive heterogeneity' which is politically useful, but the obverse of this is equally so; the 'multi' presupposes a 'mono', and is always in conflict, at some level, with the imaginary of – most – nations. Thus it can never be fully dissociated from histories of antagonism. After multiculturalism, the politics of diversity replicates its ontological reductionism while closing off this faded field of ideological contest. Diversity works to conceal and neutralize the ideas and 'histories of antagonism and struggle' central to shaping the critical space of diversity politics (Ahmed and Swan 2006: 96). These histories are doubly lost when diversity is positioned as a response to the now orthodox critique of multiculturalism's group reification and lack of attention to hetereogeneity and 'internal' power relations. As a fluid reshaping of transcendental homogeneity, as a declaration of *who we are now*, the generative histories of 'diversity', striated with occluded patterns of inequality and oppression, are lost.

While this recoding is international, it is perhaps most pronounced in the UK after the Cantle Report. Within the discourse of community cohesion, shifting elucidations of Britishness were elaborated as ways of insisting on forms of civic nationalism while recognizing the diversity of the population (McGhee 2008; Fekete 2009; Pitcher 2009). Whether related to cohesion or civic assimilationism, the importance of Britishness is its appeal to multiculturalism as a constituent feature of shared life, but also one that embodies certain values that represent the limits of good diversity (Pitcher 2009). After the London bombings of 2005, multiculturalism was held both to be responsible for the attacks, by creating the conditions for the cultivation of extremism, but also to be under attack, given that the victims had diverse backgrounds and identities. Writing in the *Guardian* in the immediate aftermath of the attacks, David Davis, then shadow Home Secretary, illustrates broad political agreement on the importance of Britishness as a rubric for unity in diversity:

Britain has pursued a policy of multiculturalism, allowing people of different cultures to settle without expecting them to integrate into society [...] Often the authorities have seemed more concerned with encouraging distinctive identities than with promoting common values of nationhood [...] Britain has a proud history of tolerance towards people of different views, faiths and backgrounds. But we should not flinch from demanding the same tolerance and respect for the British way of life. (2005)

Consequently, government authorities and New Labour think tanks searched for ways of replacing the outmoded and discredited discourse of multiculturalism with modes of recognizing difference that could be reconciled with the new focus on cohesion. A central influence on this tank-thinking was the work of David Putnam (2000) on diversity and 'bonding' and 'bridging' capital, a framework, as Crowley and Hickman argue, that in the British context peddles a nostalgia for the post-war era while privileging 'the notion that multiculturalism is the obstacle to re-achieving the social cohesion of a diversified modern world' (2008: 1222–32). Putnam's capacious concepts have become particular forms of widely recited truths. They were influential in the development of forms of 'reflexive multiculturalism' within the Commission on Integration and Community Cohesion (CICC), set up after the 7/7 attacks. Derek McGhee details how the CICC shifted its focus towards multicultural operations on the local level (2008: 98–100). This change in emphasis involved advocating moving away from single group support to initiatives that encouraged communities to be less 'insular' and more 'outward-facing', and to develop the cross-community 'bridging capital' necessary for 'shared futures' and 'community cohesion' (ibid.: 101–4). In the abstract engineering of future communities bowling together, a repudiation of the essentialism of town-hall multiculturalism makes space for the unguent of fluid identities building bridges, discovering new features and experiences in common and acting as points of reference and mediation in 'single group conflicts' (ibid.). At the same time, this fresh articulation of the cohering properties of diversity was folded into an increasingly authoritarian understanding of Britishness as involving a 'duty to integrate' into shared values (Pitcher 2009). In Tony Blair's vision, diversity within Britain may constitute a threat to cohesion unless it is subsumed to a civic integration model defined through a nationalist horizon of good and bad diversity: 'Integration is not about culture or lifestyle. It is about values. It is about integrating at the point of shared, common unifying British values. It isn't about what defines us as a people, but as citizens, the rights and duties that go with being a member of our society' (2006, quoted in McGhee 2008: 133).

Diversity does the work of transforming the divisive differences of multiculturalism into a new incorporative structure, and this has a number of important political implications in terms of Cooper's vision of diversity politics as a space of critical possibility. There is something important in government agencies promoting multiple and fluid identities, as in the case of the CICC. In challenging the 'spectre of incommensurability' (Bernstein 2010) of town-hall multiculturalism, it theoretically opens up forms of freedom from oppressive collectivities. Yet it does so without recognizing how people have long struggled to carve out these spaces and possibilities themselves, and in so doing dehistoricizes multiculturalism as nothing more than misplaced but well-meaning block thinking, a regrettable concession to minority demands. The prime elision of second-order depoliticization is a failure to acknowledge how depoliticization was inherent to multiculturalism itself. In acknowledging how multiculturalism refused diversity politics, this type of analysis calls on a long-established anti-racist critique – concerned with the denial of the political reality of racism – in order to argue that the prime legacy of culturalism is an outmoded allegiance to group politics. In foregrounding diversity as the biographical dimensions of the individual, diversity as 'bridging capital' is paradoxically individualized. The diverse subject cultivates the competences necessary to live with difference understood as a series of variegated characteristics, but not as relations of power, and thus becomes elemental to the privatization of race.

In the post-7/7 environment the understanding of diversity as a dimension of integration means that any communal expression or political mobilization becomes vulnerable to being understood as a further expression of 'insularity' and weak citizenship. Communities, as Breda Gray argues, are enlisted by governments to take charge of problems that 'cannot be entirely left to individuals' (2006: 123). However, communities that are portrayed as 'unfree' increasingly have their freedom to organize under the rubric of diversity curtailed. Thus diversity, in integration politics, acts on the individual as a counterbalance to the dangers of community. This is the most specific line of contamination of diversity politics by the politics of diversity. The language of freedom as practice has been inhabited by diversity as a form of governmentality, nudging conduct and self-management towards desired effects. The intensive state attention paid to frameworks for managing and disciplining lived diversity has resulted in the recent application of the insights of governmentality (Rose 1999) to British multicultural politics, in ways that nevertheless refuse any assumption about the 'success' of these approaches (McGhee 2008; Pitcher 2009; Fortier 2010).

Anne-Marie Fortier, most recently, has analysed how the governmental attention to 'bridge-building' and 'meaningful interaction' positions diversity as an asset but also a threat. In so doing, difference – 'in terms of the relational, material, symbolic and cultural variations and power relations that position people and groups differentially in terms of access to, and use of resources' (2010: 27) – is disqualified politically. Diversity is a rationality of integration; it ceases to be a divisive force when it is good, and anchored in shared values, and refrains from being the bad diversity that appears in the 'bonding' terms now proscribed. Good diversity, in effect, racializes the acceptable limits of adversarial politics; to criticize British foreign policy while being identified as a British Muslim, for example, is to be poorly integrated rather than critically engaged. Fortier draws attention to the forms of 'active citizenship' and 'meaningful interaction' delineated in the most recent cohesion document, the 2009 British Department for Communities and Local Government (DCLG) *Guidance on Meaningful Interaction: How encouraging positive relationships between people can help build community cohesion*. The document stresses how meaningful interaction and feeling comfortable in public are important ways of addressing the problem of 'parallel lives'. It follows from this that political antagonism is not conducive to good feelings, and thus to cohesion:

> For example, 'civic participation' such as 'taking part in a public meeting, rally, public demonstration or protest, or signing a petition' [… is] negatively associated with community cohesion. Similarly, 'tackling racism' is characterised as a 'negative activity' that would discourage people from joining and that could ultimately create new divisions. (Fortier 2010: 27)

Conclusion: the burka as bad diversity and governmental event

Far from constituting a sticky problem to be transcended in a neoliberal era, culture has become a key terrain for governmentality, control and legitimization. As Charles Hale notes, under neoliberalism the stress placed on culture within a framework that emphasizes 'the development of civil society and social capital [...] appears highly counterintuitive' (2005: 12). In his ethnographic study of cultural activism in Guatemala, Nicaragua and Honduras, Hale shows how state initiatives – what he terms 'neoliberal multiculturalism' – based on defining cultural groups and calibrating their cultural rights have become a key mode of political regulation, including the delegitimization of those groups 'who do not fit' the sanctioned shape of relations of 'intercultural equality'. Latin American elites that have long and often violently opposed cultural rights for indigenous minorities have now become 'reluctant arbiters of rights grounded in cultural difference. In so doing, cultural rights, when carefully delimited, not only pose little challenge to the forward march of the neoliberal project but also induce the bearers of these rights to join in the march' (ibid.: 13). The state cannot control or shape the meanings generated in mobilizing around struggles for recognition; however, 'the great efficacy of neoliberal multiculturalism resides in powerful actors' ability to restructure the arena of political contention, driving a wedge between cultural rights and the assertion of the control necessary over resources necessary for those rights to be realized' (ibid.).

In a discussion of US cultural politics, George Yúdice (2003) claims that, since the civil rights struggle, 'identities' have been 'incorporated into a range of governmental (in the Foucauldian sense) mechanisms' (ibid.: 48). These identities are performative and serve a particular function, not only for their performers, but more importantly for the 'state institutions and media and market projections that shape, respectively, clients and consumers' (ibid.). Given this, Yúdice claims that we need to understand culture as expedient. Culture 'has no "in itself": it is a resource for politics' (ibid.: 23). It has become the lens through which problems of community are read and prescribed, so that community – be it local, ethno-racial or national – is 'caught in a circular, tautological reasoning' where culture is 'invoked to solve problems that previously were the province of economics and politics' (ibid.). Yúdice proposes that *'cultural power'* (ibid., italics in the original) is added today to the biopower[26] implicit in governmentality because anthropological understandings of groups as cultural power have become so widespread. Culture operates through the construction of a 'fantasy structure' (ibid.: 49) within which subjects are invited to imagine and perform their action and within which their moral and political stance can be immediately read. Within this space of appearance, all marginalized groups are equivalent to each other and can be 'visibly represented as parallel forms of identity' (Warner 1993: xix, cited in Yúdice 2003: 50).

The focus of the French government on the negative effect of the burka can be read in these terms.[27] The decision, in 2010, to activate the symbolic politics of the ban through an accelerated parliamentary process must be understood in the context of the *grand débat sur l'identité nationale* conducted by Sarkozy and Éric Besson, minister for immigration and national identity, from 2 November 2009 to 2 February 2010. Minorities, as we have argued, are mobilized to mediate the uncertainties of social life (see also Appadurai 2006). What is striking is that the Great Debate hid this mediation in plain sight. Organized through a moderated website and convened through 350 town-hall meetings, the debate was structured by two questions: 'What does it mean to be French today? What has immigration contributed to France?' For Besson, the debate was precisely about reanimating a national identity under pressure from immigration, Europeanization and 'accelerated globalization'. Following the poor performance of the UMP (Union pour un mouvement populaire) in regional elections in March, Sarkozy argued that the debate had *concluded* in the need for a burka ban. This is familiar terrain; Mabel Berezin has illustrated how Sarkozy, first as interior minister in the government of Jacques Chirac, and then as presidential candidate, continued the established centrist technique of separating the message of the Front national from the messenger, appropriating not only the 'issues' of national identity, (immigrant) crime and opposition to Turkish EU membership, but more fundamentally the mobilizing possibilities of national identity in a country with such 'a tight fit between nation and state – culture and institutions' (2009: 245–8). The burka, as an object of governmental intervention in national identity, is suitably elaborate: it extends the debates concerning the headscarf in 2003/04, and the invitation to mediate the resistant boundaries of the nation through the tropes of secular neutrality and gender after the end of history. At the level of form, the shift from national debate to symbolic action indicates the increased importance of the mediated integration events discussed in the previous chapter.

In an article on the 2004 headscarf law, Emmanuel Terray locates a focal impetus for the 'hysteria' of the headscarf in public and political anxiety concerning socio-economic exclusion – 'the breakdown of integration' – and gender inequality, 'the slowdown and stagnation of any equalization of the sexes', and the convergence of these anxieties on the bodies of the young women of the dis-integrated, discontented *banlieues*. Coming as a 'brutal affront to national *amour-propre*', and 'powerless before problems that it has not the energy to master, its narcissism wounded, its self-image under assault: confronted with such difficulties, the hysterical community will substitute a fictive problem that can be solved purely in terms of discourse and symbols' (2004). Collective hysteria cannot result in collective psychological repression, but proceeds by 'doffing one's cap in passing', acknowledging and then bracketing the original problem and turning back to effective thinking upon the fictive substitute. The burka spectacle, emerging from a staged debate, doffs its cap and even straightens its tie. As an act of cultural governmentality, the burka ban specifies bad diversity as a problem of national integra-tion, and as an affront to a settled national identity. The attempt to respond to diffuse socio-political anxieties in cultural terms will not stifle the accumulating discontent with 'the degrading realities of France's survivalist economy', and from the ideological refusal to countenance the experience of racism in policing, public and private employment and the distribution of urban resources (de Beer 2010). Symbolic mobilization has become integral to neoliberal governance through a repressive twist in Yúdice's idea of culture as an expedient for socio-political and economic amelioration. Yet the elevation of culture as problem from the episteme of culture as resource, despite increasingly elaborate strategies, cannot but also draw attention to its increasingly transparent status as fictive substitute.

The casting of veiled Muslim women in the role of the subjugated female pushes familiar orientalist buttons. However, it is also com-plicit in the image of the 'good' autonomous subject versus the 'bad' dependent one mediated in neoliberal formations. This reworking of citizenship can be claimed as a national virtue; in particular, the unveiled, emancipated woman can be claimed as exemplary of a particular, national 'way of doing things'. Hence, in backing the ban on the burka in France, Sarkozy could claim: 'We cannot accept to have in our country women who are prisoners behind netting, cut off from all social life, deprived of identity. *That is not the idea that the French republic has of women's dignity*' (emphasis added).[28] Such national claims over particular notions of female emancipation, as the next chapter takes up in greater detail, both ignore the persistence of gender inequality across all societies and turn the struggles of the women's movement into something already enshrined in a particular, in this case French, culture. It thus rewrites the history of feminism and discounts the possibility that veiled Muslim women could identify both as religious and as feminist, and argues for emancipation being lived in any way other than that deemed 'correct' by dominant Western norms. Paradoxically, then, freedom and autonomy are not goals which the autonomous subject reaches alone, but can only be granted through alignment with a particular culture which portrays itself as encapsulating a promise of freedom and autonomy.

The general culturalization of politics detailed by Yúdice implies that 'choice' is arranged on a limited palette of options. The choice to veil is rarely regarded as a *real* choice, because the dominant interpretation of choice, based on particular visions of what a free woman looks like, does not include that possibility. The effective result of precluding other, minoritarian and marginalized, modes of expressing autonomy is that these voices are drowned out by the loud certainty with which liberal feminism is proclaimed a national value. Therefore, it is unsurprising that of the 200 testimonies heard by a French parliamentary commission established to examine the ban on the burka in 2009, only one contributor was a woman wearing the face veil.[29] This silencing has also been violently enacted. Marwa el-Sherbini, an Egyptian woman living in Germany, died in July 2009 after being stabbed eighteen times in thirty seconds by a twenty-eight-year-old man, Axel W., in a court in Dresden in front of her husband and three-year-old son.[30] Perhaps as a consequence of the shock and outrage the case caused in Egypt and among many in Germany, little attention was paid to the stance originally taken by el-Sherbini. She took her murderer to court for insulting her for wearing the hijab, and associating her choice to wear it with 'Islamism' and terrorism. In essence, el-Sherbini was exercising her right, as a resident of Germany, for her choice to wear the hijab to be protected. However, as Beverly Weber argues:

> Media coverage a year after el-Sherbini's death continues to portray her almost exclusively as a victim. The focus has been on an emerging acknowledgment of Islamophobia, el-Sherbini's husband, the desire of el-Sherbini's family to see the presiding judge and the intervening policeman prosecuted, newly implemented security measures in response to el-Sherbini's murder, and the appropriation of el-Sherbini's death for 'anti-West' protests (often state sponsored) in Iran and Egypt. When the focus does shift to el-Sherbini herself,

it is often to highlight her role as wife and mother, rather than the contribution she made by taking advantage of the German legal system to challenge Islamophobic speech. Presumptions made about Muslim women as victims who need to be spoken for and protected have contributed to this problem. El-Sherbini becomes either a 'special case' because she was well-educated, spoke German well, and was well-integrated; or her education and action against racism disappears entirely from the coverage. But el-Sherbini, like other Muslim women in Germany today, was more than a victim of violence. She was also a courageous woman who drew on her everyday experiences in active democratic participation and in order to combat hate speech. (2010)

This courage is effaced not only when 'debates' on the hijab and the burka create an opposition between two equal sides, the West and Islam, but when imaginaries of good and bad diversity cannot accommodate the 'contradictions' of her experience, and actions. It scarcely needs reiterating that the comparison drawn by Alice Schwarzer, in Germany, between the veil and the yellow star which the Nazis forced Jews to wear violently effaces these lives and experiences (see Chapter 3). Yet such scarcely credible soundbites further serve to illustrate how identity politics is bivalent, practised both by those 'construed as minorities' (Yúdice 2003: 48) and by the state and its champions. The resulting equation is familiar; the ethno-national variant of culture promoted by the state is legitimate and neutral, while the assertion of minoritarian cultural difference, on the contrary, has no place in the public sphere. This continues to present 'minorities' with an equally familiar double bind, as compliant integration into a prescribed national 'way of doing things' depends on being recognized as integrating, and this is a fragile basis on which to ensure equality.

SIX

On one more condition: the politics of integration today

Introduction

There is a consensus in Europe that integration is an issue, and that it is of pressing importance to the now and future nation-state. It is also a question of perspective. It is a question of freedom of speech, as Houria Bouteldja, prosecuted for a pun, knows well. It is a question of democratic values, as Asmaa Abdol-Hamid, a candidate for the Red–Green alliance in the 2007 Danish election, realizes, having been declared 'brainwashed' by the Danish People's Party, and asked not to stand by others on the 'left' because she wears a hijab (Andreassen 2010; Wheeler 2008). It is a question of the glue of shared history, as Rachid Bouchareb understands, having been faced with UMP-backed protesters at the 2010 Cannes festival screening of his film *Hors la loi*, who accused him of 'rewriting history from a militant and partisan standpoint' for dedicating six celluloid minutes to the Sétif massacre of up to 45,000 Algerians by French colonialists in 1945.[1] It is a question of undoing the fractious legacies of multiculturalism, a task understood by the Belgian parliament, which undertook to ban the burka in 2010 before a more rational set of multicultural fractures threw the federal system into crisis. It is a question of tradition, as the migrants subject to door-to-door searches in Coccaglio's 2009 'White Christmas' operation appreciate too well (Hooper 2009). In the introduction we quoted David Goldberg's idea that 'Europe begins to exemplify what happens when no category is available to name a set of experiences that are linked in their production [...] to racial arrangements and engagements' (2009: 154). In the previous chapters we have argued why experiences such as these need to be linked to racial arrangements, and why the appeals to laundered and coded problems of wrong culture, unfreedom and bad diversity still require this more categorical naming.

These problems have been specified as problems of integration; too little of it, and too many people who refuse to integrate. In the last decade, the problem of integration has been diagnosed as one of compatibility with Western societies and democracies. Integration is not a novel problematic; it is arguably the foundational question in modern sociology, and the shape-shifting problematic of the nation-state (Richmond 1984). In the post-war era of labour migration and post-colonial flow, it has been the site of fantasies of reversal. Since the 1970s, particularly in the social aftermath of economic restructuring, it has become a vexed question of national identity, and of shifting allegiances to various 'models' of immigrant integration, predicated on various status pathways, welfare arrangements and modes of cultural management. In an era of globalization, intensified mobility, European integration and lives connected across interlocking scapes of interdependence (Appadurai 1996), it took on a hint of pastness also, with influential theses detecting that post-national citizenship depended less on membership of the political community than on embeddedness in place under an extraterritorial rights regime (Soysal 1994). And, at least in the conventional narrative, after the death of multiculturalism the need to guarantee cohesion, specify and inculcate core values and cultivate new kinds of citizens has moved integration to the centre of political consciousness and state action.

Multiculturalism has flecked these pages and its osmotic properties are no closer to being contained. Even in contexts where it did actually mean something, its pathologies are still far from agreed. Whatever it was, it was abandoned loudly and, through circuits of reflex-ivity, repeatedly after 9/11. Though it is clear that the production of migrants as 'social enemies' – and the elaboration of socio-economic, securitarian and identitarian problems – was well advanced before this convenient threshold (Tsoukala 2005), this has not prevented an *era of integration* taking shape. Yet this era remains a multicultural era, both in the descriptive sense, and in the prescriptive sense of integration being shaped along a spectrum from semi-real to entirely fictitious rejections of a failed experiment, and remaining politically defined and ontologically beholden to them. Multiculturalism, after it ceased to have any semblance of programmatic meaning or cred-ibility as a social vision, however inchoate, has been important as a repository of social unhappiness, things we don't want. This is the sense of Elliot and Lemert's argument, quoted in the epigraph to Chapter 1, that the very idea of multiculturalism 'disturbs out of all proportion to what in fact it may be' (2006: 137). It is not just that, in rarefied normative conditions, multiculturalism is contentious, or that it provides, in the post-racial era, populist code for scapegoating racialized minorities as threats to social order. It is that in societies of increasing precariousness it radiates a tremulous sense of uncertainty, of lack of control. It allows those blurred cartographies of neoliberal revolution and globalized vulnerabilities to be mapped on the bodies and subjectivities of those blamed and associated, whatever their biographies, with the upheavals that now make the imagined home of the nation that bit less homely. In the absence of transformative political visions and projects, taming it offers a semblance of control, the possibility to reorder society *on our own terms*, to compensate sovereignties and the dramatic arc of political resolution on an overdetermined, culturalist terrain imagined to be the only one on which solidarity, freedom and collective purpose is possible. For political identities and projects recovering from postmodernism, or rationalizing their full and complicit acceptance of the terms of neoliberal capitalism, the discursive space of multiculturalism has provided a space of animation, the domestic pleasures of a suitable enemy, the frisson of sectoral rescue missions in intersectional lives, and the fiction that 'running around on the rugby field of rational controversy will deliver a rational universe' (MacCabe 2005). A discussion of this contemporary politics of 'integrationism' (Kundnani 2007), understood not as a break with multiculturalism but as its most significant contemporary iteration, provides the structure for a series of conclusions to the book.

In the preceding analysis, we have already encountered a range of integration discourses, frequently shaped through hybrid assemblages of cultural racism, 'assertive' liberalism and the subjectifications of neoliberal rationality. In their elaboration, there is no shortage of evidence of *dis*-integration, and stirring invocations of common cultures, lead values and liberal lifeworlds. Yet it is rare to encounter political visions of migration societies that do not hinge on the problem of compatibility, or that have a real dialogical commitment, or reflexive relation to power, beyond the unspeak of a 'two-way process'. The certainties of the post-racial terrain, the patterning of a malleable paradigm of global war to local diversities, and the political abolition of structural understanding have led to the remarkably resilient topos of a 'clash of civilizations' within integration discourses (translated from its now somewhat embarrassing origins to provide a more flexible framework of legitimized aversions). In a study of integration discourses across France, the Netherlands, Norway, Germany and

Austria, an international team of researchers at the Institute of Race Relations found significant convergence between dominant public discourses. The research also involved those integrants whose experience of being integrated is so rarely featured, never mind accounted for, in integration politics. In stark contrast to literal, liberal democratic accounts of the difference between yesterday's assimilation and the integration of today, they characterized public debates as equating integration with cultural homogeneity, as being predicated on the implicit superiority of 'western morals', as being focused through an emphasis on national identity and 'lead values', as being conducted in religio-cultural rather than socio-economic terms, and as having been heavily inflected by the securitarian concerns of the 'war on terror' (Fekete 2008: 8–23).

This research identifies how the parameters and tone of integration debates pose a significant barrier to integration. We must also recall, from Chapter 4, how integration debates and events are never just about the issues at hand. In his analysis of debates as rituals, Ghassan Hage suggests that the categorical questions proposed for debate – should we 'scrap' multiculturalism for assimilation? – are mystifications desired by dominant social groups who still imagine themselves as the sole architects of the nation and of national futures. Worrying about migrants who do not integrate, or integrate enough, may in fact be a fear of real integration. The desire for 'more integration' translates as a desire 'for more supervised integration' – that is, 'rather than integration, it is more like an instrumental insertion which positions the White Australian subject, yet again, in the role of the great supervisor of integration' (1998: 239). Contemporary integration politics in Europe is similarly fixated on this role, but the conjunctural addition of the great supervisor of civilization has allowed for the categorical questions to be endlessly multiplied. This necessitates opening out some further dimensions of integration talk as a governmental event.

In research with integration officials in the Swedish and Danish municipalities joined by the Øresund bridge, Kirsten Hvenegård-Lassen (2005) examined the order of integration and those unintegrated people and things 'deemed to be outside the insider's order of things'. Who is the 'integrant', and when are they integrated? Discussing integration, for her respondents, was inseparable from the articulation of an 'impossible and ideal notion of the good society' (ibid.: 8). There is arguably a wider truth to this reflex. 'Effective thinking upon an illusory object' (Balibar and Wallerstein 1991) is still susceptible to actual thinking. The repetitive location of anomie and globalized vulnerabilities in the relation between the integrant and society is too limited, it bleeds into thinking about self and society. In many contexts, for example, the introduction of citizenship tests was unsettled by activists asking parliamentarians to complete them, or speculating on proportions of the established citizenry who would have the requisite knowledge. Would I pass? Am I integrated? If that's a ghetto what's that gated community? Do I really have to educate a political refugee about rights and freedoms? What happens when the burkas run out?

But the Danish officials reflected not only on a general state of integration, but also on how they evaluate the integrants' progress. From their perspective, for the integrants to be integrated is to be happy as a normatively required state, a state that perforce expels unhappiness from Danish society or at least restricts it to the soul and body of the integrant. It produces an idea of society that would not be replicated if the research conversation were held otherwise (Hvenegård-Lassen 2005: 7–8). In other words, integration discourse may inflect a wider commentary on society, but both institutionally and imaginatively it is construed as a different discursive domain when it comes to the subjects of integration. This is why the critical possibilities of reversing even the most blatant double standards of integrationism are limited. It is always worth ventilating the hypocrisy of the politics of freedom; that, for example, while the Danish People's Party champions gay rights in Denmark, it formed an alliance in the European Parliament in 2009 with, among others, the Italian Lega Nord, whose deputies have called for 'an ethnic cleansing of faggots'.[2] Yet the exposure of hypocrisy breaks down on the right to unhappiness. These are recited truths, and in the structure of fantasy, they are meant to apply differently to different people. In part this relates to the representational strategies of populism discussed in Chapter 3, but not solely.

Jodi Dean's (2009) reading of Hardt and Negri's (2000) account of the shift from disciplinary society to the society of control is suggestive here. The modern disciplinary society worked through the social institutions of the workplace, the school, the family and civil society to establish determining social norms. A range of developments – the neoliberal reconstitution of the terms of the social, the individualizing and 'de-socializing of people's biographies' (Elliot and

Lemert 2006: 5), political mobilization through identity politics – lead Dean to employ Žižek's idea of the 'decline of symbolic efficiency' to characterize a transition towards fundamental uncertainty, that 'there is no ultimate guarantor of meaning, no recognized authority that stops our questioning or assuages our doubts' (2009: 64). 'Societies of control', in this reading, depend both on the cultivation of imaginary ideals of individual fitness for life and the enjoyment of life, but also a transfer from the 'social state' to the modalities of the 'garrison state' (Giroux 2002). The penal mode of racial neoliberalism discussed in the previous chapter is a dimension of an increased disciplinary reliance on surveillance, data, policing and, according to Bauman, the publicity of punishment, 'where the awesome might and steely resolution of the rulers can be effectively displayed for public admiration' (2004: 54).

This is a compressed summary, but it helps identify the double drive in the fantasy of integration, as does this illustration. In February 2010, the British immigration minister, Phil Woolas, announced that migrants would be taught to queue properly and that questions on queuing could be included in citizenship tests. According to a report in the *Daily Mail*, 'surveys show that 91% of Britons object strongly to queue-jumping'. Arguing that queue-jumping was damaging social cohesion, Woolas pointed out that 'much tension in communities is caused by foreigners not understanding they must wait in line for services rather than barging to the front as may be the custom in their own culture'.[3] A finer satire on the culturalization of everything and the governmentality of unease is hard to imagine, yet the absurdity is purposeful. Queuing is an expression of the internalized discipline of social order and civil society, and in the fantasy structure of integration, it is threatened only by the kind of dis-integrated actions that can be made subject to technologies of control. Tension, as an affect, becomes a focus of external control, of action on actions, in a context where individuals must resolve tensions autonomously, as part of the larger project of outsourcing care of the social fabric to subjects guided towards responsibility and self-regulation.

The fantasy, however, is not the exquisite essentialism of barging as custom, nor merely the dissociation of in-queue-tension from such possible causal factors as diminished public provision, or the auto-mated, deskilled and layered service culture of 'Call Centre Britain' (Bracewell 2002). It is rather a question of the powers of display, that through technologies of control they can *become* disciplined. By being held up for discipline they hint that symbolic efficiency is still possible, that anxieties have a source and they can be addressed. Christian Joppke is right to point to the fact that integration initiatives in Europe look for compliance with values, not their internalization (2009). But in a mediated politics, internalization is almost beside the point; integrants must look as if they are internalizing them, and being compelled to do so. And in this regard integration really is a 'two-way' thing. The governmentality of queuing displays the technologies of control that migrants and suspicious populations are subject to, while functioning *as* display for the 'majority', as a compensatory order. As the last chapter discussed, this governmentality of display is not restricted to queuing. Where, as Gary Younge asks in relation to the British government's anti-terror strategy, 'will we find the perfect Muslim for monocultural Britain'?

> Somewhere out there is the Muslim that the British government seeks. Like all religious people he (the government is more likely to talk about Muslim women than to them) supports gay rights, racial equality, women's rights, tolerance and parliamentary democracy. He abhors the murder of innocent civilians without qualification – unless they are in Palestine, Afghanistan or Iraq. He wants to be treated as a regular British citizen – but not by the police, immigration or airport security. He raises his daughters to be assertive: they can wear whatever they want so long as it's not a headscarf. He believes in free speech and the right to cause offence but understands that he has neither the right to be offended nor to speak out. Whatever an extremist is, on any given day, he is not it. (2009)

Where, in other words, is the desired subject of display, the subject whose radical beliefs and practices threaten the values on which social cohesion is based and can be recouped? For the immoderates and queue-jumpers, of course, the process is one of shaping not desired values, but desired behaviours. As McGhee says in his evaluation of British anti-terror initiatives, the twin-track technologies of integration and security are dedicated to shaping 'docility, moderation [...] responsibility and obedience' (2008: 7). The integrant is the stranger, a category, after Simmel, that is never integrated but instead specified and positioned in ways that regenerate institutional practices and networks of affect. The particular cultural capital of 'the Muslim', as we argued in Chapter 1, is that the repertoire of strangeness allows for a dense lattice of regeneration and animation that coincides with but is not determined by or restricted to state practices.

In this concluding chapter, we argue that it is not possible to 'have a debate' about integration without unfolding the ways in which integration discourse, and integration frameworks, work to ensure different kinds of exclusion. Given the problems generated by 'models' of multiculturalism, first buoyed and then haunted by the 'specter of incommensurability' (Bernstein 2010), it is no surprise that emerging policy frameworks of integration are bound up with the problematic of compatibility. However, it is not compatibility for belonging which has superseded the problem of incommensurability, it is compatibility for dwelling and residing. In the next section, we examine how integration policy, for all the sound and fury, is bound up in a system of barriers to entry, dwelling, settlement and citizenship – that is, by the development of integration policy in a matrix of managed migration, securitization and civic stratification. Integration is profoundly a question of control and instrumental insertion, of managing flows of good and bad diversity, and of focusing on *compatibility* as the nexus of future social cohesion.

The rise of *domopolitics*

In an essay on the securitization of migration, Mark Maguire and Tanya Cassidy (2009) suggest that a biopolitical focus on security unsettles the defining centrality accorded to the state in discussions of integration. The state as a space of mobilities, traversed by good and bad diversity, requires managing the tensions between stimulating beneficial flows and stemming and displacing risky ones. Thus, the question 'revolves less around the power of the state and more around the ways in which biopolitics is connected to new articulations of "state" power, racialization and citizenship' (ibid.: 24). While we are not fully in agreement with their argument that the '"state" provides a simple mask that prevents a full engagement with biopolitics today' (ibid.), it provides a thoughtful point of entry to considering the shifting border practices, speeds and routeways of entry and conditions of stay, and continuums of security practice, that cannot be held together in a confident rubric of 'integration'. Integration is a concern that increasingly links questions and domains of security, migration, citizenship and the labour market in a process of choosing migrants for their utility, compatibility and autonomy.

While influential accounts of integration policies eschew the abstractions of national 'models', they are predominantly state-centred, drawing attention to the innovations of 'civic integrationism'. Joppke

(2007) gives a nuanced account of the development of modes of civic integrationism that, while steering towards what he terms 'repressive liberalism', are increasingly less nationally specific, and less amenable to location on the conventional scale of 'multiculturalism' to universalistic 'assimilationism' (ibid.: 1–3). The idea of civic integrationism is closely associated with the rejection of multiculturalism in the Netherlands and the shift to coercive measures in the service of cultivating 'Dutch norms and values'. However, such measures are quite widespread. Long-term residence in France, for example, is dependent on signing an integration contract, attending language lessons and satisfying a condition of *l'intégration républicaine*, defined as '*connaissance de la langue française et des principes qui régissent la République française*' (quoted in ibid.: 10). This was augmented in 2007 with a 'Welcome and Integration Contract' obliging immigrants to respect the 'laws and values' of France and take civics lessons (Koff and Duprez 2009).

In Denmark citizenship reform, migration restrictions and integration initiatives have been a priority since the 2001–06 Venstre and Konservative Folkepartei coalition came to power through dependence on the Dansk Folkepartei. Restrictions on marriage with non-EU citizens and on family reunification, points-based residency systems and citizenship tests were introduced in this administration, and in 2006 the government introduced a compulsory 'Declaration on integration and active residency in Danish society'.[4] The declaration must be signed as part of a citizenship application, and the preamble states that 'I will actively endeavour to ensure that I and any of my children and spouse/cohabitant who reside in Denmark will be integrated and will become active citizens in Danish society', after which six principles attest that the subject 'understands and accepts' the need to comply with democratic principles; to learn the language and about society; to be self-supporting; and to accept equality between men and women. In 2007 an explicit 'Danishness test' for prospective new citizens was introduced, and in 2010 a new bill of amendments to the Aliens Act was passed which introduced a new points system for permanent residence, including eight compulsory criteria – one of which is not to have been in receipt of social welfare for three years before the application – a second points category of 'active citizenship' and a third of 'supplementary conditions relevant to integration' (Ersbøll 2010). The official reasoning behind the amendments is to allow 'well-integrated foreigners' to accede more quickly to permanent status, but according to an assessment from the EU Democracy Observatory on Citizenship, the combination of conditions around social welfare, full-time employment and language proficiency is likely to work enormously against refugees – for whom seminal status-revoking provisions[5] were also included in the act – and unskilled workers. Furthermore, there is ambiguous interpretative latitude accorded to adjudicating those who 'do not prove good will to integrate' (ibid.).

For all this recent history, the reason why the Netherlands features centrally in these debates is because its rapid accumulation of laws and instruments has proved attractive to other European and Western governments (Fekete 2009). From 1994's Integration Policy, but more particularly in the Civic Integration of Newcomers Act in 1998 (which introduced obligatory Dutch language and sociocultural orientation programmes) and the direct replacement Civic Integration Act in 2006 (which extended a 'civic integration duty' – *inburgeringsplicht* – to all non-Dutch/EU residents between sixteen and sixty-five, including 'old-comers' and select groups of naturalized Dutch citizens), Dutch integration policy has been informed by convictions concerning the problem of cultural difference, the imperative of fashioning autonomous individuals through ameliorative culturalization, and an institutional/ideological redefinition of integration as a 'law and order affair' (Entzinger 2003: 9). The 2006 act privatized the responsibility for integration by outsourcing integration courses to the private sector and making migrants pay the costs (van Wichelen and De Leeuw 2011). Moreover, it linked the granting of a residence permit to passing the exam, thus explicitly linking the domain of migration policy to the domain of integration and incorporation.

Also operational from 2006 was the stipulation of a pre-integration test for foreigners *before* they go to the Netherlands as a prerequisite for a temporary residence permit. The test, which examines knowledge of language and of Dutch society, is also outsourced to private providers, who charge prospective migrants for an instruction video and a computerized test taken over the phone (ibid.). The provision for this test was made as part of the Naturalization Test introduced in the Dutch Citizenship Law 2000, which also reintroduced a previously rescinded obligation to renounce an existing citizenship, while also making the eventual receipt of citizenship more difficult (de Hart 2007). Not every non-EU foreigner is required to take this pre-arrival exam; Swiss, Australian, Canadian, Japanese, South Korean, EEC and New Zealand citizens are exempt, and not as a happy coincidence of abnormal levels of knowledge concerning Dutch society and language. According to the Dutch Justice Ministry these exemptions would not lead to 'undesirable immigration' or 'fundamental problems with integration in Dutch society' (ibid.).

This architecture of interlocking provisions cannot be abstracted from the 'full-throated culturalism' (Demmers and Mehendale 2010) of Dutch integration politics. A political culture in which the former immigration minister Rita Verdonk could propose to introduce 'integration badges' to be worn by *allochtonen* cannot be allowed to launder itself by palming off 'failed initiatives' as slightly loopy curiosities.[6] Instead they must be remembered as iterations of what is deemed possible on the terrain of (post-)race at a given conjuncture. For this reason, while agreeing with Christian Joppke's conclusion that 'integration [...] is a world apart from classic nation-building as cultural homogenization' (2007: 17), it is not possible, in our view, to argue that interpreting repressive liberalism 'in "nationalist" or "racist"' terms is really just the smell of yesteryear' (ibid.: 16). What we have contended in this book is that the smell of yesteryear is perfumed by a more complex set of racializing modalities, for if racism is a 'scavenger ideology' (Back and Solomos 1996: 220), it is adept at picking up scents. Joppke's argument emphasizes the changes in the wind; the deployment of illiberal means in the service of liberal goals has much to do with the 'heavy dose of economic instrumentalism' underpinning integration policies and politics (Joppke 2007: 16–17). This heavy dose is intensified in the recent Danish amendments. Yet Joppke's insight draws us back to the formations of racial neoliberalism, and Cassidy and Maguire's question about the agency of the state.

The variegated 'neo-assimilationist agendas' that now seek to protect social cohesion through demands for affirmations of identity and loyalty are integral to an involved spectrum of 'managed migration regimes' and processes of civic stratification (Kofman 2005). Differentiated access to civil, economic and social rights, as well as potential citizenship, is organized according to the gradated utility of migrant labour and concomitant modes of entry, employment and residence. As Kofman summarizes, 'immigration policies are directed towards selecting those who will be most advantageous to the economy, will fit into a pre-existing national culture, and not disrupt a supposed social and community cohesion' (ibid.: 463). While Kofman clearly views the development of civic integrationism within a mode of nationalist assertion, the issue is not ultimately one of whether the thematic of integration is conventionally nationalist, avowedly liberal or, as is always the case, a protean hybrid of both. Liberalism, as Wendy Brown puts it, 'is not only itself a cultural form, it is also striated with nonliberal culture wherever it is institutionalized and practiced' (2006: 23). Integrationism is not about nation-building in culturally homogenizing terms or any others. It represents the suturing of complex, highly instrumental managed migration regimes, and the matrix of borders and modes of containment directed at asylum seekers (Agier 2009; Schuster and Welch 2005), with heavily stratified and delimited statuses and conditions of residence. Thus the terrain of integration policy is bound up in the governmental need to demonstrate, as in the example of France in the previous chapter, 'the ability to control and manage migrations and diversity' (Kofman 2005). Integration has become a border practice, beyond and inside the territorial border, and regimes in western Europe are characterized by an apparent contradiction between the expansion of stratifying systems of entry, status, residence and legitimacy, and extensive formal, symbolic and affective demands for loyalty and elective homogeneity. This is most pronounced in the ways in which pathways to citizenship have been narrowed or truncated. In a survey of compulsory integration modalities in Europe, Guild et al. (2009) draw attention to the transfer of 'civic mandatory integration' from a process of access to national citizenship through naturalization to the new matrix of integration practices:

> In the context of immigration law, integration becomes a tool to control the non-national 'inside' the nation-state and even 'abroad' [...] Integration functions as another regulatory technique for the state to manage access by the non-national – not to the status of citizen – but to the act of entry, the security of residence, family reunification and protection against expulsion [...] Integration determines the 'legality' or 'illegality' of human mobility, and constitutes another frontier to being considered as a 'legal immigrant'. (Ibid.: 16)

There is no contradiction between expansive demands for affective and symbolic integration, and structured stratification. The apparent contradiction can be resolved with reference to James Tully's discussion of subjectification (2002). Tully gives the example of what he terms *citizenization* to argue that practices of governance are also practices of subjectification, not only in that they create subjects classified and organized by legal status, but also through the development of habituated, 'practical identities' over time. Neither determining nor overdetermined, the field of citizenization involves 'the diverse kind of relational subjectivity one internalizes and negotiates through participation over time, with their range of possible conduct and individual variation' (ibid.: 539–40). In regulating and organizing the productive contribution of migrant labour and the manifold risks associated with migrants as 'social enemies' (Tsoukala 2005), integration governance seeks to detach formal status from practical identity. It produces differentiated and flexible modes of legal subjectification, while delineating acceptable ranges of possible conduct and desirable subject-positions.

These 'new hierarchies of belonging' (Back and Sinha 2011) organize the problem of good and bad diversity. The management of flow and display in the 'market state' helps to explain why, as Alessandro de Giorgi notes, market demands for cheap labour, and the anxious demographics concerning the reproduction of working-age populations in western Europe (Legrain 2009),[7] must also involve policies based on the idea that migrants are a potentially deviant social group 'whose behaviour should be planned for and prevented, whose flow should be contained and limited, and whose legal situation should almost always be determined by a context of emergency' (de Giorgi 2000: 50). Migrant labour constitutes a neoliberal rationality in the sense that it can, to paraphrase an Italian anti-racist phrase, 'be used and thrown away'. Migrant workers pay taxes and social contributions, contributing to the public good, and according to the context, receive tightly stratified social, economic and political rights in return.[8] Solely in these terms, in Europe the challenge ahead 'does not consist in dissuading migrants from seeking its hospitality, but in demonstrating itself to be a sufficiently attractive destination in order to halt its own decline' (Cette France Là 2009: 365).

The problem of good and bad diversity is that they must also learn to queue. The glow of communality tenuously sought in the idiom of queuing recalls William Walters's reconciliation of flow, state and biopolitics in his compelling theorization of 'domopolitics', a securitized politics of 'home' (2004). Walters argues that the 'figure of a coherent national economic system linked in turn to a social order [...] in an international order populated by discrete, bounded socio-economic systems engaged in mutual relations of trade' (ibid.: 244) has been largely replaced by configurations of the neoliberal state located in a space of flows, where the 'business' of governance involves tapping into and directing productive and attractive mobile goods. In this porous order, 'insecure societies' are held to be vulnerable to mobile 'bads', including such human mobilities as 'unskilled' workers, bad diversity and the delegitimized mobility of asylum-seeking – a product of the previous international order. The idea of domopolitics, in suggesting a cohering politics of the *domus*, of 'home as our place, where we belong, naturally, and where others, by definition, do not' resonates with Arjun Appadurai's discussion of compensatory cultural sovereignty focused on the proxy of the 'needed but unwelcome' (2006). Yet domopolitics does not, and cannot, seek to arrest mobility; it looks to manage, tame and discipline its costs and risks.

In the national home, invited guests must learn the house rules – a common metaphor in integration debates – and submit to cultural governance. Home must also be protected because its 'contents (our property) are valuable and envied by others' (Walters 2004: 241), implying guest self-governance and self-sufficiency. Guests should not steal; the threat of the 'immigrant' is a threat to the residual welfare state (Gingrich and Banks 2006), and domopolitics deploys rights-based notions of citizenship and distributive justice to stratify and exclude less desirable, undesirable and 'illegal' populations from social entitlements and the protections of citizenship (Tyler 2010). Domopolitics transfers (social) security to the policing of resource threats in a field of internal and transnational security: 'Hence domopolitics embodies a tactic which juxtaposes the "warm words" (Connolly, 1995: 142) of community, trust and citizenship with the danger words of a chaotic outside – illegals, traffickers, terrorists' (Walters 2004: 241). In these terms, the Danish, Dutch, French and British contexts we have examined represent a recognizable domopolitics.[9] To illustrate the flexibility of domopolitics in the context of communicative capitalism, we conclude this section with a discussion of Ireland, which closes the circle opened by the editorial anxieties discussed in the book's introduction, and provides an example of a state beyond the dominant European narrative, where policy has been intimately shaped and influenced through circuits of belief.

The development of an integration rubric in Ireland has a history that involves significant interplay between NGOs, academic researchers and state agencies from the early 1990s (see Lentin and

McVeigh 2006 for an overview). State policy, during the mid to late 2000s, was influenced by the development of non-binding common principles by the European Council in 2004. A discourse of integration substantively emerged through policy statements from the Department of Justice, Equality and Law Reform (DJELR) in 2006/07, and culminated in the establishment of the Office of a Minister of State for Integration (OMSI) in 2007 and the launch of a policy framework in 2008. At least rhetorically, integration policy was presented as a mode of 'future-proofing' the nation, and as a key priority for government. As Michael McDowell, then DJELR minister, stated: 'Standing at the integration crossroads [...] we need to carefully examine those choices because if we journey down the wrong road, it may not be easy to find our way back. Neither may we have the time for the return journey' (2007: 10). Ireland's integration leitmotif, in contradistinction to the frequently value-laden idioms of crisis countries (Fekete 2009: 64), has been framed as 'a chance to get it right'. Integration governance, in other words, is projected as bypassing this European 'failed experiment', and inserting society at an advanced point on a developmental trajectory. The idea of a 'chance' posits an ephemeral opportunity to contain multiculture's excess without the corrosive amplification of excessive multiculturalism, a narrative that is explicit in the policy framework *Migration Nation: Statement on Integration Strategy and Diversity Management*, which characterizes 'experience in other countries' as cycling governmentally through 'relatively laissez-faire [...] to compulsory engagement', which suggests that 'from Ireland's point of view, we may be able to position ourselves on a more advanced cycle rather than go through earlier cycles' (OMSI 2008: 35–6).

For all this modular precision, contemporary research and analysis have consistently focused on the disparity between a governmental vision of intercultural exchange and cohesion-building with the 'New Irish', and actual policy and its lacunae. In an encompassing critique, Gerry Boucher argues that 'official integration policy [...] is more of a collection of policy statements and piece-meal, reactive policy responses to immediate, experiential policy problems' (2008: 6), a paucity institutionalized in the politically and financially limited instruments developed under the auspices of the OMSI. The development of integration policy, in response to highly variegated migration including significant circular migration from Poland and other post-2004 EU accession states (Kropiwiec and King-O'Riain 2006), quickly overlapped with the first of a series of concerted reductions in state provision implemented during the political-economic crisis from 2008. In that year the government abolished agencies deemed central to integration governance, such as the National Consultative Committee on Racism and Interculturalism (NCCRI) and the National Action Plan against Racism (NAPR), and further removed a series of integration supports, including language support available to schools. In part justified by the widely mediated assumption that migrants will return 'home' during a recession, the political priority of integration was demobilized with instructive speed.

What is significant about this rapid demobilization and official downgrading is the mobile, strategic nature of integration as a cultural thematic and governance narrative. The rhetoric of integration in Ireland has had little of the stridency or appeal to homogeneity and cultural unity of western Europe; instead it has preferred references to diversity, intercultural dialogue and the need for a 'two-way process'. Overt nationalist rhetoric in Ireland is historically contaminated by the conflict in Northern Ireland,[10] but also, the mediation of a 'modern, liberal, progressive multicultural image' (Kirby et al. 2002: 197) has been strategically inflected in an economy predicated on foreign direct investment, and had wider cultural resonance during a period of sustained economic growth and consumerism that came to be seen as 'the end of Irish history' (Coulter and Coleman 2003). In keeping with this soft-focus rhetoric, a 2010 Migrant Rights Centre study noted government pronouncements that expressed concern about possible scapegoating of migrant workers during the recession. Yet they also noticed that actual policy has been characterized by inaction on the bonded labour facilitated by an employer-held work permit system, and by a moratorium on work permits for low-paid jobs. The problems campaigned on during the economic boom – the work permit regime and the lack of protection for domestic workers – persisted, with policy 'based on a misunderstanding of migrant workers and their families as temporary residents whose position is entirely dependent on economic circumstances. Migrant workers and their families are thus actively encouraged to leave Ireland, or not to come here in the first place' (Crowley 2010: 5).

However, as Boucher (2008) and Fanning and Mutwarasibo (2007) detail, these structured contingencies are not misunderstandings, but central to the fusions of 'systems that couple security and migration with visions of integration' (Maguire and Cassidy 2009: 7). Prior to

2002, integration governance was restricted to those granted refugee status, and labour migration was regarded as temporary (Boucher 2008: 22; Lentin and McVeigh 2006). In advance of the accession of new EU member states in 2004, immigration policy shifted to develop a system of stratification based on satisfying low-skilled labour needs from mobile EU labour, and a 'managed migration system' involving Green Cards for skilled non-EU labour and enhanced pathways to permanent residence (ibid.). Reflecting on the Citizenship Referendum of 2004, which removed the birthright of citizenship from children of 'non-nationals' in Ireland, Bryan Fanning placed Ireland firmly within the dynamics of civic stratification described by Kofman (2005), and the concomitant exclusionary reformulation of citizenship noted elsewhere (Tyler 2010):

> Gradations of rights between citizens and non-citizens, immigrant 'guest' workers, 'illegal' workers, refugees and asylum seekers have emerged [...] in such a context citizenship becomes not just a set of rights but also [...] a mechanism of civic stratification, a form of inequality in which groups of people are differentiated by the legitimate claims they can make on the state. (2009: 111)

As Fanning argues, the objectives of a viable integration project should be to work to close gaps between 'nationals' and 'non-nationals' for the sake of future social cohesion (ibid.: 3). In Ireland, however, integration discourse works to obscure the gap. As one activist in asylum-seeker and migrant rights put it in a public discussion, 'there is a soft wing talking about anti-racism and multiculturalism on the one hand, on the other there is a very hard wing of the state that has the legal basis to actually do something [... to make it] very difficult for people to get documentation, very difficult for people to gain status and which is trying to influence public opinion in a security conscious way' (cited in Titley et al. 2009: 17). This is the domopolitics of what, without irony, came to be called 'The Migration Nation', and in which the institutionalized precariousness of migrant labour shadows the suspension of asylum seekers in frequently lengthy asylum determination phases and appeals, socially and physically immobilized by a system of 'direct provision' in a 'network of hidden villages', and 'regarded as being outside of integration policy until they have been granted refugee status or other subsidiary protection' (Maguire and Cassidy 2009: 22). The glow of community was inscribed in the rebranding of multiculturalism as interculturalism (NCCRI 2002);

however, the drive of integration governmentality was clearly to prefer and shape 'self-sufficient and autonomous immigrants, who must work on themselves in order to be independent, and committed to contributing to the Irish economy and society, in order that they may be integrated' (Gray 2006: 130).

The prevailing debate as to whether or not integrationism is neo-nationalist, or a novel interpretation or repurposing of liberalism's racial supplements, neglects the fact that the logic of flow inscribed in domopolitics is also discursive. Domopolitics assembles the elements of the moment, or in the terms used in Chapter 4, it assembles contributions, not messages. Therefore the theming of home can be overtly culturalist and exclusionary, or it can fetishize integration while structurally precluding it. Recognizing the discursive flows that theme the new structures of inclusion provides a second critical dimension of engagement with contemporary integration debates, and this extends to the circuits that connect not only state action, but the actions of civil society and social movements. We now move to examine this in relation to the dominant sexual politics of integration.

Integrating the sexual nation

On Couscous Global, an online 'platform to discuss and debate for teenagers and young adults world wide',[11] Sofie, a Norwegian artist living in the Netherlands and the daughter of a Christian minister, poses a question to Sara, 'a young lady' from Iran:

> Hello people, I'm Sofie from Norway. I've done a piece in the Red Light district in Amsterdam. We were putting a woman in the window with a burka next to these women [pointing at photographs of prostitutes] on both sides of her. And it's next to the church in Amsterdam. And the reactions we got from the people outside and both in the church and from the prostitution environment was a lot. So, what do you think guys about the idea of putting a woman in a burka in the Red Light District?[12]

In Iran, Sara, who watches Sofie on a computer in her comfortable Tehran apartment, asks the Dutch interviewer whether she can see Sofie's art installation, 'not even a picture of it?' 'No,' answers the faceless interviewer, 'because the girl who did it is afraid for her life.' Musing later on Sara's responses together, the interviewer tells Sofie: 'Maybe if you have lots of restrictions, it makes you more clear. You are sort of lost, right? Even with all the freedom.' Sofie laughs: 'Yes, I'm really lost.' And later: 'this experience made me re-think a lot and also my own freedom'. Sex, gender and sexuality have emerged as the new frontiers of democracy, citizenship – and as we saw with the English Defence League (EDL) in the introduction – diverse social movements. Incessant veil debates revolve around the relationship between veiled subjectivities and feminist intervention. The final principle in the Danish 'integration and active residency' declaration asks one to 'accept that it is punishable in Denmark to commit actual violence against or threaten one's spouse and others, including children'. Yet Sofie's questioning of the burka, and herself, suggests that there is little clarity concerning what a state of 'sexual democracy' (Fassin 2010), much like a state of integration, would look like. What is clear is that 'the instrumentalization of sexual politics against immigrants has now become a European [we would say Western] reality' (ibid.) and that this concerns, not only immigrants themselves, but also their descendants.

As with the polyphony of identity liberalism, the widespread deployment of a discourse of liberation transposed from the emancipatory canon of feminism and gay rights has rendered them contaminable. Deployed by political actors with no history of activism or struggle – or even ongoing antipathy to feminist and queer politics – they also provide, in the shading of liberty into liberality, an important contouring of bad diversity in state integration practices by excluding all those considered illiterate in 'hegemonic forms of sexual politics' (Gunkel and Pitcher 2008a). The progressive yardsticks now waved at migrants, who are always already presumed backward, belies the fact that there are few Western states whose legal practices and clusters of dominant opinion are as liberal as their rhetoric when it comes to feminism, and lesbian, gay, bisexual and transgender (LGBT) rights (Butler 2009; Fassin 2010).

Nevertheless, burka and headscarf bans, and a core focus on 'honour killings', forced marriages, female genital mutilation and polygamy – all associated with 'illiberal', mainly Muslim, minorities – have been foregrounded, with different emphases, in the Nordic countries, France, the Netherlands, Germany, the UK and Belgium. As Davina Cooper argues, 'gendered minority practices receive a level of critical attention out of all proportion to their pervasiveness or influence' (2004: 193). In keeping with her treatment of diversity politics, this assessment is clearly not, as is so often projected in the fractious exchanges on these subjects, a form of 'relativism'. It is, instead, a critique of the disruption of intersectional lives by sectional politics, and an attention to the processes through which certain differences 'arise and are made to speak' while others are silenced and made invisible (ibid.: 194). The movement of sex, gender and sexuality to the forefront of integrationism involves contextual histories of gender politics and the influence of a domopolitical confluence shaped by the 'war on terror'.

The August 2010 cover of *Time* magazine featured a young Afghan woman with her face mutilated; her nose had allegedly been cut off on the orders of a Taliban court. Featuring the headline 'What happens if we leave Afghanistan', the cover did not pose a question, but rather implied a link between radical gender violence and the legitimacy of the US-led occupation. In the loops of communicative capitalism, bloggers and journalists were quick to relate the cover to declassified US military material, released on the WikiLeaks website,[13] documenting CIA advice to use the oppression of Afghan women as 'pressure points', particularly in Europe, and more particularly in France.[14] Although the story was subsequently revealed to have been falsified,[15] and despite the fact that the oppression of women in Afghanistan may have deepened in the matrix of power struggles and territorial pacts since the invasion in 2001,[16] the sight of Aisha/Nazia's mutilated face circulates in the global 'space of appearances' (Silverstone 2007) within which the spectacle of defining images has contingent political power. The post-racial force of good intentions perdures in the desire to save her: the act of trying to save (rather than actually saving) Afghan women is what is important. The mark of 'imperial feminism' (Amos and Parmar 1984) inscribes gender violence in subaltern cultural traits, positioning a hegemonic Eurocentric liberal feminism as a path-dependent politics of emancipation, and a position from which Western societies can choose to obviate the violence afflicting 'our own' mothers, sisters, wives and daughters.[17] In the world of photogenic narratives of emancipation, the struggle of organizations such as the Revolutionary Association of the Women of Afghanistan (RAWA) against a patriarchy that has been consolidated by Western triumphalism does not merit a photo-shoot. As Huda Jawad describes:

> There are currently three major parties at play in determining the fate of women in the country: the US-installed government, the Taliban-influenced insurgency, and the US itself. Here's a wild

thought: at those top secret meetings between these three altruistic set of agendas, the last thing they concern themselves with is whether or not little Fatima or Aisha is allowed to go to school without acid being thrown on her face. Instead, the rights of women becomes a breaking point only when the Afghan government and US make undignified concessions to the insurgency regarding women's rights, in order to maintain a cease-fire with the insurgents or to obtain more political leverage.[18]

There is a sapping familiarity to the exclusion of the political action of non-white women and sexual minorities that veers from the established scripts of what freedom looks like. Most often, black women's insistence on the importance of defining and resisting their own oppression (Amos and Parmar 1984; hooks 1990) is dismissed as the residue of divisive identity politics. The idea, expressed most succinctly in Audre Lorde's indictment that 'The master's tools will never dismantle the master's house' (Lorde 1984), is confined to the doll's house. In the reduction of diversity politics to the expression of the properties of the individual, the irony is that independent and radical voices are frequently dismissed as perpetuating groupism. However, work on the ways in which gender has been integrated into the nation's ongoing reproduction (Yuval Davis 1997) has been important for identifying how both women and the white, feminist movement have often been complicit in the subordination of women of colour (Carby 1982; Mohanty 1986). Similarly, black lesbian feminists have taught important lessons about the racist presumptions that often inflect white queer movements (Lorde 1984). To discuss how these complicities have become pronounced in the assemblages of integration, we focus here on a burgeoning literature and activism concerned with what Eric Fassin has termed 'sexual democracy' (Fassin 2010).

Within the context of contemporary integrationism, sex and gender politics increasingly defines who is 'with us' and who is 'against us', while the racist implications of yet another bracing divide not only go unnoticed but are actively discounted. In this new era of confronting taboos, we are encouraged to eschew political correctness towards those minorities whose multiculturalism has undermined social cohesion. But multiculturalism used to be understood as linked de facto to an identity politics that *included* feminism and gay rights (Gunkel and Pitcher 2008a). Now the co-optation of discourses of gender and LGBT equality, both by the state and in the name of a global military interventionist politics, pits them against racialized minorities who find themselves increasingly alone in the struggle for equality (Duggan 2003; Pitcher 2009; Haritaworn 2008). Something is going on, therefore, in the shift from a debate among feminists and queers about the perpetuation of racism within their movements to the reproduction of those same racisms in the terms of feminism and gay rights, also at the level of the state. Within the 'complex, contradictory cultural and political project' of neoliberalism (Duggan 2003: 70), it is insufficient to analyse the discursive demise of multiculturalism and the rise of the politics of diversity and integrationism solely as top-down impositions on social movements. The generation of understandings of society underpinning integration mechanisms does not originate with the state alone. Situating the politics of integration within the dynamics of neoliberalism reveals how the latter gives it form as a politics of ownership. Neoliberalism, generated through agendas which include 'local alliances, cultural projects, nationalist agendas, and economic policies work[ing] together, unevenly and often unpredictably, rife with conflict and contradiction' (ibid.: 70–71) undergirds an integrationist drive which is never fully unidirectional, but rather shaped by a number of unanticipated forces and disparate strands whose common interests are not always immediately apparent.

Just as anti-racism is not a 'movement' as such, expressing a unitary ideology or even commonly intelligible goals (Lentin 2004), so too the politics of feminism and LGBT rights constitutes multiple traditions and trajectories, often with widely differing political implications. Pitcher (2009) distinguishes between feminism and the 'feminism' of the state in which minority women's rights are always constructed through a 'racializing discourse' (ibid.: 131). The emancipatory drive associated with feminism, when incorporated by the state and other dominant actors, can be used to launder oppressive measures by 'providing a legitimate point of entry into a controversial realm of racial politics that would otherwise be resolutely off-limits' (ibid.: 130). While Pitcher notes how this appropriation works without the 'active support of feminists' (ibid.: 132), this does not account for the *active* collusion of feminists – as opposed to 'feminists' – in perpetuating the idea of the anti-feminism of non-whites. The 'colonial feminism' for which hegemonic white women have been consistently taken to task has its echoes in the white-led international LGBT movement, expanding with the institutionalization of the politics of diversity through more business-oriented identity politics since the 1990s in the USA, with similar processes occurring in the co-optation of social movement vocabularies in Europe through processes of supranational 'consultation'.

The movement away from civil rights traditions by proponents of a new 'neoliberal brand of identity/equality politics' may be far from complete but it attracts high visibility (Duggan 2003: 44). The development of this trend is consistent with a more general development towards transnational social movements that no longer have a broad progressive base (Keck and Sikkink 1998). In contrast, the most dominant gay and lesbian organizations in the United States have become 'the lobbying, legal, and public relations firms for an increasingly narrow gay, moneyed elite' (Duggan 2003: 45). It is this genre of organizations which objected during the invasion of Afghanistan to the publication of an AP photograph of a US warhead emblazoned with the words 'Hijack this Fags', not because of opposition to the war but because 'the message equates gays with the enemy' and dishonours gay servicemen (ibid.: 46). This 'homonormativity', expressed in the focus on 'mainstreaming gays' by appeals for social acceptability, finds echoes in the distancing of liberal and humanitarian feminisms from the mass of women worldwide on whose behalf they speak, but whom they rarely represent. According to Delphy and Bouteldja (2007), feminism's legitimacy now seems to be secured in the establishment of an opposition between white, emancipated, women and brown, subjugated, ones. Noting the consensus on 'post-feminism' (Power 2009), they remind us that while feminism had become a dirty word by the 1980s, it was resurrected in France in the 1990s after the military coup in Algeria against 'Islamism': 'an Algerian feminist was a heroine, a French feminist a frustrated bitch' (ibid.).[19]

The confluence of particular state agendas around integration, construed as a response to an ailing multiculturalism, and the rise of a 'third way' in feminism and gay rights (Duggan 2003: 48), formulates a 'sexual integrationism' that posits the illiberal subjects of multiculturalism as 'obstacles to successful "integration" within the West' (Gunkel and Pitcher 2008a). If integration is about shaping citizenships that work for neoliberal states, neoliberalism's autonomous subjects are imagined as sexually free and gender equal. The existence of bad sexual diversity, of religious Muslims in Western societies, for example, allows the hegemonic *us* to forget how far this fiction is from the social reality. In the palimpsest of aversion, they stand for a fear of losing hard-won freedoms by coming to symbolize a not so distant past of sexual repression and gendered oppression. This seems to explain why the centrality of sexual democracy to integration politics is established by states in conjunction with dominant feminists and gay rights activists who actively collaborate in foreclosing the possibility of full citizenship for 'illiberal' minorities (Haritaworn and Petzen 2010; Long 2009). Organizations representing mainstream LGBT and women's groups, including those of racialized women such as Ni putes, ni soumises ('Neither sluts nor doormats') in France, participate in scapegoating non-white men as either the perpetrators of sexism and sexual violence (Bouteldja 2007; Raissiguier 2008) or as 'non-integrated' terrorist subjects (Puar 2007). In so doing, they reinforce discourses of integration based on the discipline of homogeneity, and a uniform vision of citizenship that eschews its messy, limited reality. This creates at least three problems. It establishes unilinear visions of what being a woman or being gay or transgender entails in our societies and denies the ethno-racial heterogeneity within these categories. Secondly, it shuts down the possibilities for solidarity between racialized groups, feminists and movements of sexually non-conforming people (Erel et al. 2008). Lastly, this situation serves only to assist in the persistence of a hegemonic heteronormativity that continues despite the lip-service paid to the institutionalization of gender equality and sexual freedom.

A sound thrashing: the gender politics of integration Pym Fortuyn, in a 2002 interview entitled 'Islam is a backward culture', said, 'I want a very strong emancipation policy for Islamic women in disadvantaged neighbourhoods. In particular the highly educated Turkish and Moroccan girls get a sound thrashing from me. They leave their sisters in the lurch' (quoted in Bracke 2011). Fortuyn's assessment is interesting, as his vociferous appeal to sexual and gender equality was ultimately based on limited ideas of what has been achieved, and must be defended. Thus, as Sarah Bracke argues, he dismissed the feminist activism of a 'generation of young, well-educated and vocal Muslim women who at the time had begun raising their voices in the Dutch national debate', while also contrasting them to 'our feminists from the 1970s', from whom he claimed they should learn (ibid.). In this doll's-house argument, the temporal framework is interesting. Fortuyn relegates feminism by portraying its aims as already achieved, and claiming feminism as 'part of a "heritage" of Dutch society' (ibid.). This ignores how feminism in the 1970s was expanding to include a range of other voices – black, majority world, Muslim – that have been critical of precisely the type of white, liberal feminism that Fortuyn instrumentalized (cf. Mohanty 1986; hooks 1990; Lorde 1984). Fortuyn's argument amounts to conventional post-feminism; good for the 1970s but a thing of the past today (Bracke 2011). Returning, once again, to Fortuyn helps unfold political narratives that have subsequently become widely circulated. The script of sexual democracy allows dominant actors to promulgate the fiction that gender equality in the West has been achieved, and that where it is threatened, it is the fault of unintegrated minorities who, for crimes against feminism no less, deserve a sound thrashing.

However, Fortuyn's preferred feminist subjects are not only imagined. The French organisation Ni putes, ni soumises (NPNS), for example, follows in the tradition of dominant French anti-racist organizations, SOS Racisme in particular,[20] by reproducing the hegemonic script that pits a neutral, *laïcque* and egalitarian state against culturalist and violent, or culturally violent, men. Their patriarchal tyranny is portrayed as the primary barrier to the freedom of women and, as a consequence, to integration in general. Through its presentation of men of the *banlieues* of mainly North African origin as out of control – the *racaille* – the NPNS advances a unitary vision of integration that ultimately denies the heterogeneity that its members themselves represent. By labelling all *jeunes du cité* as misogynist and as potential (gang) rapists (Fassin 2010), NPNS participates in perpetuating the idea that it is only by integrating into the republic that non-white women can be free. It consequently assists 'this ruling class to exploit the Muslim veil, but also the questions of sexism and antisemitism, in order to literally put these overly "arrogant" "youth" in their place [...] This *colonial call to order* constitutes a kind of historical revenge, a "we told you so!", a "reconquest" of these Arabs "unjustly" emancipated by France' (Bouteldja 2007, emphasis in original). The contemporary prescription of integration as a balm for societal *dis*-integration should therefore be read as a means of regathering the subjects of colonial France, lost through emancipation, whose freedom produces unease at its heart in spite – or because – of the benevolence with which it was originally granted, and against which the disorderly *cité* now rails.

Integration represents a symbolic colonial reconquest in Bouteldja's terms, substituting for the impossibility of a real return to Algeria. NPNS launders this desire by becoming the embodiment of the 'truth' of the social tyranny inflicted on women by the *banlieusards*. NPNS developed in 2002, in response to murders such as that of Sohane Benziane, burnt by a former boyfriend in a cellar in Vitry-sur-Seine. It organized highly mediated campaigns to expose brutalities such as that suffered by Sohane, as well as instances of gang rapes and the 'constant and intolerable degradation faced by the girls in our neighbourhoods'.[21] In that these are real problems with real, and often brutal, repercussions, NPNS's formal remit to tackle the dual problems of sexism in the *banlieues* and so-called 'green fascism' is an utterly legitimate one (Bouteldja 2007). The problem Bouteldja notes is the essentialist vision of the young racialized men of the *banlieues* that underpin the organization's commitments. A banal observation in itself, this reductionist approach nonetheless serves the purpose of 'exempting the natives from all self-criticism with regards to sexism, while validating the idea of a sexism which is exogenous to and imported [into France] by Arab-Muslim immigration' (ibid.).

The force of Bouteldja's point, when connected to integration as a proposed solution to the problems highlighted by NPNS, is that by connecting sexism and 'green' – Muslim – 'fascism', the organization participates in the equation of all Muslims with sexual violence, to which the only response can be the criminalization of Muslims *tout court*. It is only a short step from combating sexism to banning various forms of Muslim dress,[22] and for a grassroots movement mobilized to protect the young women of the *cités* from becoming complicit in the denial of freedom to those who do not comply with the image of womanhood authorized by the French state. In defending *les filles de banlieue*, NPNS omits the fact that many veiled women too are *les filles de banlieue*.[23] The demands of the NPNS, described by Bouteldja as 'an ersatz feminism: stigmatising and excluding the "sluts" *and* the "doormats" (read: the veiled), [and] in so doing promoting a "femininity" which conforms to dominant norms' (2007, emphasis in original), have the effect of unveiling 'gender integration' as an insufficient form of citizenship. By integrating into a particular vision of femininity, young black and brown women do not achieve equality as befitting their status as French citizens. On the contrary, the best they can hope to achieve is a 'discount citizenship', the minimum right to wear a miniskirt, but not a veil (ibid.). In practical terms, then, to integrate is to conform rather than to gain more rights and close the material gap between *les filles de banlieue* and their white co-citizens.

The indexicality of the oppositions that underpin NPNS discourse –

universalisme/communautarisme, integrated/fundamentalist, secular/ subjugated – allows them to be rapidly integrated into institutional and mediatic frameworks. In a parallel example, the cooperation of parliamentarians and civil society organizations in the production of a civil bill on forced marriage in Britain enabled rapid connections to the separate issue of honour killings to be made in both popular and legal discourse (Wilson 2007). This presents a dilemma for many organizations. An association such as Southall Black Sisters, with a long history of struggle against both institutional racism and communal patriarchy, participated in the drafting of the bill, making a decision in full awareness of the potential uses of racialized assumptions about culturalized 'gender crimes'. In other words, nuanced understandings of internal social movement strategies may be lost when 'the linguistic manifestations of racist ideas [have] become so familiar, recurring, and generalizable that [they] hardly [seem] to count as racist' (Gaudio and Bialostock 2005, cited in D.-A. Davis 2007: 352). Thus, Mix Together, a UK network supporting 'mixed couples (mixed race/religion/caste) who face opposition from family or community to their relationship',[24] can claim that 'Free choice in marriage will help prevent extremism' and argue for forced marriage to be integrated into the UK government's anti-terrorist 'Prevent' agenda.[25]

Similarly, the entry of NPNS leaders Fadéla Amara and Rama Yade into Sarkozy's government[26] was not essential for the binaries undergirding NPNS's beliefs to pollinate the repressive integrationism of French citizenship decisions. This is evident in Nicolas Sarkozy's explicit indexing of sexual integrationism and French exceptionalism to the procedurally separate question of who has the right to French citizenship. In the indexing of gender and sexuality to integration it is not merely that the 'figure of a victimized and/or manipulated girl-woman' (Raissiguier 2008) is instrumentalized in constructing tropes for 'debates' on the 'problems of immigration' or the 'challenges of integration'. The 'overly-fecund African mother' (ibid.) or the veiled and submissive Muslim daughter are used directly in attempts to undermine their citizenship, thus putting into question not just the terms of their integration, but the consequent consideration as to who is really to be considered a citizen. In June 2008, for example, a Moroccan woman married to a Frenchman with whom she had had three children, all born in France, was denied naturalization. The official reason supplied was that, despite her knowledge of the French language, she wore the burka and had 'no idea about secularism or the right to vote. She lives in complete submission to the men in her family.' The case demonstrates the extent to which 'sexual democracy patrols the borders of French national identity – and paradoxically, it is primarily at the expense of women' (Fassin 2010). The familiar paradox, of course, was that the negative ruling by the Conseil d'État, an outcome supported by the NPNS, essentially punished a woman 'for her submission to men' (ibid.). Rather than saving the world's subjugated women from male oppression, France, the country where 'equality between men and women [...] is part of our identity' (Sarkozy, cited in Fassin 2010), rejected this woman for her lack of assimilation to a country that she was denied the chance to assimilate into in the first place.

Not free enough: sexual repression as a barrier to integration In June 2010 the renowned gender theorist Judith Butler turned down the 'Civil Courage' prize offered to her by the organization of the Berlin Pride at its annual 'Christopher Street Day' event. Acting upon an appeal from queer and trans activists of colour, she cited the organizers' complicity in perpetuating racism within the global context of the 'war on terror' but also, specifically, against the racialized, including queers of colour, and Muslims in Germany.[27] Butler declared that 'I must distance myself from complicity with racism, including anti-Muslim racism' as a result of which homosexuals, 'bi, trans and queer people can be used by those who want to wage war'.[28] She publicly offered the award to the local organizations which contacted her in the hope that she would take a stand.[29] As the organization SUSPECT documented, mainstream gay activists in Germany were quick to 'whitewash' the event, and media coverage mainly ignored her explicit condemnation of racism, focusing instead on her minor criticism of the Pride's commercialism. In reaction to cheers from the few queers of colour and their allies who gathered in the crowd to support Butler, the event's organizers, Jan Salloch and Ole Lehmann, yelled, 'You can scream all you like. You are not the majority. That's enough [...] Pride will just continue in its programme [...] No matter what [...] Worldwide and here in Berlin [...] This is how it's always been and will always be.' Yet it has not always been this way, as gay rights are not a timeless given of Western political life. The Berlin Pride affair can be set in the context of current attention to 'gay globalization' (Duggan 2003). Linked to homonormative values, 'homonationalism' – 'the utility of gay rights discourses to US/

Western imperial projects' (Puar et al. 2008) – and 'gay imperialism', the active participation of 'dominant gays' in the 'war on terror' (Haritaworn 2008), have become useful frameworks for making sense of the deployment of freedom in a politics of exclusion (Butler 2009: 104–5). Puar notes the

> *convivial* relations between queerness and militarism, securitiza-
> tion, war, terrorism and surveillance technologies, empire,
> torture, nationalism, globalization, fundamentalism, secularism,
> incarceration, detention, deportation, and neoliberalism: the
> tactics, strategies, and logistics of our contemporary war machines.
> (Puar 2007: xiv, emphasis in original).

As Butler argues in *Frames of War* (2009), the articulation of these disparate and seemingly conflictual processes, standpoints and ideologies comes about 'most frightfully when women's sexual free-dom or the freedom and expression and association for lesbian and gay people is invoked instrumentally to wage a cultural assault on Islam that reaffirms US sovereignty and violence'. A new scholarship, writing across the USA and Europe, is engaging the ways in which homonormativity has come to supplement and support the hetero-normative assumptions crucial to nation-state formations (Puar et al. 2008; Butler 2009; Haritaworn 2008). This move is pronounced in the post-civil rights context in the USA, during which what Puar calls the 'successes of incorporation' led to the emergence of a damaging binary; 'the homosexual other is white, the racial other is straight' (Puar et al. 2008). The neoliberal privatization discussed in Chapter 5 further fractured race and class alliances, thus creating a space for homonationalism to develop beyond structural critiques of power. How this binary could come to be appropriated to the civilizational discourse of the 'war on terror' is clear; just like the mutilated woman on the cover of *Time*, the brown gay Other (man) is in need of saving from the barbarians in his own society. As Jin Haritaworn notes, in the construction of brown, often Muslim, gays 'as secretive, repressed, closeted victims who are exceptionally brave and in *need* of liberation by their already-liberated (white) siblings', the uneven relations of power are more than apparent (2008).

But how did this become relevant to the partygoers at the Berlin Pride? As Butler insists, 'my point is surely not to abandon freedom as a norm, but to ask about its uses' (2009: 105). Holding a Pride party in the centre of a European capital city, and for that event to be endorsed and attended by public figures, including gay elected politicians, is rightly considered as a political achievement, and one worth struggling to keep. Yet dominant gay actors are waging the fight for freedom of sexual expression, not against a state that actively repressed and criminalized it in the very recent past, and which continues to perpetuate hegemonic heteronormative norms (Mepschen 2009b), but against a purportedly oppressive minority. Explicitly, the new frontier for the Western gay establishment is the dividing line drawn between (white) gays on one side and (straight) black and brown people on the other. In that integrationist politics over the last decade have explicitly targeted Muslims as the least assimilable among those still sequestered as immigrants, this pernicious binary pits white, secular gays against fundamentalist homophobic Muslims. The conflict between these two overdetermined sides takes place on home ground, in the *domus* (Walters 2004: 241), where the unhomely stranger is always out of place. The sense of exclusive, privatized ownership facilitated by integrationism, like a particularly blunt sign above the door in a private members' club, reads, 'Do things our way, or get out'.

But what quite would 'doing things our way' mean in Europe, where, for example, only '44% of respondents around the continent support gay marriage and 32% support the right for gay people to adopt', or in the USA, where gay marriage is legal in only one state, Massachusetts?[30] The idea that we are free has resonance only in that *they* are not; and while helping others to be free is consistent with a long history of altruistic activism going back to the civilizing mission (Goldberg 2002), today too it is necessary to construct the other as *un*-free before being able to make him 'free like me'. The integration of the sexually unrepressed nation imagines particular populations not only as sexually repressed but also as actively repressive, not only over 'their own' but, crucially, over 'us' and in violation of our rights here at home. Disciplining the repressive immigrant homophobe thus becomes a job for *domopolitical* integration, one that operates in tandem with the commitment to emancipate gay victims worldwide.

But who does the integrating in matters of sexuality is less straightforward than in the case of subjugated women, where the state can act legislatively upon headscarves and marriages to foreigners. The role of protecting sexual minorities from societal abuse and state repression has largely fallen to public figures backed by social movements. Outrage, led by the UK-based veteran gay rights campaigner Peter

Tatchell, is one such actor.[31] Here there is also troubling polyphony, as these forms of activism run the risk of being seen to converge, through their shared focus on illiberal Muslims,[32] with the instrumental adoptions of groups like the EDL, which boasts a '115-strong lesbian, gay and transgender wing'.[33] These tensions and affinities indicate how integrationism can create unanticipated alliances. If the basis of integration is shared national values, and Islam is held to pose a threat to gays in particular and the West as a whole, these disparate political voices become allies on the side of the integrationist nation struggling with its disintegrated and dis-integrating others. As in the case of NPNS, the prominence of gay activist attacks on multiculturalism[34] has legitimized state instrumentalization of the theme of gay liberation in the construction of the *domus*. The indicator of tolerance towards homosexuality provides a way of policing migration and potential citizenship. As Arun Kundnani (2007) argues with regard to New Labour's reform of UK citizenship laws, the decision to exclude or include is less dependent on the overtly racialized terms that dictated previous policies based on concepts of 'belongingness' and 'patriality' (Solomos 2003). Rather, new migrants are to be judged on their presumed fidelity, or proximity to a culturalized set of shifting British 'values' (ibid.), and tests of this fidelity have been added to the technologies of integration.

The Dutch 'civic integration examination abroad' centrally features the threshold of sexual integration. In preparation for the phone exam, prospective migrants must watch the 'Coming to the Netherlands' DVD, which includes images of two men kissing. The provision of a special edited version of the film for countries in which 'it is against the law to be in possession of films with images of this nature' anticipates its censorship and thus 'confirms the geography and geopolitics that such sexual politics reflect and simultaneously contribute to establishing' (Fassin 2010; see also van Wichelen and de Leeuw 2011). The institutional incorporation of homosexuality proceeds from the homonationalism discussed in Chapter 3, and grounds compatibility in exclusive, sometimes liberal, sometimes Dutch, sexual norms as a condition for migration. Hence the work of social movements is pre-empted by states precluding potential conflict before it arises, or even arrives. Activism thus no longer emerges through direct engagement in dialogue with different others, but is curtailed, even as a potentiality, before it can begin: social cohesion made to measure, integration pre-shrunk.

In keeping with the everyday plebiscite of immigration debates, the focus on sexually repressive migrants extends to citizens and long-term residents, including those of the second and third generation that have become the specific targets of pedagogical sexual reorientation. In the Berlin context, the invented tradition of German gay-friendliness was used by the organizations criticized by Butler to construct a vision of migrant communities in Germany as 'violently homophobic', while simultaneously casting themselves in the role of defender of gay and lesbian migrants, and thus becoming the carriers of the German state's 'integration' agenda (Haritaworn and Petzen 2010). The Lesbian and Gay Federation in Germany's (LSVD) development of 'migration projects' illustrates the dominant dynamics of 'sexual integration'.[35] The federation's inauguration in 1999 of the MILES (Centre for Migrants, Lesbians and Gays) Project had the dual goal of integrating 'gay and lesbian migrants, and combat[ting] homophobia in "migrant communities"' (ibid.). The project's main activity was to teach '"the migrants" German "core values" of sexual freedom and gay friendliness', thus establishing itself as a 'public expert' in integration, now (re)constructed as a 'sexual problem' (ibid.). Soldering the threat of homophobia to the cultural fault-lines that continue to sequester people born and brought up in Germany as 'migrants' has a deep affinity with the slippage in integration policy between arriving migrants and settled, but unsettling, populations. As Haritaworn and Petzen analyse, the LSVD invested political labour in the recited truth that homophobia among non-white youth was widespread, and a result both of a lack of integration and adherence to (Muslim) religious tradition. As a civil society actor, the LSVD is centrally placed to construct a comforting image of migrants/Muslims as both 'held back by their culture' and 'holding the rest of "us" back as well' (ibid.). In this conjunction, integration and immigration control become a prophylactic measure, a widespread reworking of the Caldwellian slippery slope in progressive terms.[36]

The rewiring of integration as being for *us* rather than for *them* cannot be held to produce more socially cohesive societies. However, it serves to reassure those historically excluded from the hetero-normative narrative that still dominates Western national formations that they too have a place at the hearth of the *domus*. Focusing on the complicity of 'progressive' activists with the divisive, racialized politics of integration draws attention to the fact that these politics are never simple, nor are they unidirectional. As Haritaworn notes in relation to Judith Butler's primary focus on the state as the 'sole actor' in the perpetuation of homonationalism, a focus on top-down initiatives 'leaves intact the notion of an innocent gay subject, who is victimized even by a state which appropriates its righteous struggles for citizenship and alienates it from its coalitions with other Others' (2008). In other words, activist participation in the demonization of 'brown homophobes' can easily be overlooked, thus participating in advancing more simplistic accounts of racialized integrationism as the project of states against which neither the progressive forces of civil society nor wider society have any power.

Further, such unidimensional perspectives do not account for the utility and affective charge of integrationism within neoliberalized societies, where the certainties of sexual democracy provide another layer of compensation for wider fragmentation. The fluidity of recited truths, and the work of assemblages that are resistant to charges of inconsistency or hypocrisy, makes the work of critiquing these circuits of racial formation difficult. In the enduring and acceler-ated assembly of what it means to be Western, competing values, ideologies and behaviours run together. The incompatibility between, for example, 'our Christian roots' and 'our sexual tolerance' is less important that the meta-incompatibility it secures. On one level, the ubiquitous rhetoric of sexual democracy does reflect the progress made in Western societies towards the greater equality of women and gay and lesbian people, and their inclusion in the imagined centre of public discourse. However, the assumption of already achieved equality is now the basis for what Sara Ahmed (2009) terms the creation of 'problematic proximities', the associations made between terms – for example, 'Muslim' and 'homophobe' – that make them essential and 'sticky'. This is where post-racialism is at right now – the reproduction of racisms through conjunctions in which an anti-racist stance is officially endorsed. By sequestering their critique of Muslim or migrant homophobia from their concomitant opposition to racism, organizations and individuals – such as the LSVD or Peter Tatchell – artificially bracket that critique from the circuits of belief and racialized context in which it is circulated. Thus, 'freedom can be what "we" have or even what we are' while 'homophobia too can be exercised as what "the others" need liberating from; it too can become attributed to others, and thus an attribute of others' (ibid.). In claiming to confront racism, these logics perpetuate the essentialisms upon which racism relies.

It is also where the attenuated politics of diversity claims ascendancy. Post-political appeals to the universal right to self-fulfilment obviate the geopolitical and gross material realities that prevent the world's majority from enjoying even its promise. Failing to engage with the difficult task of tracing and critiquing racisms leaves progressive politics vulnerable to the drive of a domopolitical order vested in this systemic inequality and injustice. Ayaan Hirsi Ali makes this connection explicit: 'as people who have never known peace and prosperity long enough to groom themselves to a state of metrosexuality assert themselves in hordes and come to possess weapons of mass destruction, manly courage becomes indispensable for survival, world peace, and order'.[37] In this identity politics, gender and sexuality become the latest grounds on which the West must tie its courage to the sticking post, and so scripted, the English Defence League's adoption of gay emancipation to rally the street-fighting man does not seem so anachronistic. Arguing for the need to mobilize 'progressive social movements by building on dynamic, interactive differences' (2003: 85) Lisa Duggan turns to the possibilities of intersectional work to mobilize for '*equality, freedom, justice,* and *democracy*' in ways that 'exceed their limited (neo)liberal meanings' (2003: 87). A dense network of resistant movements and solidarities currently work against the complicity of emancipatory struggles with integrationist domopolitics, yet these are not the movements favoured by the polished surfaces of the space of appearance. At what Duggan calls 'this moment of danger and opportunity' (ibid.), she is right to emphasize 'struggles for social justice that are respectfully affiliative and dialogic rather than pedagogical'. In the pursuit of this, diversity politics must engage the sectional horizons of a politics of diversity that works for *our* emancipation, and for *theirs*, but only on the terms that domopolitics permits. The laundering of the last decade has left us with much baggage to unpack.

Notes

1 Recited truths

1 Gary Younge, 'The crises of multiculture?' Workshop held at the Institute for Cultural Inquiry, Berlin, 15 July 2010. www.ici-berlin.org/docu/the-crises-of-multiculture/?tx_bddbflvvideogallery_pi1[video]=7, accessed 17 September 2010.

2 Captured in Silvio Berlusconi's statement that 'we don't want Italy to become a multi-ethnic, multicultural country'.

3 Since the state of emergency invoked in the UK to pass the Anti-Terrorism, Crime and Security Act in November 2001 – the 'Guantánamo Bay law' – men of Muslim appearance have been treated as potential fifth columnists (Poynting and Mason 2006: 375), and more generally in Europe the potential of hidden but networked extremism justified the ever-increasing ideological and institutional fusion of immigration, security, cohesion and integration, and questions of national belonging and loyalty (Fekete 2009). In the USA, prior to its absorption into the Department of Homeland Security, the Immigration and Naturalization Service chose the first anniversary of the 9/11 attacks to begin implementing a compulsory programme of registration for 'non-immigrant aliens' resulting in 'nothing short of a massive roundup of out-of-status and visiting Arabs and Asians from predominantly Muslim countries' (Cainkar 2003). Discussing the range of profiling, internments and forced registry enabled by the USA Patriot Act of 2001, Winant argues that 'race offers the most accessible tool to categorise the American people politically: who is "loyal" and who is a "threat", who can be trusted and should be subject to surveillance, who should retain civil rights and who should be deprived of them' (2004: 130). According to Stoler, the state coercion of the Bush administration, and the exhortation of everyday vigilance for 'enemies in disguise', recalls that 'fear of an omnipresent, invisible "hidden force" and the desire for a secret intelligence apparatus to combat it [...] standard features of imperial administrations' (2006: 145).

4 The 'Ground Zero' mosque gave it the chance to connect in the USA also.

5 www.englishdefenceleague.org/index.php?option=com_content&view=article&id=209:edl-in-newcastle-no-commies-no-violence&catid=42:feature-stories.

6 Now linked up with and in relation to the Ground Zero mosque.

7 This culturalism persists, as can be seen in how, twenty years ago, British 'Asians' were seen as socially cohesive because of their purportedly strong cultural identity, an idea now parlayed as the source of societal segregation, unrest and threat (Solomos 2003).

8 As Kundnani (2007) has shown, the geographical separation between whites and 'Asians' in Oldham and Bradford can be traced back to the deindustrialization of these old mill towns. Following the unemployment of swathes of workers, discriminatory housing policies run by the councils allocated homes on housing estates to whites, leaving Asians in the run-down terraced housing originally built for the mill workers. Asians who did get houses on the white-dominated housing estates were often the victims of racial abuse, leading them to congregate in neighbourhoods where they soon became the majority. Housing segregation led to segregation in education, with some catchment areas containing nearly 100 per cent members of one ethnic group.

9 In his review, in the *London Review of Books*, of *Family Britain* by David Kynaston, Nicholas Spice makes the following observation about post-war social segregation: 'At its most blatant – and ugly – the effects of this system approached a kind of apartheid, as in the notorious "Cutteslowe Walls" in North Oxford, seven feet high and topped off with iron spikes, built in the 1930s but still standing 20 years later, for the purpose of separating a middle-class suburban enclave from the neighbouring working-class housing estate. But the need for hierarchy seems to have been pervasive, expressing itself across society through superfine class distinctions which everyone understood: "We had a street party that our parents were insistent should not include the children from the terraced houses,"

Michael Burns wrote, recalling VE Day celebrations in Tolworth near Kingston. And it was much the same eight years later in New Malden at the Coronation festivities ("They're much too posh for street party" was the headline in the *People*).' 'Don't look down', *London Review of Books*, 32(7): 13.

10 The idea of 'community' in British race relations, as Ben Pitcher points out, 'has become the main site at which the state and its agencies have sought to understand and construct policies designed to" affect or influence racialized minorities in particular socio-geographical contexts' (2009: 76).

11 The agreement to hold an inquiry into the murder of black teenager Stephen Lawrence, resulting in the finding of the London Metropolitan Police as institutionally racist (Macpherson 1999).

12 Quoted by Richard Seymour, 'Marxism talk on "The changing face of racism in Britain"', *Lenin's Tomb*, 6 July 2010, leninology. blogspot.com/2010/07/marxism-talk-on-changing-face-of-racism.html, accessed 6 September 2010.

13 Goodhart developed his argument over a series of essays in *Prospect* between 2004 and 2006, and in a pamphlet for the think tank Demos entitled 'Progressive nationalism' in 2007. However, it is his 2004 *Prospect* piece which is normally referenced.

14 Whatever the actual influence on his thought, attention to the circularities of recitation would suggest there is some significance in the profound overlap between Goodhart's arguments and 'welfare state

nationalism' in Scandinavia (Keskinen et al. 2009). Proponents of neoliberal 'reform' of welfare provisions and populist appeals to 'welfare chauvinism' tie the legitimacy of the welfare state to the *deservingness* and utility of migrant populations; the problem of a welfare-dependent ethnic 'underclass'; the need to prevent racism by undermining the case of the far right through limiting immigrant access to the state and to public resources; and the dilution of the national solidarity and cultural affinities underpinning the credibility of the system (Andersen 2006).

15 'Is this man the left's Enoch Powell?', BBC News, 26 April 2004, news.bbc.co.uk/1/hi/magazine/3652679.stm, accessed 6 September 2010.

16 For a discussion of the emergence of ideas of 'white working-class culture', and the abandonment of the white working class, in part because of multiculturalist hegemony, see Vron Ware (2008). Ware also discusses the reinterpretation and partial rehabilitation of Powell in documentaries during the BBC's 2008 White Season and Channel 4 dispatches. For a hugely critical review of how Denys Blakeway's 'Rivers of blood' BBC documentary sought to link the London bombings of 7 July 2005 to 'multiculturalism', see O'Neill (2008).

2 Let's talk about your culture

1 Comment on the Pickled Politics blog, www.pickledpolitics.com/archives/5603, accessed 14 April 2010.

2 The Parti des indigènes de la République's spokesperson

Houria Boutledja notes the other euphemisms used to describe them: '«Français musulmans», «nord-africains», «immigrés», «deuxième, troisième ... cent trente et unième génération», «issus de l'immigration maghrébine ou africaine» puis à nouveau «Français musulmans» et enfin «issus de la diversité» sans parler dans un registre moins soutenu par les «sidis», «bougnoules», «rats», «ratons», «crouilles», «melons», «bicots», «gris» ou encore l'intemporel «négros».' 'Petite leçon de français d'une sous-sous-chienne aux souchiens malentendants', 7 July 2007, www.indigenes-republique.fr/article.php3?id_article=188, accessed 6 May 2010.

3 www.guardian.co.uk/books/2009/jun/13/christopher-caldwell-revolution-in-europe, 13 June 2009.

4 According to Finney and Simpson, who have carried out statistical studies challenging myths about race and migration in the UK and the myth of 'minority white cities', the widely predicted assumption that several British cities will shortly become the first to be majority non-white 'needs to be interpreted as "predicted wide of the mark"' (Finney and Simpson 2009: 142). Examining a 2006 report in the *Sunday Times* that claims that Leicester, followed by Birmingham, Oldham and Bradford, will become minority white cities by 2011 and 2016 respectively, they show that these predictions are based on scant evidence. The article in *The Times* references only a Commission for Racial Equality report which itself

is based on references, three of which 'give no claim about Minority White Cities in Britain'. Four – from the *Mirror* and *Daily Telegraph* newspapers, from the Leicester Partnership and from the Benefit Fraud Inspectorate – make a claim of Leicester becoming minority white in 2011 or 2010 but give no source. A government-sponsored doctoral student's report claims that Leicester 'is to become the first "minority-majority" city in the UK, but sources a newspaper article that refers not to population but to school rolls'. Finally, the ninth source is an academic article that refers to unsourced claims about Leicester's future plural status, but concludes that 'Data for the 2001 Census indicate that the anticipated demographic changes are taking place at a lower rate than some of the more alarmist projections would appear to suggest' (Finney and Simpson 2009: 147–8). Finney and Simpson then go on to examine the quantitative evidence regarding plural cities and conclude that five key factors will determine the outcome: immigration and emigration, which is impossible to predict precisely as it depends on a host of factors including government policy; internal migration within the country; fertility, which is initially high among ethnic minorities but then evens out; momentum of a young age structure, which can change with Leicester's children, for example, being as proportioned between ethnic minorities and whites as other cities despite predictions to the contrary; and perceptions of ethnicity, which change over time, particularly with respect to mixed-parentage children whose future ethnic identification cannot be predicted at the present time.

5 For a discussion of 'deterritorialised, global Islam', see Roy (2004).

6 *Sunday Times*, 13 December 2009, www.timesonline.co.uk/tol/news/uk/article6954571.ece, accessed 16 February 2010.

7 Similarly, Caldwell dismisses accusations of police brutality by reference to the fact that 'not a single rioter was killed by the police', without explanation as to how this is the single, arbitrating indicator of brutality (2009: 113). As Sophie Body-Gendrot has established, young people in the racialized suburbs regard police surveillance and brutality as their *defining* relationship with the state. As she argues, the marginality of the *banlieues* extends to some extent also to the police, who, in a highly centralized command structure, and in a context where discussions of 'institutionalized racism' are taboo, are, like the residents, left to operate in spaces of exception (2010).

8 For a superb summary of the image of the *banlieues* in relation to the burka debates of 2010, see the article 'Burqas and banlieues: disguising France's integration problems' on the anti-racist blog Creeping Durkadurkastan, durkadurkistan.wordpress.com/2010/07/26/burqas-and-banlieues-disguising-frances-integration-problems/, accessed 5 August 2010.

9 www.germanbookreview.com/jan-fleischhauer-among-leftists/.

10 Translated from the French. Unless otherwise stated, all translations in the book are by the authors.

11 '"Souschiens" ou "sous-chiens": Une (sombre) histoire de tiret', 12 June 2008, www.montraykreyol.org/spip. php?article1269, accessed 19 November 2009.

12 The AGRIF is described as 'one of the satellites in the constellation of the Catholic and traditionalist, ultranationalist and racist Right; an influential widespread current which converges with notorious anti-Semitic former collaborators of the Vichy regime, fervent supporters of colonization, former members and sympathizers of the terrorist group of ultraright bent OAS [from the French, Organization de l'Armée Secrète], Christian fundamentalists, and others nostalgic for the Crusades'. 'Party of the Indigenous of the Republic threatened in France', 8 June 2010, readersupportednews. org/pm-section/21-21/2149-party-of-the-indigenous-of-the-republic-threatened-in-france, accessed 5 August 2010.

13 Of course, this does not deny the fact that an item of clothing, such as a veil, may be removed, while skin colour is almost impossible to conceal, rendering black and brown people as still the most likely victims of racism.

14 In 1950, UNESCO brought together a panel of social and natural scientists to draft the UNESCO Statement on Race and Racial Prejudice. This work, which asserted the lack of scientific basis

to the concept of race, proposed the use of terms such as ethnicity to describe cultural differences between human groups that have no grounding in biology or genetics, and proposed the term ethnocentrism as a better descriptor of the discrimination faced by 'minorities'.

15 Rush Limbaugh on Obama's nomination of Sonia Sotomayor to the Supreme Court, cited on *The Politics Daily*, www.politicsdaily. com/2009/05/26/rush-limbaugh-calls-sonia-sotomayor-president-obama-racists/, accessed 5 August 2010.

16 The Tea Party Movement emerged from the Tea Party protests that took place in 2009 against the US government's bank bailouts and healthcare reform initiatives. According to Gary Younge in the *Guardian* on 28 February 2010, 'If you were looking for one thing that unites them, it would not be an agenda, but anger. Many are regular anti-tax, small-government social conservatives. But there are some serious Mad Hatters at this Tea Party: they believe Obama is a Muslim communist who was not born in the US – and they tend to be the loudest'; www.guardian.co.uk/ commentisfree/cifamerica/2010/ feb/28/obama-tea-party-republicans-opposition, accessed 7 August 2010.

17 For a discussion of who is behind the Birther Movement, see 'Anti-Obama "birther movement" gathers steam', *Guardian*, www. guardian.co.uk/world/2009/ jul/28/birther-movement-obama-citizenship.

18 Gary Younge, 'To engage the birther fantasists is futile; to dismiss

them, reckless', *Guardian*, 2 August 2009.

19 www.centerforsecuritypolicy.org/p18466.xml?genre_id=1004, accessed 10 August 2010.

20 Those who oppose the building of the mosque claim that the imam behind the initiative, Feisal Abdul Rauf, hides behind a moderate exterior to promote a 'Shariah doctrine', 'the same program that animated the jihadists who destroyed the World Trade Center and many of its occupants on 9/11'; bigpeace.com/fgaffney/2010/08/13/obamas-ground-zero-mosque/, accessed 17 August 2010.

21 'Republicans battle over and about Sonia Sotomayor's "racism"', *This Week in Race*, 1 June 2009, raceproject.org/2009_06_01_archive.html.

22 In their excellent blog, *This Week in Race*, Stephen Maynard Caliendo and Charlton McIlwaine analyse the Skip Gates affair and in particular Gates's purported overreaction to his interpellation. Paying attention to the lived experience of everyday racism, they write, 'Even without all the details, I do believe that Gates reacted exactly as the officer said. I believe he said the things he did and in the tone the officer said he did. But I think that to say that Gates "overreacted" is very subjective. As a person who has been harassed by cops for absolutely nothing other than the color of my skin (like the Shawnee [Oklahoma] cops who would routinely pull me over when driving in some of the nice neighborhoods, but never give me a reason why they stopped me,

and including on two occasions having the cops called because I was "breaking in" to my own apartment, then doing searches of my apartment for no reason), I think Gates's reaction was somewhat mild – hardly an overreaction. Was it a reasonable reaction? Probably not, but we're not talking about the realm of reason here. It's the emotional feeling one gets at this kind of personal injustice.'

23 Chris Hallquist, uncrediblehallq.blogspot.com, 18 February 2007, accessed 12 June 2010.

24 For example, Hege Storhaug, of the Norwegian organization Human Rights Service, has argued that the bad patriarchies and cultural differences of illiberal immigrants present an integration challenge of such dimensions that immigration from non-Western countries should be 're-thought' (Storhaug 2003; see Fekete 2009: 93–4). Given Norway's history and humanitarian reputation, it would be possible to reject multiculturalism without the 'colonial guilt' felt in France and the UK. The degree to which gender equality has been claimed as a defining cultural value of Nordic societies, and often deployed to position Muslims as an integral threat to gender equality and human rights standards, has led to the formation of a group of activists and academics exploring *Nordic colonialism*. All Western countries have benefited from the economics of colonial expropriation, and they are also marked by its gendered and racialized power relations. To mark these societies as post-racial, or

never raced, is to ignore dense and latticed lines of colonial complicity, and how 'the lure of an enterprise as powerful and authoritative as the western civilizing project attracts even those who never belonged to its centre or were its main agents' (Keskinen et al. 2009).

25 D'Souza modifies his discussion of 'Black Culture' to 'African American culture' in the second edition, taking on board criticisms of the essentialism of the former category. It is arguable, of course, to what extent this relabelling has a substantive impact on his specification of 'cultural pathologies'. See D'Souza (1995: xxvi–xxviii).

26 Quote from a White House press release; see 'Right blasts Obama speech to students', www.politico.com/news/stories/0909/26711.html, accessed 2 August 2010.

27 (1) 'Don't talk to strangers: Obama as other', *This Week in Race*, raceproject.org/2009/09/dont-talk-to-strangers-obama-as-other.html; (2) 'Critics take aim at Obama's speech to kids', MSNBC News, www.msnbc.msn.com/id/32673334/ns/politics-white_house/.

28 blacksnob.blogspot.com/2008/04/ward-connerly-likes-obama-but-would.html.

3 Free like me

1 It is telling that Schmittian liberalism, as Triadafilopoulos argues, is articulated along a continuum from state-centred integrationism to the military adventures of the 'war on terror' (2011). Beyond the home front to the loosely encompassing war, an appeal to intentionality over practice and consequence is also pivotal. As Talal Asad has forcefully argued, the politics of intentionality, most clearly expressed in the 'accidental' killing of civilians, depends on a moralized distinction between humanitarian war and terrorism that belies the scale of devastation involved in the deployment of modern warfare technologies, and the conduct of war in spaces that are neither fully spaces of war or peace but instead a 'single space of violence': '"just war" claims to follow clear legal and moral rules but belligerent nations do not agree on how these are to be applied in concrete cases; it seeks to humanize war but accommodates the massive killing of civilians and it cannot hold powerful states accountable for atrocities; it refuses the terror threatened by insurgents but accepts the terror of a nuclear option by the state. Although theorists seek to present liberalism as consistent, unified and universal, and polemicists seek to separate it clearly from doctrines and attitudes that are illiberal, the ways in which self-styled liberals deal with questions of military violence are not so easily classifiable' (2010).

2 In all three instances – 1989, 1994, 2003 – the particular *affaire du foulard islamique* focused on the *studium*, or public school, and on fears concerning the grip of Islam on student subjectivities and the consequent implications of headscarf-wearing for the ideology of *laïcité* and the social reproduction of the nation. Anthias and Yuval-Davis have famously argued that

women are a particular focus of the nation-state's concerns, positing, but not determining, roles as the reproducers of group boundaries, and as 'signifiers of ethnic-national differences – as a focus and symbol in ideological discourses used in the construction, reproduction and transformation of ethnic/national categories' (1989: 7). Paul A. Silverstein echoes this in his exploration of how the headscarf came, in the 1980s, to represent a threat to the national and moral order. As the agents of what is problematically termed social reproduction, women can be held to represent the continuity of the 'cultural nation', while also having the instability of that identity projected on to them, becoming symbols of threat (2004: 139–49).

3 It is useful to note the inverted commas around the idea of exclusion. Liberalism is not only a post-racial politics; its fixations on differences deemed intolerable do not really constitute, or result in, exclusion.

4 'Islam stuck in the Middle Ages, says Professor Hans Kung', *The Times*, 17 June 2008, www.timesonline.co.uk/tol/comment/faith/article4150391.ece, accessed 1 September 2010.

5 Life, as Didier Fassin argues, 'is not only a question of politics seen from the outside, through the lenses of the state, of institutions, of immigration policies [...] but should also be seized from the inside, in the flesh of the everyday experiences of social agents, immigrants, and refugees' (2005: 57).

6 'Argument 9: les acquis de la

laïcité', Les mots sont importants, October 2003.

7 For example, Leila, a mother of five children, describes being physically attacked while taking a Metro with her children in Lille. During another altercation, a woman told her, '"with your headscarf there, you can go back home!" "Madame, I am at home." "At home? This will never be your home!" "Oh yes? Why are you more French than I?" "The headscarf, it's not French! Here, this is a republic! Be warned! If something bad happens to you, I will have warned you!"' (Chouder et al. 2008: 167).

8 Haute Autorité de Lutte contre les Discriminations et pour l'Égalité.

9 'Racism and Islamophobia are the real problems', 20 April 2006, miriyamaouragh.blogspot.com/2006/04/racism-and-islamophobia-are-real.html, accessed 5 April 2010.

10 The piecemeal cultural support that existed was oriented towards maintaining the cultural fitness of migrant labourers for seamless reintroduction to their home environment. See Vink (2007).

11 Prins and Saharso (2008) point to the ambivalence of this in the Dutch context, particularly in relation to the 'feminist political entrepreneurship' of Ayaan Hirsi Ali and her argument that the emancipation of Muslim women could only be achieved by explicitly rejecting Islam through the adoption of secular liberal values. Hirsi Ali's intervention resulted in significant policy attention on 'migrant women', a development the authors regard as a 'blessing and curse'. It configured Muslim women in public

discourse as 'either the victims of their own culture and religion, or in the case of women who actively identify themselves as Muslim [...] as accomplices to a culture which is oppressive to women and a threat to the cohesion of Dutch society and to the values underlying the Netherlands as a liberal democratic state' (ibid.: 380). The irony of Hirsi Ali's focus on voiceless and nameless 'victims', however, was to mobilize Muslim women's networks to publicly reject being spoken for and to 'express their own views of and desires for emancipation' (ibid.).

4 Mediating the crisis

1 cnn.tv/2009/WORLD/europe/10/08/switzerland.poster.campaign/index.html.

2 A complementary perspective is given by Nicholas Mirzoeff in his discussion of the war in Iraq and its global visual representation. Mirzoeff is uninterested in both the political redundancy of Baudrillard's analysis of the 1991 Gulf War (1991), and equally in what he describes as the tendency to 'unmask these images for their deceitful intent' (2005: 13). Instead, he argues that a constant inchoate flow of images has become part of the weaponry of the 'military-visual complex' which operates to construct war as a network of events perceived from a multiplicity of positions that immediately defies intelligibility (ibid.: 10–14). Central to this elliptical limitlessness is a reflexive media sense of a fragmented audience, an audience that has come to expect the technical manipulation of image and is comfortable with the polysemy of imagery. This results in: 'banality of images [...] in which the very awareness of the input of the viewer in creating meanings has paradoxically weakened that response. For if all meanings are personal response, the argument goes, then no one meaning has higher priority. It is however important to stress that this banality of images is no accident, but the result of a deliberate effort by those fighting the war to reduce its visual impact by saturating the senses with non-stop indistinguishable and undistinguished images' (ibid.: 14).

3 Though many of the paradigms brought to bear on 9/11 and the invasion of Iraq and Afghanistan as media events are also indebted to Paul Virilo's work on the 1991 Gulf War; see *Desert Screen: War at the Speed of Light* (2002 [1991]).

4 Ralph Negrine, in a historically informed discussion of transformations in political communication, notes that while transformations vary in degree, scale and intensity according to different political systems, it is possible to summarize main vectors of recent change at the level of *media* (the privileging of 'media logic' over 'political logic' through deregulation and globalization, the competitive power of market-oriented media actors, technological change and the dynamics of instantaneous transnational networking); at the level of *media practice* (the interplay of media logic and proactive political strategizing and communications management); at the level of the *media–politics juncture* (the field of negotiation for coverage, angle and access between media, political, corporate and civil

society actors); and at the level of the *political party* (organizational changes within parties involving less dependency on members, greater centralization of communications and public relations, issue-based strategization to capture 'floating voters' and key demographics) (2008: 157–61).

5 As Wendy Brown notes, key to understanding neoliberal rationality is understanding how it becomes dominant as governmentality without being dominant as ideology (2006: 49).

6 Writing in the the *Guardian* in June 2010, the Labour leadership candidate Ed Balls called for an open debate on immigration to the UK, and distanced himself from his 'mentor' Gordon Brown. While Balls was attempting to capitalize on Brown's image as 'out of touch' with ordinary people's concerns following what came to be known as 'Bigotgate', his vigorous populism came less than a month after a general election campaign in which candidates spent considerable energies attempting to position themselves as tough but, in a nod to anti-racialism, as a little bit loving as well. Thus Brown had, in a key policy speech at the end of March 2010, employed the rhetorical equivalent of Lord Kitchener's First World War recruitment poster, and speaking directly to migrants, informed them that our country doesn't need you: 'To those migrants who think they can get away without making a contribution; without respecting our way of life; without honouring the values that make Britain what it is – I have only one message – you are not welcome.' To possess such exalted

values is also to live them, and after deploying images of the parasitical alien, Brown called for the debate on migration to be conducted 'responsibly'. In the struggle to appropriate the experience of Gillian Duffy, the 'Rochdale pensioner, on her way for a loaf of bread', this episode confirms the enduring utility of immigration/integration to populism as a mode of representation (Arditi 2008). Commenting on the arms race dynamics of the UK election migration debate, Gary Younge noted that 'there can be no meaningful debate about immigration in Britain (or anywhere else) that does not address neoliberal globalisation, trade policy, development, aid, colonial legacy, the European Social Fund, the dependency ratio and the low paid. But that is not the debate we have been having. Indeed, it is not a debate we have ever had. It's not accusations of racism that are stopping that conversation, but racism itself. For if there is a liberal elite out there thwarting discussion on immigration, it is doing a very bad job. The tabloids and middle-market papers seem to talk about little else, and whenever they play their inflammatory tunes the politicians duly dance'; 'Yes we need an honest immigration debate, but this tough talk isn't it', 'Comment is Free', *Guardian*, Monday, 26 April 2010.

7 Both events also depended heavily on a performative appeal to anti-racialism that has its roots in the 'commonsense' self-protection discourses of new racism (Barker 1981). The Howard government argued in effect that, as representatives of the people,

their actions could never be racist as the people are not racist, thus also leaning on post-race moralization of the worthy and unworthy. The Irish government presented their actions as in fact anti-racist, as 'the greatest contribution to racism and xenophobia would be if it was perceived that the Government could not control immigration' (politician quoted in Lentin 2007: 620); and through a similar populist trope of transparency, if the people voted for this in a referendum, and the people are intrinsically not racist, how could this be racist?

8 As Didier Fassin has argued in relation to the periodic media event of moving asylum seekers from the Sangatte Red Cross camp near Calais, and from an informal encampment known as '*le jungle*', the ambivalence of the camp in French political culture renders this kind of event ambivalent in itself; Sangatte became the emblematic 'camp' among many on the north coast of France, but it also conjured with the camps of the Second World War period (2005: 228).

9 The image of the minarets on the Swiss flag has been 'loaned' by the SVP to other right-wing groups, and it has appeared in protests in Germany, Austria and Poland. See Charles Hawley, 'International right-wingers gather for EU-wide minaret ban', *Der Spiegel International*, 26 March 2010, www.spiegel.de/international/germany/0,1518,685896,00.html, accessed 18 April 2010.

10 For example, Julia Onken: '[m]osques are male houses, minarets are male power symbols

[...] The building of minarets is also a visible signal of the state's acceptance of the oppression of women.' See Mairéad Enright, 'Swiss minaret ban: key points', *Human Rights in Ireland*, blog, 7 December 2009, www.humanrights.ie/index.php/2009/12/07/the-swiss-minaret-ban-key-points/.

11 www.cbc.ca/arts/film/story/2009/04/16/wilders-geert-fitna-sequel.html.

12 Westergaard sued Wilders for using the cartoon without copyright permission, and it was removed in a subsequent edit.

13 Liesbet van Zoonen's project on the life of *Fitna* has focused on how it provoked a huge range of viral responses; cut 'n' mix political engagements, video testimonials of personal experience in relation to the film or themes, and responses made to 'tag and jam' the film and obstruct its viral dissemination. See van Zoonen et al., 'Fitna: the video battle' (2010), paper available at www.lboro.ac.uk/.../FITNA/.../BJoS%20Fitna%20Van%20Zoonen,%20Muller,%20Hirzalla.pdf.

14 www.spiegel.de/international/germany/0,1518,667158,00.html.

15 In January 2010 an attempt was made on the life of Kurt Westergaard, when a man with an axe attacked him in his home in Arhus. Prior to that, the cartoons were reprinted by all the major Danish newspapers in February 2008 as an act of solidarity following the arrest of three men in connection with a conspiracy to murder Westergaard. A long interview in *Der Spiegel* gives an account of the traumatic personal cost of the cartoon's aftermath for

Westergaard, which he continues to understand purely in universalist terms, casting voices critical of the political gestation of the cartoons crisis as an 'intellectual class [...] that spends its time drinking coffee and polishing its cultural relativism'. See Henryk M. Broder, 'Muhammad cartoonist defiant after attack', *Der Spiegel*, 20 January 2010, www.spiegel.de/international/europe/0,1518,672716,00.html. The case of the Swedish cartoonist Lars Vilks, a self-described 'freedom of speech activist', has also come to be intertwined with the narrative after he published cartoons of a dog with the head of Muhammad in the regional newspaper *Nerikes Allehanda* in 2007, also as a protest at what he saw as self-censorship. 'Brothers jailed for Vilks arson attack', *The Local*, 15 July 2010, www.thelocal.se/27806/20100715/.

16 In an interview with *Index on Censorship* concerning her book *The Cartoons that Shook the World* (2009), Jytte Klausen points to the difficulties involved in relating violent deaths to the cartoons outside of their instrumentalization in pre-existing local and regional conflicts; www.eurozine.com/articles/2010-01-25-klausen-en.html.

17 www.danielpipes.org/7808/swiss-minarets-european-islam.

18 See, for example, the 2010 campaign by the European Federation of Journalists protesting against the 'spiral of decline' in news investment, working conditions and editorial prerogatives; europe.ifj.org/en/articles/unions-of-journalists-pledge-fight-back-over-spiral-of-decline-in-european-media.

19 Bauder's (2008) quantitative study of news coverage of proposed changes to immigration law in Germany examines the possible influence of media coverage, between 2001 and 2004, on the shift in orientation from a seminal assertion of Germany as an 'immigration society' to a 'rather conservative piece of legislation' focusing on integration (ibid.: 95). He examined how reportage where 'external events were discursively linked to migration', in particular after the terrorist attacks in Madrid in 2004, resulted in a 'danger topos' where news routinely associated immigration and immigrants with risk and terrorism (ibid.: 108).

20 Speculative in the sense that there is significant scope here for future qualitative research on media coverage, institutional processes and procedures and journalistic practices and understandings on the examples under discussion. However, here we draw on existing qualitative research and theoretical frameworks to advance the discussion.

21 See '*Résultats par région linguistique et par type d'habitat: interdiction de minarets*' in the report '*Votation populaire du 29 novembre 2009, Office fédérale de la statistique*', www.bfs.admin.ch/bfs/portal/fr/index/themen/17/03/blank/key/2009/05.html, accessed 15 July 2010.

22 The True Finns Helsinki city councillor Jussi Halla-aho, for example, was convicted in September 2009 of 'violating the sanctity of religion' for blogging that the Prophet Muhammad was a paedophile, and Islam a religion that sanctifies

paedophilia. See 'Court finds City Council member guilty of insulting religion', *Helsingin Sanomat International*, 9 September 2009, www. hs. fi/english/article/Court+finds+ City+Council+member+guilty+of+ insulting+religion/1135249190300. The court case arose from an original complaint by the women's organization of the Finnish Green Party, on account of Halla-aho's musings on the pedagogy of rape by immigrants for deluded female multiculturalists: 'The number of rapes will increase in any case. Therefore, as more and more women will undoubtedly get raped, I sincerely hope that at least the right women, the green-leftist reformers and their voters, will find themselves in the clutches of the rapists, who randomly select their victims. Rather them than anyone else. With people like that nothing else works, except when their own multiculturalist views turn against them.' See 'Green women's organization considers filing criminal report against True Finns Jussi Halla-aho', *Helsingin Sanomat International*, 14 November 2008, http://www.hs.fi/ english/article/1135241093602.

5 Good and bad diversity

1 For a genealogy of the events, see bang.calit2.net/2010/03/bang-lab-edt-update-call-for-accountability-and-the-criminalization-of-research/.

2 bang.calit2.net/.

3 The petition text specifies the difference between the potential of a virtual sit-in to really disrupt website activity and the more damaging Distributed Denial of Service Attack (DDOS). 'There are several critical differences between a virtual sit-in and a DDOS: a DDOS is prolonged and unending, used by various governmental groups to censor a wide variety of free speech groups, activist groups, etc, and non-transparent (the creators of the DDOS set up virtual robots to blast a given site with millions of hits, and hide the creators behind various firewalls and filters. A virtual sit-in is open, does not use such "robots," and the creators are identified freely)'; www.thepetitionsite.com/1/ stop-the-de-tenuring-of-ricardo-dominguez.

4 For example, in November 2009 students involved in an occupation of a university building at the University of Sussex in the UK were beset by police and issued with injunctions in addition to being disciplined by the university.

5 www.viceland.com/int/ v16n11/htdocs/follow-the-gps-225. php?page=2.

6 blog.art21.org/2010/06/04/ uc-crisis-post-3-try-not-to-do-this-again/.

7 www.migrationinformation. org/feature/display.cfm?ID=407.

8 www.signonsandiego.com/ news/2010/mar/07/taxpayers-should-be-outraged-use-funds/.

9 For example Mohammad Sidique Khan, described as the ringleader of the London '7/7' bombings of 2005, was typically referred to as being well integrated into British society. According to a BBC report, Sidique Khan lived a 'Westernized' life, going by the name 'Sid' and even shunning his Pakistani-Muslim origins. 'Suicide bombers' "ordinary" lives', BBC

News, news.bbc.co.uk/1/hi/4678837.
stm, accessed 8 September 2010.

10 Omi and Winant (1994)
describe racial formation as 'a
permanent process in which
historically situated projects
interact: in the clash and connect,
as well as the accommodation and
overlap of these projects, human
bodies and consciousness as well as
social institutions and structures,
are represented and organized. We
argue that in any given historical
context, racial signification and
racial structuration are ineluctably
linked. To represent, interpret, or
signify upon race, then, to assign
meaning to it, is at least implicitly
and often explicitly to locate it in
social structural terms.'

11 In a July 2010 *Counterpunch*
article, Bill Quigley gives fourteen
examples of how the US criminal
justice system is one in which
'African-Americans are directly
targeted and punished in a much
more aggressive way than white
people'. Showing how, statistically,
African-Americans are far more
likely to be arrested and incarcerated
than whites, he concludes that the
US prison system functions like
a new Jim Crow, 'creating legal
boundaries between them and
us, allowing legal discrimination
against them, removing the right to
vote from millions, and essentially
warehousing a disposable population
of unwanted people'; www.counter
punch.org/quigley07262010.html.

12 TANF 'clients' are subjected
to 'stricter work requirements,
narrower exemption criteria, an
expanded menu of behaviours
subject to sanction, and stronger

penalities for noncompliance'
(Schram et al. 2008: 19).

13 This is despite the fact that,
as Bill Quigley (2010) shows, in
the USA, 'if poor whites or others
get out of line, they will be given
the worst possible treatment,
they will be treated just like poor
blacks'; www.counterpunch.org/
quigley07262010.html, accessed
23 August 2010.

14 Dana-Ain Davis notes that,
whereas in 1992 welfare recipients
were 39 per cent white, 37 per cent
African-American and 18 per cent
Hispanic, by 2001 the figures had
become 30, 39 and 26 per cent
respectively. She notes that the
shift in the racial composition of
the recipients accelerated after the
introduction of new welfare policies
in 1996.

15 This politics is complicated
by the 'progressive' attack on
diversity, as evidenced by the work
of David Goodhart, where the
broadly symbolic commitment
to diversity is enlisted to provide
a materialist gloss to culturalist
aversion (see Chapter 1). Too much
diversity is incompatible with social
solidarity, and with solidarity only
conceivable in ethno-cultural terms,
diversity weakens the legitimacy
of the welfare state. Ultimately,
however, there is no conflict between
the celebration of diversity and its
restriction in these terms, as both
have abstracted difference from
socially structured asymmetries.

16 'Sarkozy dégaine les clichés
et cible les immigrés', *Libération*,
31 July 2010.

17 Article 1 of the French
constitution declares all citizens to

be equal before the law regardless of their origin.

18 The video can be viewed at www.20minutes.fr/article/586841/Societe-La-video-d-une-expulsion-a-La-Courneuve-fait-polemique.php, accessed 20 August 2010.

19 The Hungarian far-right party Jobbik (Movement for a Better Hungary) captured 17 per cent of the national vote in a 2010 election on an explicitly anti-Semitic and anti-Roma platform. It linked its most recent policy proposal, for compulsory 'public order protection camps' for Roma, to the ongoing action in France. On Jobbik, see Paul Hockenos, 'Inside Hungary's anti-Semitic right wing', *Global Post*, 1 June 2010, www.globalpost.com/dispatch/europe/100528/hungary-jobbik-far-right-party, accessed 15 August 2010, and on the public order integration camp proposals, see Daniel McLaughlin, 'Far right party calls for camps for Hungary's Roma', *Irish Times*, 3 September 2010.

20 'Nicolas Sarkozy gets tough on France's itinerant groups', *Guardian*, 27 July 2010, www.guardian.co.uk/world/2010/jul/27/france-nicolas-sarkozy-roma-gypsy.

21 For an overview, see Steve Erlanger, 'Expulsion of Roma raises questions in France', *New York Times*, 19 August 2010, www.nytimes.com/2010/08/20/world/europe/20france.html, and for Sweden, 'Tiggeri inte en rimlig försörjning' [Begging is not sufficient support], *Dagens Nyheter*, 31 July 2010, www.dn.se/nyheter/sverige/tiggeri-inte-en-rimlig-forsorjning-1.1146195.

22 For an overview of twentieth-century French administrative action against Roma, see Olivia Miljanic and Robert Zaretsky, 'France: behind the expulsion of the Roma', *Le Monde Diplomatique*, 3 September 2010, mondediplo.com/blogs/france-behind-the-expulsion-of-the-roma.

23 It should also be noted that there is a total lack of historicized contextualization of the types of measures proposed by Sarkozy, although the Parti des Indigènes de la République reminds us of the existence of precedents: the Vichy regime 'denaturalized' French citizens going back to 1927 ('Qui ose encore dire qu'il n'y a pas d'indigènes en France?', *PIR*, 3 August 2010, www.indigenes-republique.fr/article.php3?id_article=1048). Nevertheless, there is the distinct impression that recalling this, or indeed the racial classifications of Jews or Gypsies under Nazism, is completely unnecessary in the face of the apparently unbounded threat to France being posed by alien outsiders. As has already been pointed out, the failure to call to mind these very historical references is, on the face of things at least, stranger still given the ease with which they trip off the tongue when the urgency *not* to evoke race is insisted upon. Historical memory becomes expedient only when it can serve in sustaining the order of things.

24 By recalling, but also tempering, Žižek's (1997) well-known dismissal of liberal multiculturalism as 'the form of appearance of its opposite, of the

massive presence of capitalism as universal world system', the widespread appeal to diversity emerges as a dimension of capitalism's 'routes to survival in critiques of it', particularly the ingestion of the 'artistic critique' of the uniformity and regulation of Fordist capitalism. As a value of the 'connexionist world', diversity provides a thematic dimension to the neoliberal individualization of working conditions, but also, with its inscription in the project of the actualizing self, elective community and putative freedom from hierarchy, diversity is a moral promise (Boltanski and Chiapello 2005). That 'diversity' is primarily attuned to the space of appearances is also a familiar critique. In a rather more nuanced account than Žižek's, Henry Giroux has drawn attention to the ambivalence of this promise in the marketization of culture. As every teenager knows, any sign can be appropriated. However, as Giroux argues, 'difference is also a dangerous marker of those historical, political, social and cultural borderlands where people who are considered the "other" are often policed, excluded and oppressed' and thus it is never without the 'legacy of possible disruption' (2009). The depoliticization of difference in diversity is in its rendering through the act of recognition, in being interpolated as the solution to the problem it references, in being made available within a consensus on the harmony made possible through recognition. The moral promise of diversity is a recursive promise, an idea Ron Becker echoes in analysing the emergence of gay-themed television in the 1990s as signifying the 'affordable politics of social liberalism' for baby boomers and Generation Xers. Shorn of class and systemic exclusion, the gay freedom and economic prosperity of acceptable gay archetypes naturalizes the primacy of cultural over political-economic struggle, fusing 'a cutting edge allure dulled just enough by [...] assimilationist goals' (2006: 184). Prosperous gay characters, in Becker's argument, signify an acceptable diversity that serves to obscure racialized economic inequality through commitment to a 'more easily digested Other' (ibid.: 204).

25 The first dimension of this turn is quite obvious. Thomas Faist (2009), for example, while welcoming what he sees as the extension of multiculturalism into an emerging idea of diversity, recognizes its attraction as a rebranding opportunity, thus appealing to neoliberal emphases of autonomy and reflexive competence, and the general incorporation of 'cultural factors' into organizational management (ibid.: 173–4; see also Wrench 2004). Rebranding does just that, so as well as smuggling back the insistent reifications of experimental failure, diversity programmes are disconnected from 'actual political developments and societal practices' (Faist 2009: 186). In some contexts the process of rebranding is more involved. Public service broadcasters in Europe, for example, have indirectly – and sometimes directly – responded

to the 'crisis of multiculturalism' by reworking multicultural programming as diversity, while seizing on to the discourse of integration as a legitimizing narrative for national broadcasters decentred by digitalization, media transnationalization and audience fragmentation (Larsen 2010). In Roger Silverstone's theorization of *media work as boundary work* (2007), the modern centripetal phase of public service broadcasters involved the work of 'boundary and community construction at national [...] levels' (ibid.: 19). In the network society, where the integrative role of national broadcasting is disturbed, boundary work becomes more difficult but, from the broadcasters' perspective, also more pressing. As a consequence, the governmental fusion of diversity and integration has significant elective affinity, proposing both a renewed institutional role, but also a way of conceptualizing audience fragmentation as 'diversity', a move which, for example, has provided 'reality television' formats with a form of socio-political justification. In the UK, Ben O'Loughlin (2006) has demonstrated how BBC policy shifted from an essentialist vision of multiculturalism to a 'concept of cultural diversity' influenced by community cohesion agendas, and the knowledge economy goal of increasing individual social capital (ibid.: 15).

26 Biopower refers to the state's role in fostering life or letting die. This stands in contrast to the old sovereign power which administered death, but did nothing to promote life. The biopolitical state, thus, is concerned with the life of its population, seeing it as a single organism that must be kept alive. It therefore disciplines individual bodies within it and regularizes the population in general.

27 The burka has been appropriated to culturalist governmentality elsewhere also. In 2009, the Conservative Party in Denmark called for the burka to be banned in public places, citing its un-Danish oppression of women. The government established a commission of inquiry, and research conducted by Copenhagen University for the commission revealed that three women in Denmark wear the burka, with between 150 and 200 wearing the niqab (over one third of them are Danish converts). After, in conjunction with the Danish People's Party, accusing the research team of 'poor scientific method', the Conservative Integration spokesperson Naser Khader admitted that while a ban on dress in public space would be unconstitutional, it would be necessary to enact legislation for certain circumstances, such as driving buses. Andreassen's research (2010), cited in Chapter 3, noted how the recited truth of the burka informed a debate in 2007 concerning the problem of employing burka-wearing women in kindergartens, and extended to those who opt for a life on benefits by choosing to wear the burka. As one Liberal (Venstre) politician summarized: 'If one is at the labour market's disposal, then one needs to send a signal that one wishes to

enter the labour market, and one does not do that if one is covered and wearing a burka' (ibid.).

28 'Sarkozy speaks out against burka', 22 June 2009, news.bbc. co.uk/1/hi/8112821.stm.

29 'France moves toward partial burqa ban', 26 January 2010, edition.cnn.com/2010/WORLD/ europe/01/26/france.burqa.ban/ index.html.

30 The murder took place during a court hearing of Axel W.'s appeal against the 750-euro fine he incurred for calling Sherbini terrorist, 'Islamist' and 'bitch' when she asked him to make room for her son to play on swings at a local park in 2008. While stabbing Marwa, Axel W. shouted, 'You have no right to live.' Her husband was also injured when he was shot in the leg by a German security officer while he was trying to protect his wife.

6 On one more condition

1 The exact death toll at Sétif in the weeks following the outbreak of violence on 8 May 1945 (VE Day) has always been disputed, a dispute that owes much, as Alistair Horne has argued, to the enormously different significances accorded to the massacre: 'For all the general ignorance in metropolitan France of what happened at Sétif, the impact on Algerians was incalculable, and ineradicable' (2006 [1977]: 277]).

2 Leigh Philips, 'UKIP, Lega Nord form hard-right bloc in the EU Parliament', euobserver.com/9/28394.

3 'Immigrants to be taught the fine British art of how to queue', Daily Mail, 14 February 2010, www.dailymail.co.uk/news/

article-1250946/They-havent-got-queue-Government-teach-immigrants-British-art-lining-up. html#ixzz0zOmQUlEJ.

4 'Declaration on integration and active citizenship in Danish society', www.nyidanmark.dk/en-us/coming_to_dk/permanent-residence-permit/integration-and-active-citizenship.htm.

5 Anne Andlauer, 'Le Danemark durcit sa politique d'immigration', RFI, 16 March 2010, www.rfi.fr/contenu/20100316-le-danemark-durcit-politique-immigration.

6 'Minister scraps integration "Jewish star"', Expatica, 22 June 2004, www.expatica.com/nl/news/local_news/minister-scraps-integration-jewish-star---8753.html. In 2003, for example, the Dutch justice minister, Piet Hein Donner, proposed a two-tier justice system for foreigners and Dutch nationals; the PvdA (Labour) party debated a ban on child benefits for foreign families with more than one child (van Stokrom 2003).

7 The Cette France Là collective (2009: 365) cites a 2008 European Commission report, 'Employment in Europe', which notes that 'recently arrived immigrants have generally contributed to the global growth of the economy and of employment (by almost a quarter) in the Union since 2000 without there having been any major repercussions for salaries and national employment levels'.

8 As remarked by the Cette France Là collective's report into the work done by Sans papiers in France, most undocumented migrants do in fact work, using a false identity, meaning that they thus pay into the

national taxation and social security system on a basis equal to that of any other French worker.

9 Another example is the ways in which citizenship tests and 'reform' were seamlessly linked to terrorism, immigration controls and the integration of Muslims in Australia after the London bombings in 2005. According to Kuhn (2009), for all the marked accretion of anti-Muslim racism to forms of multicultural backlash (Hage 2003; Poynting and Mason 2006, 2007) a governmental focus on the domopolitical problem of Muslims – that is, on a continuum from global terrorist to potential migrant to existing citizens – was rapidly mobilized during 2006/07, and presented as responsibility for the shared home. According to one government minister: '[A]fter months of discussions with Muslim communities I believe that [their] unfair stigmatisation will not change materially until all Australian Muslims take responsibility for addressing the situation they find themselves in. Each Australian Muslim in their own way and in their own circumstance should seek to address the fears and misunderstandings of the broader community' (quoted in Kuhn 2009: 66).

10 It is also interesting to note that the Good Friday Agreement has been thoroughly criticized for institutionalizing a multicultural model of 'two communities' coexisting through a 'parity of esteem', a phrase that in turn found its way back into mainstream 'interculturalism' in Ireland. On the first point, see Coulter (1999); on the latter see Lentin and McVeigh (2006).

11 www.couscousglobal.com/page/81/en.

12 www.couscousglobal.com/page/3356/en.

13 In July 2010, the whistleblowing website WikiLeaks published more than 90,000 records of incidents and intelligence reports about the war in Afghanistan, revealing 'how coalition forces have killed hundreds of civilians in unreported incidents, Taliban attacks have soared and Nato commanders fear neighbouring Pakistan and Iran are fuelling the insurgency'; 'Afghanistan: the war logs', *Guardian*, 25 July 2010.

14 Priyamvada Gopal, 'Burqas and bikinis', *Guardian*, 3 August 2010, www.guardian.co.uk/commentisfree/2010/aug/03/burkas-bikinis-reality-afghan-lives, accessed 11 September 2010.

15 Aisha's story has now been revealed to be falsified by the Revolutionary Association of the Women of Afghanistan (Rawa). Aisha, who is in fact called Nazia, had her nose and ears mutilated by her husband, 'an old man who had already killed his first wife', and not by the Taliban, as *Time* alleges. Taliban misogyny and hostility to gender equality not denied, this was nevertheless a case of domestic, not political, violence. 'Is *Time*'s Aisha story fake?', *Huffington Post*, 29 August 2010, www.rawa.org/temp/runews/2010/08/29/is-time-s-aisha-story-fake.html, accessed 11 September 2010.

16 Huda Jawad reports that 'the numbers sold to the media paint an upbeat picture of the state of Afghan women. In reality, these statistics are a cruel joke and

do nothing to improve the social standing of women. Ten years and 300 billion dollars later, the United States has done little to empower females in the war-torn country. In the Uruzgan province there are officially 220 schools, but only 21 of them function. According to researcher Rachel Reid in Kabul for Human Rights Watch, "only four per cent of secondary school age girls reach grade 10"'; *Dissident Voice*, 9 August 2010, www.rawa.org/temp/runews/2010/08/09/liberating-the-women-of-afghanistan.html, accessed 11 September 2010.

17 For example, 160 women a year are said to be killed by their partners in France every year; 'Violent French husbands "may be tagged"', BBC News, news.bbc.co.uk/1/hi/world/europe/8537591.stm, accessed 11 September 2010.

18 Huda Jawad, op. cit.

19 'Soumise à l'ordre postcolonial: "Quand Fadéla rallie Sarko": trahison politicienne, continuité politique', Les Mots Sont Importants, lmsi.net/Soumise-a-l-ordre-post colonial, accessed 31 August 2010.

20 NPNS is exemplary of the particularity that is official French anti-racist politics, first seen with the rise of SOS Racisme in the 1980s. Generally understood as a crucial junior ally of the French Socialist Party under Mitterrand, SOS Racisme, by founding itself upon an unwavering commitment to republican universalist values, wholeheartedly rejects the *communautarisme* of 'Anglo-Saxon' multiculturalism as divisive and detrimental to an anti-racism that seeks to incorporate, rather than alienate, the greatest

number of people (Lentin 2004). Indeed, the NPNS leader, Fadéla Amara, joined SOS Racisme in the 1980s, seeing it as more welcoming to women activists than the autonomous anti-racist movement around the '*Marche des beurs*'. Amara rose to become president of the Fédération Nationale des Maisons de Potes, a spin-off organization of SOS Racisme (Raissiguier 2008).

21 www.niputesnisoumises.com/mouvement-presentation/, accessed 11 September 2010.

22 www.niputesnisoumises.com/laicite/, accessed 12 September 2010.

23 Les Mots Sont Importants, 'Argument 5: la protection des "non-voilées"', October 2003, lmsi.net/Argument-5-la-protection-des-non, accessed 12 September 2010.

24 www.mixtogether.org/, accessed 16 September 2010.

25 'Using forced marriages for your own agenda', *Pickled Politics*, 8 November 2009, www.pickled-politics.com/archives/6493, accessed 16 September 2010.

26 Delphy and Bouteldja (2007) note that its success in helping to bring a woman of North African descent, Fadéla Amara, to power as a minister in Nicolas Sarkozy's government is not a sign of the more generalized success of integration policies. Rather, it is cynically political, representing a 'win-win' situation for the dominant order. Amara's ascent to power has two positive effects for the maintenance of a 'politics of gender typical of colonial orders': 'one for whites as a dominant group, the other for those who dominate as a function of being men' (ibid.). In other words, what could

be regarded as a coup by a relatively young, racialized woman leading to her becoming a government minister is belied by the function that Amara and her co-ministers, Rama Yade and Rachida Dati, served for perpetuating the notion of the French state as egalitarian, which in turn allowed the sexist and racist status quo to remain unaltered.

27 'Judith Butler refuses Berlin Pride Civil Courage Prize 2010', *No Homonationalism*, nohomo nationalism.blogspot.com/2010/06/ judith-butler-refuses-berlin-pride. html, accessed 13 September 2010.

28 The text of Butler's speech can be found at www.egs.edu/faculty/ judith-butler/articles/i-must-distance-myself/, accessed 13 September 2010.

29 The organizations are GLADT, LesMigraS, SUSPECT and ReachOut.

30 Gary Younge, 'Gay equality can't yet be claimed a western value, but it is a human right', *Guardian*. 7 June 2010, www.guardian.co.uk/ commentisfree/2010/jun/07/racism-islamophobia-homophobia-far-right, accessed 13 September 2010.

31 Among countless other initiatives (Puar 2007: 19), Tatchell states that 'for nearly four decades I have worked with the leading black, Muslim, anti-racist, anti-imperialist and left-wing campaigners in the UK [...] I was one of the original endorsers of the Palestine Solidarity Campaign UK in 1982 and a keynote speaker at its founding conference, and I have supported oppressed Muslims from Palestine, to Iraq, Chechnya and Kashmir'; www.petertatchell.net/, accessed 13 September 2010.

32 Tatchell is careful not to paint all Muslims with the same brush, coming out on the side of 'our Muslim brothers and sisters in countries like Saudi Arabia and Iran'. However, he participates in perpetuating the view of Islam as particularly, and uniquely, repressive by couching what he sees as the left's refusal to come out against Muslim fundamentalism as 'political correctness': 'Most liberals and left-wingers would protest loud and strong if these persecutions were perpetrated by a western regime or by Christian fundamentalists. But they get squeamish when it comes to challenging human rights abuses done in the name of Islam.' While he claims that the reason for this is that left-wingers 'confuse protests against fundamentalist, political Islam, which seeks to establish a religious dictatorship, with an attack on Muslim people and the Muslim faith', he fails to acknowledge the fact that, within the context of the 'war on terror', both Muslim people and brown people generally are treated as representatives of the fundamentalist Islam he opposes, whether or not they identify with it. Peter Tatchell, 'Just say no to Sharia law', *Guardian*. 19 November 2009, www.guardian.co.uk/commentisfree/ belief/2009/nov/19/islam-religion, accessed 13 September 2010.

33 Gary Younge, op. cit.

34 While being careful to defend the advances brought about by multicultural policies, Peter Tatchell opposes multiculturalism's 'excesses' to individual human rights: '[By] asserting and celebrating difference, multiculturalism can also divide people on racial, religious and other

grounds. It risks emphasising divergences between different communities that may evolve into rivalries and antagonisms. We have in Britain, for instance, witnessed riots between factions of Afro-Caribbean and Asian youths, and tensions between sections of the Muslim and Jewish communities. Too much emphasis on difference can easily spill over into separateness, which subverts an understanding of our common humanity and undermines notions of universal rights and freedoms. It can produce a new form of tribalism, where societies are fragmented into myriad communities, each loyal primarily to itself and with little interest in the common good of society and the collective welfare of humankind as a whole'; 'Their multiculturalism and ours', *Democratiya*, 8, Spring 2007, www.petertatchell.net/multiculturalism/democratiya8.htm, accessed 13 September 2010.

35 As Haritaworn and Petzen explain, the term 'migrant', originally born out of anti-racist struggle, has come to replace that of 'foreigner' in Germany, used to describe 'not only the contracted labourers who came in the post-war period from North Africa and southern Europe (most of whom were from Turkey), but also their German-born or raised children, or indeed anyone whose non-white parentage is visibly written on their bodies' (2010).

36 Dominant gay organizations such as the LSVD and the COC, the premier gay rights organization in the Netherlands, have become the mouthpiece for a discourse that becomes progressively more entrenched, eventually becoming a fundamental part of the integration strategies of several European states. In what Gunkel and Pitcher refer to as 'an act of audacious historical revisionism', the LSVD participates in mobilizing gay rights 'as a key signifier of European cultural superiority, as (white) gay Germans assert their membership of the national community through the construction of the figure of the homophobic Muslim' (2008a). From this, it is a short step to the institutionalization of 'gay-friendliness' as a prerequisite for integration. In what came to be known as the Muslim Test, the Christian Democrat-led government of the German *Land* of Baden-Württemberg introduced a questionnaire given exclusively to citizenship applicants from Muslim countries. The majority of the questions relate to gender and sexuality and include the following: 'Imagine your son comes to you and declares that he's a homosexual and would like to live with another man. How do you react?' (cited in ibid.). The Berlin chapter of the LSVD came out in favour of the test and appealed to the Berlin Senate to adopt it (Haritaworn and Petzen 2010). Although this particular battle was ultimately lost and the test abandoned, the media debate served the purpose of inserting the idea of migrants/Muslims in Germany as intrinsically homophobic and, thus, no longer in need of being integrated, but rather as posing a threat to integration reconfigured as a society-wide right.

37 'Is courage a masculine value?', *In Character, a Journal of Everyday Virtues*, incharacter.org/pro-con/is-courage-a-masculine-virtue/.

Bibliography

Abbas, Tahir (ed.) (2005) *Muslim Britain: Communities under Siege*, USA: Palgrave Macmillan.

Afshar, Haleh (2008) 'Can I see your hair? Choice, agency and attitudes: the dilemma of faith and feminism for Muslim women who cover', *Ethnic and Racial Studies*, 31(2): 411–27.

Agamben, Giorgio (1998) *Homo-Sacer: Sovereign Power and Bare Life*, Stanford, CA: Stanford University Press.

— (2005) *State of Exception*, Chicago, IL: University of Chicago Press.

Agier, Michel (2009) 'The camps of the twenty-first century: corridors, security vestibules and borders of internal exile', *Irish Journal of Anthropology*, 12(3): 39–44

Ahmed, Sara (2004) 'Declarations of whiteness: the non-performativity of anti-racism', *Borderlands e-journal*, 3(2), www.borderlands.net.au/vol3no2_2004/ahmed_declarations.htm.

— (2007) 'You end up doing the document rather than doing the doing: diversity, race equality and the politics of documentation', *Ethnic and Racial Studies*, 30(4): 590–609.

— (2008) 'Liberal multiculturalism is the hegemony: it's an empirical fact – a response to Slavoj Žižek', *Darkmatter: In the Ruins of Imperial Culture*, 19 February.

— (2009) 'Problematic proximities, or why critiques of "gay im-perialism" matter', www.alanalentin.net/2009/11/09/problematic-proximities-or-why-critiques-of-gay-imperialism-matter/, 9 November, accessed 17 September 2010.

Ahmed, Sara and Elaine Swan (eds) (2006) 'Doing diversity work', *Policy Futures in Education*, 4(1).

Ahmed, Sara, Shona Hunter, Sevgi Kilic, Elaine Swan and Lewis Turner (2006) 'Race, diversity and leadership in the learning and skills sector', Commissioned by the Centre for Excellence in Leadership.

Ali, Ayaan Hirsi (2009) 'Swiss ban on minarets was a vote for tolerance and inclusion', *Christian Science Monitor*, www.csmonitor.com/Commentary/Opinion/2009/1205/p09s01-coop.html.

Aly, A. and D. Walker (2007) 'Veiled threats: recurrent cultural anxieties in Australia', *Journal of Muslim Minority Affairs*, 27(2): 203–14.

Amir-Moazami, Schirin (2007) *Politisierte Religion. Der Kopf-tuchstreit in Deutschland und Frankreich*, Bielefeld.

Amiraux, V. (2001) *Acteurs de l'Islam entre Allemagne et Turquie. Parcours militants et expériences religieuses*, Paris: L'Harmattan.

— (2010) '"L'affaire du foulard" en France: retour sur une affaire qui n'en est pas encore une', *Sociologie et sociétés*, 41(2): 273–98.

Amiraux, V. and P. Simon (2006) 'There are no minorities here: cultures of scholarship and public debate on immigrants and integration in France', *International Journal of Comparative Sociology*, 47(3/4): 191–215.

Amirthalingam, Kumaralingam (2007) 'Free speech and religious sensitivity', *Media, Culture and Society*, 29: 509–15.

Amos, Valerie and Pratibha Parmar (1984) 'Challenging imperial feminism', *Feminist Review*, 17: 3–19.

Andersen, Jorgen Goul (2006) 'Immigration and the legitimacy of the Scandinavian welfare state: some preliminary findings', AMID Working Papers series 53/2006.

Anderson, Perry (2007) 'Depicting Europe', *London Review of Books*, 29(18): 13–21.

Andreassen, Rikke (2010) 'Sing a song but stay out of politics. Two cases of representation in the Danish media', in Kaarina Nikunen and Elisabeth Eide (eds), *Media in Motion*: Cultural Complexity and Migration in the Nordic Region, Aldershot: Ashgate.

Andreassen, R. and D. Lettinga (2011) 'Veiled debates: gender and gender equality in European national narratives', ch. 3 in S. Rosenberger and B. Sauer (eds), *Politics, Religion and Gender. Regulating the Muslim headscarf*, New York: Routledge.

Ang, Ien and Brett St Louis (2005) 'The predicament of difference', *Ethnicities*, 5(3): 291–304.

Anthias F. and N. Yuval-Davis (eds)

(1989) *Woman, Nation, State*, Basingstoke: Macmillan.

— (1992) *Racialized Boundaries; Race, Nation, Gender, Colour and Class and the Anti-Racist Struggle*, London: Routledge.

Anthony, Andrew (2008) *The Fallout: How a Guilty Liberal Lost His Innocence*, London: Vintage.

Aouragh, Miriyam and Anouk de Koning (2006) 'Racism and Islamophobia are the real problems', miriyamaouragh. blogspot.com/2006/04/racism-and-islamophobia-are-real.html.

Appadurai, Arjun (1996) *Modernity at Large: Cultural Dimensions of Globalization*, Minneapolis: University of Minnesota Press.

— (2006) *Fear of Small Numbers: A Geography of Anger*, Durham, NC: Duke University Press.

Appiah, A. and Amy Gutmann (1996) *Color Conscious: The Political Morality of Race*, Princeton, NJ: Princeton University Press.

Applebaum, Anne (2009) 'Don't blame the Swiss: the ban on minarets wasn't driven by bigotry; it was about fear of extremists', *Slate Magazine*, www.slate.com/id/2237635/.

Aradau, Claudia (2008) 'Forget equality? Security and liberty in the "war on terror"', *Alternatives: Global, Local, Political*, 33(3): 293–314.

— (2009) 'The Roma in Italy: racism as usual?', *Radical Philosophy*, 153: 2–6.

Arditi, Benjamin (2008) *Politics on the Edges of Liberalism. Difference, Populism, Revolution, Agitation*, Edinburgh: Edinburgh University Press.

Arendt, Hannah (1966) *The Origins of Totalitarianism*, new edn,

New York: Harcourt Brace Jovanovich.

Asad, Talal (2010) 'Thinking about terrorism and just war', *Cambridge Review of International Affairs*, 23(1): 3–24.

Austrian Freedom Party (1997) 'Our programme', www.fpoe.at/fpoe/bundesgst/programm/chapter4.htm, accessed 14 August 2004, quoted in Gavan Titley (2004), 'Resituating culture: an introduction', in Gavan Titley (ed.), *Resituating Culture*, Strasbourg: Council of Europe Publishing.

Back, Les (1996) *New Ethnicities and Urban Culture: Racisms and Multiculture in Young Lives*, London: Routledge.

Back, Les and Shamser Sinha (2011) 'New hierarchies of belonging', in Alana Lentin and Gavan Titley (eds), 'The European crisis of multiculturalism?', Special issue of *The European Journal of Cultural Studies* (forthcoming).

Back, Les and John Solomos (1993) 'Doing research, writing politics: the dilemmas of political intervention in research on racism', *Economy and Society*, 22(2): 178–99.

— (1996) *Racism and Society*, Basingstoke: Palgrave Macmillan.

Back, Les, Michael Keith, Azra Khan, Kalbir Shukra and John Solomos (2002) 'New Labour's white heart: politics, multiculturalism and the return of assimilation', *Political Quarterly*, 73(4): 445–54.

Badiou, Alain (2009) *The Meaning of Sarkozy*, London: Verso.

Balibar, E. and I. Wallerstein (1991) *Race, Nation, Class: Ambiguous Identities*, London and New York: Verso.

Barker, Martin (1981) *The New Racism: Conservatives and the Ideology of the Tribe*, London: Junction Books.

Barry, Brian (2001 *Culture and Equality: An Egalitarian Critique of Multiculturalism*, Cambridge, MA: Harvard University Press.

Bauder, Harald (2008) 'Media discourse and the new German Immigration Law', *Journal of Ethnic and Migration Studies*, 34(1): 95–112.

Baudrillard, Jean (1991) *La Guerre du Golfe n'a pas eu lieu*, Paris: Galilée.

Bauman, Zygmunt (1989) *Modernity and the Holocaust*, Cambridge: Polity Press.

— (1991) *Modernity and Ambivalence*, Cambridge: Polity Press.

— (2004) *Identity: Conversations with Benedetto Vecchi*, London: Polity Press.

Beck, Ulrich (2006) *Cosmopolitan Vision*, Cambridge: Polity Press.

Becker, Ron (2006) 'Gay-themed television and the slumpy class. The affordable, multicultural politics of the gay nineties', *Television and New Media*, 7(2): 184–215.

Benbassa, Esther (2010) 'Inventer des "sous-Français", jeu dangereu de Sarkozy', *Rue 89*, 1 August, www.rue89.com/passage-benbassa/2010/08/01/inventer-des-sous-francais-jeu-dangereux-de-sarkozy-160655.

Berezin, Mabel (2009) *Illiberal Politics in Neoliberal Times: Culture, Security, and Populism in the New Europe*, Cambridge: Cambridge University Press.

Bernstein, Richard J. (2010) 'The specter haunting multiculturalism', *Philosophy and Social Criticism*, 36(3/4): 281–94.

Bhabha, Homi (ed.) (1990) *Nation and Narration*, London: Routledge.

Bhambra, Gurminder (2007) *Rethinking Modernity: Postcolonialism and the Sociological Imagination*, Basingstoke: Palgrave Macmillan.

Bhattacharyya, Gargi (2010) 'Social justice and ethnic status: the questions that matter', MCB reply dossier to Prospect, www.mcb.org.uk/comm_details.php?heading_id=121&com_id=2#gargi.

Bigo, Didier (2002) 'Security and immigration: toward a critique of the governmentality of unease', *Alternatives*, 27: 63–92.

Bilge, Sirma (2010) 'Beyond subordination vs. resistance: an intersectional approach to the agency of veiled Muslim women', *Journal of Intercultural Studies*, 31(1): 9–28.

Blaagaard, Bolette (2010) 'Media and multiplicity: journalistic practices and the resurgence of xenophobia in Europe', *Translocations*, 6(2).

Bleich, Erik (2009) 'Muslims and the state in the Post-9/11 West', *Journal of Ethnic and Migration Studies*, 35(3): 353–60.

Blommaert, J. and J. Verschueren (1998) *Debating Diversity: Analysing the discourse of tolerance*, London: Routledge.

Blum, Laurence (1994) *Moral Perception and Particularity*, Cambridge: Cambridge University Press.

Body-Gendrot, Sophie (2010) 'European policies of social control post-9/11', *Social Research: An International Quarterly*, 77(1): 181–204.

Bolaffi, G., R. Bracalenti, P. Braham and S. Gindro (eds) (2003) *Dictionary of Race, Ethnicity and Culture*, London: Sage.

Bolt, G., S. Ozuekren and D. Phillips (2010) 'Linking integration and residential segregation: editorial', *Journal of Ethnic and Migration Studies*, 36(2): 169–86.

Boltanski, Luc and Ève Chiapello (2005) *The New Spirit of Capitalism*, New York: Verso.

Bonjour, Saskia (2005) 'The politics of migration and development: the migration–development connection in Dutch political discourse and policy since 1970', Paper presented at the Florence School on Euro-Mediterranean Migration and Development, September.

Boucher, Gerard (2008) 'Ireland's lack of a coherent integration policy', *Translocations: Migration and Social Change*, 3(1): 5–28, www.translocations.ie.

Boukhars, Anouar (2009) 'Islam, jihadism, and depoliticization in France and Germany', *International Political Science Review*, 30(3): 297–317.

Bourdieu, Pierre (1998) *On Television*, London: Pluto Press.

— (1999) *Acts of Resistance: Against the Tyranny of the Market*, New York: New Press.

Bourdieu, Pierre and Loïc Wacquant (1999) 'On the cunning of imperialist reason', *Theory, Culture and Society*, 16(1): 41–58.

Bourne, Jenny (2001) 'The life and times of institutional racism', *Race and Class*, 43(2): 7–22.

Bouteldja, Houria (2007) 'De la cérémonie du dévoilement à Alger (1958) à Ni Putes Ni Soumises: l'instrumentalisation coloniale et néo-coloniale de la cause des femmes: Ni putes ni soumises, un appareil idéologique d'état', Les Mots Sont Importants, June, lmsi.net/De-la-ceremonie-du-devoilement-a, accessed 11 September 2010.

Bouteldja, Naima (2009) 'France: voices of the banlieues', Race and Class, 51(1): 90–99.

Bracewell, Michael (2002) The Nineties: When Surface was Depth, London: Flamingo.

Bracke, S. (2011) 'Subjects of debate. Secular and sexual exceptionalism, and Muslim women in the Netherlands', Feminist Review, forthcoming.

Brah, Avtar (1996) Cartographies of Diaspora, Contesting Identities, London: Routledge.

Brahm Levy, Geoffrey (2009) 'What is living and what is dead in multiculturalism', Ethnicities, 9(1): 75–93.

Braidotti, Rosi (2009) 'Fitna, or: the pornography of representation', Unpublished paper.

Brittain, Victoria (2009) 'Besieged in Britain', Race and Class, 50(3): 1–29.

Broder, Henryk M. (2010) 'Westergaard's life sentence: Muhammad cartoonist defiant after attack', Spiegel Online International, www.spiegel.de/international/europe/0,1518,672716,00.html.

Brown, Malcolm (2006) 'Comparative analysis of mainstream discourses, media narratives and representations of Islam in Britain and France prior to 9/11', Journal of Muslim Minority Affairs, 27(3): 297–312.

Brown, Wendy (2005) Edgework: Critical Essays on Knowledge and Politics, Princeton, NJ: Princeton University Press.

— (2006) Regulating Aversion: Tolerance in the Age of Identity and Empire, Princeton, NJ: Princeton University Press.

Bruckner, Pascal (2010) The Tyranny of Guilt: An Essay on Western Masochism, Princeton, NJ: Princeton University Press.

Brun, Ellen and Jacques Hersh (2008) 'The Danish disease: a political culture of Islamophobia', Monthly Review, June.

Burnett, J. (2004) 'Community, cohesion and the state', Race and Class, 45(3): 1–18.

— (2007) 'Review of community cohesion: a new framework for race and diversity by Ted Cantle', Race and Class, 48(4): 115–18.

Buruma, Ian (2006) Murder in Amsterdam: The Death of Theo van Gogh and the Limits of Tolerance, New York: Penguin Press.

Butler, Judith (2009) Frames of War. When is Life Grievable?, London: Verso.

Cainkar, Louise (2003) 'Targeting Muslims at Ashcroft's discretion', Middle East Report Online, www.merip.org/mero/mero031403.html.

Caldwell, Christopher (2009) Reflections on the Revolution in Europe: Can Europe be the same with different people in it?, London: Allen Lane.

Carby, H. (1982) 'White women listen! Black feminism and the boundaries of sisterhood', The Empire Strikes Back, Centre for Contemporary Cultural Studies, London: Hutchinson.

Carr, Matt (2006) 'You are now entering Eurabia', Race & Class, 48(1).

— (2009) 'Christopher Caldwell

dissected', Institute of Race Relations, www.irr.org.uk/2009/july/ha000011.html.

Castells, Manuel (2000) *The Information Age: Economy, Society and Culture*, vol. 1: *The Rise of the Network Society*, London: Wiley/Blackwell.

— (2004 [1997]) *The Power of Identity, the Information Age: Economy, Society and Culture*, vol. II, 2nd edn, Oxford: Blackwell.

Cette France Là (2009) *Vol. 1 06 05 2007/30 06 2008*, Paris: La Découverte.

— (2010) *Vol. 2 01 07 2008/30 06 2009*, Paris: La Découverte.

Chanock, Martin (2000) 'Culture and human rights: orientalising, occidentalising, and authenticity', in Mahmood Mamdani (ed.), *Beyond Rights and Culture Talk: Comparative Essays on the Politics of Rights and Culture*, New York: St Martin's Press.

Chouder, I., M. Latrèche and P. Tévanian (2008) *Les Filles voilées parlent*, Paris: La Fabrique.

Cleary, Tim (2006) 'France inflamed: riots and reactions', *European Race Bulletin*, 54, Institute of Race Relations.

Coene, Gily and Chia Longman (2008) 'Gendering the diversification of diversity: the Belgian hijab (in) question', *Ethnicities*, 8: 302–21.

Cole, Mike (2009) 'A plethora of "suitable enemies": British racism at the dawn of the twenty-first century', *Ethnic and Racial Studies*, 32(9): 1671–85.

Comaroff, Jean and John L. Comaroff (2000) 'Millennial capitalism: first thoughts on a second coming', *Public Culture*, 12(2): 305.

Confiant, Raphaël (2008) '"Souschiens" ou "sous-chiens": une (sombre) histoire de tiret', 12 June, www.montraykreyol.org/spip.php?article1269, accessed 19 November 2009.

Connolly, William E. (1995) *The Ethos of Pluralization*, Minneapolis: University of Minnesota Press.

Cooper, Davina (2004) *Challenging Diversity: Rethinking Equality and the Value of Difference*, Cambridge: Cambridge University Press.

Cottle, Simon and M. Rai (2006) 'Between display and deliberation: analysing TV news as communicative architecture', *Media, Culture and Society*, 28(2): 163–89.

Couldry, Nick (2008) 'Form and power in an age of continuous spectacle', in David Hesmondhalgh and Jason Toynbee (eds), *The Media and Social Theory*, London: Routledge, pp. 161–77.

Coulter, Colin (1999) *Contemporary Northern Irish Society: An Introduction*, London: Pluto Press.

Coulter, Colin and Steve Coleman (2003) *The End of Irish History? Critical Reflections on the Celtic Tiger*, Manchester: Manchester University Press.

Craft, Stephanie and Silvio Waisbord (2008) 'When foreign news remains foreign: cartoon controversies in the US and Argentine press', in Elisabeth Eide, Risto Kunelius and Angela Phillips (eds), *Transnational Media Events: The Mohammed cartoons and the imagined clash of civili-

zations, Gothenburg: Nordicom, pp. 133–48.

Crary, Jonathan (1999) *Suspensions of Perception: Attention, Spectacle, and Modern Culture*, Cambridge, MA: MIT Press.

Cronin, Anne M. (2004) *Advertising Myths: The strange half-lives of images and commodities*, London: Routledge.

Crouch, Colin (2004) *Post Democracy*, Cambridge: Polity Press.

Crowley, Helen and Mary Hickman (2008) 'Migration, postindustrialism and the globalized nation state: social capital and social cohesion re-examined', *Ethnic and Racial Studies*, 31(7): 1222–44.

Crowley, Niall (2010) *Hidden Messages, Overt Agendas*, Dublin: Migrants Rights Centre Ireland.

Davis, Aeron (2007) *The Mediation of Power: A Critical Introduction*, London: Routledge.

Davis, Angela (1998) 'Masked Racism: reflections on the prison industrial complex', *ColorLines*, Autumn, www.thirdworldtraveler. com/Prison_System/Masked_ Racism_ADavis.html, accessed 8 September 2010.

Davis, D.-A. (2007) 'Narrating the mute: racializing and racism in a neoliberal moment', *Souls*, 9(4): 346–56.

Davis, David (2005) 'The Tories will champion the poor', *Guardian*, 12 June.

De Beer, Patrice (2010) 'France's other worlds: burqa and abyss', Open Democracy, 3 March, www. opendemocracy.net/patrice-de- beer/frances-other-worlds-burqa- and-abyss.

De Certeau, Michel (1984) *The Practice of Everyday Life*,

Berkeley: University of California Press.

De Giorgi, Alessandro (2000) *Zero Tolleranza: Strategie e Pratiche della Società del Controllo*, Roma: Derive Approdi.

De Hart, Betty (2007) 'The right to domicile of women with a migrant partner in European immigration law', in Sarah Katherine van Walsum and Thomas Spijkerboer (eds), *Women and Immigration Law: New variations on classical feminist themes*, London: Routledge-Cavendish, pp. 142–63.

De Laforcade, Geoffroy (2006) '"Foreigners", nationalism and the "colonial fracture": stigmatized subjects of historical memory in France', *International Journal of Comparative Sociology*, 47(3/4): 217–33.

De Vries, Bald (2010) 'Anger and courage: Fitna and the politics of disengagement', *Sfera Politicii*, XVIII(4): 146.

De Zengotita, Thomas (2005) *Mediated: How the Media Shapes Your World and the Way You Live in It*, London: Bloomsbury.

Dean, Jodi (2009) *Democracy and Other Neoliberal Fantasies: Communicative Capitalism and Left Politics*, Durham, NC: Duke University Press.

Debord, Guy (1992 [1967]) Society of the Spectacle, Detroit, MI: Black and Red.

Debray, Régis (1993) *L'Etat séducteur. Les révolutions médiologiques du pouvoir*, Paris: Gallimard.

Delphy, Julie and Houria Bouteldja (2007) 'Soumise à l'ordre post-colonial. Quand Fadela rallie Sarko: trahison politicienne, continuité politique', Les Mots Sont Importants, lmsi.net/Soumise-a-l-ordre-postcolonial.

Demmers, Jolle (2009) 'Fitna: othering and belonging in the Dutch market society', Unpublished paper.

Demmers, Jolle and Sameer S. Mehendale (2010) 'Neoliberal xenophobia: the Dutch case', *Alternatives: Global, Local, Political*, 35(1): 53–71.

Douzinas, Costas (2007) 'The many faces of humanitarianism', *Parrhesia*, 2: 1–28.

D'Souza, Dinesh (2005) *The End of Racism: Principles for a Multiracial Society*, New York: Free Press.

Duggan, Lisa (2003) *The Twilight Of Equality?: Neoliberalism, Cultural Politics, and the Attack on Democracy*, Boston, MA: Beacon Press.

Durham Peters, John (2005) *Courting the Abyss: Free Speech and the Liberal Tradition*, Chicago, IL: University of Chicago Press.

Duyvendak, J. W., T. Pels and R. Rijkschroeff (2005) 'A multicultural paradise? The cultural factor in Dutch integration policy', Paper presented at the 3rd ECPR conference, Budapest, 8–10 September.

Dyer, Richard (1997) *White*, London and New York: Routledge.

Eagleton, Terry (2000) *The Idea of Culture*, Oxford: Blackwell.

Edgar, David (2009) 'In the new revolution, progressives fight against, not with, the poor', *Guardian*, 24 August.

Eide, Elizabeth, Risto Kunelius and Angela Phillips (eds) (2008) *Transnational Media Events: The Mohammed cartoons and the imagined clash of civilizations*, Gothenburg: Nordicom.

Elliot, Anthony and Charles Lemert (2006) *The New Individualism: The Emotional Costs of Globalization*, London: Routledge.

Entzinger, Hans (2003) 'The rise and fall of multiculturalism: the case of the Netherlands', in C. Joppke and E. Basingstoke Morawaska (eds), *Towards Assimilation and Citizenship: Immigration in Liberal Nation-States*, New York: Palgrave Macmillan, pp. 59–86.

— (2006) 'Changing the rules while the game is on. From multiculturalism to assimilation in the Netherlands', in Y. Michal Bodemann and Gökçe Yurdakul (eds), *Migration, Citizenship, Ethnos: Incorporation Regimes in Germany, Western Europe and North America*, New York: Palgrave Macmillan, pp. 121–44.

Erel, Umut, Jin Haritaworn, Encarnación Gutiérrez Rodríguez and Christian Klesse (2008) 'On the depoliticisation of intersectionality talk: conceptualising multiple oppressions in critical sexuality studies', in Adi Kuntsman and Esperanza Miyake (eds), *Out of Place: Interrogating Silences in Queerness/Raciality*, York: Raw Nerve Books.

Eriksen, Jens-Martin and Frederik Stjernfelt (2010) 'Culturalism: culture as political ideology', Open Democracy, 29 July, www.opendemocracy.net/page/jens-martin-eriksen/culturalism-culture-as-political-ideology._

Eriksen, Thomas Hylland (2001) *Tyranny of the Moment: Fast and Slow Time in the Information Age*, London: Pluto Press.

— (2006) 'Diversity versus difference: neo-liberalism in the minority debate', in Richard Rottenburg, Burkhard Schnepel and Shingo Shimada (eds), *The Making and Unmaking of Difference*, Bielefeld: Transaction, pp. 13–36.

Ersbøll, Eva (2010) 'Denmark: new rules on access to permanent residence passed in Parliament on 25 May 2010', European Union Democracy Observation on Citizenship, eudo-citizenship.eu/citizenship-news/316-denmark-new-rules-on-access-to-permanent-residence-passed-in-parliament-on-25-may-2010, accessed 12 September 2010.

Essed, Philomena (1991) *Understanding Everyday Racism: An Interdisciplinary Theory*, London: Sage.

Essed, P. and K. Nimako (2006) 'Designs and (co)incidents: cultures of scholarship and public policy on immigrants/minorities in the Netherlands', *International Journal of Comparative Sociology*, 47(3/4): 281–312.

Etzioni, Amitai (1993) *The Spirit of Community: Rights, Responsibilities and the Communitarian Agenda*, New York: Crown.

Eyerman Ron (2008) *The Assassination of Theo Van Gogh. From Social Drama to Cultural Trauma*, Durham, NC: Duke University Press.

EYF (European Youth Foundation) (2006) *Youth Opinion*, 1: 6.

Faist, Thomas (2009) 'Diversity – a new mode of incorporation?', *Ethnic and Racial Studies*, 32(1): 171–90.

Fakhraie, Fatemeh (2009) 'An open letter to white non-Muslim feminists', *Muslimnista*, muslimnista. org/2008/10/13/an-open-... tern-feminists/.

Fanning, Bryan (2009) *New Guests of the Irish Nation*, Dublin: Academic Press.

Fanning, Bryan and Fidele Mutwarasibo (2007) 'Nationals/non-nationals: immigration, citizenship and politics in the Republic of Ireland', *Ethnic and Racial Studies*, 30(3): 439–60.

Fanon, Frantz (1986) *Black Skin, White Masks*, London: Pluto Press.

Fanshawe, S. and D. Sriskandarajah (2010) 'You can't put me in a box: superdiversity and the end of identity politics in Britain', London: Institute for Public Policy Research.

Fassin, Didier (2005) 'Compassion and repression. The moral economy of immigration policies in France', *Cultural Anthropology*, 20(3): 362–87.

— (2008) 'Compassion and repression: the moral economy of immigration policies in France', in J. Xavier Inda and R. Rosaldo (eds), *The Anthropology of Globalization*, Oxford: Blackwell.

Fassin, Didier and Eric Fassin (eds) (2006) *De la question sociale à la question raciale? Représenter la société française*, Paris: La Découverte.

Fassin, Eric (2010) 'National identities and transnational intimacies: sexual democracy and the politics of immigration in Europe', *Public Culture*, 22(3): 507–29.

Fekete, Liz (2006) 'Enlightened fundamentalism? Immigration, feminism and the right', *Race and Class*, 48(2): 1–22.

— (2008) 'Integration, Islamophobia and civil rights in Europe', London: International Race Relations.

— (2009) *A Suitable Enemy. Racism, Migration and Islamophobia in Europe*, London and New York: Pluto Press.

Fenton, Natalie (ed.) (2009) *New Media, Old News: Journalism and Democracy in the Digital Age*, London: Sage.

Finkielkraut, Alain (1988) *The Undoing of Thought*, trans. Dennis O'Keeffe, London: Claridge Press.

Finney, Nissa and Ludi Simpson (2009) *'Sleepwalking into Segregation'? Challenging the Myths about Race and Migration*, Bristol: Policy Press.

Fleischhauer, Jan (2009) *Unter Linken. Von einem, der aus Versehen konservativ wurde*, Hamburg: Rowohlt Verlag.

Fleras, Augie (2009) *The Politics of Multiculturalism: Multicultural Governance in Comparative Perspective*, Basingstoke: Palgrave Macmillan.

Fortier, Anne-Marie (2008) *Multicultural Horizons: Diversity and the Limits of the Civil Nation*, London: Routledge.

— (2010) 'Proximity by design? Affective citizenship and the management of unease', *Citizenship Studies*, 14(1): 17–30.

Foucault, Michel (2001) *Madness and Civilization*, London: Routledge.

— (2004 [1969]) *The Archaeology of Knowledge*, London: Routledge.

Fraser, Nancy (2004) 'Social justice in the age of identity politics: redistribution, recognition, and participation', in Nancy Fraser and Axel Honneth, *Redistribution or Recognition: A Political-Philosophical Exchange*, London: Verso.

Geisser, Vincent (2003) *La nouvelle islamophobie*, Paris: La Découverte.

Ghannoushi, Soumaya (2006) 'The bigger cultural picture', *Guardian*, 5 September.

Gilmartin, Mary and Gerald Mills (2008) 'Mapping migrants in Ireland: the limits of cartography', *Translocations: Migration and Social Change*, 4(1): 21–3.

Gilroy, Paul (1987) *There ain't No Black in the Union Jack: The Cultural Politics of Race and Nation*, London: Hutchinson.

— (2000) *Between Camps: Nations, Culture and the Allure of Race*, London: Allen Lane.

— (2004) *After Empire: Melancholia or Convivial Culture?*, Abingdon: Routledge.

Gingrich, Andre and Marcus Banks (2006) *Neo-Nationalism in Europe and Beyond: Perspectives from Social Anthropology*, London: Bergahn Books.

Giroux, Henry (2002) 'Global capitalism and the return of the garrison state', *Arena*, 19: 141–60.

— (2006) 'The politics of disposability', National Association for Urban Debate Leagues, Chicago, IL, www.urbandebate.org.

— (2009) 'Benetton's "world without borders": buying social change', www.csus.edu/indiv/o/obriene/art7/readings/Benetton.htm.

Goldberg, David Theo (1993) *Racist Culture: Philosophy and the Politics of Meaning*, Oxford: Blackwell.

— (2002) *The Racial State*, Malden, MA: Blackwell.

— (2009) *The Threat of Race: Reflections on Racial Neoliberalism*, Oxford: Wiley/Blackwell.

— (2010) 'Call and response', *Patterns of Prejudice*, 44(1): 89–106.

Göle, Nilüfer (2010) 'Mute symbols of Islam', *The Immanent Frame*, 13 January, blogs.ssrc.org/tif/2010/01/13/mute-symbols/.

Goodhart, David (2004a) 'Too diverse?', *Prospect*, 20 February.

— (2004b) 'The discomfort of strangers: part I', *Guardian*, 24 February, www.guardian.co.uk/politics/2004/feb/24/race.eu/print, accessed 6 September 2010.

Goodwin, C. (2007) 'Participation, stance and affect in the organization of activities', *Discourse and Society*, 18(1): 53–73.

Gopal, Priyamvada (2010) 'Burqas and bikinis', *Guardian*, 3 August.

Gray, Breda (2006) 'Migrant integration policy: a nationalist fantasy of management and control?', *Translocations: The Irish Migration, Race and Social Transformation Review*.

Gray, John (2000) *The Two Faces of Liberalism*, Cambridge: Polity Press.

Greenfield, Cathy and Peter Williams (2001) '"Battlers" vs. "elites": mediating democracy', *Southern Review: Communication, Politics and Culture*, 34(1).

Gregory, Derek (2004) *The Colonial Present*, Oxford: Blackwell.

Gresch, Nora, Leila Hadj-Abdou, Sieglinde Rosenberger and Birgit Sauer (2008) 'Tu felix Austria? The headscarf and the politics of "non-issues"', *Social Politics*, 15(4): 411–32.

Grewal, Kiran (2007) '"The threat from within": representations of the *banlieue* in French popular discourse', in Matt Killingsworth (ed.), *Europe: New Voices, New Perspectives*, University of Melbourne: Contemporary Europe Research Centre, e-book, pp. 41–67.

Grieshaber, Kirstin (2010) 'Thilo Sarrazin, German banker, under fire for racist remark', *Huffington Post*, 29 August, www.huffingtonpost.com/2010/08/29/thilo-sarrazin-german-banker-jewish-remark_n_698301.html.

Grillo, Ralph (2007) 'An excess of alterity? Debating difference in a multicultural society', *Ethnic and Racial Studies*, 30(6): 979–98.

Guild, Elspeth, Kees Groenendijk and Sergio Carrera (2009) 'Understanding the contest of community: illliberal practices in the EU?' in E. Guild, K. Groenendijk and S. Carrera (eds), *Illiberal States: Immigration, Citizenship and Integration in the EU*, Farnham: Ashgate.

Gunew, Sneja (2004) *Haunted Nations: The colonial dimensions of multiculturalisms*, London: Routledge.

Gunkel, Henriette and Ben Pitcher (2008a) 'Editorial', in 'Racism in the closet: interrogating postcolonial sexuality', *Darkmatter*, 3.

— (2008b) 'Q&A with Jasbir Puar', *Darkmatter*, 3, www.darkmatter101.org/site/2008/05/02/qa-with-jasbir-puar/, accessed 13 September 2010.

Hage, Ghassan (1998) *White Nation: Fantasies of White Supremacy in a Multicultural Society*, New York: Routledge.

— (2003) *Against Paranoid Nationalism: Searching for Hope in a*

Shrinking Society, Annandale, VA: Pluto Press.

Hale, Charles (2005) 'Neoliberal multiculturalism: the remaking of cultural rights and racial dominance in Central America', *PoLAR: Political and Legal Anthropology Review*, 28(1): 10–28.

Hall, Stuart (1997) *Representation: Cultural Representations and Signifying Practices: Culture Media and Identities*, Milton Keynes: Open University.

— (2003) '"In but not of Europe": Europe and its myths', in L. Passerini (ed.), *Figures d'Europe: Images and Myths of Europe*, Brussels: Peter Lang, pp. 35–46.

Hall, Stuart and Les Back (2009) 'At home and not at home: Stuart Hall in conversation with Les Back', *Cultural Studies*, 23(4): 658–87.

Hallin, Daniel (2008) 'Neoliberalism, social movements, and change in media systems', in D. Hesmondhalgh and J. Toynbee (eds), *The Media and Social Theory*, London: Routledge, pp. 43–58.

Hallin, Daniel and Paolo Mancini (2004) *Comparing Media Systems: Three Models of Media and Politics*, Cambridge: Cambridge University Press.

Haneke, Michael (2005) *Caché*, Sony Pictures Classics.

Hänggli, Regula and Hanspeter Kriesi (2010) 'Political framing strategies and their impact on media framing in a Swiss direct-democratic campaign', *Political Communication*, 27: 141–57.

Hannaford, Ivan (1996) *Race: The History of an Idea in the West*, Woodrow Wilson Center Press.

Hardt, Michael and Antonio Negri (2000) *Empire*, Boston, MA: Harvard University Press.

Hargreaves, Alex and Mark McKinney (eds) (1997) *Post-Colonial Cultures in France*, London: Routledge.

Haritaworn, Jin (2008) 'Loyal repetitions of the nation: gay assimilation and the "war on terror"', *Darkmatter*, 3, www.darkmatter101.org/site/2008/05/02/loyal-repetitions-of-the-nation-gay-assimilation-and-the-war-on-terror/, accessed 13 September 2010.

Haritaworn, Jin and Jennifer Petzen (2010) 'Sexual representations of Islam', in Chris Flood, Stephen Hutchings, Galina Miazhevich and Henri Nickels (eds), *Islam in Its International Context: Comparative Perspectives*, Cambridge: Cambridge Scholars Publishing.

Harvey, David (1996) *Justice, Nature and the Geography of Difference*, Oxford: Wiley/Blackwell.

— (2005) *A Brief History of Neoliberalism*, London: Oxford University Press.

Held, D., A. McGrew, D. Goldblatt and J. Perraton (1999) *Global Transformations: Politics, Economics and Culture*, Stanford, CA: Polity and Stanford University Press.

Hervik, Peter (2008) 'The original sin and its side effects: freedom of speech as Danish news management', in Elisabeth Eide, Risto Kunelius and Angela Phillips (eds), *Transnational Media Events: The Mohammed cartoons and the imagined clash of civilizations*, Gothenburg: Nordicom, pp. 59–80.

— (2011) 'Ending tolerance as a solution to incompatibility: the

Danish "crisis of multicultural-ism"', in Alana Lentin and Gavan Titley (eds), 'Question-ing the European crisis of multiculturalism?', Special issue, *European Journal of Cultural Studies* (forthcoming).

Hervik, Peter, Elisabeth Eide and Risto Kunelius (2008) 'A long and messy event', in Elisabeth Eide, Risto Kunelius and Angela Phillips (eds), *Transnational Media Events. The Mohammed Cartoons and the Imagined Clash of Civilizations*, Gothenburg: Nordicom, pp. 29–38.

Hesmondhalgh, David and Jason Toynbee (eds) (2008) *The Media and Social Theory: Culture Economy and the Social*, London: Routledge.

Hesse, Barnor (ed.) (2000) *Un/settled Multiculturalisms*, London: Zed Books.

— (2007) 'Racialized modernity: an analytics of white mythologies', *Ethnic and Racial Studies*, 30(4): 643–63.

Hewitt, Roger (2005) *White Backlash and the Politics of Multicultural-ism*, Cambridge: Cambridge University Press.

Hind, Dan (2007) *The Threat to Reason*, London: Verso.

Hondius, Dienke (2009) 'Race and the Dutch: on the uneasiness surrounding racial issues in the Netherlands', in Sharam Alghasi, Thomas Hylland Eriksen and Halleh Ghorashi (eds), *Paradoxes of Cultural Recognition: Perspec-tives from Northern Europe*, Farnham: Ashgate.

hooks, bell (1990) *Yearning: Race, gender, and cultural politics*, Boston, MA: South End Press.

— (1992) *Black Looks: Race and Representation*, Boston, MA: South End Press.

Hooper, John (2009) 'Italian town where a White Christmas is a police matter', *Guardian*, 20 December.

Horne, Alistair (2006 [1977]) *A Savage War of Peace: Algeria 1954–1962*, New York: New York Review Books.

Horsti, Karina (2010) 'Polarized views on migration: impact of the changing journalistic field on immigration debate in the Nordic countries', Paper presented at 'Populist mobilisation in Europe', IMISCOE 7th Annual Confer-ence.

Huggan, Jane (2001) 'Virtual multiculturalism: the case of contemporary Britain', *European Studies*, 16: 67–85.

Huntington, Samuel (1993) 'The clash of civilizations?', *Foreign Affairs*, Summer.

— (1996) *The Clash of Civilizations and the Remaking of World Order*, New York: Simon & Schuster.

Husain, Fatima and Margaret O'Brien (2000) 'Muslim commu-nities in Europe: reconstruction and transformation', *Current Sociology*, 48(4): 1–13.

Hvenegård-Lassen, Kirsten (2005) 'Realistic grown-ups? A comparative analysis of how the formation of an integrated subject is conceived in Sweden and Denmark', AMID Working Paper Series 44/2005.

Hyland, Matthew (2006) 'Proud scum: the spectre of the ingrate', in *Dis-Integrating Multicultural-ism*, London: Central Books.

Ibrahim, Yasmin (2007) '9/11 as a new temporal base for Islam: the narrative and temporal framing of Islam in crisis', *Contemporary Islam*, 1(1): 37–51.

Isin, Engin F. (2004) 'The neurotic citizen', *Citizenship Studies*, 8(3): 217–35.

Jacobs, D. (2004) 'The challenge of minority representation in Brussels', in G. Aubarell, A. Nicolau and A. Ros (eds), *Immigració i qüestió nacional. Minories subestatals i immigració a Europa*, Barcelona: Mediterrània, pp. 51–64.

Jallon, Hugues and Pierre Mounier (1999) *Les Enragés de la République*, Paris: La Découverte.

Jespersen, Karen and Ralf Pittelkow (2006) *Islamisten en näivisten*, Copenhagen: People's Press.

Joppke, Christian (2007) 'Beyond national models: civic integration policies for immigrants in western Europe', *West European Politics*, 30: 1–22.

— (2009) *Veil: Mirror of Identity*, Cambridge: Polity Press.

Jordan, B. and F. Düvell (2003) *Migration: The Boundaries of Equality and Justice*, Cambridge: Polity Press.

Judt, Tony (2008) 'The problem of evil in post-war Europe', *New York Review of Books*, 14 February.

Kalra, Virinder (2002) 'Riots, race and reports: Denham, Cantle, Oldham and Burnley inquiries', *Sage Race Relations Abstracts*, 27(4).

Karner, Christian (2007) *Ethnicity and Everyday Life*, London: Routledge.

Kastoryano, Riva (2008) 'Review symposium: contested citizenship', *Ethnicities*, 8: 133.

Keck, Margaret E. and Kathryn

Sikkink (1998) *Activists beyond Borders: Advocacy Networks in International Politics*, Ithaca, NY: Cornell University Press.

Keskinen, Suvi (2009) 'Honour-related violence and Nordic nation-building', in Suvi Keskinen, Salla Tuori, Sari Irni and Diana Mulinari (eds), *Complying with Colonialism. Gender, Race and Ethnicity in the Nordic Region*, Aldershot: Ashgate.

— (2010) 'Borders of the Finnish nation. Media, politics and rape by "foreign" perpetrators', in Elisabeth Eide and Kaarina Nikunen (eds), *Media in Motion. Cultural Complexity and Migration in the Nordic Region*, Aldershot: Ashgate.

Keskinen, Suvi, Salla Tuori, Sari Irni and Diana Mulinari (eds) (2009) *Complying with Colonialism. Gender, Race and Ethnicity in the Nordic Region*, Aldershot: Ashgate.

Khiari, Sadri (2006) *Pour une politique de la racaille: immigrés-es, indigènes, et jeunes de banlieues*, Paris: Textuel.

— (2009) *La contre-révolution coloniale en France: de De Gaulle à Sarkozy*, Paris: La Fabrique.

Kiliç, Sevgi, Sawitri Saharso and Birgit Sauer (2008) 'The veil: debating citizenship, gender and religious diversity', Special issue, *Social Politics: International Studies in Gender, State and Society*, 16(4).

Kirby, Peader, Michael Cronin and Luke Gibbons (2002) *Reinventing Ireland: Culture, Society and the Global Economy*, London: Pluto Press.

Klausen, Jytte (2006) 'Rotten judgment in the state of Denmark',

Spiegel Online, 8 February, service.spiegel.de/ache/international/0,1518,399653,00.html.

— (2009) *The Cartoons that Shook the World*, New Haven, CT: Yale University Press.

Klein, N. (2007) *The Shock Doctrine: The rise of disaster capitalism*, New York: Penguin.

Koff, H. and D. Duprez (2009) 'The 2005 riots in France: the international impact of domestic violence', *Journal of Ethnic and Migration Studies*, 35(5): 713–30.

Kofman, Eleanore (2005) 'Citizenship, migration and the reassertion of national identity', *Citizenship Studies*, 9(5): 453–67.

Koopmans, Ruud, Paul Statham, Marco Giugni and Florence Passy (eds) (2005) *Contested Citizenship: Immigration and Cultural Diversity in Europe*, Minnesota: University of Minnesota Press.

Kramer, Jane (2006) 'Letter from Europe: the Dutch model', *New Yorker*, 3 April.

Kropiwiec, Katarzyna and Rebecca Chiyoko King-O'Riain (2006) *Polish Migrant Workers in Ireland*, Dublin: National Consultative Committee on Racism and Interculturalism.

Kuhn, Rick (2009) 'Xenophobic racism and class during the Howard years', *Marxist Interventions*, 1: 53–82.

Kundnani, Arun (2001) 'From Oldham to Bradford: the violence of the violated', Institute of Race Relations, 1 October.

— (2002) 'The death of multiculturalism', Institute of Race Relations, www.irr.org.uk/2002/april/ak000001.html,

— (2004) 'The rise and fall of British multiculturalism', in Gavan

Titley (ed.), *Resituating Culture*, Strasbourg: Council of Europe.

— (2007) *The End of Tolerance? Racism in 21st Century Britain*, London: Pluto.

— (2011) 'Multiculturalism and its discontents: left, right and liberal', in Alana Lentin and Gavan Titley (eds), 'The European crisis of multiculturalism?', Special issue of *The European Journal of Cultural Studies* (forthcoming).

Kunelius, Risto and Amin Alhassan (2008) 'Complexities of an ideology in action: liberalism and the cartoons affair', in Elisabeth Eide, Risto Kunelius and Angela Phillips (eds), *Transnational Media Events: The Mohammed Cartoons and the Imagined Clash of Civilizations*, Gothenburg: Nordicom, pp. 81–98.

Kymlicka, Will (2007) *Multicultural Odysseys: Navigating the New International Politics of Diversity*, Oxford: Oxford University Press.

Laden, Simon and David Owen (eds) (2007) *Multiculturalism and Political Theory*, Cambridge: Cambridge University Press.

Langvasbråten, Trude (2008) 'A Scandinavian model? Gender equality discourses on multiculturalism', *Social Politics*, 15(1): 32–52.

Larsen, Håkon (2010) 'Legitimation strategies of public service broadcasters: the divergent rhetoric in Norway and Sweden', *Media, Culture and Society*, 32(2): 267–83.

Lash, Scott (2002) *Critique of Information*, London: Sage.

Lee, Spike (2006) *When the Levees Broke: A Requiem in Four Acts*, HBO.

Legrain, Philippe (2009) *Immigrants:*

Your Country Needs Them, London: Abacus.

Lentin, Alana (2004) *Racism and Anti-Racism in Europe*, London: Pluto Press.

Lentin, Alana and Gavan Titley (eds) (2008) *The Politics of Diversity in Europe*, Strasbourg: Council of Europe Publishing.

Lentin, Ronit (2007) 'Ireland: racial state and crisis racism', *Ethnic and Racial Studies*, 30(4): 610–27.

Lentin, Ronit and Robbie McVeigh (2006) *After Optimism? Ireland, Racism and Globalization*, Dublin: Metro Éireann Publications.

Lerman, Anthony (2008) 'In defence of multiculturalism', *Guardian*, 22 March.

— (2010) 'In defence of multiculturalism', *Guardian*, 22 March.

Les mots sont important (2003) 'Argument 9: les acquis de la laïcité', lmsi.net/Argument-9-les-acquis-de-la, accessed 2 September 2010.

Lettinga, D. (2009) 'Rethinking national constellations of citizenship. Situating the headscarf debate in the Netherlands', in S. Alghashi, T. Hylland Eriksen and H. Ghorashi (eds), *Paradoxes of Cultural Recognition*, Farnham and Burlington, IN: Ashgate, pp. 243–64.

Lettinga, Doutje and Rikke Andreassen (2008) 'Gender equality as a tool in European national narratives', Paper presented at the VEIL conference, Vienna, 28/29 November.

Lévi-Strauss, C. (1979 [1975]) *The Way of the Masks*, London: Cape.

— (1981 [1971]) *The Naked Man* (Mythologiques IV), London: Cape.

— (1991) *The Story of Lynx*, trans. Catherine Tihanyi, Chicago, IL: University of Chicago Press.

Lévi-Strauss, C. and D. Eribon (1991 [1988]) *Conversations with Claude Lévi-Strauss*, Chicago, IL: University of Chicago Press.

Lex, S., L. Lindekilde and P. Mouritsen (2007) 'Public and political debates on multicultural crises in Denmark', Report for the project 'A European Approach to Multicultural Citizenship. Legal, Political and Educational Challenges' (EMILIE), central.radiopod.gr/en/wp-content/uploads/2008/05/denmark_report_multicultural_discourses_final.pdf.

Liddle, Rod (2004) 'How Islam has killed multiculturalism', *Spectator*, May.

Lippert, Randy (1998) 'Rationalities and refugee resettlement', *Economy and Society*, 27(4): 380–406.

Livingstone, Sonia (2009) 'On the mediation of everything', *Journal of Communication*, 59(1): 1–18.

Long, Scott (2009) 'Unbearable witness: how Western activists (mis)recognize sexuality in Iran', *Contemporary Politics*, 15(1): 119–36.

Lorde, Audre (1984) *Sister Outsider: Essays and Speeches*, Darlinghurst, NSW: Crossing Press.

MacCabe, Colin (2005) 'Mumbo-jumbo's survival instinct', *Open Democracy*, 1, February.

MacMaster, Neil (2000) *Racism in Europe 1870–2000*, Basingstoke: Palgrave Macmillan.

Macpherson, William (1999) 'The Stephen Lawrence Inquiry', Report of an Inquiry by Sir William Macpherson of Cluny. Presented to Parliament by the Secretary of State for the Home Office by Command of Her Majesty, London: Stationery Office.

Maguire, Mark and Tanya Cassidy (2009) 'The new Irish question: citizenship, motherhood and the politics of life', *Irish Journal of Anthropology*, 12(3): 18–29.

Maguire, Mark and Fiona Murphy (2009) 'Management, truth and life: an introductory essay', *Irish Journal of Anthropology*, 12(3): 6–11.

Mamdani, Mahmood (2005) *Good Muslim, Bad Muslim: America, the Cold War and the Roots of Terror*, New York: Doubleday.

Manji, Irshad (2005) 'Why tolerate the hate?', *New York Times*, 9 August.

Mazower, Mark (2009) 'Reflections on the revolution in Europe', *Financial Times*, 4 May.

McDowell, Michael (2004) 'The proposed Citizenship Referendum', *Sunday Independent*, 14 March.

— (2007) *Address by an Tánaiste at the Conference on Integration Policy – Strategies for a Cohesive Society*, Dublin: Department of Justice, Equality and Law Reform, 1 February, www.justice. ie/en/JELR.

McGhee, Derek (2008) *The End of Multiculturalism? Terrorism, Integration and Human Rights*, Milton Keynes: Open University Press.

Mepschen, Paul (2009a) 'Against tolerance: Islam, sexuality, and the politics of belonging in the Netherlands', *International Viewpoint*, June.

— (2009b) 'Erotics of persuasion: sexuality and the politics of alterity and autochtony', Unpublished paper.

Mielants, Eric (2006) 'The long-term historical development of racist tendencies within the political and social context of Belgium', *International Journal of Comparative Sociology*, 47: 313–34.

Mihelj, Sabina (2008) 'National media events: from displays of unity to enactments of division', *European Journal of Cultural Studies*, 11(4): 471–88.

Miles, R. (1989) *Racism*, London: Routledge.

Miller, Peter and Nikolas Rose (2008) *Governing the Present. Administering Economic, Political and Social Life*, Cambridge: Polity Press.

Mills, Charles W. (1997) *The Racial Contract*, Ithaca, NY: Cornell University Press.

— (2007) 'Multiculturalism as/and/or anti-racism?', in Anthony Simon Laden and David Owen (eds), *Multiculturalism and Political Theory*, New York: Cambridge University Press, pp. 89–114.

Minogue, Kenneth (2005) 'Introduction: multiculturalism: a dictatorship of virtue', in Patrick West, *The Poverty of Multiculturalism*, London: Civitas.

Mirza, Munira (2010) 'Introduction: rethinking race', *Prospect*, 175, 22 September.

Mirzoeff, Nicholas (2005) *Watching Babylon: The War in Iraq and Global Visual Culture*, London: Routledge.

Mitropoulos, Angela (2008) 'The materialisation of race in multiculture', *Darkmatter*, 2, February, www.darkmatter101.org/site.

Mohanty, Chandra Talpade (1986) 'Under Western eyes: feminist scholarship and colonial discourses', *Boundary 2*, 12(3): 333–58.

Mudde, Cas (2004) 'The populist Zeitgeist', *Government and Opposition*, 39(4).

Murray, Graham (2006) 'France: the riots and the Republic', *Race and Class*, 47(4): 426–45.

NCCRI (National Consultative Committee on Racism and Interculturalism) (2002) *Guidelines on Anti-Racism and Intercultural Training*, Dublin: NCCRI.

Ndiaye, Pap (2008) *La Condition noire. Essai sur une minorité française*, Paris: Calmann-Lévy.

Negrine, Ralph (2008) *The Transformation of Political Communication*, Basingstoke: Palgrave Macmillan.

Nolan, David (2003) 'Media governmentality, Howardism and the Hanson effect', *International Journal of the Humanities*, 1: 1367–77.

Nossek, H. (2004) 'Our news and their news. The role of national identity in the coverage of foreign news', *Journalism*, 5(3): 343–68.

Nousianinen, Anu (2010) 'Kukkahattutäti kohtaa kriitikkonsa', *Kuukausiliite*, 454.

Nyers, Peter (2004) 'What's left of citizenship?', *Citizenship Studies*, 8(3): 203–15.

O'Cinneide, Colm (2004) 'Citizenship and multiculturalism: equality, rights, and diversity in contemporary Europe', in Gavan Titley (ed.), *Resituating Culture*, Strasbourg: Council of Europe.

Ohmae, Kenichi (1995) *The End of the Nation State*, New York: Free Press.

O'Loughlin, Ben (2006) 'The operationalization of the concept of cultural diversity in British television policy', ESRC CRESC Working paper no. 27.

Omi, Michael and Howard Winant (1994) *Racial Formation in the United States*, 2nd edn, London: Routledge.

OMSI (Office of the Minister of State for Integration) (2008) *Migration Nation: Statement on integration strategy and diversity management*, Dublin: Government of Ireland.

O'Neill, Martin (2008) 'Echoes of Enoch Powell', *New Statesman*, 10 March.

Örnebring, Henrik (2009) 'Introduction: questioning European journalism', *Journalism Studies*, 10(1): 2–17.

Outhwaite, William (2005) *The Future of Society*, Malden, MA: Wiley/Blackwell.

Owen, David and A. S. Laden (eds) (2007) *Multiculturalism and Political Theory*, Cambridge: Cambridge University Press.

Parekh, B. (2000) *Rethinking Multiculturalism: Cultural Diversity and Political Theory*, Cambridge, MA: Harvard University Press.

Pateman, Carole and Charles W. Mills (2007) *Contract and Domination*, Malden, MA: Polity Press.

Pathak, Pathik (2007) 'The trouble with David Goodhart's Britain', *Political Quarterly*, 78(2).

— (2008) 'Making a case for multiculture: from the "politics of piety" to the politics of the secular?', *Theory, Culture and Society*, 25(5): 123–41.

Pautz, H. (2005) 'The politics of identity in Germany: the Leitkultur debate', *Race and Class*, 46(4): 39–52.

Penninx, Rinus (2005) 'Integration

processes of migrants: research findings and policy challenges', Background paper for the European Population Conference 2005, 'Demographic Challenges for Social Cohesion', 7/8 April, Strasbourg, www.coe.int/t/E/social_cohesion/Population/European_Population_Conference/.

Phelan, Sean (2009) 'Irish neoliberalism, media, and the politics of discourse', in Debbie Ging, Michael Cronin and Peadar Kirby (eds), *Transforming Ireland: Challenges, Critique and Resources*, Manchester: Manchester University Press, pp. 73–88.

Philips, Leigh (2010) 'Prospect of French anti-Roma summit disturbs EU Presidency', *EU Observer*, 24 August, euobserver.com/22/30668.

Phillips, Anne (2007) *Multiculturalism without Culture*, Princeton, NJ: Princeton University Press.

Phillips, Anne and Sawitri Saharso (2008) 'The rights of women and the crisis of multiculturalism', *Ethnicities*, 8(3): 2–12.

Phillips, Coretta (2007) 'The re-emergence of the "black spectre": minority professional associations in the post-Macpherson era', *Ethnic and Racial Studies*, 30(3): 375–96.

Pilkington, Ed (2010) 'Mosque near 9/11 site likely to go ahead despite rightwing fury', *Guardian*, 3 August.

Pipes, Daniel (2008) 'Will Europe resist Islamization?', *Jerusalem Post*, 3 April, www.danielpipes.org/5503/will-europe-resist-islamization.

Pitcher, Ben (2009) *The Politics of Multiculturalism: Race and Racism in Contemporary Britain*, Basingstoke: Palgrave Macmillan.

Power, Nina (2009) *One-Dimensional Woman*, Ropley: Zero Books.

Poynting, Scott and Victoria Mason (2006) '"Tolerance, freedom, justice and peace"? Britain, Australia and anti-Muslim racism since 11 September 2001', *Journal of Intercultural Studies*, 27(4): 365–91.

— (2007) 'The resistible rise of Islamophobia: anti-Muslim racism in the UK and Australia before 11 September 2001', *Journal of Sociology*, 43(1): 61–86.

Poynting, S., G. Noble, P. Tabarand and J. Collins (2004) *Bin Laden in the Suburbs: Criminalising the Arab Other*, Sydney, NSW: Sydney Institute of Criminology.

Pred, Allan (2000) *Even in Sweden: Racisms, Racialised Spaces and the Popular Geographical Imagination*, Berkeley: University of California Press.

Prins, Baukje (2002) 'The nerve to break taboos: new realism in the Dutch discourse on multiculturalism', *Journal of International Migration and Integration*, 3(3/4): 363–80.

Prins, B. and S. Saharso (2008) 'In the spotlights. A blessing and a curse for immigrant women in the Netherlands', *Ethnicities*, 8(3): 365–84.

Puar, Jasbir (2007) *Terrorist Assemblages: Homonationalism in Queer Times*, Durham, NC: Duke University Press.

Puar, Jasbir, Ben Pitcher and Henriette Gunkel (2008) 'Q&A with Jasbir Puar', *Darkmatter*, 3, www.darkmatter101.org/

site/2008/05/02/qa-with-jasbir-puar/.

Putnam, Robert David (2000) *Bowling Alone: The Collapse and Revival of American Community*, New York: Simon & Schuster.

Quigley, W. (2010) 'Rampant racism in the criminal justice system', *Counterpunch*, www.counterpunch.org/quigley07262010.html.

Raissiguier, Catherine (2008) 'Muslim women in France: impossible subjects?', *Darkmatter*, 3, www.darkmatter101.org/site/2008/05/02/muslim-women-in-france-impossible-subjects/.

Raj Isar, Y. (2006) 'Cultural diversity,' *Theory, Culture and Society*, 23: 2–3.

Ramadan, Tariq (2009) 'My compatriots' vote to ban minarets is fuelled by fear', *Guardian*, 29 November, www.guardian.co.uk/commentisfree/belief/2009/nov/ 29/swiss-vote-ban-minarets-fear.

Rana, Juanid (2007) 'The story of Islamophobia', *Souls: A Critical Journal of Black Politics, Culture, and Society*, 9(2): 1–14.

Rhodes, James (2010) 'White backlash, "unfairness" and justifications of British National Party (BNP) support', *Ethnicities*, 10(1): 77–99.

Richmond, Anthony (1984) 'Ethnic nationalism and postindustrialism', *Ethnic and Racial Studies*, 7(1): 4–18.

Rieff, David (2005) 'The dream of multiculturalism is over', *New York Times*, 23 August, www.feldmeth.net/ethics/rieff.html.

Robbins, Christopher G. (2004) 'Racism and the authority of neoliberalism: a review of three new books on the persistence of racial inequality in a color-blind era', *Journal for Critical Education Policy Studies*, 2(2).

Rose, Flemming (2006) 'Europe's politics of victimology', *SignandSight.com. Let's Talk European*, www.signandsight.com/features/782.html.

Rose, Nikolas (1999) *Powers of Freedom: Reframing Political Thought*, Cambridge: Cambridge University Press.

Rosenberger, Sieglinde and Birgit Sauer (2006) 'Governing cultural, religious and gender differences: the case of Muslim headscarves', Paper presented at the Third Pan-European Conference on EU Politics, ECPR Standing Group on the European Union, Istanbul, September.

Rostock, P. and S. Berghann (2008) 'The ambivalent role of gender in redefining the German nation', *Ethnicities*, 8(3): 345–64.

Roth, Joseph (2001) *The Wandering Jews*, trans. Michael Hoffman, New York: Norton.

Rottmann, Susan B. and Myra Marx Ferree (2008) 'Citizenship and intersectionality: German feminist debates about headscarf and antidiscrimination laws', *Social Politics*, 15(4): 481–513.

Roy, Olivier (2004) *Globalized Islam: The Search for a New Ummah*, New York: Columbia University Press.

Said, Edward (1991) *Covering Islam: How the Media and Experts Determine How We See the Rest of the World*, London: Vintage.

Salmi, Iikka and Jorma Vuorio (2009) 'DEBATE: Time running out on immigrant integration', *Helsingin Sanomat*, International

edn, www.hs.fi/english/article/
DEBATE+%E2%80%9CTime+
running+out+on+immigrant+
integration%E2%80%9D/
1135246620673.

Salmon, Christian (2010) *Storytelling: Bewitching the Modern Mind*, London: Verso.

Sarkozy, Nicolas (2009) 'Respecter ceux qui arrivent, respecter ceux qui accueillent', *Le Monde*, 8 December.

Sarrazin, Thilo (2010) *Deutschland schafft sich ab*, Deutsche Verlags-Anstalt.

Scheffer, Paul (2000) 'The multicultural drama', *NRC Handelsblad*, 19 April.

Schlesinger, Philip (1992) 'Europeanness – a new cultural battlefield?', *Innovation*, 5(1).

Schram, Sanford F., Richard C. Fording and Joe Soss (2008) 'Neo-liberal poverty governance: race, place and the punitive turn in US welfare policy', *Cambridge Journal of Regions, Economy and Society*, 1: 1–20.

Schuster, Liza and John Solomos (2001) 'Introduction: citizenship, multiculturalism, identity', *Patterns of Prejudice*, 35(1): 3–12.

Schuster, Liza and Michael Welch (2005) 'Detention of asylum seekers in the US, UK, France, Germany, and Italy: a critical view of the globalizing culture of control', *Criminal Justice: The International Journal of Policy and Practice*, 5(4): 331–55.

Scott, Joan Wallach (2007) *The Politics of the Veil*, Princeton, NJ: Princeton University Press.

Sennels, Nicolai (2009) *Blandt kriminelle muslimer: en psykologs erfaringer fra Københavns Kommune* [Among criminal Muslims: a psychologist's experience in the Copenhagen Municipality], Copenhagen: Free Press Society.

Seymour, Richard (2008) *The Liberal Defence of Murder*, London: Verso.

— (2010) 'The changing face of racism', *International Socialism*, 126.

Shohat, Ella and Robert Stam (eds) (2003) *Multiculturalism, Postcoloniality and Transnational Media*, New Brunswick, NJ: Rutgers University Press.

Shooman, Yasemin and Riem Spielhaus (2010) 'The concept of the Muslim enemy in the public discourse', in Jocelyn Cesari (ed.), *Muslims in the West after 9/11. Religion, Politics and Law*, London and New York: Routledge, pp. 198–228.

Siapera, Eugenia (2009) 'Theorizing the Muslim blogosphere: blogs, rationality, publicness, and individuality', in A. Russell and N. Echchaibi (eds), *International Blogging: Identity, Politics, and Networked Publics*, New York: Peter Lang, pp. 29–46.

Siim, Birte and Hege Skjeie (2008) 'Tracks, intersections and dead ends: multicultural challenges to state feminism in Denmark and Norway', *Ethnicities*, 8(3): 322–44.

Silverman, Maxim (2007) *Deconstructing the Nation: Immigration, Racism and Citizenship in Modern France*, London: Routledge.

Silverstein, Paul (2004) *Algeria in France: Transpolitics, Race, and Nation*, Bloomington: Indiana University Press.

Silverstein, Paul A. and Chantal Tetreault (2006) 'Postcolonial urban apartheid', *Riots in France*, riotsfrance.ssrc.org/Silverstein_ Tetreault/.

Silverstone, Roger (2007) *Media and Morality: On the Rise of the Mediapolis*, Cambridge: Polity Press.

Singer, Peter (2004) *The President of Good and Evil: The Ethics of President George W. Bush*, London: Granta.

Sivanandan, A. (2003) 'Racism and the market-state: an interview with A. Sivanandan', *Race and Class*, 44(4): 71–6.

Skenderovic, Damir (2007) 'Immigration and the radical right in Switzerland: ideology, discourse and opportunities', *Patterns of Prejudice*, 41(2): 155–76.

Solioz, Christophe (2009) 'Switzerland in Wonderland', *Open Democracy*, 1 December, www.opendemocracy.net/christophe-solioz/switzerland-in-wonderland.

Solomos, John (2003) *Race and Racism in Britain*, London: Palgrave Macmillan.

Soysal, Levant (2009) 'Introduction: triumph of culture, troubles of anthropology', *Focaal*, 55: 3–11.

Soysal, Yasemin (1994) *Limits of Citizenship*, Chicago, IL: University of Chicago Press.

Spongenberg, Helena (2010) 'Populism on the rise in the Nordic region', *EU Observer Online*, 16 September.

Stabile, Carole and Deepa Kumar (2005) 'Unveiling imperialism: media, gender and the war on Afghanistan', *Media, Culture and Society*, 27: 765–82.

Stehle, Maria (2006) 'Narrating the ghetto, narrating Europe: from Berlin, Kreuzberg to the banlieues of Paris', *Westminster Papers in Communication and Culture*, 3(3): 48–70.

Stolcke, Verena (1995) 'Talking culture: new boundaries, new rhetorics of exclusion in Europe', *Current Anthropology*, 36(1): 1–24.

Stoler, Ann Laura (1997) 'On political and psychological essentialisms', *Ethos*, 25(1): 101–6.

— (2006) 'On degrees of imperial sovereignty', *Public Culture*, 18(1): 125–46.

Storhaug, Hege (2003) *Feminin integrering. Utfordringer i et fleretnisk samfunn* [Feminine integration. Challenges in a multiethnic society], Oslo: Kolorfon Verlag.

Strömbäck, Jesper, Adam Shehata and Daniela V. Dimitrova (2008) 'Framing the Mohammad cartoons issue: a cross-cultural comparison of Swedish and US press', *Global Media and Communication*, 4(2): 117–38.

Taggart, Paul (2000) *Populism*, Buckingham: Open University Press.

Taguieff, Pierre-Andre (1989) *La Force du prejugé: essai sur le racisme et ses doubles*, Paris: La Découverte.

Taguieff, Pierre-Andre et al. (1991) *Face au Racisme*, 2 vols, Paris: La Découverte.

Tarlo, Emma (2005) 'Reconsidering stereotypes: anthropological reflections on the jilbab controversy', *Anthropology Today*, 2(6): 13–17.

— (2010) *Visibly Muslim: Fashion, Politics, Faith*, Oxford: Berg.

Taylor, Charles (1992) *Multiculturalism and 'The Politics of Recognition'*, Princeton, NJ: Princeton University Press.

— (1994) *Multiculturalism*, Princeton, NJ: Princeton University Press.

Taylor, Matthew (2010) 'English Defence League targets Bradford as "The Big One"', *Guardian*, 10 August.

Tebble, Adam James (2006) 'Exclusion for democracy', *Political Theory*, 34(4): 463–89.

Terray, Emmanuel (2004) 'Headscarf hysteria', *New Left Review*, 26: 118–27.

Tévanien, Pierre (2005) *Le Voile médiatique. Un faux débat: 'l'affaire du foulard islamique'*, Paris: Éditions Raisons d'agir.

Tissot, Sylvie (2008) 'French suburbs: a new problem or a new approach to social exclusion?', Centre for European Studies Working Paper Series 160.

Titley, Gavan (2007) 'Backlash! Just in case: "political correctness", immigration and the rise of pre-actionary discourse in Irish public debate', *Irish Review*, Spring.

Titley, Gavan and Alana Lentin (eds) (2008) *The Politics of Diversity in Europe*, Strasbourg: Council of Europe Publishing.

Titley, Gavan et al. (2009) 'What do we mean when we say "integration"? A discussion', *Irish Journal of Anthropology*, Special issue: *Managing Migration: The Politics of Truth and Life Itself*, 12(3).

Toscano, Alberto (2010) *Fanaticism: On the Uses of an Idea*, London: Verso.

Traynor, Ian (2009) 'Swiss vote to ban construction of minarets on mosques', *Guardian*, 29 November, www.guardian.co.uk/world/2009/nov/29/switzerland-bans-mosque-minarets.

Triadafilopoulos, Phil (2011) 'Illiberal means to liberal ends? Understanding recent immigrant integration policies in Europe', *Journal of Ethnic and Migration Studies*, Special issue on 'The limits of the liberal state', 37(6).

Tsoukala, Anastassia (2005) 'Looking at immigrants as enemies', in D. Bigo and E. Guild (eds), *Controlling Frontiers. Free Movement into and within Europe*, Aldershot: Ashgate, pp. 161–92.

Tully, James (2002) 'Political philosophy as a critical activity', *Political Theory*, 30(4): 533–55.

Tyler, Imogen (2010) 'Designed to fail: a biopolitics of British citizenship', *Citizenship Studies*, 14(1): 61–74.

UNESCO (1968) 'UNESCO statement on race and racial prejudice', *Current Anthropology*, 9(4): 270–72.

Urry, John (2003) *Global Complexity*, Cambridge: Polity Press.

Van Bruinessen, M. (2006) 'After Van Gogh: roots of anti-Muslim rage', Paper presented at the 7th Mediterranean Social and Political Research Meeting, European University Institute, 22–26 March.

Van den Brink, Bert (2007) 'Imagining civic relations in the moment of their breakdown: a crisis of civic integrity in the Netherlands', in Anthony Simon Laden (ed.), *Multiculturalism and Political Theory*, Cambridge: Cambridge University Press, pp. 350–73.

Van der Veer, Peter (2006) 'Pim Fortuyn, Theo van Gogh, and the politics of tolerance in the Netherlands', *Public Culture*, 18(1): 111–25.

Van Dijk, Teun A. (2002) 'Denying racism: elite discourse and racism', in Philomena Essed and David Theo Goldberg (eds), *Race Critical Theories: Text and Context*, Oxford: Blackwell, pp. 307–25.

Van Stokrom, Robin (2003) 'Netherlands: anti-immigration and the road to intolerance', *IRR News*, 2 December, www.irr.org.uk/2003/december/ak000005.html.

Van Wichelen, Sonja and Marc de Leeuw (2011) 'Civilizing migrants: integration, culture and citizenship', in Alana Lentin and Gavan Titley (eds), 'The European crisis of multiculturalism?', Special issue of *The European Journal of Cultural Studies* (forthcoming).

Vasta, Ellie (2007) 'From ethnic minorities to ethnic majority policy: multiculturalism and the shift to assimilationism in the Netherlands', *Ethnic and Racial Studies*, 30(5): 713–40.

Vertovec, Steven and Susanne Wessendorf (2009) 'Assessing the backlash against multiculturalism in Europe', MMG Working Paper 09-04.

Vihavainen, Timo (2009) *Länsimaiden tuho*, Helsinki: Otava.

Vink, Maarten (2007) 'Beyond the pillarization myth', *Political Studies Review*, 5: 337–50.

Virilio, Paul (2002 [1991]) *Desert Screen: War at the Speed of Light*, Wiltshire: Continuum.

Von Rohr, Mathieu (2009) 'Swiss minaret ban reflects fear of Islam not real problems', *Spiegel International*, 30 November, www.spiegel.de/international/europe/0,1518,664176,00.html.

Vries, Bald de (2010) 'Anger and courage: Fitna and the politics of disengagement', *Sfera Politicii*, XVIII(4): 146.

Wacquant, Loïc (2008) *Urban Outcasts: A Comparative Sociology of Advanced Marginality*, Cambridge: Polity Press.

Wade, Peter (2010) 'The presence and absence of race', *Patterns of Prejudice*, 44(1): 43–60.

Walters, William (2004) 'Secure borders, safe haven, domopolitics', *Citizenship Studies*, 8(3): 237–60.

Ware, Vron (2008) 'Towards a sociology of resentment: a debate on class and whiteness', *Sociological Research Online*, 13(5): 9.

Weber, Beverly M. (2010) 'Playing the victim: media coverage of Marwa el-Sherbini', *Muslimah Media Watch*, 27 July, muslimah mediawatch.org/2010/07/playing-the-victim-media-coverage-of-marwa-el-sherbini/.

Weeks, Jeffrey (1995) *Invented Moralities: Sexual Values in an Age of Uncertainty*, Cambridge: Polity Press.

Werbner, Pnina (2005a) 'The translocation of culture: "community cohesion" and the force of multiculturalism in history', *Sociological Review*, 53(4): 745–68.

— (2005b) 'Islamophobia: incitement to religious hatred – legislating for a new fear?', *Anthropology Today*, 21(5): 5–9.

Werbner, Pnina and Muhammed Anwar (1991) *Black and Ethnic Leaderships in Britain: The cultural dimensions of political action*, London: Routledge.

Wheeler, Jacob (2008) 'Caricaturing Danish Muslims', *In These*

Times, 28 March, www.inthese
times.com.

Wilson, Amrit (2007) 'The forced
marriage debate and the British
state', *Race and Class*, 49(1):
25–38.

Wimmer, A. (2008) 'The
left-Herderian ontology of
multiculturalism', *Ethnicities*,
8(1): 254–60.

Winant, Howard (1997) 'Racial
dualism at century's end', in
W. Lubiano (ed.), *The House that
Race Built: Black Americans, US
Terrain*, New York: Pantheon.

— (1998) 'Racism today: continuity
and change in the post-civil rights
era', *Ethnic and Racial Studies*,
21(4): 759.

— (2004) *New Politics of Race:
Globalism, Difference, Justice*,
Minnesota: University of Min-
nesota Press.

Witschge, Tamara, Natalie Fenton
and Des Freedman (2010) *Protecting the News: Civil society and
the media*, London: Carnegie UK.

Woollacott, Martin (2009) 'Europe's
risky experiment: reviewing the
effects of immigration', www.
guardian.co.uk/books/2009/
jun/13/christopher-caldwell-
revolution-in-europe.

Worley, C. (2005) '"It's not about
race. It's about the community":
New Labour and "commu-
nity cohesion"', *Critical Social
Policy*, 25(4).

Wren, Karen (2001) 'Cultural racism:
something rotten in the state of
Denmark?', *Social and Cultural
Geography*, 2(1): 141–62.

Wrench, John (2004) 'Managing
diversity, fighting racism or
combating discrimination? A
critical exploration', in Gavan

Titley (ed.), *Resituating Culture*,
Strasbourg: Council of Europe
Publishing.

Yilmaz, Ferruh (2006) *Ethnicized
Ontologies: From foreign worker
to Muslim immigrant*, San Diego:
University of California.

— (2011) 'The Danish Cartoon
Affair: a provocation that went
away? Or did it?', Forthcoming
paper.

Young, Robert (1995) *Colonial
Desire: Hybridity in Culture,
Theory and Race*, London and
New York: Routledge.

Younge, Gary (2009) 'When you
watch the BNP on TV, just
remember: Jack Straw started all
this', *Guardian*, 21 October.

— (2010a) *Who We are and Should
It Matter in the 21st Century?*,
New York: Viking.

— (2010b) 'Yes we need an honest
immigration debate, but this
tough talk isn't it', Comment is
Free, *Guardian*, 26 April.

Yúdice, George (2003) *The Expediency of Culture: Uses of Culture
in the Global Era*, Durham, NC:
Duke University Press.

Yuval Davis, Nira (1997) *Gender and
Nation*, London: Sage.

Žižek, Slavoj (1997) 'Multiculturalism, or, the cultural logic of
multinational capitalism', *New
Left Review*, I: 225.

— (2008) *Violence*, London: Verso.

— (2010) 'Liberal multiculturalism
masks an old barbarism with
a human face', *Guardian*,
3 October.

Zuquette, Jose Pedro (2008) 'The
European extreme-right and
Islam: new directions?', *Journal
of Political Ideologies*, 13(3):
321–44.

Index

About Zed Books

Zed Books is a critical and dynamic publisher, committed to increasing awareness of important international issues and to promoting diversity, alternative voices and progressive social change. We publish on politics, development, gender, the environment and economics for a global audience of students, academics, activists and general readers. Run as a co-operative, Zed Books aims to operate in an ethical and environmentally sustainable way.

Find out more at:

www.zedbooks.co.uk

For up-to-date news, articles, reviews and events information visit:

http://zed-books.blogspot.com

To subscribe to the monthly Zed Books e-newsletter, send an email headed 'subscribe' to:

marketing@zedbooks.net

We can also be found on **Facebook**, **ZNet**, **Twitter** and **Library Thing**.